# Promising Rituals

# Promising Rituals

## Gender and Performativity in Eastern India

Beatrix Hauser

Routledge
Taylor & Francis Group
LONDON NEW YORK AND NEW DEHLI

First published 2012 in India
by Routledge
912 Tolstoy House, 15–17 Tolstoy Marg, Connaught Place, New Delhi 110 001

Simultaneously published in the UK
by Routledge
2 Park Square, Milton Park, Abingdon, Oxfordshire OX14 4RN

First issued in paperback 2015

*Routledge is an imprint of the Taylor & Francis Group, an informa business*



*Typeset by*
Star Compugraphics Private Limited
5, CSC, Near City Apartments
Vasundhara Enclave
New Delhi 110 096



British Library Cataloguing-in-Publication Data
A catalogue record of this book is available from the British Library

ISBN-13: 978-1-138-66503-3 (pbk)
ISBN-13: 978-0-415-62585-2 (hbk)

# Contents


*List of Plates and Maps* vii
*Glossary* ix
*Notes on Transcription* xvii
*Acknowledgements* xix

Introduction: Doing Gender in Southern Orissa 1

1. Tasting Ritual: How to Fast for a Good Husband 36
2. Shared Pain — Shared Joy: On Ritual Composition and Authority 62
3. Periodically Untouchable: Female Bodies and the Performance of Impurity 93
4. Contested Bodies: Deity Possession as a Religious Idiom 118
5. (Re-)Calling the Goddess: The Emergence of Divine Presence 144
6. Nocturnal Encounters: Living Mothers and Divine Daughters 169
7. Divine Play or Subversive Comedy? On Costuming, Gender, and Transgression 195
8. The Limitations of Ritual: Female Politics and the Public 216

Afterword 236

*Bibliography* 250
*About the Author* 271
*Index* 272

# List of Plates and Maps

## Plates




1.1 Brahmin college girls perform the churning of curd 44
1.2 Joint prayer to the goddess Bṛndābatī 52

2.1 Altar of Mā Maṅgaḷā: the turmeric idol, sacred jars and lamps 71
2.2 While ringing a bell, Māusī offers fruit to the goddess 73

4.1 & 4.2 A votary impersonates the goddess Bṛndābatī and becomes possessed by Bāṭa Maṅgaḷā 127

5.1 A Tuesday Pageant with two giant *ṭhākurāṇī*-masks, a ritual specialist in the costume of Kāḷī (here unmasked) and two married women carrying sacred pots 149
5.2 Kāḷī, impersonated by a dancing ritual specialist 151
5.3 Possession by Kānduri Mā, the Crying Mother 157
5.4 Possession by Tārā-Tāriṇī and, in front, Durgā 159
5.5 Buṙhī Ṭhākurāṇī in her temple, attended by Bhaṇḍārī priests 164

6.1 Buṙhī Ṭhākurāṇī, embodied in a sacred pot, attended by Dāmalā priests 175
6.2 The Deśībeherāṇī carries the main goddess pot 179
6.3 Private altar with 32 sacred pots in honour of the goddess 184
6.4 Divided into groups of hundreds, pot bearers approach the temple 184

7.1 Painted to resemble a smallpox victim, the boy is taken to the goddess 200
7.2 Dancing as tiger, the favourite animal of Buṙhī Ṭhākurāṇī 201

7.3 A parody of priests, spiced up with 'sacred' potatoesand inflated condoms 204

8.1 Dāmalā priest seals the body of the Deśībeherāṇī, documented by a local television reporter 224

Between pages 194 and 195

Plate 1 Girl adopting the role of goddess Bṛndābatī on the occasion of Jahni Oṣā

Plate 2 *Oṣā-brata* rites performed by senior women (here Bālukā Pūjā) serve as paradigm versions for the younger generation

Plate 3 Female pot bearer at the Tuesday Pageant

Plate 4 During the Tuesday Pageant a devotee places the loose end of her sari on the road to let the living embodiment of *ṭhākurāṇī* walk on it

Plate 5 Telugu devotee offering a cock on the occasion of Jhāmu Yātrā

Plate 6 Female devotees carrying sacred pots on the outskirts of Berhampur

Plate 7 Various types of processions employ a giant mask representing Buṙhī Ṭhākurāṇī

Plate 8 Daily pot processions are the main feature of Ṭhākurāṇī Yātrā: the pots embody Buṙhī Ṭhākurāṇī (highly decorated pot at the left) and her eight sisters

## Maps

Map 1 Berhampur, Orissa 14
*Source:* Prepared by the author

Map2 Orissa and its Shakta centres 69
*Source:* Adapted by the author from a documents provided by Orissa Research Programme, German Research Foundation

# Glossary

| | |
|---|---|
| *ājñā phula* | flower of consent, refers to a flower garland that shows divine permission |
| *ahya* | married woman whose husband is alive |
| *akhaṇḍa dīpa* | unfading light |
| *āmiṣa* | non-vegetarian |
| *ārati* | an offering which involves waving light in front of the deity |
| *asṭhāẏī mandira* | temporary shrine/temple |
| *āśvina* | name of the Hindu lunar month which corresponds to September/October |
| *āṭha bhauṇī* | eight sisters (of Buṙhī Thākurāṇī), a group of eight female divinities |
| *bāgha beśa* | tiger costume |
| *bāgha nāca* | tiger dance |
| *bāhuṙā yātrā* | return journey, refers to the final night of Thākurāṇī Yātrā |
| Bāidhara | male god, Buṙhī Thākurāṇī's son |
| *baiśākha* | name of the Hindu lunar month which corresponds to April/May |
| *bandanā* | prayer, invocation which includes the offering of *ārati* |
| *basanta* | smallpox |
| Bāṭa Maṅgaḷā | Maṅgaḷā at the roadside, refers to a form of the goddess which preferably dwells near (cross)roads |
| *bauddha sannyāsī beśa* | (Buddhist) monk costume |
| Bāurī | (agricultural) labourers, caste of labourers, one of the predominant Scheduled Castes |
| *beśa* (Sanskrit: *veśa* Telugu: *veśam*) | costume, attire, guise, disguise |
| *bhāba* | emotion, thought, meaning |
| *bhāgya* | fate |

| | |
|---|---|
| *bhakti* | (unrestrained) devotion |
| Bhaṇḍārī | barber, name of the Oriya barber caste |
| *bhoga* | sacrificial food, blessed food given back by the deity (synonym: *prasāda*) |
| *bhūta* | ghost, demon |
| *bhūta-preta* | ghosts and spirits, demons |
| *bidhi-bidhāna* | rules and regulations, religious custom |
| *brata* (Sanskrit: *vrata*) | set of rites based on a religious promise |
| Bṛndābatī (Sanskrit: Vṛndāvatī) | name of a goddess, epithet of the goddess Tuḷasī |
| Buṙhī Ṭhākurāṇī | old lady, name of the tutelary goddess of Berhampur |
| *caitra* | name of the Hindu lunar month which corresponds to March/April (or April/May according to the Telugu calendar) |
| Caitra Maṅgaḷabāra | *caitra*-Tuesday, name of the Tuesday Pageant |
| *cāndā* | subscription, donation |
| Caṇḍī | name of a goddess |
| Caṇḍī-Cāmuṇḍā | names of two goddesses, here derogatively to refer to two disturbing attendants of Buṙhī Thākurāṇī |
| *cāṅguṙi pūjā* | basket worship, refers to the sanctification of a basket and its ingredients |
| *chānda* | poetic metre, verse, song |
| *chuā-achuā* | touchable–untouchable, refers to matters of purity |
| *dādhimanthana* | churning of curd, here in reference to Kṛṣṇa mythology |
| *ḍāhāṇī* | female demon or ghost |
| *ḍākiṇī* | female spirit, witch |
| *dakṣiṇā* | fee, money given to a priest for his services |
| Dāmalā | Telugu name for temple servants who blow a conch (Oriya: Jānī) |
| Daṇḍa Nāṭa | stick dance, name of a ritual performance which includes physical exercises, acrobatics, skits and drama |

| | |
|---|---|
| Daśaharā | tenth day of the bright fortnight in the month of *āśvina*, name of a festival |
| Ḍerā | weaver, Oriya name of the weaver caste (Telugu: Devāṅgī) |
| Deśībeherā (Deśabeherā) | native carer, title of the headman of the Devāṅgī |
| Deśībeherāṇī (Deśabeherāṇī) | wife of the Deśībeherā |
| Devāṅgī (Telugu) | weaver, Telugu name of the weaver caste (Oriya: Ḍerā) |
| *dharma* | socio-cosmic order, nature, religion, duty |
| *dharma jhāṇḍa* | religious flag pole |
| *digabandhana* | literally: 'binding the directions', refers to the ritual act of banning evil spirits |
| *dīpa* | earthen lamp filled with oil or clarified butter (*ghia*) |
| *dūdha-cāuḷa* | milk and rice grains, refers to a specific offering |
| *ghaṭā parikramā* | processional movement with big earthen pitchers/pots |
| *ghia* | clarified butter |
| *gotra* | family, lineage |
| *guā* | betel nut |
| *guṇa:* | quality/nature: |
| *tāmasa (Sanskrit: tamas)* | darkness, lethargy |
| *rājasa (Sanskrit: rajas)* | passion, activity |
| *sattva (Sanskrit: sattva)* | purity, light |
| *guṇiā* | magician, exorcist |
| Hāṙi | sweeper/scavenger, caste of sweepers/scavengers, one of the predominant Scheduled Castes |
| *huḷahuḷi* | auspicious ululating sound women produce with their tongue |
| *iṣṭadebatā* | chosen personal deity, tutelary deity |
| *iṭāmallī (iṭimaḷā, iṭāmāḷa)* (Telugu) | orange jasmine, name of a flower (*Crossandra infundibuliformis*) |
| Jagannātha | name of a god |

| | |
|---|---|
| *jahni* | ridge gourd |
| Jahni Oṣā | ridge gourd fast, name of a votive rite |
| *jaṇāṇa* | prayer |
| Jāṙī Mā | dumb mother, name of a goddess |
| *jāti* | birth, caste |
| Jhāmu Yātrā (Jhāmi Yātrā) | fire-walking (festival) |
| *jhaṙā-phunka* | literally 'sweeping and blowing', refers to the ritual act of banning evil spirits with a peacock-feather whisk |
| *jhoṭi* | drawing made from rice powder |
| *jhūṇā* | resin, smoke from glowing resin |
| *kaḷākuñja* | artistic display of scenes, diorama |
| Kāḷī (Kāḷikā) | black one, name of a goddess |
| Kāḷimukhī | black-faced one, name of Buṙhī Thākurāṇī's daughter-in-law |
| Kanaka Durgā | golden (-faced) Durgā, name of a goddess |
| Kānduri Mā | weeping mother, name of a goddess |
| *kārttika* | name of the Hindu lunar month which corresponds to October/November |
| *kathā* | story, legend |
| Kātyāẏaṇī | name of a goddess, a female attendant of Buṙhī Thākurāṇī |
| *kauṙi kheḷa* | cowry game, refers to a game played with seashells |
| Khulaṇā Sundarī | beautiful Khulaṇā, title of a legend |
| Kṛṣṇa | name of a god |
| Kumāra Pūrṇṇimā | young full moon, refers to the full moon in the month of *āśvina* |
| *kumbha* | jar, pot, refers to a sacred pot filled with different items |
| Kumuṭi | merchants and moneylenders, caste of Telugu merchants |
| Lakṣmī | name of a goddess, consort of Nārāẏaṇa |
| *lāñcuā* | bribe, temptation |
| *laṇḍā beśa* | literally 'tonsure costume', refers to people wearing the disguise of a Vaishnava priest |
| *laukika* | common, folk |

| | |
|---|---|
| *līḷā* (Sanskrit: *līlā*) | eternal play, divine play, re-enactment of divine play on a stage |
| *mā* | mother, common way of addressing a goddess |
| Mādigā (Telugu) | cobbler, name of the Telugu cobbler caste, classified as a Scheduled Caste (Oriya: Moci) |
| *mahāpuru* | Almighty, Lord (also used in reference to feminine deities) |
| Mahurī Rājā | ruler (local chief, 'king') of Mahurī |
| Māḷī | gardener, florist, caste of florists |
| *mānasika* | conditional vow, desire for a divine favour |
| *mānasika ghaṭa* (Telugu: *mānasika ghaṭam*) | a sacred pot carried to fulfill a *mānasika* |
| Maṅgaḷā | beneficial one, bestower of well-being, name of a goddess, epithet of a goddess |
| *maṅgaḷa* | auspicious, beneficial; name of the planet Mars |
| *mantra* | sacred or magico-mystic formula |
| *mārā* | polluted, impure |
| *māsika* | monthly period |
| *nāca* | dance |
| Nārāẏaṇa | name of a male god |
| *niśā* | night, darkness, nocturnal |
| Niśā Maṅgaḷabāra Oṣā | nocturnal Tuesday fast, name of a votive rite |
| *niśācara* | roaming around at night, quality of a goddess |
| *Narasiṃha* | man-lion incarnation of Nārāẏaṇa |
| *oṣā* (Sanskrit: *upavāsa*) | religious fast |
| *osā bidhāna* | rules of the fast |
| *osā-brata* | votive rites, religious observances |
| *paṇā* | milk-based drink |
| *pāp* | sin |
| *paramparā* | tradition, transmission |
| Pārbatī | name of a goddess |
| *pāṭa* | silk, silk cloth |

| | |
|---|---|
| *patibrata* (Sanskrit: *pativrata*) | loyalty to one's husband, chaste |
| *paurāṇika* | mythological, related to epics |
| *penṭha* | habitat, district, trade centre |
| *pilākhāi ḍāhāṇī* | child-eating female demon |
| *pīṭha* (Telugu: *pītham*) | seat, shrine, refers to centres of goddess worship; the Telugu version commonly indicates the seat of Buṙhī Thākurāṇī in the Deśībeherā's house |
| *pūjā* | act of worship |
| *pūjā bidhi* | rules of worship |
| *puṇyā* | religious merit, virtuous act |
| *puṣpadāna* | offering of flowers |
| *raja* | menstrual blood, female sexual secretion |
| *ratha* | chariot, here it refers to mostly moveable statues of divinities |
| *sāāntāṇī* | mistress |
| *sādhaka* | practitioner of austerities, scholar of *tantra* |
| *sajība debatā* | living deity |
| *śākta* | related to the divine feminine |
| *śakti* | power, ability, female divine energy personified in the goddess |
| *sāmājika* | social |
| *saṃkrānti* | planetary constellation, movement of the moon from one zodiac to another |
| Senāpati | general, commander, title of a local Devāṅgī sub-chief |
| *Śiba* (Sanskrit: Śiva) | name of a god |
| *śraddhā* | affection, devotion |
| *staba* | praise, prayer |
| *sthāpana* | installation, refers to the invocation of a deity into a pot, stone or idol |
| *strīdharma* | women's duty/religion |
| *stuti* | prayer, praise |
| *śubha* | auspicious, beneficial |
| *śubha khuṇṭi* | auspicious pole |
| Śyāma Kāḷī | dark (-skinned) Kāḷī |

| | |
|---|---|
| *tantra* | class of sacred scriptures, body of esoteric knowledge, mode of worship/ritual practice, black magic |
| *tāntrika* | practitioner of tantra, well-versed in tantra scriptures/practices, magician |
| *tapasyā* | penance |
| Tārā-Tāriṇī | a twin deity, Tārā and Tāriṇī |
| *ṭhākura* | god, lord |
| *ṭhākurāṇī* | goddess, lady, mistress, often refers to 'village goddesses' and 'plague goddesses' |
| *Ṭhākurāṇī Yātrā* | (Buṙhī) Thākurāṇī's journey/procession |
| Tuḷābuṇī (Tuḷābhiṇā) | name of an Oriya caste which processes raw cotton |
| Tuḷasī | sacred basil plant, personified as a goddess |
| *tuḷasī caurā* | Tuḷasī altar |
| *veikallu ghaṭam* (Telugu) | thousand-eyed pot |
| Yaśodā | name of Kṛṣṇa's foster mother |
| *yātrā* | journey, procession, movement, festival, theatre |
| *yoginī* | female companion of the goddess, group divinities |

# Notes on Transcription

This book includes several terms from Indian languages, in particular from Oriya. Generally this vocabulary is presented according to the standard system for transliterating words from Indo-Aryan languages. This transliteration has been modified in order to also approximate the pronunciation:

- As in Sanskrit, the final consonant of most Oriya words evokes the sound of 'a'. If necessary, this letter also occurs in the transcription.
- Oriya has only one letter to signify what in several other Indo-Aryan languages is either 'b' or 'v'. I shall transcribe this letter as 'b', unless it is pronounced otherwise (as the second part of a conjunct letter, or in case of words of Telugu origin).
- The Oriya alphabet distinguishes 'l' and 'ḷ'. Therefore several terms are spelt slightly differently than in neighbouring languages, for instance *maṅgala* (Sanskrit) or *maṅgal* (Hindi) becomes *maṅgaḷa*. In general, I use the Oriya version and, when deemed necessary, add the Sanskrit or Hindi spelling in brackets. When referring to scholarly debates that concern pan-Indian concepts and practices, I shall use the respective Hindi or Sanskrit version.
- Words of Telugu origin (indicated in the glossary) are given according to their spelling in Oriya. However, strictly speaking Telugu is not a foreign language as southern Orissa is bilingual with Oriya and Telugu being used.

Some very rough guidelines may be given concerning the pronunciation of Oriya for readers already familiar with Hindi or Sanskrit. In spoken Oriya

- 's', 'ś' and 'ṣ' are pronounced approximately like 's';
- both 'j' and 'y' are pronounced like 'j';
- 'ẏ' and 'y' as a second conjunct sound like 'y';
- the vowel 'ṛ' (in words of Sanskrit origin) is pronounced like 'ru'; and
- in many words 'a' is almost spoken as 'o' (as in Bengali).

Personal names (including pseudonyms of individuals I interviewed) and geographic names are given in their standardized English version, similar to common Indian words that appear in the *Oxford English Dictionary* (Vaishnava, Shakta, sari, etc.) The official spelling of the Indian state Orissa was changed by the end of 2011 to 'Odisha'; the city of Berhampur is now referred to as 'Brahmapur'. Since the present ethnography is based on fieldwork conducted between 1999 and 2003, the former spellings are used throughout the book.

Names of deities and rituals are transliterated in the manner presented earlier. The names of Oriya publications are given with diacritics.

In reference to secondary literature, terms from Sanskrit, Hindi, Bengali, Telugu or Tamil are given in the spelling used by the respective author.

# Acknowledgements

This book resulted from ethnographic research that shaped many years of my intellectual life. Without doubt several people contributed to its present form, knowingly and unknowingly. First of all, my sincerest thanks to the Oriya women who not only invited me to join their rituals, but also shared their thoughts, worries and moments of joy. For the sake of anonymity, I do not mention their real names and use synonyms throughout the book. However, some interlocutors are well-known and hence it would neither make sense to conceal their names nor do I wish to belittle their help. I was deeply honoured by the support I received from Srimati P. Devaki and Sri P. Durga Prasad Desibehera, the adopted 'parents' of goddess Buṙhī Ṭhākurāṇī, from the present Mahurī representative Sri Asok Kumar Narendra Dev as well as from the priests at the main Buṙhī Ṭhākurāṇī temple in the old town of Berhampur: Sri Narayan Gantayat, Sri Babula Gantayat and his brothers. Without their patience in explaining and illustrating every detail of religious ceremonies and their ability to introduce me at several ritual occasions I would have never gained the insights that allowed me to write this book. In Berhampur there were several other women and men who helped me in various ways — by sharing their memories from religious festivals, personal accounts of local history and reflecting on their commitment to the goddess. Many thanks to all of them, in particular to Prof. Gagan N. Dash, Nila Mani Prushti as well as D. V. Srinivas and his family. Moreover, the local channel ETV as well as K. Nageswar Rao from the Telugu daily Eenadu, were extremely helpful by opening their archives on the performance of Ṭhākurāṇī Yātrā.

In Bhubaneswar I would like to thank Professor Prasanna Kumar Nayak at Utkal University, who not only enriched my research work with his vast knowledge on Orissa, he also offered practical help and encouragement whenever needed. For being warmly received I am also grateful to his wife, his daughter Dipa and his nephew Niranjan. During the various phases of my research work in Berhampur and its rural surroundings, several university graduates helped me as field assistants. My sincere thanks go to Madhumita Das, Dr Sarmistha Choudhury, Bandita Panda, Gayatri Vinodh Ayyangar, Ranjan Das, and

Manas Ranjan Kar. In particular I want to mention Kamini Krishna Panda and Y. Ramakrishna Rao in Gopalpur, for being my Oriya teachers, advisers in several matters, a mine of information, and above all, friends. They made my stay in Orissa not only productive, also intensely pleasurable.

In Germany, my thanks go first of all to Professor Dr Burkhard Schnepel at the University of Halle-Wittenberg. He drew my initial interest to the subject of 'contested identities', supported my research work at every stage, and in particular, offered his professional expertise to get a sound financial basis for doing so. I am grateful to my colleagues at the Orissa Research Project, namely, Prof. Dr Hermann Kulke (University of Kiel), Dr Georg Berkemer (Humboldt University of Berlin), Prof. Dr Angelika Malinar (University of Zurich) and Prof. Dr Georg Pfeffer (Free University of Berlin). I would like to acknowledge Prof. Dr Rahul Peter Das (University of Halle-Wittenberg) for his valuable suggestions related to language and semantics, and Prof. Dr William S. Sax (University of Heidelberg) for his careful and rigorous reading of the final manuscript. I am also indebted to Prof. Dr Erika Fischer-Lichte (Free University of Berlin), for her stimulating thoughts on theatricality and aesthetics that, after all, helped to rethink the theoretical foundations of this book, and thus inspired its completion.

During the seemingly endless process of data interpretation and writing chapters, several colleagues and academics spread around the globe offered helpful comments and suggestions. I wish to thank Prof. Dr Ursula Rao (University of New South Wales, Sydney), Prof. Dr John Hutnyk (Goldsmiths, University of London), Prof. Dr Klaus Peter Köpping (University of Heidelberg), PD Dr Michael Schetsche (IGPP, Freiburg), Prof. Dr Alexander Henn (Arizona State University), Dr habil. Bettina J. Schmidt (University of Wales Trinity Saint David), and PD Dr Lale Yalçın-Heckmann (University of Halle-Wittenberg), for their feedback on earlier drafts and sections of this book. I also gained a lot from the constructive comments by Routledge's anonymous referees. For their careful proofreading I also wish to thank Dr Christoph Kucklick, Martina Elsner, Elisabeth Bergner, Jutta Burger, Christina Knüllig, and Ursula Münster. Last, but not least, I would like to thank Oliver Woolley who copyedited the manuscript and the editorial team at Routledge for their thorough support and competent suggestions while preparing this book. The German Research Council generously supported my research and writing from 1999 to 2001 and again from 2002 to 2004.

Several sections of this book were published previously, in academic journals and as part of conference volumes. I am grateful to the editors as well as the publishers Peter Lang (Frankfurt/Main), Ergon (Würzburg) and Kohlhammer (Stuttgart) for allowing the reproduction of these articles. I would also like to thank Manohar (Delhi) for publishing earlier versions of chapters 2 and 4. In line with the overall structure of this book these texts were thoroughly revised, partly extended and translated into English. Full bibliographical details of these earlier versions are given in the respective chapters.

The book is dedicated to my daughter Jana.

# Introduction: Doing Gender in Southern Orissa

This study is about Hindu women and their religious practices. It shows how the performance of rituals influences the self-understanding of women, their sense of femininity, and their position in the lived-in world. I shall focus on how women perceive, realize and reflect on religious ideas, how they engage in ritual and, by doing so, also negotiate gender norms. In this respect the book addresses the active part women play in the perpetuation and social negotiation of gender differences. What is more, the study is essentially about ritual as a cultural site that alters perception and in turn transforms social reality. I shall explore how the performance of ritual affects and relocates the sense of self, for instance, by empowering the participants in a way that spills over into non-ritual spheres. The experiential space provided by the framing of the event, I assume, invokes self-images that vary and at times challenge everyday notions of identity. Thus, the aim of this study is to shed some light on the relationship between religion and women, together with the influence of Hindu doctrines on present-day conceptions of gender. With regard to non-Western contexts, religion is often understood to hinder female self-esteem and gender equality. Focusing on the worship of Hindu goddesses, some feminist theologians also hold the opposite view. What is missing in both generalizations, however, is the diversity and ambivalence of experiences gained by women who follow the respective religious traditions.

This study is, first of all, an ethnography based on fieldwork in southern Orissa. It shows the immense popularity of goddess worship in this region and also how women come to share the divine agency, above all, in the case of deity possession. By means of their female body women serve as essential intermediaries to please the powerful and threatening goddesses, who in turn protect the region and its inhabitants. Although each chapter of the book takes a close look at a specific ritual practice, at semi-private processions or at a Hindu festival that attracts hundreds of thousands of visitors, I do not discuss only regional phenomena. In analyzing academic interpretations concerning votive rites, the concept of pollution, and possession by supernatural beings, I shall link the ethnographic findings to various general debates related to Hinduism. Nevertheless, the underlying question is, in what respect Hindu rituals offer women in southern Orissa the opportunity of verifying the self vis-à-vis the world. What incentives do ritual practitioners obtain about their everyday reality, on personal crisis and suffering, or regarding their status as women in society? How does it matter whether the performance of a ritual is dedicated to the well-being of others, for instance, the long life of a husband? In which ways do women perceive and consider goddess theology? By what means do rituals manipulate emotions, reframe bodily dispositions, inspire social relations, and thus may alter the self-understanding and position of practitioners?

This study also suggests a theoretical argument about ritual and the specific ways it influences the constitution of identity. In its course, I shall engage two bodies of theory: first, regarding cultural performance as a site for memorizing, (re-)enacting, embodying and negotiating shared values, attitudes and concepts; and second, on gender-identity as a routine achievement that results from seen, but mostly unnoticed, everyday activities, marking a person as female or male. After looking in each chapter at the practice of 'doing gender' during framed events, and ritual in particular, I shall round off the study by making a heuristic distinction of performance as representational practice, discursive practice and aesthetic practice. On the basis of these contrasting perspectives, I argue that the experience of the gendered self during the participation in rituals is not only determined by women's degree of awareness (i.e., self-presentation), and limited by discursive structures (for instance, Brahminical doctrine). It is also constituted by the somatic attention given to performative effects – such as the excitement or joy while being confronted with gender/ed images – and thus determined by the ontology of an event, in this case a ritual. Whereas each of these analytic views on performance illuminates different facets of social reality, their *difference* allows some conclusions on the faculty of framed events to alter self-understanding, and thus the experiences of practicing Hindu women in southern Orissa. The three perspectives on performance also inform my appraisal of the human subject and her (or his) agency. However, one should note that these theoretical assumptions on the human subject position are an intellectual device and should, therefore, be distinguished from culture-specific ideals of personhood and also from the actual status given or claimed in a certain context. Similarly, gender-identity is not a 'category of practice' (Bourdieu) popular among women in southern Orissa. Rather than participating in *specific* discourses on women's rights, gender equality or femininity, several women certainly reflect on social constraints imposed upon them, whether conveyed in terms of gender or other affiliations, within the realm of ritual and beyond.

## Women and Hinduism

The portrayal of Indian women and their position in society is mostly characterized by either silencing their capacity to influence living conditions at all, or by an idealization of their rich symbolic role. Media and social activists rightly focus on the alarming discrimination against women; the high female mortality rate is only one indicator. Yet Indian scholars have also pointed towards the politics of gender representation, and how the idea of the voiceless and submissive woman is deployed for particular purposes in a given historical context (see Sangari and Vaid 1989; Sunder 1993). The obedient wife who passively follows obsolete traditions, for instance, is regarded as a cultural trope that emerged from colonial discourse – best exemplified by British reports on the burning of widows. Following Partha Chatterjee (1989) these early nineteenth-century accounts served to demonstrate the 'barbaric' social customs that, so it was believed, derived from Hindu doctrine. The atrocities perpetrated on Indian women also came to legitimize British intervention and colonial rule. In this rhetoric, the pitiable status of women was taken as an index of India's backwardness. Despite its contrasting political agenda, the nationalist movement for its part promoted a notion of femininity that alluded to religious ethics. Values like chastity, self-sacrifice and submission again qualified women as representatives of modern Indian culture (Chatterjee 1989: 629).

The figure of the subservient Hindu woman has not originated from colonial discourse, and to explain it as an Orientalist construction reveals only one side of the coin. The historian of religion, Madhu Khanna (2000: 109) rather states: 'Feminist critiques of classical Hinduism unequivocally assert that Hinduism betrayed women'. Along the same line, Renate Syed (2001) showed how several old Indian scriptures also enforced gender-based social inequality. Although there is not enough room to express the variety and implications of Sanskrit teachings in regard to the social position of women, I will briefly present a few of the significant arguments on the relationship between women and Hinduism (for a condensed historical treatment of this matter, see Young 2002).[1]

According to the notorious *Laws of Manu* (200 BCE–200 CE), for instance, a woman was to do nothing independently. Rather she should be subjected to male control, by her father, her husband or by her son.[2] In this compilation of moral guidelines the mere fact of femaleness is seen to prove the sins of a previous life. In the social hierarchy, women were hence ranked as low as servants (identified as Shudra) and, like them, not eligible to study the sacred texts, to perform sacrifices or actually to attain salvation without being reborn in a higher male form (McGee 1991: 76). The only spiritual exercise open to women (allegedly) consisted of their *pativrata* (Sanskrit) – the wifely devotion to a husband – thus assuming marriage as normative for women's religiosity and cosmological disposition (Sanskrit *strīdharma*).[3] In this

---

[1] The assessment of Sanskrit literature is a challenge for several reasons. First of all, evidence is lacking as to the usage of these scriptures, for instance, whether they described social reality, moral ideals or selected practices ignored by the masses. In addition, some English editions of those texts have been criticized for the ethnocentric bias implicit in the translation. However, it is also not self-evident that these treatises can be subsumed as part of a 'Hindu religion'. Hinduism is a historically new concept. Originally the term 'Hindu' was used to describe the inhabitants of the Indian subcontinent. It was in the colonial period that 'Hinduism' was first used as an umbrella term to classify several modes of worship, forms of living and philosophical traditions, vis-à-vis those explicitly associated with Islam, Christianity, Sikhism, Jainism or Buddhism. On the problem of defining the Hindu religion, see, for instance, Flood (2003).

[2] The compilation of laws ascribed to the sage Manu (*manusmṛti*) belongs to a text genre that focuses on codes of conduct (*dharmaśāstra*); it is one of the most controversial Hindu scriptures. According to feminist historians, the *Laws of Manu* exemplify women's loss of status, a process that started about 400 BCE, and gradually reduced whatever power or equality women might have had in ancient times (see Young 2002: 11). According to Bose (2000: 3–4) the restrictive impetus of the *manusmṛti* is largely due to exegetic commentaries composed in the eighth century. Other scholars claim that the colonial rediscovery and interpretation of this text brought about its discriminating notion of women (see Doniger and Smith 1991 in their introduction to *The Laws of Manu*).

[3] The Hindu concept of *dharma* – a guideline to ethical orientation, often translated as 'religion' or 'duty' – does not assert a universal moral code, but its relativity, i.e., variable notions of righteousness according to a person's sex, caste, age and other circumstances.

respect, Brahminical Hindu doctrine was regarded as weakening the autonomy of women and as perpetuating a 'theology of subordination' (Khanna 2000: 110).

By the beginning of the 1980s, scholars working on women's religious roles became increasingly critical of a supposedly male bias of their colleagues.[4] They started to explore ritual practices and theological treatises in search of alternative concepts of femininity and the female subject position. With respect to Hinduism, the research interest shifted from topics like purity and pollution – as an hierarchical axis that disparaged women – towards the relevance of 'auspiciousness' (Sanskrit *maṅgala*), and hence also contributed to the (academic) recognition of female religious practices (Carman and Marglin 1985; Marglin 1985a; 1985b). Moreover, it focused on the concept of *śakti*, the ultimate generative energy, as a substantially female power that influenced living women within and beyond ritual practice (Wadley 1980b). Studies from this gendered perspective emphasize the autonomy of women's religious identity and their self-esteem as creators and maintainers of life, and as a source of prosperity and well-being. Apparently, conservative Hindu doctrines were deconstructed as androcentric fiction and several scholars explicitly aimed at reassessing Sanskrit scriptures on religious traditions as a source of women's empowerment (see Bose 2000; Leslie 1991; Leslie and McGee 2000). The ideal of *pativrata*, for instance, was understood to represent male wishful thinking, rather than a description of social practice in the history of the subcontinent (Leslie 1989). Similarly, researchers focused on female saints, ascetics and ritual specialists, who, in spite of Brahminical ideology, hold a respected position in Hindu society (Ojha 1981; Ramaswamy 1997; Denton 2004).[5]

---

[4] Due to the lack of adequate sources, conservative scholars used to legitimize the previous inattention to women in the academic discipline of religious studies as a consequence of women's lesser degree of involvement in the religious domain. They also subscribed to the view of a generic masculine that included the feminine viewpoint. At the beginning of the 1980s this paradigm was significantly challenged by Falk and Gross' (1980) pioneering compilation of women's religious lives in non-Western cultures.

[5] Significantly, the question as to whether and in what way religious doctrines serve to empower Indian women was rarely asked with reference to Islam, Sikhism, Christianity or Buddhism. With respect to popular religion in India, Muslim women in fact often share and also influence several of the religious practices relevant to Hindu women, though within their own interpretative framework.

Another prominent issue of this academic pursuit was the focus on goddess worship. In comparison to other religions, the variety of female deities in Hinduism is particularly elaborate. It thus attracts not only local devotees, but also women in the West, towards a theological and scholarly 'rediscovery' of the divine as female.[6] Special attention was given to the fierce and awesome aspect associated with some Hindu goddesses, exemplified by the worship of Kālī. Owing to her creative violence she appeared to feminists as a potential destroyer of present-day social evils, above all, patriarchy (L. Gupta 1991).[7] Several scholars addressed the question of whether and in what respect the powerful goddess can be viewed as a model for living (Hindu) women. The answers were rather reserved.[8] Whereas in *some* religious contexts female worshippers are regarded as manifestations of the divine generative power by virtue of their sex, Hindus clearly distinguish between women and goddesses, who, after all, can be impersonated by male ritual specialists as well. Furthermore, it has been questioned whether, to whom, and in what situations, 'wild' goddesses appear terrifying at all (McDermott 1996a; Michaels, Vogelsanger and Wilke 1996).

In general, scholars assume that women's position in society has not benefited from the theology and symbolism of Hindu goddesses (Chitgopekar 2002a: 32; Hiltebeitel and Erndl 2000a: 17; Pintchman 1994: 194–98; Sunder Rajan 2000: 272). The choice to adore a goddess would neither reflect nor evoke a particular consciousness towards gender issues (Coburn 1991: 172), but rather relate to the purpose of

---

[6] On the conceptualization of Hindu goddesses in terms of an explicitly feminist spirituality, see L. Gupta (1991); Kripal (2000); Kurtz (2000); McDermott (1996b). For a theological view that regards the worship of Hindu goddesses as liberating for (Western) women see, for instance, Dobia (2000).

[7] Hence the first feminist publishing house in India was named 'Kali for women'.

[8] To follow the arguments of this debate see King (1997) – specifically the contributions by Erndl, Humes, Wulff, and L. Gupta – as well as Hiltebeitel and Erndl (2000b): *Is the Goddess a Feminist?* and in particular Pintchman (2000). For a historical study on the rising goddess theology and its influence on the social status of women in medieval times, compare Khanna (2000). In more recent publications on goddess worship and its impact on women, the question of empowerment has not lost its attraction to scholars (see the compilations edited by Chitgopekar 2002b and Sharma 2005). Unfortunately several of these (text-based) explorations do not refer to a shared debate.

worship, family tradition or the fame of a deity. In this respect the social implications of goddess devotion would not differ from those worshipping male deities. Some scholars argue that although divine gender models and particular forms of worship influence human relationships in the lived-in world, they generally secure gender inequality and do not promote any form of resistance. The worship of a goddess such as Kālī was seen to serve men by expressing their interests, anxieties and religious experiences.[9] However, Rita Sherma (2000: 25), Kathleen Erndl (1997: 30–31, 2000: 101), Rita Gross (2000: 107), Lina Gupta (1997: 96) and Cynthia Humes (1997: 60) claim that from the perspective of *some* female devotees and ritual specialists, the worship of a goddess can indeed raise one's self-esteem and social status. Such religious engagement could transform a woman's sense of gender, while simultaneously garnering her respect and authority. Though any general conclusions are rejected as a simplification of social practice and gender roles, these scholars assume a relation between the power of a goddess and the empowerment of women. Yet they also point to the misleading connotations of the 'Western' notion of power. *Śakti* does not refer to control and subjugation; it implies potentiality rather than agency, and also includes the ability to tolerate suffering. To understand power in terms of domination would, thus, limit the understanding of *śakti* and its impact on Hindu women (Humes 2000: 141; L. Gupta 1997: 85–86; Gross 1997: 106). At any rate, these studies suggest that Hindu rituals serve as a cultural site where women are confronted with encouraging notions of femininity, and thus are able to verify their self-understanding as gendered beings.

In what ways and roles women are able to manipulate gender models according to their own perspective of the social reality is explored in studies about women's expressive forms, and particularly their verbal arts (legends, oral epics, poetry, and songs).[10] Furthermore, women's personal narratives are analyzed in their capacity to reflect on gender

---

[9] The psychoanalytic influence is most explicit in the arguments of Caldwell (1999), Kripal (2000: 240–41) and Menon and Shweder (2000: 151).

[10] There are several studies on this subject, see: Appadurai, Korom and Mills (1991); Bose (2000); Flueckiger (1996); Kumar (1994b); Leslie (1991); and Raheja and Gold (1994). On the works of female writers, compare Tharu and Lalita (1993). Scholars also explored gender representations in 'classical' Hindu scriptures and how a female audience reacts to these (see, for instance, Flueckiger 1991).

stereotypes, and as a way of bringing about self-awareness. In line with the historian's agenda of 'subaltern studies', this academic debate concentrates on a distinct female perspective of the world, assuming that women, like the weaker sections of society, are to subscribe to everyday forms of resistance in order to criticize hegemonic order and patriarchy.[11] Drawing on fieldwork in Uttar Pradesh and Rajasthan, Gloria Raheja and Ann Gold (1994) argue that women's verbal arts indeed display alternative models of femininity, and these contrast with the ideologies of gender and kinship that place women in subordinate positions. At marriage celebrations, for instance, women commonly gather and enjoy themselves with 'insult songs' (*gālī*). This genre makes fun of the bridegroom and his family, and the obscenities that go with it are widely heard (Gold 1994). In this respect some female arts are 'subversive' — at least they are reminiscent of transgressive rites of reversal. Raheja and Gold (1994: 185) conclude that '[s]uch expressive forms are not of course always or regularly successful in permanently altering the structures of dominance or deprivation they critique'. Although the authors presuppose a correlation between aesthetic genre and female identity, they rightly avoid giving a straight answer. Nevertheless, this area of research deserves the credit for pointing towards women's agency in the perpetuation and interpretation of cultural repertoire. Women neither follow tradition blindly nor always share the male view.

In respect to religious practices and its influence on the performer's perception of gender, the debate on female art forms is only partly helpful. It suggests that there are some genres that are more likely than others to express a critical female view, as if a specific type of event assures its affirmative or subversive character. This is problematic for two reasons. First, it implies that specific forms of worship *generally* improve or deteriorate the self-perception, confidence and status of women. Though each ritual will indeed affect participants in some ways, the results are not entirely related to its discursive meaning (purpose, content) and generic form. The experience also depends on the individual's perspective and role in the ritual, on her (or his) emotional and somatic experiences at this time, and on contingent issues that emerge from the performance itself. How social reality is finally altered by means of ritual or verbal arts can thus be understood and

[11] The subaltern studies group was shaped by scholars such as Ranajit Guha (1998) and Partha Chatterjee (1989), to name only a few.

systematized only with respect to its actual performance. Moreover, the vision of specific subversive art forms also raises methodological problems. Joyce Flueckiger (1996) has pointed out that from a local perspective, genre distinctions are anything but clear. Rather women's oral repertoire is thought to be part of diverse caste-specific and regional practices, and hence fails to be objectified as genre by itself. Yet she also shows that verbal arts are often conceptualized within the realm of ritual. Following her perspective from Chhattisgarh (a state neighbouring Orissa) right away annihilates any attempt to distinguish fairly repetitive and collective traditions from rather creative and aesthetic ones, i.e., to transfer the post-Enlightenment separation of the religious domain and the arts.

## The Scope of Research

The question of the *potential* of Hindu rituals, in altering the self-understanding of women and their notion of femininity, has been raised in all its aspects and continues to be a motive of several debates. Although all answers come with a series of methodological problems (how to define and assess self-identity, human agency, power, and change), to think about religious practice in terms of improving the self-esteem of performers and their capacity to act on the world is intriguing (cf. McGee 2000: 4; Sered 1994: 7). Certainly, recognizing how Hinduism bestows women with hitherto unknown powers also reflects the feminist vision of a society beyond the devastating excesses of patriarchy. However, changing research paradigms have replaced the simple question of empowerment in favour of historicizing reflections on 'discursive power' (Foucault) and femininity. Recent studies focus, for instance, on practices that 'discipline' the body or on 'invented identities' (for India, see Leslie and McGee 2000; Thapan 1997). In comparison, my interest rather concerns women's *views* of power and agency, i.e., their perception and self-images as well as the diversity and ambivalence of experiences that result from the regular participation in rituals and influence the gendered self.

Hence this study aims at exploring how the performance of rituals, processions and festivals shapes gender-identity and affects female performers in their sense of self. Concentrating on one ethnographic site, I focus on experiences 'ordinary' women — rather than female priests or ascetics — may gain about themselves as gendered beings, about femininity and 'female' traits in and through several elaborate forms of worship and related semi-religious events.[12] How do women deal with apparently restrictive and also, to the contrary, omnipotent role expectations? My analysis will show the various ways in which women perceive, enact and legitimize gender stereotypes, and also how they, at times, modify or reject these images. It will indicate in what respect they become agents to negotiate these objectifications of womanhood, and also when and how alterations are made explicit and taken as a challenge.[13]

With the term 'gender-identity' (or 'female identity') I refer to a complex of intersecting categories such as women's self-understanding, self-images, self-esteem, sense of femininity, sense of gendered self, etc., i.e., *ideas and feelings* that generally derive from acts of identification with ideal constructions, role expectations, ideologies, and social practices.[14] This usage of 'identity' does not necessarily imply discursive articulation, yet it may become manifest in self-presentation. This understanding neither presumes the sameness of women in southern Orissa nor of Hindu women in general. Yet it refers to a collective phenomenon in that it hints at an inherently social imagination rather than a merely subjective category (though sensed individually). Furthermore, the term 'gender-identity' is not employed in an exclusive sense; the self-understanding of women cannot be

---

[12] I do not assume that within the realm of Hindu society one can clearly separate secular and religious events. Here the term 'semi-religious' refers to social practices that are not defined by the worship (*pūjā*) of deities, for instance, the subtle communication of menstrual impurity (Chapter 3) or the provocative masquerades associated with Ṭhākurāṇī Yātrā (Chapter 7).

[13] To think of Indian women as creators of their lived-in world risks translating a concept of subjectivity, reason and free will that is heavily influenced by the European heritage of the Enlightenment. Several scholars are quite critical concerning whether personhood in India can be judged in terms of individual action. I shall return to these conceptual points in the following section when I discuss theoretical approaches concerning the performativity of the self.

[14] This view on identity is fairly consonant with George Herbert Mead's (1934) notion of the self as a result of two interrelated and dynamic dimensions: the 'me' consisting of internalized attitudes of 'significant others' and the 'I', understood as the individual and creative response to the 'me'. In his view identity emerges from the never-ending interplay of external ascription and internal response (see Jenkins 1996: 30). On the difficulties associated with the inflationary use of 'identity' as an analytic category in Social Anthropology and related disciplines, see Brubaker and Cooper (2000).

separated from social, linguistic, regional or religious affiliations. (Nevertheless, in order to speak of 'identities' in plural form one should not ignore that commonalities with diverse entities are rarely clearly separated.) I conceive of gender-identity as an embodied faculty, i.e., a vision that encodes the sentient body, habitual routines and tacit knowledge. Occasionally it becomes accessible to the reflecting mind (for instance, in case of conflict).

I assume that the implicit knowledge about oneself as a gendered being is conveyed, first of all, by means of *performative* practices of everyday life.[15] From this angle, gender is a matter of 'doing' rather than passive being – an ongoing achievement. The concept of 'doing gender' was coined by the ethno-methodologists Candace West and Don Zimmerman (1987: 126): 'Doing gender involves a complex of socially guided perceptual, interactional, and micropolitical activities that cast particular pursuits as expressions of masculine and feminine "natures".'[16] Initially this concept referred to the analysis of linguistic features such as voice (pitch, tone), prosody (intonation patterns, accent, rhythm) and conversation style ('genderlect'). Meanwhile scholars make use of this phrase in the broader sense and also focus on the presentation of the body, for instance ornamentation, dress practices, hair style; on habitual routines and taste, on etiquette and, of course, on self-conscious activities, statements and behaviour.[17] Gradually the concept came to reflect the reconceptualization of gender as a process rather than as category. 'Doing gender' thus stresses the subtle and observable, but mostly unnoticed, activities that in a given situation not only indicate but rather produce the gender of the self. As a result, our understanding of who we are is always encoded or 'gendered'. Unlike Erving Goffman (1979), who thought of gender display as an optional dramatization that is played out for an audience, 'doing gender' refers to a permanent activity without being cognitively involved. It appears natural to social actors. In this respect 'doing gender' is in line with

[15] Although I would not categorically exclude the impact of genetics or sexual characteristics, as an anthropologist I am primarily concerned with the socially shaped dimension of gender/ed identity.

[16] The social constructivist approach to gender was in fact substantiated by anthropological research in the 1970s, see Ortner and Whitehead (1981) or MacCormack and Strathern (1980). For a retrospective view on feminist anthropology and *Making Gender*, compare Ortner (1996).

[17] The scholarly approaches to 'doing gender' vary as to what features are to be included in this process (Kotthoff 2002).

the philosopher Judith Butler (1990, 1993) and her theory on gender performativity. Yet, whereas Butler regards gender constructs as discursive products rather than as human creations, the concept of 'doing gender' does not intend to question the assumption of a pre-existing subject.

In the shape of performative practices, notions about the gendered self are accessible to the anthropologist, although they rarely take the character of indexical signs waiting to be deciphered. Nevertheless, they are materialized as 'habitus' (Bourdieu) or in histrionic form, and thus are conveyed in visual, aural and tactile ways that can be sensed and recognized during participant observation. They are collective and 'contagious' in that they suggest the possibility of sharing. As a result, fieldworkers often acquire a second set of moral standards, emotions and routines (an anthropological gaze, or rather sensorium, subjected to time and place, see Howes 1990, 1991).[18] Depending on context and convention, ideas about the gendered self are objectified and verbalized. First-person narratives and language use certainly invite one to consider notions of gender and serve to verify interpretation. Instead of engaging in conversation analysis (like ethno-methodologists), anthropologists aim to explore communication patterns in a broader sense. They pay attention to the ways in which their interlocutors classify the lived-in world, and search for taxonomies of experience.[19] In any case, informal and semi-structured interviews not only reveal previous thoughts and feelings of 'informants', they also advance and bring about self-awareness, self-reflection and self-reflexivity (i.e., to consider self-presentation and its effects on others).

'Doing gender' not only accompanies everyday routines, it is also a side effect of framed events such as rituals, processions and festivals. In Social Anthropology it is widely assumed that cultural performances are particularly prone to shape practices and processes of identity formation (as argued in the following discussion). In what respect these occasions actually differ from everyday interaction in their capacity to outline, shape and verify self-understanding remains basically unclear.

---

[18] This is a general phenomenon, yet I believe from personal experience that it is more relevant to female anthropologists whose personal notion of self-identity contrasts with gender norms met at the site of fieldwork.

[19] Nevertheless, the act of converting the 'other' into one's own language and categories always risks missing the point. The epistemological problems of translating 'cultures' are well represented by Srubar, Renn and Wenzel (2005).

To anticipate some of the arguments explained further down, in this study I conceive of meta-communicative framing as a mode to open up an additional experiential space, that does not only produce alternative realities – possibly classified as sacred – but also seduces participants to reconsider and relocate the self. Thus, I focus on Hindu rituals in their capacity to affect the gendered self in *exceptional* rather than in common ways and, for this reason, to alter women's self-understanding and position in non-ritual times as well. However, it is not sufficient to merely claim that framed performances vary in their impact on the self from everyday performativity. Therefore, this study will also consider performative practices that are not part of a specific religious event. Taking the example of the non-verbal display of menstrual pollution in day-to-day communication, Chapter 3 will emphasize the theatrical dimension of these interactions and explore how they manipulate the self-understanding of women, and in what respect these routine enactments (social conventions) vary from framed performances (rituals) in their impact on the gendered self. I shall come back to the concept of cultural performance and how anthropologists have theorized about its effects on identity formation, but first let me proceed with some background information on the field research.

This study is based on ethnographic fieldwork in the city of Berhampur[20] and its rural surroundings, located on the eastern coastline of the Indian subcontinent (Map 1). The area, called Ganjam District (8,070 sq. km), belongs to the state of Orissa and borders Andhra Pradesh to the south. Ganjam is known as a cultural melting pot, with influences from northern and southern India as well as from the indigenous population (Adivasi) in the mountainous hinterland (the Eastern Ghats). Considering the economic and social development statistics, the district is rather backward, though more advanced than the hilly regions towards the west of Orissa (see Government of Orissa 2004). Berhampur is the main commercial and trading centre in southern Orissa. The prosperity of the town, famous for its silk manufacture, is attributed to the power of the goddess Buṙhī Ṭhākurāṇī. This indicates the significance of goddess worship in this region (see Brighenti 2001). The popularity of Buṙhī Ṭhākurāṇī only competes with that of Lord Jagannātha, whose temple in Puri, 120 km to the north of Berhampur,

[20] In 2001 Berhampur had approximately 300,000 inhabitants. Like several other Indian towns of this size it continues to have a rather provincial character.

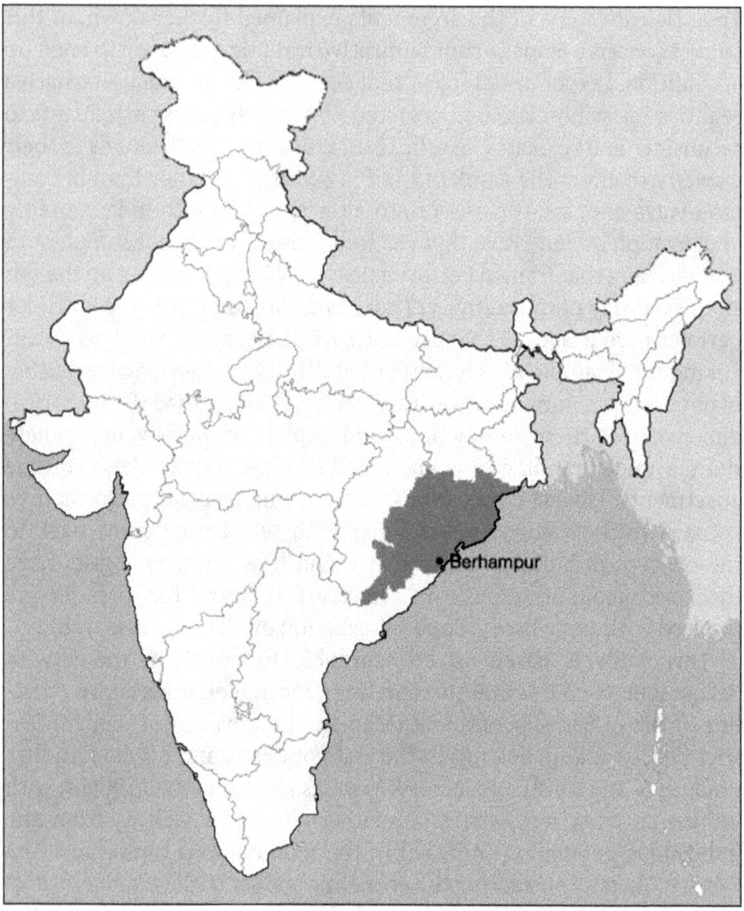


**Map 1:** Berhampur, Orissa
Not to scale.

serves as one of the major pan-Indian sites of pilgrimage. Located in the heart of Orissa, the Jagannātha temple is closely linked to the history and identity of the state (see Eschmann, Kulke and Tripathy 1978; Kulke and Schnepel 2001). In Ganjam the cultural norms still vary in many respects. For instance, the mother tongue of almost a quarter of the population in Berhampur is not Oriya but Telugu, the language spoken in Andhra Pradesh.[21]

[21] Linguistically Oriya belongs to the eastern group of the new Indo-Aryan languages, whereas Telugu is the most widely spoken 'Dravidian' language.

The field research was arranged in five sequences, commencing in September 1999, when it was immediately interrupted by a devastating cyclone. After returning in 2000 (twice), 2001 and finally in 2003, the fieldwork made up 16 months in total. Initially, I was not looking at Hindu ritual as a cultural institution influencing female self-understanding; rather my interest concerned women's expressive forms. After being told that in coastal Ganjam there is no such genre, I realized that women's verbal and visual arts were almost exclusively classified as part of votive rites and seasonal festivals.[22] This turned out to have heuristic value. I gradually recognized that in this region the religious domain was indeed central to the life of many women – offering not only a realm of self-expression, but also the most evident, accessible and important field in which to gain confidence and respect. The following chapters will illustrate and thus specify this finding.

In general, women responded very positively to my request to attend their rituals. Though clearly a guest, I was often asked to participate actively, i.e., to join the prayers or to offer flowers. In this respect, my presence was similar to that of neighbourhood women who dropped in occasionally. My curiosity in female forms of worship was appreciated as a consequence of my own gender and in response to

---

For a brief account on the Telugu diaspora in present-day Orissa, see Raja Rao (1999). The language distribution is given according to the *Orissa District Gazetteer* (Behuria 1995: 165), based on data from 1981.

[22] Considering Flueckiger's (1996) study on gender and genre in Chhattisgarh, I could have anticipated this categorization. Yet following K. B. Das' *Folklore of Orissa* (1991) I expected a vast tradition of oral narratives, dances and theatre forms. Many of these genres were either of sub-regional importance and not known in Ganjam, or they had already vanished. Female religious practices, however, were subsumed as folklore.

Besides this, there are few substantial studies on Oriya women: Marglin's (1985b) exploration on the now extinct tradition of temple dancers in Puri; L. N. Dash's (1993) survey on the socio-economic situation of rural women; and Seymour's (1999) study on education and its impact on the social status of women in urban Bhubaneswar (in chronological order). Meanwhile Tokita-Tanabe (1999a) has submitted a thesis on women's ritual practices in a village in Khurda District. This ethnography not only invites regional comparison, her theoretical approach was also very stimulating while reconsidering my own research assumptions. Recently, Schömbucher (2006) presented an in-depth study about deity possession among Telugu-speaking women in Puri, and Otten (2006) on women's healing practices among the Ronā, an indigenous community (Adivasi) living in the mountain area of Orissa.

a deity's reputation and power. Being of 'foreign caste' and Christian origin was no obstacle. However, finding suitable accommodation as a paying guest proved to be difficult. Providing accommodation for a woman raised several problems concerning the maintenance of ritual purity within the home (see Chapter 3) and also regarding my 'safety'. For an ethnographer this was indeed illuminating. Nevertheless, after the first intervals of fieldwork I moved to a guesthouse. One reason for this change was that I needed to attend rituals at night (see Chapter 6). My late return would have been a tremendous challenge to the honour of any host family. Although I gradually acquired some basic knowledge of Oriya (after language training in Hindi and Bengali in earlier years), I preferred to visit the rituals in the company of a female research assistant from the locality. This not only increased the pleasure of fieldwork and was helpful in a practical way, it also introduced another level of discursive reflection. Again, at night I had to rely on a male assistant.

Although this study invites to look at a female-centred world largely defined by religion, this perspective is not representative of *all* women, either at the sub-regional level or with respect to Orissa. Some Hindu women only rarely participate in religious activities, mostly due to pragmatic reasons such as workload, lack of time or expense. In this respect, social status matters. However, the following chapters will show that caste is hardly a factor that determines how rituals affect the gendered self. Brahminical and 'low-caste' values may differ but do not constitute contrastive ethical codes, as Karin Kapadia (1995) observed in southern India. Although the degree to which women identify with their religious practices varies, it would be misleading to draw an opposition of 'religious women' and their 'non-religious' counterpart. Even young, educated and—according to local classification—'modern' women do not (openly) criticize the female occupation with rituals. At some point in time, they would have also visited a temple, participated in a Hindu festival or joined a family celebration. However, Western or global values and lifestyles do influence not only women in Mumbai or Delhi, but have gradually come to reached regions such as southern Orissa (lately via the Internet). As in any other work by social anthropologists, the ethnographic present might thus refer to a rather short time-span. At any rate, the following study shows the satisfaction, joy and excitement female participants gain through the *regular* performance of rituals. I argue that women who abstain from the religious domain lose not only a sense of agency legitimized by their pious engagement, but also a source of self-esteem that allows for reframing and also practically influencing the lived-in world. Unless they do achieve any other source of power (for instance through work opportunities), women are much more tied by gender restrictions that, after all, shape secularized spheres and sections of society as well. Before I develop my argument in detail and with respect to different cultural performances, let me briefly sketch out the guiding theoretical assumptions of this study and introduce some key concepts of my research.

## The Self Performed

To conceive of women in southern Orissa as co-creators of their gendered reality might raise a certain scepticism about the assumed human subject position and the cross-cultural validity of analytic concepts. Most of these questions result, I believe, from two academic discourses that in recent decades received immense attention: first, the debate over the social construction of identities, and second, the concept of performance as the paradigm of postmodern society.[23] Both debates have produced diverse and also contested notions about the performativity of the self. In this section I shall clarify assumptions relevant to my own research approach, against the background of these ongoing debates.

The concept of 'doing gender' does *not* refer to the *intentionality* of action in the first place. In this respect, to 'negotiate' identity does not imply an interest in change. Although the display of gendered qualities of behaviour can include strategic articulation and identification with ideal constructs, in general it is anything but a self-conscious process. Conceptualizing gender as a performative category rather draws the scholarly attention to embodied practices, i.e., pre-reflective and somatic modes of expression and learning (see Csordas 1990, 1993, 1994). From this perspective, the human body is not looked at as a pre-discursive entity (a culturally neutral object), but is by itself 'socially informed' (Bourdieu 1977: 124), i.e., variable and shaped by living conditions. Conversely, the political gender debate that regards the self-fashioning of identities as liberating for all is, in my view, a particularly Western trope. In post-traditional society, the sociologist Anthony Giddens (1991)

---

[23] There is a vast body on literature on both subjects. See, for instance: Calhoun (1994); Giddens (1991); Hall and du Gay (1996); Jameson 1991; McKenzie (2001); Willems and Jurga (1998).

has argued, the active creation and refinement of the self came to define the human being. Unlike kinship and social roles that used to determine personhood in pre-modern times, self-identity emerged as a 'reflexive project' with the individual being responsible. This predominantly European and Anglo-American practice is based on the assumption that the individual can select from a variety of lifestyles, role models and cultural codes in order to achieve a consistent narrative about her- or himself. Historically, the relevance of this specific awareness was reflected by the popularization of the term 'identity' from the 1950s onwards, and culminated in postmodern debates on 'multiple', 'fragmented', 'fluid', and 'contested' identities.[24] This vision has also coined gender and queer studies, two emerging academic disciplines that are based on the assumption that gender-identity and sexual desire are constrained by hegemonic power structures. From their angle, the self-conscious play on gender stereotypes (such as in drag or camp) reveals the imitative nature of apparently given realities, and thus causes 'interstices' that are potentially subversive (see Butler 1990, 1993). The concept of gender performativity is taken as a political agenda, and thus related to the problematic notion of a voluntarist interpretation of gender (Morris 1995: 373; for explicitly feminist performance strategies, see Hart and Phelan 1993).

There is no Indian counterpart to this culture-specific discourse on the self.[25] Moreover, unlike the Cartesian notion of the autonomous person as a cognizing subject, a concept that served as prerequisite to (post-) modern debates on identity, Indian philosophical theories dismiss the everyday self with its ego obsession (Bharati 1985). According to this literature, caste, class, gender, personality, and subjectivity are to be regarded as ephemeral, contingent effects influenced by antecedent karmic causes. In the course of two thousand years

---

[24] For a recent overview on the history and career of the term 'identity', see Kaufmann (2005, part one), for the debate on identity in social anthropology, see Sökefeld (1999), a critical appraisal of the term is given by Brubaker and Cooper (2000).

[25] I am aware that holding such an opposition risks to invite trouble, not only because several recent scholars in the US are of Indian origin (Gayatri Spivak, to name a prominent example), but also because there are several scholars in South Asia who relate in their works to postmodern theories. However, even the latter criticize the Western bias in models of the self (Sunder Rajan 1993: 119–20); for a discussion on Indian feminist notions of agency and the collective see Gedalof (1999, Chapter 2).

philosophers have rather focused on the *eternal* self (see Bharati 1985; Butzenberger 2002). In reference to present-day social reality, however, the anthropologist Frédérique Marglin (1995: 128) claims that the 'bounded unitary self does not exist for . . . Oriya villagers, nor does an essentialist construction of personhood'. Indeed, the denial of individualism in Hindu teachings often serves academic scholars as a paradigm to distinguish 'Western' and 'Indian' society (see Dumont 1970). The absence of an equivalent concept is understood as a reflection of social reality rather than a moral ideal, best exemplified by McKim Marriott's (1976) conception of the 'dividual' person (rather than individual). According to Marriott, Indians conceive of themselves as divisible units – constantly transformed compositions of elementary coded substances exchanged and shared with others. Ronald Inden (1990) modifies this notion of 'collective agency', yet he also unmasks the emphasis on non-individuality as an Orientalist construct going back to the colonial encounter, when it was an attempt to deny Indians any agentive status of their own. However, ethnographers like Mattison Mines (1994) indeed show how personal autonomy is pursued within Indian society. The debate about individuality and its relevance to South Asia will probably go on.[26] From an anthropological angle, it is thus problematic to generalize the idea of the 'Western self'. Also, it is equally misleading to pursue the opposite and to deprive the other self-reflexive monitoring of action (Sökefeld 1999: 430).[27]

At any rate, the absence of a similar idea of personhood does not suggest that women in India are not able to consider their own position with respect to others. Although discourses on identity differ historically and culturally, reflections on who we are, on the diversity of being human and on categories in which one may associate with, are universals (Jenkins 1996: 9). The sociologist Veena Das (1976) has shown, for instance, how Punjabi women (and men) routinely consider the effects of their own behaviour on other family members, and thus actively 'mask' their intentions and engage in 'impression management' (Goffman 1959). Nevertheless, the form and dynamism

[26] If not stated otherwise, I employ the term 'individual' to address a discrete human being rather than the moral and cultural notion of individualism.

[27] However, during fieldwork ethnographers tend to overlook the egocentric behaviour of the individual and rather focus on its socio-centric dimension. For the debate on self-consciousness in social anthropology, see Cohen (1994) and Rapport (1997).

of 'doing gender' seems to vary according to region, as several authors have pointed out. According to Kapadia (1995), the social negotiation of gender in southern India is largely determined by caste and class, as opposed to reflecting a clear-cut category of its own. Erndl (cited from McGee 2000: 38) argues that in South Asia *gender identities* are fairly loosely defined and variable, whereas *gender roles* are fixed – contrary to the modern West where it is the other way round. Hence Indian women were faced with explicit expectations concerning their gender-specific duties, and comparatively unrestrained in delineating what it is to be feminine or masculine. Here Erndl follows the social historian and psychologist Ashis Nandy and his theory of gender fluidity. Nandy (1980: 42) asserts that 'in Hindu thought' there is no rigid dichotomy of masculinity and its inferior other; unlike in Western societies, the feminine is not perceived as an inversion of a male normative. Rather there is a large repertoire of moral qualities ascribed to women that also includes activism, aggression, competition, and intrusiveness. Conversely, 'the softer forms of creativity and the more intuitive and introspective styles of intellectual and social functioning are not strongly identified with femininity.' (Nandy 1980: 38) Thus the images, gestures and traits employed in 'doing gender' seem to vary as well as their sign quality itself. Similarly, Nita Kumar (1994a: 3) emphasizes that the protest of Indian women often does not take well recognized forms but appears in various other permutations of the everyday, such as evasive tactics or a distinct language use.

'Doing gender' describes socially appropriate mimetic forms of action, i.e., the re-enactment of conventions. It is about making belief rather than make-believe or play-acting. Accordingly, notions such as 'performance' and 'theatricality' are employed to suggest that gender *is* acted out and put into force, rather than with the intention of asking *why* it is done and whether for the sake of an (imagined) audience or not. To the contrary, to think of the social world as a form of theatre is basically a culture-specific metaphor. It relies heavily on the Cartesian dichotomy of mind and body, and also on a distinct perspective on truth and reality. Therefore Edward Schieffelin (1997: 202) argues that it is problematic to assume a *homo performans* in those communities who do not conceive of the world as a stage. This is partly true for India. In Hindu terms, the world emerged from divine play (*līlā*) and mortals are in principle able to participate in this divine play for a limited duration, for instance, during a ritual performance of the same name: *līlā*. Yet to do so, they should ignore, if not abandon, their ordinary self, defined by false consciousness. In other words, whereas the everyday reality is considered fictitious in character (*māyā*), the *līlā* stage is associated with eternal truth in that the human performer is turned into a divine vessel. Not self-conscious play-acting but submission to supernatural powers constitutes the ideal behaviour of an actor.[28] Thus the distinction of appearance and reality, and the qualities associated with both, resemble cultural categories rather than human universals. Schieffelin's critique is particularly relevant to those scholars who follow the sociologist Goffman and his approach to self-presentation (see Srinivasan 1990). Goffman regards gender display as a form of coding that is basically subjected to the reflecting mind. As mentioned before, the notion of 'doing gender' is different since it addresses a permanent process that mostly escapes human control. If gender identification is shown intentionally, it is likely to appear artificial. To sum up, one can say that the acting involved in 'doing gender' is manifest in the reproduction of, participation in and shaping of cultural practices and tacit knowledge.

Considering the performative in respect to the constitution of gender, several scholars have criticized the ambiguity of the academic terminology, and the intermingling of performance and performativity in particular.[29] In the social sciences the notion of performance and related terms is indeed used in various ways (see Carlson 1996; Schieffelin 1997; Parker and Sedgwick 1995; Wirth 2002). First, it addresses intentional bounded productions that involve a certain consciousness of the performer(s), highlight symbolic and aesthetic features, and have specific purposes or qualities for the people who observe them (Schieffelin 1997: 195). Thus, the term performance refers to those events that can be loosely classified as theatre or (secular) ritual. Several scholars would include everyday enactments, supposing

[28] For a further discussion on the implicit theories of acting perpetuated by the Rāmlīlā tradition in contrast with events classified as possession see Hauser 2008a. On the concept of *līlā*, see Sax (1995a), who elsewhere (2002) also analyzed ritual theatre (Pāṇḍav līlā) as a cultural site to enact collective identities.

[29] Meanwhile studies that focus on theatrical practices shaping gender have mushroomed across several academic disciplines. The idea of gender being 'carved out' through performance is not entirely new, but was antedated by anthropological studies on initiation. In this context, becoming a social and gendered persona was enforced by intense psychophysical experiences, such as self-induced pain or the isolation of adepts.

one or more persons assume responsibility to address an audience, such as in the ironic display of gender stereotypes (on this 'breakthrough' into performance, see Hymes 1975). Second, performance addresses the expressive dimension of everyday interaction rather than a class or subset of behaviour. In this case, the term alludes to the realization of culturally pre-structured forms, and thus to episodes that potentially differ from incorporated sets of disposition, i.e., habitus (Bourdieu 1977; see Bal 2002: 263). From this angle, performance embraces the theatricality and contingency inherent to social practice. Following a third line of thinking, performativity is opposed to expressiveness. Here the focus is on non-referential acts, i.e., a type of behaviour that, like illocutionary speech, becomes effective not due to its semiotic potential but rather by means of its conventionalized form. Moreover, performative acts are conceived as an instrument to bring about subjectivity, instead of a (creative) product of a pre-existing 'author' or self. Thus performance alludes to the power of discourse to bring about the effects that it designates (Butler 1990, 1993: 2). It emphasizes cultural norms that authorize gender enactments, and also the process of their 'naturalization'.

All three ways of employing the term performance in the exploration of gender constitution refer to different epistemological categories. Broadly speaking, in my research I concentrate on framed enactments (the first notion of performance) in order to show how its realization (including the second notion) interferes with day-to-day performativity (the third idea of performance) of the gendered body, and by doing so gives impetus to women's self-understanding. For this purpose I use the term performativity in a general sense to signify the efficacy of enactments on the embodied mind. The distinction of social practice on one hand, and framed events on the other, is to some extent artificial – both are prone to mutual influence (see U. Rao 2006: 13–14). This will become particularly clear when analyzing the routine display of menstrual pollution in social interaction. These enactments are embedded in day-to-day activities, and thus have only a loosely defined beginning and end. They cannot be considered as cultural performance in a strict sense (as discussed later). Still these episodes visualize and perpetuate religious doctrines and have tremendous effect on women's self-understanding. Their analysis will emphasize the agentive dimension of the human body itself, i.e., the force of embodied practices to shape emotions vis-à-vis one's self and the social world. Yet, the majority of this book will focus on framed events, where the subtle process of 'doing gender' continues or is even heightened, as the following section will show in detail.

## Performance and Transformation

Anthropologists seek to explore public events and performances for different reasons: (*a*) as 'total social facts' (Mauss) allowing insight into all aspects of society; (*b*) as sites of collective self-definition and memory; (*c*) as social meta-commentary on normative ideas and incidents; and (*d*) as institutions that shape specific ways of seeing, listening and understanding (tacit sensibilities). In this respect, rituals, lectures, concerts, plays, festivals, theatre, political rallies, sporting events, etc., are classified as 'cultural performance'. This term goes back to Milton Singer (1959: xiii) who thought of ultimate units of observation that each have 'a definitely limited time span, a beginning and end, an organized program of activity, a set of performers, an audience, and a place and occasion of performance.' Yet, Singer not only introduced an umbrella term that henceforth could compensate ethnocentric genre classifications (for instance, regarding connotations such as authenticity), he rather conceived of these events as collective forms of self-presentation. Singer was convinced that 'perhaps all peoples . . . think of their culture as encapsulated in such discrete performances, which they can exhibit to outsiders as well as to themselves' (ibid.), and that these genres were 'interrelated so as to constitute "a culture"' (Singer 1972: 72). Although in retrospective his understanding of culture as a summary of separate self-presentations has become highly questionable, Singer deserves the credit for pointing towards the theatricality of social practice as an inherent constituent of culture.[30] In this respect Singer's notion antedates recent theories on the performative construction of reality (Fischer-Lichte 2002: 290). However, he also shows the impact of meta-communicative frames on the

[30] More than 30 years later, Singer had not verified his concept of self-consciously performed culture as the following statement shows: '"Cultural performances" . . . were, first of all, performances, that is, enactments of some episode or feature of a myth or legend, or historical story-plot, whether they were songs, dances, dramas, recitations, prayers, festivals or the like. Secondly they were . . . observable units of a feature of a cultural tradition in these various media. A third, . . . they were *identified and exhibited by members of the society as encapsulating forms of their culture which they considered suitable to display for themselves and outsiders.* In other words: the cultural performances were for them expression of a cultural self-image' (Singer 1992: 23, my emphasis).

self-awareness of social actors, like the emphatic display of self-images (or their abandonment, I should like to add) during bounded and culturally pre-structured events. This aspect is particularly relevant to my own research on the performative negotiation of the gendered self.

In fact, framing produces several interrelated effects. It marks off space and time of special significance, thus making it possible to view and evaluate what is inside, like dramatic and social scripts and their mode of realization. In this respect cultural performances are more than entertaining or functional, they also invite performers to memorize, re-enact and to reflect on shared experience, cultural paradigms and history (see J. Assmann 1992). 'Whether this program is flexible or fixed, conscious or unconscious, consensual or conflictive, or, as is usually the case, a little of each, there is no performance without preformance,' John MacAloon (1984: 9) explains. Although this original could exist merely in the realm of the imaginary, a cultural performance is never only a 'model of' but also a 'model for' reality, to use Clifford Geertz' terminology. Scholars think of them as particularly apt occasions to evaluate imaginative qualities, and to manipulate meanings in order to bring about new perceptions of oneself and one's social relationships in the lived-in world.

Furthermore, framing produces an essentially 'subjunctive mood'.[31] While turning into a performer — a ritual specialist, stage character or football player — a person is invited to assume a supposed state and to follow a pre-structured program. Thus framing orients the attention towards another reality and imposes special rules of reception, for instance, to assess gestures and facial expressions as suffering or, conversely, as triumph. Simultaneously performance evokes real feelings — leaving behind participants with legs turned to jelly or with hitherto unknown energetic powers, in happiness or awestruck. Moreover, the reference to an imagined reality provides performers with the freedom of invention and interpretation that is not envisaged with regard to the social reality.[32] This hints to the political impact of, for instance, carnivalesque allusion or satire. Here subjunctivity creates real effects, including pain; although, and precisely *because*, the actors draw on the realm of imagination.

[31] This term was coined by Victor Turner (1991: 11) who defines cultural subjunctivity as 'the mood of maybe, might-be, as-if, hypothesis, fantasy, conjecture, desire'.

[32] Bailey (1996: 13) convincingly shows this mechanism with reference to village politics in Orissa.

For some scholars cultural performance is primarily a *form of representation*. The major premise is that these enactments are effective since their symbols 'express' and instill meaning to particular problematic situations, and then reframe, transform or intensify this sense, leading to a new orientation of the participants with respect to their situation (Schieffelin 1985: 707). The task of the ethnographer is then to analyze the logic of symbols and to decipher their meaning. From this perspective it appears to be the human psyche that is influenced by the power of symbolism in order to (re-)produce a feeling of shared values and communality. However, this approach fails to consider how cultural performance can transform participants through (among other things) interpersonal dynamics, contingent factors and unforeseen external influences, so that it becomes authoritative in offering new perspectives on the social world.[33] Hence anthropologists such as Schieffelin (1997: 194) locate the generative potential of cultural performance in its presences and suggest regarding *performance as self-referential act*:

> Performance deals with actions more than text: with habits of the body more than structures of symbols, of illocutionary rather than propositional force, with the social construction of reality rather than its representation (. . .) Performances, whether ritual or dramatic, create and make present realities vivid enough to beguile, amuse or terrify. And through these presences, they alter moods, social relations, bodily dispositions and states of mind.

Rather than searching for the 'meaning' of a certain sequence the challenge thus is to sense emergent effects and forces that shape the reality of performance. Shifting the focus on the aesthetics of an event, we may ask how non-discursive aspects of Hindu rituals possibly recode the corporeal knowledge of female performers about themselves as gendered beings. This ability to influence the embodied mind also shows why cultural performance is a particularly forceful agent in identity politics.

---

[33] The notion of performance as representation is also problematic in other respects. Can anthropologists indeed anticipate ontologically prior meanings, on gender, power, etc., that are communicated during performance, and to what extent are these cognitively understood by participants? This methodological challenge cannot be resolved by alternative modes of relating performance and reality, as Handelman (1990) suggests, when differentiating between public events that: (*a*) mime; (*b*) reflect on; or (*c*) confront and play with the social world.

The importance of aesthetics as a cause of transformation in the self-understanding of participants is well-known among scholars working on ritual.[34] They acknowledge ritual experience as an outcome of (also) dramaturgical features, for instance the sequencing of an event, the rhythm of prayers, the use of high-pitched music, and fast drum beating, or the systematic interweaving of comedy and transgression. These features culminate in the 'liminal' phase of ritual. Drawing on Arnold van Gennep's three-stage model of rites of passage, Victor Turner (1982, 1984, 1991) has argued that this transitory phase – 'between-and-betwixt' the positions assigned – essentially involves aesthetic means to mark and to effect transition. In this condition a person is aware of nothing but her or his own experience and state. This temporary suspension (and occasionally inversion) of social reality, basic values and moral truths – in short, liminality – allows participants to reconsider and also to reorient themselves. The impact of ritual aesthetics on perception and everyday self-understanding is particularly explicit in case of healing ceremonies (see Desjarlais 1992; Kapferer 1983; Laderman and Roseman 1996).

In Turner's view, only rituals are designed to enforce *collective* and *permanent* transformation. In this respect they differ from drama performance where, according to him, the reorganization of the self is optional. Yet the contrast of ritual and theatre and their respective effects is not that clear, as the theatre director and leading performance-studies scholar Richard Schechner (1985) has pointed out. Schechner is committed, primarily, to the similarity of both genres, concerning the structure of the event, the function of aesthetics and also the process from preliminaries to aftermath. He also shows that the boundaries of ritual and theatre are flexible, in a historical respect and also within one and the same performance. Thus, ritual can turn into theatre, whereas 'social drama' and play may interfere with and dominate ritual. From this angle, any performance is effective, yet the transformative capacity is not only directed to a given purpose (as it is in healing rituals or in the case of initiation), but rather concerns a variety of phenomena that are characterized by the ambiguity, oscillation and metamorphosis

[34] According to Tambiah's (1979) 'performative approach' to ritual, dramaturgical features constitute one of three dimensions in which ritual becomes effective. His theory in fact inspired several anthropological studies; see, for instance, Emigh (1996); Hobart and Kapferer (2005); Kapferer (1983); Köpping (1997); Köpping and Rao (2000); Sax (2002); Turner (1982); and Williams and Boyd (1993).

of theatrical, perceptual and ontological issues. Therefore, the theatre historian Erika Fischer-Lichte (2004: 307) proposes the conception of liminality as the essential precondition of aesthetic experience in general. However, scholars have only just started to give systematic consideration to the physiological, affective, energetic, and motorial states caused by performance, for instance with respect to the nexus of music and emotion (see Becker 2004; Friedson 1996).

Whereas Turner regards the liminal as a transitory phase of the ritual process, Bruce Kapferer (2005, 2006) proposes that aesthetic features induce a reality of their own – namely virtuality – that is to spill over into the non-ritual life.[35] Virtuality, in Kapferer's sense, is neither a reproduction of external realities nor a reflection of these, but is characterized by their radical suspension, the 'pleasure of forgetfulness' so to speak. Thus, Kapferer turns the conventional understanding of ritual as a symbolic representation upside down; what matters according to him is ritual's very disjunction from the world. (Yet he does not reject that rituals may also represent meaning.) In other words, ritual creates a kind of 'phantasmagoric space' with its own modalities of human experience. This situation allows the re-imagining and redirection of the self. According to Kapferer (2006: 672), virtuality serves as 'a technological dynamic for the (re)creation, (re)generation, (re)production, redirection, or intervention within the circumstances and continuity of personal realities and social and political forms of human life.' And yet the virtual is not simply auto-suggestive but the perceptual ground for the construction of meaning and the extension towards new horizons. In this respect, aesthetics are thoroughly constitutive for the emergent result of ritual rather than merely a decorative addition.

To sum up, the debate on ritual and cultural performance offers a variety of arguments concerning the means in which framed events create extraordinary experiences and give impetus to identity and self-understanding. However, several issues are taken for granted rather

[35] In his explorations on virtuality Kapferer draws on the works of Gilles Deleuze and Felix Guattari and also on the philosopher Susan Langer. Kapferer's interest in virtuality was antedated by his previous studies on exorcism and sorcery in Sri Lanka. In this context he had already realized that rituals work through the performative manipulation of their frames, their organization of space and time, aesthetic distance, interactions of the audience and finally commitment to the performance reality (Kapferer 1983).

than addressed systematically: how do personal, emotional and somatic experiences during performative acts become authoritative, and thus influence the perception of self and reality even after the end of the event? What means foster these sensations so as to leave permanent imprints on the self-identity of performers and participants alike? In concluding this section on cultural performance and transformation, I wish to add two points on the function of ritual in processes of identity formation: first, regarding the release from individual utilitarian acting associated with the social persona, and second, concerning the authority given to subjunctivity and contingency in the realm of religion.

Whoever joins a cultural performance is invited to follow certain pre-established patterns of behaviour and to assume a 'subjunctive mood'. In this regard the performer is, partly or substantially, set free from her or his everyday subject position and the fulfillment of related role expectations. Theorizing on the quality of ritualized action, Caroline Humphrey and James Laidlaw (1994) call this new personal stance 'ritual commitment'. It is defined by the suspension of ordinary logics of acting, and converted by means of appropriating and reproducing archetypical, apprehensible and stipulated sequences. This encounter with 'non-intentional' action endows performers with reflective distance, and is therefore an invitation to 'work on' the self in various ways (ibid.: 249). It reminds performers not only of their own agency but also demands imaginative input. According to Humphrey and Laidlaw, the ritualized mode of action implies an *ontologically produced vacuum* that makes it particularly appropriate to be loaded with interpretation (ibid.: 168, chapter 7).[36] Rather than focusing on the mode of action, Peter Köpping, Bernhard Leistle and Michael Rudolph (2006b) differentiate ritual as 'an object of identity construction' employed by social actors to negotiate external ascription and internal response and, what is more, ritual as a *type of perceptual situation* that shapes the 'field of identity constitution'. In the latter case, the authors

[36] Humphrey and Laidlaw do not assume that ritual performers are free to invent whatever ritual meaning they like. Rather devotees always strive to make sense of their program of ritual acts, and since there is rarely an explicit or rational reason for certain movements, forms of uttering or the sequencing of an event, they are left on themselves to recognize why to fold hands or circulate a sacred light.

stress the impact of pre-conscious modes of meaning production and argue, in reference to Humphrey and Laidlaw, that the attention towards repetitiveness allows those traits of habitual behaviour that usually escape awareness to be considered. 'What ritual performances seem to achieve is a distinctive way of relating the individual person to super-individual structure, while at the same time realizing that structure by means of individual embodiment.' (Köpping, Leistle and Rudolph 2006a: 23)

Thus, rituals provoke and raise self-reflection in cognitive terms. At the same time, they privilege the body as an experiencing agent – psychophysical reactions and expressions that are beyond human control. According to Thomas Csordas (1993), the 'somatic mode of attention' allows a person to perceive and identify hitherto non-specific bodily sensations and, as in the realm of spirit healing, to regard them as meaningful or rather as indexical signs of non-human origin. This exposure to unintended and often uncontrolled forms of somatic learning is also described by the concept of 'passiones', revived by Fritz Kramer (1993, drawing on Godfrey Lienhardt). In fact many religious traditions employ the physicality of the body to provoke experiences beyond the self. The technique is based on the dialectics of agency and patiency, as Burkhard Schnepel (2006: 125, 2008: 123–27, 2009) has argued in reference to Dando Nato (the author's spelling of Daṇḍa Nāṭa), a ritual dance in Orissa. Here male adepts self-consciously offer their human agency, verbalized as submission to the divine, and as a result, are in the position to fully experience the 'passiones' – the effects caused by the rules, restrictions and the dynamics of this performance. The sensation of ritual empowerment is thus based on the voluntary abandoning of social persona and individuality.

From a theoretical perspective, it remains unclear whether only ritual, rather than framed events in general, operates on the meta-communicative suspension of individual agency in favour of pre-established patterns of action and perception. This is partly a problem of analytic classification. Scholars hardly agree on the concept of ritual, for instance, whether the term exclusively addresses forms of worship and thus religious events, or rather specific patterns and strategies of social practice, like routine behaviour and, alternately, 'secular rituals'.[37] Following the ethnographic accounts mentioned earlier in the discussion, the credibility and authority given to the

[37] On the problem of conceptualizing ritual see, exemplarily: Goody (1977); Bell (1992); and Humphrey and Laidlaw (1994).

sentient body and aesthetic experiences, in regard to the everyday self-understanding of the ritual performer, seems to be inherently linked to and caused by the religious realm. These sets of embodied practices and beliefs, legitimized with reference to transcendent or divine powers, not only generate a privileged discourse, they also provide a rationale to *locate* contingent influences and incidents that create the specific yet ephemeral experience of performance. Unlike in theatre, art, sport or political events – occasions that may produce equally intense affective and corporeal reactions – the notion of the sacred, divine or supernatural seems to endow devotees with tacit knowledge about the origin of non-intended modes of experience and their potentially meaningful character, or at least with the *option* to assess psychophysical reactions in this regard. Furthermore, religion not only has the authority of the divine but also of tradition. From this angle, the religious domain is prone to create perceptual situations that legitimize and privilege non-intended somatic modes of experience. Hence, I assume that religious performances are more likely, than other framed events, to challenge self-understanding vis-à-vis the social world.

## The Structure of the Book

In the following chapters I shall analyze several religious or semi-religious events, in order to trace bodily, affective and reflective moments that influence the perception of ritual reality and its effects on women's gendered identities. Each chapter also advances related conceptual issues concerning the theoretical nexus of cultural performance, transformation and identity, i.e., the field of scholarly investigation I briefly outlined earlier in the discussion.[38]

Chapter 1 looks at the Jahni Oṣā, a religious fast that pro-mises adolescent girls a good husband – at the turn of the twenty-first century a religious practice that raised several doubts. I am interested

---

[38] Several of these case studies have been published elsewhere (Hauser 2004a, 2004b, 2005, 2006b, 2006d, 2008c, 2011b). They have been composed gradually over the past few years and have received where necessary thorough revisions and extensions for the purpose of this book. For the discussion of related issues that go beyond the structure of this book, see Hauser (2007, 2008a, 2010b, 2011a).

in the ways young women understand this ritual and what psychophysical experiences they gain by their participation. It will turn out that the Jahni Oṣā is not only understood as a ritual confining teenage girls to a very narrow gender role, but participants find it attractive since it conveys a sudden social recognition as an (almost adult) woman. It introduces girls to a major gender-specific form of worship (namely votive rites/fasts), and invites them to consider religion as a sphere of self-realization. In conclusion, the doubts about the objectives of the Jahni Oṣā are traced to the novelty of this religious practice in the biography of its performers, who at this time only get a first taste of their gender-specific ritual agency. From a theoretical aspect, this chapter looks at the process of embodiment with respect to the emergence of ritual credibility. It shows that the observance of this votive rite cannot be reduced to a hegemonic practice enforcing female passivity. Rather, teenagers discuss their ideas and worries concerning love and their future life on other occasions.

Chapter 2 turns to the observance of another votive rite, the Niśā Maṅgaḷabāra Oṣā. Here the female potential to bring about well-being reveals its ambivalent character and conveys a heavy burden. In the centre of my investigation lies the seasonal worship of the goddess Maṅgaḷā by married women in a particular neighbourhood. This ritual is fairly new in the region. It was introduced in the early 1990s on the initiative of an elderly lady. I am interested in the self-governing of this ritual, i.e., in women's practical and tacit knowledge of the proper design and direction of worship. Unlike priestly ceremonies, the ritual acts are hardly outlined by written sources (apart from the recitation of a legend). Rather the religious procedure is authorized by the convincing performance of the pious leader, whose bodily presence absorbs any doubts about the legitimacy of her inventions. Mutual conviction to follow the 'rules and regulations' is also achieved by what I conceptualize as the 'personalization' of worship, thus connecting individual motives to observe the votive rite with qualities ascribed to the goddess, in this case, the ability to ease the suffering of her devotees. In the course of the ritual, this resonates in the double-edged notion that women are able to bear more burdens than men, compensated only by the pleasures of worship.

Chapter 3 is an excursus on everyday performativity and its impact on women's self-understanding. It focuses on social practices that from an emic perspective are conceived neither as self-contained events nor as religious practices. Still these actions stress a quality or rather condition that informs the performance of any Hindu ritual – the concept of purity and pollution. Considering (im-)purity as a performative category, the chapter shows how this idea achieves the status of social reality. I analyze the subtle ways in which women communicate the impurity caused by their menstruation, and also how they reflect on this construct. It shall argue that rather than blindly following obsolete menstrual taboos, Hindu women engage in a continuous process of marking their body's ritual qualification. Turning to the other side of the coin, I show how the display of purity and auspiciousness in everyday life is crucial for women's self-image, and compensates for the limitations during menses. Since menstrual restrictions vary according to caste and region, women are likely to reflect on their observance. While the practical consequences of impurity are subject to interpretation and manipulation (for instance by means of pharmaceuticals), the association of menstruation with pollution is beyond question. In any case, this does not allow any straightforward conclusions on women's self-esteem. No matter how they assess menstrual bleeding, the regular repetition of body practices rather than a cognitive decision brings about the power and persistence of the 'periodic' feeling of being untouchable. In comparison to cultural performances and their potential to verify identity, this excursus shows the continuum of theatricality.

The following two chapters deal with the socio-religious practice of goddess possession, i.e., female behaviour that is rationalized in terms of divine agency. Chapter 4 introduces different social settings that invite possession in southern Orissa. Although moments of possession are thought to be extraordinary events, the idea of a woman being overwhelmed by a spirit or deity is quite common. Generally, the respective female host and her family appreciate this occasion. In spite of the exhausting physical side effects, the divine encounter raises the reputation of a woman. This dimension is hardly recognized in the academic discourse on (divine and demonic) possession in South Asia, where the women involved are almost exclusively seen as passive victims. They appear to be vulnerable to being controlled by exterior forces, in their daily lives or in an altered state of consciousness. Previously scholars have analyzed possession in terms of mental disorder, personal distress and subversive critique. The apparently disparate assessment of divine overpowering in Orissa partially reflects the regional manifestation of goddess worship. Furthermore, I suggest, it has derived from the dynamics of ethnographic knowledge production itself. Whereas the psychological and socio-political rationale of possession relate to common local arguments, the religious experience of divine possession is a matter of social contestation. Since it is far less articulated in public discourse, scholars are less likely to take it into consideration. With respect to women in southern Orissa (if not elsewhere), goddess possession constitutes one of the major types of ritual behaviour, and legitimates their engagement in rituals as well as their perspective on Hinduism.

In Chapter 5, I take a further step towards the analysis of goddess possession. Assuming that the somatic recognition of a super-natural agent is a cultural construct that evokes real experiences, I explore how possessed women, in retrospect, identify and appreciate a deity's pursuit of their body, and thus, give shape to and materialize otherness. These women personify the divine generative power (*śakti*) by carrying a sacred pot on their head as part of private processions undertaken on the roads of Berhampur. This type of procession includes huge masks or rather statues of goddesses, a ritual specialist costumed as Kāḷī, one or two married women carrying a sacred pot each, and finally their family on whose behalf the procession is held. The analysis of two possession episodes, and also their evaluation by the respective mediums, shows the diversity of individual perception while realizing normative ideas on the iconography, moods and behaviour of a goddess. The personal experience of being possessed needs to be confirmed by the ritual specialist, who employs a mask to interact with the embodied goddess and mediates divine orders. This social negotiation of divine presence is sustained, and at times challenged, by the visible reactions of devotees. Therefore, whether possessed or as spectators, women are actively involved in perpetuating the discourse on religion, personhood and gender, and thus facilitate the reality of divine possession.

The remaining portion of the book concentrates on Ṭhākurāṇī Yātrā, a festival that is celebrated in honour of Buṙhī Ṭhākurāṇī, the tutelary deity of Berhampur. Every second year she is made to leave her temple for about three weeks in order to visit her parents, identified with the head of the weaver community and his wife, the Deśībeherāṇī. Chapter 6 explores the festival as a ritual site and focuses on the prominent role of women in respect to the daily conduct of nocturnal processions. Similar to Buṙhī Ṭhākurāṇī and her eight sisters, the Deśībeherāṇī and selected women proceed through the old town, gradually outlining and identifying the goddess' parental village. Once Buṙhī Ṭhākurāṇī enters a neighbourhood, women come and worship her on behalf of their families. On the final night the goddess is given a farewell and ten thousand women accompany the divine return journey, each of them carrying a sacred pot. Crowds of spectators follow. This primacy of women during the festival contrasts not only with their general absence in nocturnal life, but also with the privacy of their ritual activities at other times. The analysis shows that women's public ritual role is required to cope with the 'dark' quality of Buṙhī Ṭhākurāṇī, who preferably 'travels through the night' and alludes to dangerous supernatural beings.

Chapter 7 considers the ludic dimension of Ṭhākurāṇī Yātrā, and evaluates masquerades performed to please the goddess. Unlike the carrying of a sacred pot, to put on a disguise is a purely male practice. Young men dress as tigers, deities and various social characters. People invent all kinds of pious, funny and also provocative costumes. I argue that these disguises are not only understood in their semiotic sense, but role-taking is also considered as a body practice initself, serving the temporary annihilation of the self and thus a devotional exercise. Similar to women's nocturnal processions, the male practice of masquerading implies transgression, yet there are clearly gender-specific ways to cross the boundaries and, following Bataille, to prove the transcendental quality of time and place. Whereas women appropriate the night and, not only in the case of possession, are identified with the goddess, men need to modify their bodies in order to achieve transformation. In both cases, the link between the individual and her or his actions is resolved, yet only male transgressions provoke public debate. Furthermore, the convention of costuming sustains the notion of a gender-specific permeability of the self. Whereas men are considered as rather sealed entities, eligible to disguise and still made responsible for their provocations, the female self is thought prone to be absorbed and overwhelmed by the experience of divine presence.

Chapter 8 turns to Ṭhākurāṇī Yātrā as a field of communal politics involving various personal and collective interests. The twentieth-century history of the festival is marked by legal disputes about privileges, obligations and the correct ritual procedure. Rather than by shared cultural memories, Ṭhākurāṇī Yātrā is constituted by fragmented, complementary and at times competing bodies of knowledge that are advocated by different groups in the name of tradition. In this context, women may make a choice of identities and engage in (communal) politics or become subject to the politics of others. The debate stirred up after the 'faked' possession of the Deśībeherāṇī during one of the processions exemplarily shows the risk and ambivalence of public exposure. Although the Deśībeherāṇī fulfilled a prescribed ritual role, the publicity of the event invited spectators to think of her behaviour in terms of strategic self-presentation. Here the ultimate androcentric assessment of deviant female behaviour suspended the authorization women commonly achieve by means of their submission to the divine. Nevertheless, the ritual role bestowed the Deśībeherāṇī with 'social immunity'.

The ethnographic exploration shows how the performance of rituals constitutes a cultural field where women in southern Orissa can learn about themselves as powerful ritual and social actors. They can explore a variety of subject positions that exceed the religious gender role allotted to them by conservative Brahminical rhetoric. In this respect, the regular performance of religious functions not only brings about a 'sense of ritual' (Bell, following Bourdieu), but also a sense of being in control and acting upon the social world, a potential that is publicly legitimized by women's commitment to supernatural powers. Hence, ritual provides the agency (i.e., 'ritual agency') that allows women to make decisions and to behave in a way that cannot be denied by social superiors. This effect of ritual is supplemented by what I call 'personalization' — the validation of ritual acts on the basis of personal circumstances. To make it clear: I do not argue that performers are free to change rituals according to their liking, rather this form of authentication gives consideration to the personal dimension as an integral part of ritual. Some female ritual specialists (if not all) seem to modify religious scripts in order to create a feeling of resonance to their own self-understanding, a basically pre-reflective process. Conversely, the ritual roles may evoke experiences beyond the self and as a result foster awareness and reflectivity. Thus, empowerment through ritual is neither related to the intention of subverting religious doctrine nor to the internalization of a subaltern political discourse. The confidence of participants in ritual results rather from the pleasure, joy and excitement of its performance. I argue that certain seemingly restrictive religious practices create highly satisfactory experiences, regardless of the fact that they explicitly address helpless women, virgins in search of a husband or divine mothers.

# 1

# Tasting Ritual: How to Fast for a Good Husband

Once a year, girls in southern Orissa observe the Jahni Oṣā, a month-long votive rite in honour of the goddess Bṛndābatī. Her worship unites the girls from a particular street, who for this occasion create a temporary altar at a suitable semi-public site in their neighbourhood. This ritual is commonly thought of as an attempt 'to get a good husband', and is therefore repeated several times until the marriage of a girl is finalized. At the beginning of the twenty-first century, many participants did not believe in the purpose and efficacy of this votive rite. They performed the Jahni Oṣā with mixed feelings, if not as mere imitation of what they considered as tradition (*paramparā*). In local discourse, this attitude was understood as a result of improving female education and as a negative side effect of globalization. From this perspective, girls in earlier times did not reflect on the meaning of this votive rite. Their sincere devotion, rather than convention, motivated the performance. There is in fact no historical data to verify this hypothesis. Considering the practice of child marriage prevailing in the countryside of Orissa until recent decades,[1] one might assume that the votaries were at least young enough to approach the ritual in a playful manner.[2] Conversely,

[1] Statistically, even in 1998/1999 about half of the women in Ganjam District had an early marriage; according to the Government of Orissa (2004: 206) 50.7 per cent married before the age of 18. Unfortunately this governmental report does not reveal the basis of its evaluation, i.e., whether it refers to all registered marriages in 1998/1999 or a survey among married women in general.

[2] In nineteenth-century Bengal, girls were introduced to the performance of a similar votive rite by the age of five (S. C. Bose 1883: 35). To my knowledge there is no comparable data from Orissa. Senior women told me that in earlier times the Jahni Oṣā was done before menarche so as to guarantee the uninterrupted

doubts about the credibility of a comparable ritual that serves to find a good husband were already observed in the early 1960s among urban Bengali girls.[3] Regardless of how the attitude towards the Jahni Oṣā may have changed, in this chapter I shall approach the doubts about its efficacy from another angle.

Recent anthropological theorizing on ritual practice in South Asia has shown that a critical or even uninformed perspective on the significance of a ritual does not enforce its abandonment. Devotees rather consider and actively search for a variety of interpretations in order to make sense of their own ritual performance. Starting from this observation (and also with reference to the academic debate on ritual), Caroline Humphrey and James Laidlaw (1994) propose understanding ritual as a particular *mode* of action, rather than a type of event that conveys meaning. According to their theory, ritualized action is defined by a specific personal attitude and awareness of the participants ('ritual commitment'), i.e., a particular stance with respect to one's action. To think of ritual in this way raises the question of how rituals achieve credibility. This does not mean considering the success of a ritual literally, if this could be estimated at all, rather following this approach encourages us to look at the process of embodiment – the psychophysical experiences provoked by ritual, and their capacity to bring about a sense of truth, well-being and trust which encourages performers and others to undergo the ritual procedure again on another suitable occasion. Moreover, assuming that several votaries are critical as to the purpose and effects of the Jahni Oṣā, what alternative

---

performance during the complete month (on menstrual restrictions, see Chapter 3). The stories and songs recited during the Jahni Oṣā indeed address the votaries as 'children' (*pilāmāne*). However, this term also characterizes the kind of relationship devotees have with a 'mother' goddess. In one of the earliest English sources on votive rites in Orissa, Rājaguru ([1895] 1992: viii–ix) explains: 'Johni-Osa: It is held in the month of Bhadrapada, commencing on the 4th of the bright half and ending with the day of Dasara. It is confined exclusively to young unmarried girls. Every evening, they assemble together near the Tulasi basin and worship the goddess, Sarwa-Mangala, with *luffa acuttangula* flowers. The object of the Pooja is to secure immunity from widowhood and [sic] gain a large family of sons.' As will be shown further in this section, the present-day motivation and the time of the Jahni Oṣā varies slightly.

[3] Śibarātri Brata, the equivalent Bengali ritual to find a good husband is devoted to the worship of the god Śiba. During the fieldwork of Roy (1975: 38) in the early 1960s, girls in Calcutta openly discussed their doubts about the aim and effectiveness of this votive rite.

meanings do they identify with this religious act? Do they regard its performance as mere play-acting or social obligation?

Taking the example of the Jahni Oṣā, I wish to explore how the performance of a contested votive rite actually influences young women in their commitment to religion and also in their perception of femininity.[4] In what ways do they reflect on the Jahni Oṣā and rationalize their own participation? To what extent do the participants' intentions on performing the ritual differ, and how does this influence its experience? As a social and bodily practice, collective worship produces not only religious feelings, the observance of the Jahni Oṣā, like similar votive rites, also invites the social negotiation of gender stereotypes. 'Boys are not able to fast', several votaries mentioned to me and referred to the 'male' lack of self-discipline. Similarly, they were convinced that 'girls have more strength (*śakti*) than boys'. In the following sections I shall evaluate the experiences by seven groups performing the Jahni Oṣā.[5] It will be discussed how the performance of the ritual turns into an act which resonates with the adolescent's understanding of themselves as gendered beings, and also in what ways it guides girls' personal visions of adulthood. Does the pious image of women perpetuated by the discourse on the Jahni Oṣā compete, for instance, with the desire for love (marriage) or alternative role models that are not at all based on the institution of marriage?

Girls are made responsible for the independent performance of a class of rituals (votive rites), which makes them agents guaranteeing the well-being of others, most importantly their own prospective family. The performance of these religious observances invites girls to frame and legitimize their activities in terms of religion, and hence to follow their interests in such a way that escapes the control by social superiors. To follow this line, however, means to reconcile oneself to the traditional female role model. However, the perspective of those girls who completely avoided the observance of the Jahni Oṣā is not included in my exploration.

---

[4] A previous version of this chapter is published in Hauser (2008c).

[5] In the years 1999 and 2000 I joined seven groups performing the Jahni Oṣā. The social composition of these groups could be characterized as: (*a*) urban, middle class, high-caste; (*b*) urban, upper class, Brahmin; (*c*) rural, high-caste; (*d*) rural, multi-caste; (*e*) urban, untouchable; (*f*) urban, multi-caste; (*g*) urban, multi-caste, lower class. The participant observation was followed by narrative interviews with some of the devotees. These statements were verified in discussions with other people.

## The Performance of the Jahni Oṣā

In general, Hindu women perform a wide range of domestic religious duties: they take care of the house altar, worship the family deity and ancestral spirits, arrange and prepare offerings presented to deities, and organize the celebration of seasonal festivities. Moreover, in the northern half of the Indian subcontinent, the paradigm of female religiosity is the observance of votive rites (Oriya: *brata*, Sanskrit: *vrata*).[6] The term *brata*, literally 'promise' or 'vow', refers to particular sets of rituals initiated by the formal decision of a devotee, and performed to achieve well-being in the lived-in world. These ritual sets are distinguished and named according to: (*a*) the deity to whom the worship is directed; (*b*) the date and time when it is carried out; (*c*) the procedure of worship; or (*d*) particular food restrictions. Due to the dietary requirements, these sets of rituals are also known as fasts (Oriya: *oṣā*, Sanskrit: *upavāsa*). Although from the perspective of religious scholars there is a slight difference in the meaning and performance of a 'vow' and, respectively, a 'fast', women use these terms as synonyms.[7] This is also expressed by the colloquial Oriya appellation *oṣā-brata*. Which of the votive rites is actually called by either of these names depends on convention. Moreover, there are various types of religious vows that differ in their form of instrumentality. In Orissa people distinguish two types: (*a*) *brata*, signifying a promise in relation to women's votive rites; and (*b*) *mānasika*, a conditional pledge to win the favour of a deity (see Chapters 6 and 7). Occasionally the latter also takes place in conjunction with the performance of a votive rite.[8]

There are a great number of fasts distributed throughout the year. Each month, each weekday and other prominent dates of the Hindu calendar (for instance full moons) have their suitable votive rite, some

---

[6] Several studies show the popularity of votive rites in different regions of India: on fasting in Bengal see Fruzetti (1982), S. Gupta (1999) and McDaniel (2003), on fasting in Uttar Pradesh see Pearson (1996), Pintchman (2005), Tewari (1991) and Wadley (1980a), on fasting in Maharashtra see McGee (1987, 1991) and on fasting in Chhattisgarh see Babb (1975). There is little scholarly evidence on fasting (Tamil: *nōnpu*) in southern India (see Duvvury 1991, Reynolds 1980), Pearson (1996) provides some comparative data from Kerala.

[7] On the different classes of soteriological and 'mundane' vows in South Asia, see Raj and Harman (2006).

[8] In English publications this class of rituals is also termed as 'votive observances', 'domestic rituals' or 'fasts and festivals'. Indeed, most Hindu festivals include food restrictions.

limited to half a day, others lasting up to one month. Some are carried out alone, some are observed in a group. Most of them are intended for married participants, some for unmarried girls and some for senior women (after menopause) and widows. While some votive rites are limited to a certain stage in life, others are performed yearly or, to the contrary, only once in a lifetime. In this respect, the performance of votive rites corresponds to seasonal and biographical phases. An Oriya manual lists altogether 83 different types of *oṣā-brata* (Miśra 1994).[9] At the beginning of the twenty-first century, some of them were hardly known and others had merely sub-regional importance. At any rate, most Oriya women considered only a selection of these *oṣā-brata*, corresponding to their personal liking, family tradition and social circumstances (and hence also caste). After all, the performance of votive rites had to be arranged to fit in with other duties, whether household chores, agricultural labor or an office job.[10]

The Jahni Oṣā is embedded in this Hindu tradition of votive rites. Its performance is limited to Orissa, specifically popular in the southern part, where it is observed by both Oriya and Telugu speaking girls between the ages of 10 and 25.[11] It is usually the first *oṣā-brata* in a woman's ritual biography and is followed by several others in later years. Although the Jahni Oṣā transmits a particular local flavor, it has some parallels with religious practices followed in other parts of India. On the one hand, it corresponds to similar votive rites as Śiba (-rātri) Brata in northern Orissa and Bengal, that are performed to find a good

[9] In the pilgrim centre of Benares religious compendiums include up to 134 votive rites (Pearson 1996: 89). According to Wadley (1983: 92), who compared nine compilations of fasts and festivals published in northern India, these books mention between 12 and 144 rituals, amounting to a total of 184 *different* events.

[10] The most popular votive rites among women in southern Orissa are Lakṣmī Pūjā, Somnātha Brata, Sābitrī Brata, Bālukā Pūjā (Rāi Dāmodara Brata), Polari Oṣā, Kedāra Brata, Khudurūkuṇī Oṣā, Āmḷā Nabamī, Boita Bandanā (Baṙa Oṣā), Nāgala Cauṭhi Oṣā and Rabi Nārāẏaṇa Brata.

[11] In publications on Orissa, there is little reference to the Jahni Oṣā. Recently, Tokita-Tanabe (1999a: 35–37) described the performance of this votive rite in a village in Khurda District. Apart from her study, authors represent the Jahni Oṣā according to its songs and legends as if these dealt with timeless social and historical facts (for instance K. B. Dash 1991: 114; Raut 1988: 82), i.e., in fact similar to devotional digests that describe this fast for prospective votaries (like Miśra 1994: 81–84).

husband (see S. Gupta 1999: 94; Roy 1975: 37). On the other hand, it alludes to the popular worship of *tuḷasī*, the Indian basil plant that is revered all over the subcontinent as the personification of a goddess by the same name. Hindu women take the utmost care of this sacred plant, which is commonly grown on a small platform in the courtyard of their house (see Huyler 1994). *Tuḷasī* leaves are considered to be very pure and serve as offerings to a deity, to avoid evil spirits and as a home remedy for many forms of sickness. According to Hindu mythology, the goddess Tuḷasī is associated with the male deities Nārāẏaṇa, Kṛṣṇa and Jagannātha.

The celebration of the Jahni Oṣā is scheduled in the Hindu month of *āśvina* (September/October). It promotes the intense worship of the goddess Bṛndābatī, a manifestation of Tuḷasī. Between five and 15 girls from one neighbourhood join forces to construct a temporary altar where they pray to the goddess twice a day, from the first to the last day of the month. The main worship (*pūjā*) takes place in the evening and may last for approximately one hour. Throughout the month, votaries have to be particularly strict to maintain ritual purity. To make their body eligible for the performance of the ritual, they follow a vegetarian diet and avoid garlic, onions and hot spices (besides a variety of other items). The main point is, however, the prohibition of cutting, preparing or eating ridge gourd (*jahni*). Although the blossoms of this gourd vegetable are essential for the worship of the goddess Bṛndābatī and thus the performance of the Jahni Oṣā – literally the 'ridge gourd fast' – girls are not allowed to pluck them. To get these flowers, which blossom only in the evening, they rely on the help of others.

The Jahni Oṣā is celebrated outdoors on a terrace or some other (semi-) public site that achieves religious status for the duration of this month. This location has to accommodate a temporary altar with a basil plant, a number of sacred pots and, of course, the votaries. The daily maintenance and arrangement of this site constitutes a major part of the evening ritual. It serves to invite the goddess. First, the floor has to be purified and covered with red soil. This base is decorated with abstract and floral ornaments (*jhoṭi*) made of coloured rice powder. The centre is reserved for a highly decorated pot of raw clay that contains the basil plant (*tuḷasī caurā*). It is raised on a small platform and surrounded by the sacred pots (*kumbha*). At the beginning of the month, every girl who aims to join the Jahni Oṣā has to contribute and consecrate one of them. In front of the *tuḷasī* plant, girls place a small wooden pedestal, heap up some sand and put sacred betel nuts inside.[12] All other items required for the *pūjā* are kept within hand's reach: a small basket, a booklet with songs, a bowl of curd, milk with rice grains, cowry shells, a bell, etc. The whole area is decorated with *jahni* and other kinds of flowers. Vermilion and sandalwood powders are used to draw auspicious signs. Fruits, puffed rice, cakes and other sweets are arranged on special plates, ready to be offered to the deity. Finally, small earthen butter lamps (*dīpa*) and some incense sticks are lit. The participants sit down in front of the altar and start the evening ritual with a *huḷahuḷi*, the shrill sound that characterizes female worship.

On the background of seven groups who performed Jahni Oṣā in 1999 and 2000, the procedure of the ritual can be divided into three fairly consecutive but usually intermingling parts: First, the singing of the Jahni Oṣā legends and associated religious hymns, second, the performance of mythological episodes, and third, the presentation of offerings and other general features that characterize the Hindu *pūjā*.[13]

At the beginning of the evening one girl personifies Bṛndābatī. (Like any other ritual task, this role may alternate among the girls.) She will fold her hands in a prayer, focus her mind on the goddess and balance a basket containing a small burning *dīpa* and several *jahni* blossoms on her head. The remaining girls fan smoke of glowing resin (*jhūṇā*) towards her face and sing why and how one should celebrate the Jahni Oṣā. A total of five episodes (classified as *chānda*, literally: stanza, meter) narrate incidents when the votive rite was *not* performed properly, either due to mistakes or because a girl was ridiculed and prohibited to participate in the worship. Out of anger the goddess sent a deadly snake, crippled hands and employed other forms of punishment so that people realized her power. The verses stress that a girl's wish to worship Bṛndābatī is a legitimate concern that cannot be denied by anybody without serious consequences. Additional prayers and hymns highlight the religious significance of Tuḷasī, of related sacred plants (like *jahni*) and deities, particularly the goddess Maṅgaḷā. The girls call

---

[12] This arrangement suggests that the betel nuts represent deities, but there was no agreement as to their identity. Some girls recognized them as Jagannātha, Subhadrā and Baḷarāma (the divine trio adored in Puri); others regarded them as Kṛṣṇa, Tuḷasī and Baruṇa.

[13] In comparison to Tokita-Tanabe's (1999a: 35–57) description of Jahni Oṣā in a village near Khurda town (Puri District), the south Orissan performance seems to be much more elaborate.

on the glory of Bṛndābatī and request her to save them from disease and widowhood, and also to answer their desire for prosperity and a place in heaven. Most of the prayers and recitations follow an 11-page booklet available in the market.[14] Some girls keep notebooks with additional hymns and devotional songs, self-composed and copied down from others.

In the following part, verses are not only recited but at the same time enacted with gestures and movements that visualize their meaning. In this way, the girls narrate and mime popular incidents from Hindu mythology.[15] The first scene is known as the 'churning of curd' (*dādhimanthana*), and describes an episode from the childhood of Kṛṣṇa. This god is notorious for his pranks and desire for curd and butter. The song illustrates how Kṛṣṇa, in his sweet and naughty way, urges his foster mother Yaśodā to interrupt her work and feed him. During the evening ritual, one girl from the group plays her role. To imitate Yaśodā's housework (the churning of curd) the girl takes a small flower and stirs milk in a tiny pot.

Meanwhile, the rest of the group tries to touch her body and chants the matching verses that should provoke feelings of motherly affection (Plate 1.1). Finally, the fresh 'butter' is offered to Kṛṣṇa, personified by a consecrated betel nut on the altar. Next, the group begins to stage another heavenly scene, the 'game of cowry shells' (*kauṙi kheḷa*). This episode narrates how Nārāẏaṇa gambles with his wife Lakṣmī and by doing so loses not only his ornaments and wealth to her, but also his heart. While the girls collectively chant the witty dialogue between this exemplary divine couple, one by one each takes the cowries with her right hand, gives them a shake and passes them on to the next person in the row. This game is usually performed at a wedding ceremony,

---

[14] Here is an excerpt of this booklet: 'This fast will be in the month of āśvina. For thirty days it is celebrated in a group, with puffed rice (*liā*), puffed rice with molasses (*ukhuṙā*) and *jahni* flowers offered by every girl. The *pūjā* is performed along with *huḷahuḷi*. What sort of benefit is gained by the fasting? Whatever you desire (*mānasika*) you shall get. If you perform the Jahni Oṣā, the body will be cured of all kinds of diseases. (. . .) Oh *jahni* flower, I have worshipped you, would you give me a boon?' (*Jahni oṣā bā tulasī pūjā kathā*, n.d.: 1)

[15] In Orissa, episodes illustrating the pranks of Kṛṣṇa are performed during various votive rites and thus also by senior women (see J. M. Freeman 1980, on a similar votive rite in Benares see Pintchman 2005). Theatrical modes of worship are in fact advertized in the Vaishnava theology so that devotees get a chance to share the divine play (*līḷā*, Sanskrit *līlā*) of the gods.

**Plate 1.1:** Brahmin college girls perform the churning of curd

where it should help the newly-wed couple to approach each other in a less formal way. Playing cowries during the Jahni Oṣā, however, brings about the vision of one's own prospective marriage as well as romantic feelings about a lover, who in his enthusiasm forgets his own self (as Nārāẏaṇa does). In this way, the performance of both episodes evokes strong emotions towards maternal and conjugal affection, realized and intensified through the bodily involvement of the girls and also their aesthetic experience.

The remaining part of the evening ritual is dominated by sequences that are constitutive of any *pūjā*, such as the offering of food, incense, flowers, rice grains or *ārati* (the respectful waving of a flame in front of the deity). Girls have to water the basil plant and also circle around the altar (circumambulation), two ritual acts that are required whenever women worship Tuḷasī.[16] Besides this, the purity of the site

[16] According to the devotional booklet, these ritual acts should be accompanied by the recitation of two sacred formulas (*mantra*) in Sanskrit. During the watering of the plant, the girls should pray: 'Beloved of Govinda, oh goddess, you are the basis of devotional love and consciousness, I pray obedience to you, goddess of the universe (Jagaddhātrī), offering devotional love for Viṣṇu'. The second *mantra* highlights the capacity of Tuḷasī to forgive all the sins committed during childhood and should be chanted during the circumambulation.

has to be renewed every now and then by sprinkling sacred water in all directions. The performance of the evening ritual is completed by a final *huḷahuḷi*, and then the participants prostrate themselves on the ground. The blessed offerings (*bhoga*) are distributed among the girls and their family members.

Every morning in the month of *āśvina*, one or two girls repeat the ritual in a very condensed form, on behalf of the others who mostly attend school. Some of the votaries may also skip the evening ritual due to menses, sickness or some other duty. In this case, the remaining girls take care of the unattended sacred pot and in this way help each other to fulfill the observance of the Jahni Oṣā. On certain occasions none of the participants will miss the *pūjā*. This is above all at the beginning of the month when the sacred pots are installed, and also on the final day that ends with their immersion. Then the girls observe a 'complete fast', i.e., for the whole day they will eat nothing besides the blessed food (*bhoga*) in the evening. Since the concluding days of the Jahni Oṣā overlap with the most important festive period of the Hindu year (Durgā Pūjā, Daśaharā), the general spirit of celebration encourages them to carry on and complete the fast. At Daśaharā they arrange baskets with a mixture of seeds that gradually start to sprout.[17] Five days later, the month *āśvina* commences on the night of the full moon called Kumāra Pūrṇṇimā, known all over India as an occasion to play and gamble. The votaries prepare seven kinds of cakes as offerings, and are also given a new dress. After the evening ritual, the whole group takes the sacred items and proceeds to a river or pond, accompanied by their family members and, perhaps, by music and fireworks. At the waterside the girls repeat their worship of Bṛndābatī. Finally, the *tuḷasī* altar, the sacred pots, the seedlings, etc., are immersed and the goddess is given a farewell (*bisarjana*). Back home, the votaries enjoy the cakes and also a great variety of fruits. They spend the whole night in singing, playing cards and other forms of entertainment.

While girls say that their way of doing the Jahni Oṣā follows the prescribed 'rules and regulations' (*bidhi-bidhāna*), in practice, the ritual performances differ from one *pūjā* site to another. These variations concern the required items to conduct the ritual, the order and kind of

---

However, both Sanskrit formulas were hardly known to the performers of the Jahni Oṣā.

[17] In elaborate forms of worshipping a Hindu goddess, the sprouting of seedlings is a widespread ritual act.

ritual acts, as well as the number and variety of devotional songs. Most girls do not search for the meaning of these and other ritual features, although some openly wonder why they should abstain from eating ridge gourd and not perhaps tomato. None of the votaries I met was able to explain the logic behind the cowry game or why the performance of the Jahni Oṣā is associated with the goddess Maṅgaḷā (rather than with Lakṣmī, as it is in mythology).[18] What mattered to them was not the cognitive knowledge about the ritual and its performance, but their feeling of carrying out every action according to a paradigm version. However, the differences in the design and procedure of the ritual were recognized. Some girls openly competed against other groups in their neighbourhood for the most appealing altar and celebration of the Jahni Oṣā. Aesthetic features were considered a legitimate strategy to attract deities, and also, devotees. The concept of competition did not disturb the girls' understanding of religiosity.

## Rationalizing Ritual

According to public discourse, girls observe the Jahni Oṣā to find a good husband. Conversely most votaries stress slightly different reasons and some even reject this rationale at all. '[The Jahni Oṣā] gives peace of mind (*manara santoṣa pāi*)', they would say, or simply 'I feel happy by doing so'. Following their view, the performance of the fast is motivated by convention, the mere pleasure of its performance, or by the wish for a divine favour (*mānasika*). Indeed, many girls start to do the Jahni Oṣā without giving it a second thought. They simply follow the example of an elder sister or remember the colourful and lively *pūjā* site from their neighbourhood. The occasion easily attracts onlookers, since the mimetic play and the chanting of songs not only evoke a religious spirit but also laughter, enjoyment and a feeling of communal togetherness. Some girls observe the Jahni Oṣā because their family recommended them to do so. While they feel obliged to meet their parents' expectations, the recited verses emphasize the opposite. Significantly, the sacred lines call on the individual choice of a performer. The daily repetition of these verses thus teaches a girl that the aim to serve the gods cannot be denied. To stop a young woman from taking a decision to observe an *oṣā-brata* properly is considered a sin (*pāp*). The narrative also suggests

[18] Even according to a nineteenth-century description of Jahni Oṣā, the worship of the goddess Maṅgaḷā is essential (Rājaguru [1895] 1992: viii–ix, see also note 2 at the beginning of this chapter).

framing personal longings in terms of a religious concern. While the verses enumerate all kinds of desirable amenities, including material gains like 'rice for the year . . . gold for the ear', they do not mention the boon of a (good) husband.[19] Similarly, the votaries did not express this wish by themselves. Upon my persistent questions some girls referred to friends who could have this intention. Another votary reinterpreted that 'by doing this *pūjā*, one can get good in-laws' rather than merely a decent spouse.

To pass over this well-known reason for observing Jahni Oṣā is partly a rhetorical strategy to avoid the topic of one's own wedding. It is considered shameful for a girl to speak about her desire for a life partner, to show interest in a particular person or to take any steps to meet someone. Usually parents arrange the marriages of their children, and girls (as well as boys) trust in their experience and selection. However, marriage negotiations are a very common topic for gossip, so girls get to know at a very early age how people judge the ranking of prospective candidates. They realize whether they meet the relevant criteria or whether people consider them 'too dark' in complexion or 'too modern' in their behaviour. Everybody knows about the politics of dowry, the social stigma of an unmarried daughter and the ambivalent image of female higher education among some strata. No matter whether girls observe the Jahni Oṣā or not, they certainly have their own ideas about a good husband. He should come from a respectable and kind family, follow a promising career and be free of 'bad habits' like drinking, smoking and chewing betel. Above all, he should be 'very understanding', Uma explained in the bosom of her friends. In accordance with romantic Hindi movies or foreign productions like *Titanic*, several Oriya girls dream of a male hero who would introduce them to a world totally different from their own. At best, he might take them to one of the Indian metropolises that promise a rather new way of life, at least with respect to the amenities of a nuclear family.[20]

---

[19] Although the Oriya term *bara* means not only 'divine boon' but also 'bridegroom', in the case of these songs the reference is clear and does not invite misunderstanding.

[20] The desire to migrate to a distant place seems to be rather new. In earlier times, girls used to express their sorrow about the coming separation from their natal family in so-called lamenting songs (*kāndaṇā*) that were intoned at the time of marriage.

'Wherever I go [after marriage], I want to move *freely*. I don't want to remain in one [shared] place [like my mother did].' Like this Brahmin teenage girl, many wish to avoid the joint family system where a young daughter-in-law cannot 'move *freely*' but has to show obedience to affines in the form of veiling and other restrictive practices. These role expectations are regarded as a large burden: '[The duty of] veiling the face [at the in-laws' place] is a big problem for us (*oṙhaṇā deba āmapāi gote problem*)'. In this context it can take several years – and the birth of a son – before a woman feels accepted.

The votaries' considerations about a good husband often implied the idea of love marriage. As I was told in almost every group, 'all girls' dream about falling in love. In southern Orissa, this type of marriage is a highly contested issue. It is understood to oppose the Indian value system – similar to the 'dangers' of globalization – and like the latter threat it is anything but a new social phenomenon.[21] However, by the turn of the twenty-first century, fashion magazines, satellite television and Internet had come to reach even provincial towns, and gradually influenced the public discourse on female role models and gender relations. Still, girls were hardly aware of the Indian Miss World, of female social activists agitating in national politics, or the 25-year-old sportswoman who won India's only medal in the 2000 Olympics (bronze in weightlifting). The modern media aim to reach India's upper middle class, but the performers of the Jahni Oṣā had rarely access to such sources. Their considerations about the female subject position were challenged within their own locality. In one neighbourhood the police had to reprimand a teenage girl because, it was said, she did not stop following a boy and harassing him with declarations of love. A few female students started to use the Internet in the market and discussed the prospects of virtual dating.[22] Everybody knew several couples who had married against the norms of an arranged marriage. Similarly, some performers of the Jahni Oṣā clearly expressed that they would rather go for a love marriage, although their own social

[21] The bad habits associated with 'modern' times, such as love affairs, disrespect, deceit and intoxication, were already satirized in nineteenth-century popular culture (Chatterjee 1989: 625; Banerjee 1989: 111 and Chapter 3).

[22] In Berhampur the first commercial Internet service started in 1999. Two years later the town was dotted with similar shops, yet only some of them had female customers.

environment did not enable them to do so.[23] 'In our family, we are not *allowed* to do so', Kavita told.

> If we marry according to our parents' wish we also make them happy. As part of our *family* we have to consider everyone's happiness. In case of *love marriage*, if parents give their consent, then there is no *objection*. We would certainly also like this since you get the chance to know the other. Yet if at home this idea is not appreciated, then we have to *adjust* [the English words used are italicized].

Many girls felt safer trusting their parents' choice. At any rate, young women wanted to have a voice in the selection of their husband and secretly hoped for their parents' permission if they fell in love with someone. They were aware of the fact that the responsibility for the happiness of their natal family was loaded upon them. Occasionally somebody mentioned a sister who was not allowed to visit her parental home anymore since she had insisted on choosing a 'good husband' on her own. Once a girl marries against her parents' will, she risks her basic kinship ties.

The performance of the Jahni Oṣā does not invite discussions on these burning questions about love and future. 'It is not in our mind at that times . . .' The participants rather pay attention to the different ways of serving Bṛndābatī, Maṅgaḷā, Kṛṣṇa and others. Their central question is whether the gods are satisfied. No matter how faithfully girls follow the ritual procedures, they cannot escape the public rationale for their devotion: the wish for a good husband. This was obvious in their day-to-day self-presentation. Many girls tried to hide their commitment to the Jahni Oṣā because they feared the comments of young men. Once college mates heard about this ritual, they teased the girl mercilessly. Performers with higher education were also afraid of being considered backward. A 25-year-old graduate of medicine recalled the final procession at Kumāra Pūrṇṇimā:

> Everyone was wondering: a doctor performs the Jahni Oṣā? And we passed the whole street, this lane, that lane; everyone got to know that

[23] Recently Orsini (2006) published a cultural history of love in South Asia that also includes a section on 'contemporary lovescapes'. This part clearly shows how romantic ideals influence not only 'post-liberalisation urban India' but also rural discourses.

> I am doing it. I was feeling so awkward. I told God: I cannot take the sacred pot on the top of my head, I will just hold it in front.

Seemingly she felt more confident without this posture that contradicted her everyday habitus. Even among themselves girls displayed a reflective distance from the public rationale about the Jahni Oṣā. Once in a while everybody made fun of others who apparently exaggerated the power of the fast. 'Some women do this *pūjā* also to bring their husbands on the right path', a girl remarked with a smile. Upon my question whether it had worked, the whole group started to laugh: 'Oh no, it remained just the same!'[24] To make jokes in this manner once more stresses how the general reason to perform the Jahni Oṣā is regarded as a normative formula, rather than an expression that resonated with the girls' intentions. Still, their attitude towards the ritual performance was anything but subversive. They considered the Jahni Oṣā as an appropriate, gendered way to worship god, and, above all, a pleasant experience.

> I am just doing it because it makes me happy . . . some girls perform this ritual to get a good husband, but I don't have this notion in mind. I simply started to do the *pūjā* because everyone else did so. Out of happiness (*khusi*).[25]

In public discourse, however, the religious pursuit of women and their performance of votive rites were inseparably associated with female modesty and dedication towards their (marital) family. Following this line of thinking, the only imaginable motive for unmarried girls to engage in religious affairs was their desire for a good husband.

## Bodily Experiences

The experience of the Jahni Oṣā is basically a positive one. The girls enjoy their daily gatherings, the collective decoration of the altar, the

---

[24] Yet this laughter is ambivalent. Obviously, the person who was made fun of had been critical about her husband's character and hence stood out against the stereotype of a modest wife. In this respect, the laughter could also signify an attempt to expose her from a hegemonic (male) perspective. Indeed, those women who do not meet social expectations seem to be the most serious followers of the Jahni Oṣā.

[25] This statement was given by an unmarried 30-year-old woman who had performed the Jahni Oṣā for the previous 15 years.

singing of songs, and the taste of the fruits offered to the goddess. In contrast to restrictions and worries associated with the life of a married woman, the mood at the *pūjā* site can be characterized in terms of release, abandon and independence, rendered by the English adjective 'free'. Kavita describes: 'I felt happy once I got to know that tomorrow the Jahni Oṣā and the worship will begin. . . . I don't feel anything particular [during that time]. I feel *free* . . . I don't feel tired, I feel fine.' Junni explains: 'I am feeling good by doing so. During these days I keep myself busy only with worship!' To meet in the evening and sit around a nicely illuminated altar (while all the others continue with their daily routine) constitutes an atmosphere that stimulates several senses. At first, there is the aesthetic dimension: the beauty of the altar with its line-up of sacred pots, pictorial ornaments, blooming flowers and auspicious signs (Plate 1.2); the sound of hymns, prayers and other devotional songs; the smell of incense and the glowing *jhūṇā*; the mimetic performance; the playful approach to worship. What is more, the ritual evokes a strong feeling of affection. This is not only due to the mythological episodes that stress maternal and conjugal love literally, rather participants are in the mood for devotional love (*bhakti*), which is directed towards and identified with the god Kṛṣṇa.[26] In the same spirit, the collective worship deepens the friendship between the girls. They eagerly try to form a big group, since the performance of the *pūjā* would be more fun (*majā*). After concluding the Jahni Oṣā, Uma and her friends remarked: 'Now we feel lonely. Since we are not doing any *pūjā* we feel bored.' Nevertheless, the votaries may also feel some tension as to whether everything has been done according to the 'rules and regulations'. What they fear is not the critical comment of an elderly lady but rather the provocation of the goddess. Unlike in childhood days, when rituals were performed on their behalf, girls have to gain their own religious merit (*puṇyā*) and by doing so may also benefit others. The Jahni Oṣā is the first occasion in their life when they are faced with this religious responsibility.

Once in a while, during the worship of the goddess Bṛndābatī, a votary gets absorbed in the ritual act to such an extent that her loss of control over her own body is considered a form of divine possession. In this region, several women (and also a few men) watch such altered states of consciousness closely, as well as experiencing them themselves

[26] On the transcendent erotic imagery in teenage girls' oral tradition compare Tokita-Tanabe (1999b).

**Plate 1.2:** Joint prayer to the goddess Bṛndābatī

(I come back to this phenomenon in Chapter 4). During the Jahni Oṣā the possessed medium is mostly the girl who personifies the goddess in the first part of the evening. Through her body Bṛndābatī may express her (dis-) satisfaction about a particular feature of worship. The possibility of this energetic peak of the ritual contributes to the seriousness of the event, even if girls have only heard rumors about the emergence of divine presence in other groups.[27] Yet most of the time, the performance of the Jahni Oṣā provides votaries with the feeling that jointly they are more or less in control of the situation. This impression is supported, after all, by the process of fasting that directs the somatic attention towards self-control while producing a gradual independence from ordinary food habits and longings.

Being exposed to these kinds of sensorial experiences, the observance of the Jahni Oṣā also helps in the acquisition of ritual competence. The different acts of worship, which girls had merely watched during their childhood, now turn into a variety of concrete operations relevant to their own religious self. The girls practice general techniques of worship (when to purify the altar, how to perform *ārati*, etc.), and also those manual skills that are associated with the religiosity of women. Whoever performs the Jahni Oṣā will learn how to prepare the different food offerings, to arrange a sacred pot,[28] when to utter the shrill *huḷahuḷi* or how to draw delicate ornaments (*jhoṭi*) by sifting coloured rice powder through the fingertips. 'I am very fond of doing these *jhoṭis*', Deepa told, 'every day I used to invent new patterns. Sometimes I did it in this way [gesticulating], only ornaments. Then again the Tuḷasī goddess, looking like this, and ornaments . . . in this way I was doing it.' Whereas many features of the fast are memorized with the help of the legends (and their printed version), these techniques have to be learnt by heart. The ritual expertise is transmitted among the performers themselves. There is no priest who might intervene. After watching the ceremony for a while, a girl may imitate the behaviour

---

[27] In five out of seven groups there were girls who had experienced goddess possession themselves. The extensive literature on votive rites in other parts of India, however, does not mention the occurrence of deity possession at all.

[28] To arrange a sacred pot, for example, girls have to fill an earthen jar with water, close it with an old coconut and add mango leaves, a piece of red cloth, red bangles and red cotton thread. Then they apply auspicious signs and flowers. Although the procedure might sound simple, to assemble the items smoothly needs some manual skill. To do it the wrong way is considered inauspicious.

of others and gradually take the initiative in singing, decorating the altar or structuring the ritual. This routine will help her to perform any other votive rite. Moreover, it serves as a pre-condition for marriage, since in her marital home a young wife is expected to conduct several religious functions on her own. Therefore, whoever does the Jahni Oṣā receives a lot of attention and social recognition. Whereas a girl's initiative in other cultural spheres, such as an interest in fashion or higher education, is often discouraged and criticized as selfish, any attempt to improve a *pūjā* site will raise her reputation. Hence, she starts to experience the religious domain as a major sphere of self-realization — or rather as one of her rare options. Later it becomes a matter of self-esteem to refine this ritual competence.

In the long run, the regular performance of the Jahni Oṣā will contribute towards a subtle change of a girl's embodied self. She will gain a 'sense of ritual' (Bell), i.e., establish a permanent disposition that serves as a matrix for any further religious actions, feelings and thoughts. Following Pierre Bourdieu (1977) and his concept of habitus, Catherine Bell (1992) has argued that ritual practices mould the human being similarly as other forms of practice. Hence, the body is not only the object of 'inscription', but becomes an agent by itself and structures the way people perceive and understand the world. The circular character of embodied practices to bring about what they denote is particularly apparent once the girls have to utter the shrill *huḷahuḷi*. Although everybody is aware that women create this sound at very auspicious moments, at first girls feel awkward doing so themselves. It needs a forceful trembling of the tongue to produce this high-pitched and penetrating sound. Only after regular practice will their voices blend into one vibrating tone. The *huḷahuḷi* will come spontaneously and by itself create a feeling of auspiciousness. Similarly, there are other practices that start to appear natural to the votaries, such as the impulse to cover one's head with a scarf (or the end of a sari) as a sign of respect, or the sprinkling of water to purify the site, a practice that gradually inscribes (and objectifies) the danger of pollution. One could even consider the religious diet and its impact on the visceral feelings as well as on the taste of food. In this regard, the sentient body will realize and 'feel' the sacred quality of the respective time span. After all, ritual routines not only contribute to mould habitual patterns, they also influence one's perspective on the world, and how to relate to the self vis-à-vis others. In this regard, the most important transformation initiated by the Jahni Oṣā concerns the girl's identification with their gender-specific religious potential as a ritual performer. When asked for typical 'female' traits, the interviewees claimed not only that girls were cleverer than boys, but also mentioned their superiority in terms of *śakti* (strength, divine female energy) and *śubha* (auspiciousness). Hence 'ritual agency' not only bestows women with an experiential site of their own where they may exercise a variety of subject positions, it may also endow women with self-confidence.

## Votive Rites in Hinduism

In the academic discourse on South Asia, the performance of votive rites is a highly ambivalent issue. First of all, these ritual sets outline a basically *female* religious practice that is, with exceptions, oriented towards the well-being of *male* kin. The chief purpose of votive rites is, after being blessed with a husband, the good health and prosperity of the spouse, the protection of sons and the welfare of brothers.[29] The paradigm of a *vrata* in northern India is Karvā Cauth, when the wife beautifies herself like a bride and for the whole day keeps a fast to secure the long life of her husband (*pati*).[30] This pious service is regarded as a proof of her virtue and chastity, and thus contributes towards her reputation as a true *pativratā* (Oriya: *patibratā*), a devoted wife. Its equivalent in Orissa, Somnātha Brata, is celebrated a few weeks later.[31] While several scholars understand votive rites to symbolize the wife's submission and therefore a representation of orthodox Hindu doctrine, there are different interpretations as to the female perspective on them. According to Sanjukta Gupta (1999: 96) women incorporate a largely Brahminical male bias. The frequent observance of a fast would serve as a female strategy to overcome and compensate

---

[29] See Pearson (1996: 235–37) for an exemplary calendar of votive rites, supplemented with brief comments on their objectives and character. There are also votive rites intended for male observers. These rites appear to be more self-directed; at least they do not serve the explicit well-being of women but rather general aims like good crops and prosperity (Pearson 1996: 125–28; McDaniel 2003: 97–104).

[30] The literal translation 'Pitcher Fourth' refers to the ritual usage of a sacred pot and also to the date of this rite (the fourth day of the dark half in the lunar month of *kārtik [Oriya: kārttika]*). See Poggendorf-Kakar (2002: 97–105) for the celebration of Karvā Cauth in a metropolitan middle-class context.

[31] Women observe Somnātha Brata on the tenth day of the bright fortnight in the month of *āśvina*, thus it culminates with the festival Daśaharā. 'Somnātha' is an epithet of god Śiba, who is worshipped on this occasion.

pollution caused by menstruation and childbirth (see Chapter 3). A more pragmatic view is sketched out by Laxmi Tewari (1991: 16–17). Since indeed, women's living conditions mostly depend on male relatives, Tewari argues, the performance of rituals in favour of their prosperity, good health and kind-heartedness makes absolute sense. By contrast, Anne Pearson (1996: 9–10) and other authors claim that women follow these votive observances mainly for themselves. These ritual sets give them the opportunity to express their piety and personal faith in God, to get control of their lives, to gain religious merits (*puṇyā*), and to achieve 'peace of mind' (see J. M. Freeman 1980: 126; Pearson 1996: Chapter 7; Pintchman 2005; Wadley 1980a: 109).

A related point of discussion concerns the voluntariness of votive rites. According to Hindu theology, a *vrata* offers men and women alike the option to look after their own spiritual development without leaving their family relationships behind. In this respect, votive observances are thought to be optional. Yet Mary McGee (1991: 73–74) has shown that this view contrasts with women's own experiences. At her research site in Maharashtra, they perceived the performance of votive rites as *strīdharma*, i.e., as their (religious) duty as wives and mothers for the welfare of their male kin. Their observance served to maintain a happy family rather than to acquire additional merits. If women are said to be responsible for the (possibly bad) fate of a family, they are indeed bound to care for their self-presentation as pious wives. This is particularly relevant in the case of a joint family household, where the social control of female kin enforces the regular performance of votive rites. So Tewari (1991: 13, 18) noticed that Brahmin girls in Uttar Pradesh are subjected to strong psychological pressure to fast, whereas the rising popularity of nuclear families contributes to the decrease in votive rites.

Another issue in the academic debate on votive rites deals with their classification and socio-religious significance. Although there is a written discourse on *vrata* going back to about three thousand years, in comparison to other Hindu forms of worship (in which men participate) this practice is often belittled as a commonplace activity that does not deserve any particular attention.[32] Some scholars, including K. B. Dash (1991: 114), prefer even to subsume votive rites as folklore,

---

[32] On the difference between the *vrata*-theology in Hindu scriptures and women's performance of votive rites at the end of the twentieth century, see Pearson (1996: 4, 6, Chapter 2).

taking into account their often highly elaborated aesthetic form. Most votive rites require the creation of floor or wall paintings, and of ritual objects shaped out of clay, foodstuffs or kitchen utensils. Furthermore, each fast has its own songs and stories. Yet the classification of votive rites as folklore underplays their religious relevance. What is more, scholars stress the subversive character of these observances. This religious practice is believed to offer a sort of cultural resistance to Brahminical domination since it can be performed without dependence on temples and male priests (Jayakar 1989: 117–18). According to Susan Wadley (1980a: 109), votive rites are also a source of women's empowerment: 'Such rituals may give psychological support to the women themselves, because they allow women to have active control of events rather than depend completely on their male kin.' Whether in terms of folklore or subversion, women's votive rites are understood to be separate from the Brahminical Sanskrit tradition. This opposition of so-called 'popular' (*laukika*) and 'scriptural' (*śāstrika*) rites is still highly disputable. While some scholars (and devotees) believe that present-day women's rituals are 'corrupted' forms of those *vratas* described in the ancient literature, others argue that they represent an autonomous religious practice that Brahmins tried to gain control of by claiming a relationship with 'scriptural' votive rites.[33] Indeed in some of the *oṣā-brata*, at least in their present-day version, a Brahmin priest performs the final sequence (compare Pearson 1996: 141–43). Hence K. B. Dash (1991: 107) suggests that the aim of classifying women's rituals shows the socio-political interest of priests, who wish to 'exploit' certain local forms of worship, 'greedy of fees and good dinner'. In any case, the matter of classification is a highly political issue that says more about present-day religious hierarchies than about the 'origin' of votive rites.

A fourth point in the discussion on votive rites concerns the implications of fasting. In Hindu India the observance of a fast hardly refers to non-eating but rather to a religiously motivated prohibition against certain kinds of food, and thus an interruption of ordinary

[33] The political aspect is also clear in case of Abanindranath Tagore, who in the anti-colonial spirit of the beginning of the twentieth century searched for an indigenous Indian tradition. His research on Bengali *bratas* contributed significantly to their reputation as a genuine female form of worship that also involves folk stories and artistic expressions (McDaniel 2003: 34–39; Pearson 1996: 142, 272–74).

eating habits. Generally, fasting people (whether ascetics or female votaries) avoid meat, fish, eggs, onions, garlic and, depending on the occasion, other specific items (for instance, ridge gourd). There are different logics to rationalize this diet (compare Khare 1976: 82–86). At first, there is a preference for so-called 'cooling' food, i.e., unprocessed (raw) or merely boiled preparations of particular grains and vegetables, rather than spicy and fried dishes that are believed to negatively affect one's mood. This dichotomy, based on traditional medical concepts, overlaps with a philosophical distinction of three general qualities of matter (*guṇa*) which influence the spiritual disposition of a human being. In this regard, fasting implies a preference for *sattva* nutrition, i.e., preparations associated with moral or ritual purity (rather than with passion/*rājasa* or lethargy/*tāmasa*). Therefore, a religious diet often includes milk or replaces oil with clarified butter (*ghia*). In any case, the fast should bring about a psychophysical state that promotes religious attentiveness. Fasting requirements also include the hour for breaking the fast ('after sunset', etc.) and whether she (he) is allowed to drink water. Hence fasting can be either hard or quite easy.

In the debate on female religiosity, fasting is often evaluated as a form of self-restraint.[34] Pearson (1996: 10) concludes: 'Paradoxically, Hindu women who are culturally placed in a position where they must practice self-denial . . . manage to achieve a measure of control over their own lives by practicing further forms of self-denial.' However, scholars also stress the complementary aspect of dieting, i.e., the feasting that is to follow the breaking of the fast. Indeed, most votive rites demand the offering of a variety of fruits, specific kinds of cake, or sweets in an auspicious number. At the end of the worship these blessed delicacies are distributed and enjoyed by the votaries. There is a whole body of recipes associated with the performance of votive rites so that each deity can be pleased with her or his favourite dish. Leigh Minturn (1993: 178–79) noticed

> 'The women most frequently began the description of their ceremonies by saying: "We cook *halwar* [carrot candy] and *puri* [fried chapattis stuffed with vegetables] on this day". This description was so frequent

---

[34] From a 'Western' perspective the religious necessity of fasting might even raise doubts as to what extent the self-imposed abstinence from food euphemistically hides the fact that women's nutrition is regarded as secondary.

> that I teased the women by saying that they used their ceremonies as an excuse to eat special food. They laughingly agreed that this was partly true.'[35]

Thus fasting can also be a welcomed change to the monotony of simple nourishment, especially among the poorer sections of society. Furthermore, some votive rites are occasions to buy and wear new clothes.

## Conclusion: The Joy of Ritual

The academic debate surrounding votive rites suggests that there is hardly a general conclusion with regard to their capacity to endow women with self-esteem and control over their lives, or conversely, whether votive rites contribute to women's submission. At the same time there is no reason to believe that Hindu women are mere passive recipients of a hegemonic gender ideology. The case study about the Jahni Oṣā vividly shows in what ways young women and even girls interact with tradition, and how the religious observance is made to resonate with their own sense of self and gender. Carrying a sacred pot in front of the body rather than on top of the head can be regarded as a visible token of this process.

Structurally seen, the Jahni Oṣā serves as a paradigmatic votive rite for young women to rehearse important ritual acts. Moreover, it entitles them for the first time in their life to not only watch but also perform a ritual by themselves, independently and with sole responsibility for the religious consequences. Like any other votive rite that comes first in a girl's life, the performance of the Jahni Oṣā can thus be regarded as an accumulative female initiation. That is to say, girls already start to acquire ritual competence and responsibilities before they get married, similar to upper-caste ('twice-born') boys who undergo a sacred thread ceremony. However, this practice-informed anthropological understanding of initiation differs from the Hindu concept of a purely male sacrament that accompanies adolescence. In Brahminical perspective, a woman will obtain a comparable status as ritual agent only by means of her marriage.

Considering the present-day rationalization of Jahni Oṣā, the goal of finding a good husband is apparently a formula from the public

[35] A similar experience is narrated by McDaniel (2003: 112); McGee (1987: 852–55) has collected a number of recipes related to the observance of votive rites.

discourse on femininity, and not taken as an imperative by the performers. It reflects the general belief that teenage girls have no other (religious) concern than their future marriage. 'A girl would wonder how she might live a happy life – is there anything else?' From the perspective of adolescent girls, the Jahni Oṣā provides an occasion to assess and personally experience the power of ritual agency. At this age the discourse on the religious significance of a wife and mother is already familiar, and also the notion that women are to observe *oṣā-bratas* so as to guarantee the well-being of others, predominantly their male kin. From the votaries' point of view, this does not belittle their self-esteem as women but rather invites them to consider the complementary insight, i.e., to recognize and appreciate one's inherently female ritual competence (in terms of *śakti* and *śubha*) for the maintenance of society. An English-speaking girl explained: 'A man is nothing; the woman is the force (*śakti*). If he is good it is so because of his wife. Whatever prosperity he gains in his life, it is because of her.' The development of such a gendered awareness allows practicing Hindu women to frame several of their desires and actions within a theological matrix. At times this may raise the suspicion of others, in particular husbands. Although the concept of *strīdharma* is suggested by the hegemonic discourse, it is hence nourished and at the same time counteracted by women's autonomous performance of votive rites. However, the empowerment of female ritual specialists is subjected to a wider patriarchal structure (see Chapter 8) and also to socio-historical conditions, for instance, the anti- and post-colonial making of women as the bearer of tradition (Tokita-Tanabe 1999a: 3–12).

During the first years of the Jahni Oṣā the concept of ritual agency is not yet fully embodied. It competes with other forms of self-realization that girls fancy during adolescence – even if they are discouraged from doing so. In regard to the somatic process initiated and sustained by the performance of the Jahni Oṣā, the ethnographic exploration of the religious practice has shown that the mere participation in this votive rite creates pleasant and also exciting experiences. It is not possible to merely pretend the worship of Bṛndābatī. Even a girl's critical rationalization of her participation in the ritual does not prevent her from enjoying the aesthetic and psychophysical experiences in front of the *tuḷasī* altar. Theoretically speaking, the repetition of these psychophysical routines contributes towards a corporeal memory that constitutes some resonating background against which the action itself becomes meaningful and valid. It produces 'socially informed bodies' (Bourdieu 1977). In this respect, an ambivalent stance towards the performance of the Jahni Oṣā, i.e., its 'imitation' to please one's family, only gradually detracts from this process of embodiment. What I aimed to emphasize in this chapter is that the doubts about the Jahni Oṣā (as a particular type of ritual) result, after all, from the novelty of this religious practice in the biography of its performers, i.e., from inexperienced bodies rather than a general scepticism about religious values and practices. This first taste of female ritual agency provides the girls an experience that might be deepened by the observance of other votive rites after marriage. This tasting not only allows a tempting vision of the world, it also invites an inherently bodily transformation process that concerns the gendered and religious self alike. If the ritual is repeated in the following years, the lived-in body will contribute by itself to the emergence of ritual commitment and credibility.

# 2

# Shared Pain – Shared Joy: On Ritual Composition and Authority

While in the previous chapter the emphasis was on the psychophysical effects that ritual performances have on young women, now the major focus will be the other way around. I shall discuss in what respect and to what extent women contribute to the composition and design of a votive rite, and thus locate meaning and verify religious discourse. The following case study illustrates the ritual practice of experienced votaries who have already incorporated *oṣā-bratas* as a part of their female identity. Both perspectives could be regarded as the opposite sides of a coin and allude to ritual performance as a 'model of' and 'model for' reality (Geertz 1966). As mentioned in the Introduction of this book, to reduce cultural performance to mere representation of pre-given structures and collective memory risks overlooking its self-referential emerging effects (presences), and thus the full potential of its generative force. When writing ethnography, I rather prefer to consider both perspectives as a narrative strategy to reveal the disparate potentials of cultural performances as sites for the social negotiation of gender and religion.

During my first weeks in Berhampur, women mentioned the worship (*pūjā*) of the goddess Maṅgaḷā and invited me to join them. This celebration was the major constituent of a votive rite called the Niśā Maṅgaḷabāra Oṣā. On four consecutive Tuesdays in the month of *āśvina* (September/October), married women gathered in order to pray for the well-being of their husband and children. Although this motive did not come as a surprise (see Chapter 1), I had to learn that the particular form of worship was quite new to the region, becoming popular only in the 1990s. A votary needed a small picture of Maṅgaḷā, to consecrate a betel nut and to recite the legend of the 'Beautiful Khulaṇā' (*Khulaṇā Sundarī*). Furthermore, the performances I attended consisted of a highly elaborate sequence of ritual acts, and also included the construction and weekly renewal of an approximately 70-centimetre-high relief of the goddess made out of turmeric paste. One participant proudly remarked: 'Nobody does this *pūjā* the way we do!' My curiosity was awakened. On the one hand, this emphasis of singularity challenged common — local and academic — statements on the necessity to perform a ritual in conformance with the laws of tradition rather than individual liking. On the other hand, women en-thusiastically followed a ritual in favour of their marital family, whereas several people claimed that 'nowadays' such expressions of *strīdharma* (women's religious duty) was gradually decreasing. What actually motivated women to engage in this seemingly conservative ritual practice? I wondered about the origin of this new ritual and how the participants considered and legitimized individual inventions.

The most common way of acquiring ritual competence and authority in Hindu India is through the process of observation and imitation, because the validity of a ritual act results from its continuity with the past. Additionally, one may study the sacred scriptures with the guidance of a Brahmin, yet this education is specified for 'twice-born' men. How would women dedicated to the goddess Maṅgaḷā discover how to perform the *pūjā*? 'Ah, it will be written in a book', Oriya friends answered. This seemed to me quite natural since it corresponded to my own view of how to learn something. Moreover, in the bazaar I had seen piles of booklets that addressed the worship of various deities, and one of these narrated the legend of the beautiful Khulaṇā. Did this story include a description of the Maṅgaḷā Pūjā? Were there any other textbooks available and in what way did they determine the ritual practice? How did women assess these religious scriptures and their teachings? In this chapter, I shall concentrate on the role of written sources and their impact on the performance of the Maṅgaḷā Pūjā, as well as on the development of this ritual.[1]

Apart from the intriguing question of how new rituals emerge, the very fact that women employ devotional books at all also has a religio-political dimension. In the first section I show how little is actually

[1] Some sections and passages from this chapter have been published elsewhere. One article explored the Maṅgaḷā Pūjā with respect to the interdependence of text and context, i.e., as a situated process that brings about both performative scripts and a very selective view on printed religious narratives (Hauser 2004a). In another article I considered the agentive dimension of women while celebrating the Maṅgaḷā Pūjā (Hauser 2010b).

known about this recent practice. I then turn to the worship of the goddess Maṅgaḷā and introduce a specific ritual site and performance. Analyzing corresponding religious textbooks it will turn out that: (*a*) besides a few clues on the worship of Maṅgaḷā, the *Khulaṇā Sundarī* is hardly authoritative in defining the ritual; (*b*) although the votaries consult religious treatises they do not actively search for written guidance; and (*c*) the character of the ritual performance grew from mutual understanding between the participants on appropriate visualizations, ritual acts and structures of organization. This collective and mainly pre-reflective process was induced by, and connected to, the notion of suffering. Central sequences in the *Khulaṇā Sundarī* resonated to the women's personal urge to overcome distress and crisis; like Khulaṇā they approached the goddess Maṅgaḷā to ease their burden. Several features of the ceremony were suggested and implemented by one senior lady. She generally denied her initiative and regarded herself as a divine instrument. I argue that her authority resulted not only from this rhetoric but rather from her convincing performance. Finally I propose considering this process as a way of 'personalizing' ritual rather than recognizing it in terms of individual creativity or the 'invention of tradition' (Hobsbawm and Ranger 1983). This act serves as a popular way to sense and recognize ritual authenticity, a mode that differs from the legitimizing functions of sacred scriptures.

## The Consumption of Text

With respect to Hinduism, sacred scriptures and their impact on the social division of the religious domain cannot be overestimated.[2] The most prominent among them are the Vedas. Until recently, the study of these ancient Sanskrit literature was the privilege of Brahmin men. According to conservative theologians women were not pure enough to be educated in the conduct of rituals. Akin to people from lower castes, women regularly faced pollution and thus disqualified themselves. However, the exclusiveness of scriptural knowledge has been put in perspective throughout Indian history, particularly by the popularity of *bhakti* (devotion). This concept privileges an individual's path

[2] In this chapter I am concerned with 'text' as a specific (written) medium of communication. Yet in ancient India sacred literature (as a body of knowledge) was preferably conveyed orally and only later, gradually, put into writing (Michaels 2004b: 458–59). However, this does not change the argument presented here.

to salvation, defined by emotion (especially love), and thus open to anybody regardless of sex, caste or literacy.[3] Moreover, the development of the Indian printing press in the nineteenth century allowed for the spread of theological manuscripts and their translations among larger audiences. Nevertheless, what may be called a democratization of religious knowledge by means of mass printing became socially relevant only after the independence of India (1947).[4] This is due to the low literacy rate, and in this case southern Orissa serves as an example from the periphery of education. According to the census of 1951, less than five per cent of the women in Orissa (and less than 27 per cent among men) knew how to read and write. In 1991, the female literacy rate in Ganjam District had risen to 30 per cent, and in 2001 it was about 48 per cent; being comparatively higher in urban areas where 67 per cent of women were literate (Government of Orissa 2004: 102, 137).[5]

Some present-day Brahmin priests react very critically to the idea of religious texts as consumer goods. From their perspective the marketing of cheap editions opposes the proper transmission of sacred knowledge — and in fact their ritual monopoly. In northern India an increasing number of people who hired a Brahmin to recite the Devī Māhātmya — probably the most sacred scripture used to worship the goddess — have started to perform it themselves. According to Cynthia Ann Humes (1997: 43–44) religious authorities in Benares warn that this practice can be ritually dangerous (if not a curse) for those who are not authorized, i.e., for women and persons of low-caste status.[6]

---

[3] The popularity of *bhakti* increased in different historical periods and locations of India. It can be traced back to the seventh century and to regions as distant as Tamil Nadu and Kashmir, yet it is not one singular religious reform movement.

[4] Recently, scholars have explored how new media have contributed to the mobility of religious practices in terms of spatial and social distance (Babb and Wadley 1995). Unfortunately this volume skips printing since it is based on the assumption that the influence of the press on religious discourse was basically at the *beginning* of the twentieth century. In 1901, however, the literacy rate of women in Ganjam was less than 1 per cent (males 9 per cent), though it was comparatively higher in the coastal area than in the mountains (*The Imperial Gazetteer of India*, Vol. XII, 1908: 157).

[5] Since comparatively more men are able to read and write, the overall literacy rate in Ganjam District was 63 per cent (2001).

[6] From this perspective, Gita Press, one of the largest publishers of religious texts in India, was understood to be the result of a colonial plot to ruin Hindu

The huge number of religious textbooks, paperback collections and pamphlets that are available on the footpath and in the market of Berhampur, however, vary in ambition and sanctity. A whole branch of this devotional literature is intended for female readers (see McGee 1987: 375–79 and Wadley [1983] regarding other regions). Several of these booklets are dedicated to particular deities and votive rites (for instance, to the Jahni Oṣā, see Chapter 1). These publications inform their readers in between 10 and 50 pages about relevant prayers, hymns and, above all, the (hi-) story (*kathā*) of a religious observance. This legend commonly explains how a certain person started to worship a god or goddess and how her (or his) faith was proven by a variety of divine encounters. This genre of devotional literature is neither of recent date nor based on exclusive authorship; most booklets are regularly reprinted. They spread with the appearance of an indigenous Oriya press at the end of the nineteenth century.[7] According to the historian Biswamoy Pati (2001: 148) this development 'virtually reinvented' legends about female devotees from lower castes. Thus, this genre addressed women from a wide range of social strata. Yet, several *kathās* are much older. On the basis of linguistic evidence, Laksmi Narayan Raut (1988: 78) claims that they originated as early as the thirteenth and fourteenth century.[8]

Scholars working on female religiosity assume that the usage of written instructions for the conduct of votive rites is of recent date. Regarding the devotional book market in a village in Uttar Pradesh, Susan Wadley (1983: 83) concludes: 'In the period from 1967 to 1975, the choice of offerings expanded considerably – texts of songs sung only by women are more widely available'. Mary McGee (1987: 376), who in the 1980s carried out an extensive study on religious observances in Pune (Maharashtra), recognized that the increased literacy of women had contributed to the reliance on popular *vrata* manuals. 40 per cent of the women (n. = 108) said that on occasion they consult

religion by publishing corrupted manuscripts and selling sacred works to improper people (Humes 1997: 44). However, upper-caste Hindu scholars were among those first involved in the publishing, either as sources and translators for the British or as proprietors of printing shops (Wadley 1983: 82).

[7] The publication of Oriya books rose from 31 volumes in 1890 to 1190 books in 1900 (Pati 2001: 32). Unfortunately the author does not clarify whether the category 'book' also refers to devotional treatises of merely a few pages.

[8] Some of the religious digests used in women's votive rites in Maharashtra are also known to go back as far as the thirteenth century (McGee 1987: 231).

religious digests; for the recitation of the relevant *kathā* over 80 per cent relied on a book. Both Wadley (1983: 81) and McGee (1987: 375) are concerned that the spread of standardized printed versions will threaten the regional diversity of women's oral tradition that comes with the performance of votive rites.[9] Other scholars prefer to stress the positive effects of women's access to religious literature. On the basis of interviews with Bengali women in 1994/5, June McDaniel (2003: 41) argues that 'with Westernization' people are forgetting the details of votive rites and therefore prefer books to maintain a link with tradition. Moreover, the usage of religious digests by women is also a challenge to religious authorities (McGee 1987: 375). In Benares of the 1980s, Anne Pearson (1996: 142) observes: 'women are *just starting* to be their own priests *because* of the wide availability of *vrat* pamphlets in which the details of the procedure for the rite are provided, including appropriate mantras, allowing literate women to bypass priestly involvement, if they so choose' (my emphasis). In other words, the spread of devotional literature does not only reflect the transition from oral tradition to a rising emphasis on religious digests, it also raises the question about the role of texts for the empowerment of ritual performers. Do women indeed rely on scriptural knowledge to achieve authority in conducting rituals? Do they regard text as mandatory, as male priests claim in regard to their own practice? No matter whether female ritual authority is definitely increasing, and whether it derives from the ability to read and write, to what extent and in what respect women follow the instructions offered by the religious digests is quite another story – as will be shown in the following section.

## The Worship of Mā Maṅgaḷā

Although hardly known in others parts of India, throughout Orissa the worship of the goddess Maṅgaḷā (literally: The Bestower of Well-Being) is very popular.[10] Basically she is a village goddess, classified by the

---

[9] Whereas the diversity of these narratives might in fact decrease, women also come to share the religious tradition of reciting sacred texts like the Ramayana. In the 1980s this was still a new phenomenon among women (Flueckiger 1991: 44).

[10] Although several scholars translate the meaning of Maṅgaḷā as 'The Auspicious One', I prefer to render her name as 'The Bestower of Well-Being', since she, by herself, is not absolutely auspicious. With reference to the worship of Shakta goddesses, Samanta (1992: 54–56) makes clear that the term *maṅgal* refers to

generic term *ṭhākurāṇī* (mistress, lady). Like her she is adored as a protector, defender and savior, best exemplified by her invocation as 'mother' (*mā*). Furthermore, Maṅgaḷā is believed to cause and cure diseases, particularly pox and fever associated with the hot season.[11] The appropriate time to appease this kind of goddess is on Tuesdays (*maṅgaḷabāra*).[12] Some scholars believe that Maṅgaḷā was originally a 'tribal' goddess who underwent a process of Hinduization in (at the latest) the sixteenth century (Eschmann 1978: 86, Brighenti 2001: 185, 189). In any case, today she is considered both a Shakta as well as a Vaishnava goddess.

From the perspective of Shaktism, Maṅgaḷā is regarded as a form of Caṇḍī or Durgā.[13] In this capacity she is identified with a group of eight goddesses who outline the goddess topography of Orissa. Thus Maṅgaḷā (and her temple in Kakatpur) is associated with Śāraḷā of Jhankada, Birajā of Jajpur, Carchikā of Banki, Bimaḷā of Puri, Bhagabatī of Banpur, Hiṅguḷā of Talcher and Samaḷāi of Sambalpur, a list that may vary (Map 2). According to Vaishnavas of Orissa, Maṅgaḷā is primarily connected to the god Jagannātha, whose claim to supremacy she efficiently supports (Fischer and Pathy 1996: 28). His temple in Puri is one of the major Hindu sites of pilgrimage. The close relationship between both deities is recalled by the ritual of *nabakaḷebara*, i.e., the

---

the uninterrupted change and flux of life, including periods of suffering and distress, and hence a *condition* for the experience of well-being rather than an absolute quality. Similarly, the worship of the goddess Maṅgaḷā qualifies her devotees to achieve bliss. Thus her name alludes to the beneficial effect of her worship. On the concept of auspiciousness as a non-hierarchical quality beyond the purity–pollution axis, see Marglin (1985a).

11 Marglin (1985b: 268–69) and Eschmann (1978: 86) mention the offering of *paṇā*-juice to Maṅgaḷā on the roads in the month of *caitra* (March/April). This type of worship should protect the family and the village from all kinds of disease. In and around Berhampur I have not come across this practice. Instead, women offer *paṇā* in the temple of Buṛhī Ṭhākurāṇī for the same purpose.

12 According to folk etymology, this 'Auspicious Day' (*maṅgaḷabāra*) is linked to the goddess Maṅgaḷā ('The Auspicious One' compare note 10). This is misleading. Any goddess who is worshipped as a divinity in her own right (rather than as the spouse of a male god) should be worshipped on Tuesdays. Moreover, Tuesday is related to Mars (*maṅgaḷa*) as each other weekday is linked to another planet god.

13 Besides, *maṅgaḷa* also serves as an epithet of Caṇḍī and Durgā and thus conveys the idea that the worship of the deity is beneficial. The Bengali poetry in praise of Caṇḍī and several other deities is classified as *maṅgalkabya*, literally 'verses of divine beneficence'.

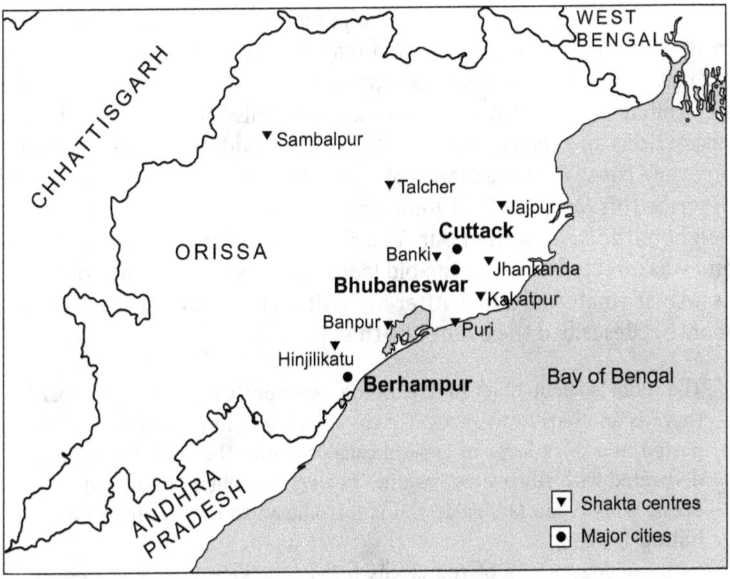


**Map 2:** Orissa and its Shakta centres

replacement of the divine wooden statues in the Jagannātha temple that happens approximately every 19 years. In the search for new logs, the priests have to visit Maṅgaḷā's temple in Kakatpur, and it is the goddess herself who transmits to them in a dream how to locate the appropriate logs (Hardenberg 1998: 240–77). According to her Vaishnava identity, Maṅgaḷā of Kakatpur is a vegetarian and purely benevolent goddess. Only Brahmins may serve as her priests.[14]

From a sub-regional perspective, it is mainly women who worship Mā Maṅgaḷā. They rarely visit Kakatpur but rather worship this goddess in their own locality, often in an aniconic form, for example in the shape of an earthen pot. To them Maṅgaḷā is the bestower of physical and economic well-being and, as will be shown further in

[14] The regional importance of the goddess Maṅgaḷā is recognized by several scholars: Mahapatra (1981/1982) focused on the religious tradition in the Maṅgaḷā temple of Kakatpur and also its fire-walking festival; Marglin and Misra (1991) discussed the competing Brahminical and low-caste discourses on the goddess; Fischer and Pathy (1996) evaluated wall paintings that serve to worship her; Preston (1983: 238–40) and Brighenti (2001: 185–93) situate the worship of Maṅgaḷā in the realm of Shaktism in Orissa.

the discussion, a protector who helps one overcome a present crisis in life. To win her favour, women may observe different votive rites, for instance the 'Nocturnal Tuesday Fast' (Niśā Maṅgaḷabāra Oṣā). Like any religious observance, it includes a promise to the deity, dietary restrictions and the regular worship of the goddess, in this case twice on every Tuesday in the month of *āśvina*. In the following section I shall describe this Maṅgaḷā Pūjā among a particular group of women in one neighbourhood of Berhampur. The ritual took place in a private house and was directed by a 52-year-old lady, who was respectfully addressed as 'Māusī' (maternal aunt). After my visit on the second Tuesday of the month, I described the event like this:

> The room is about 12 $m^2$ in size. In the lower portion of a wall cupboard there is an altar. I can recognize the image of a four-handed goddess, pasted in a thick layer of ground turmeric onto the wall. The relief is decorated with silver eyes, jasmine flowers, vermilion, kajal, and a red dress. 'This is Mā Maṅgaḷā,' she is introduced to us, 'she lives on the hilltop' (*pāhāṙa*).
>
> In analogy a pile of red cloths (*pāhāṙā*) is kept on a low wooden stool. On top of this pile, a bowl of consecrated betel nuts, lemons and a bunch of red bangles have been placed. Besides there are 23 auspicious *kumbhas*, i.e., earthen jars with coconuts on top, all decorated with a pair of red bangles, flowers and vermilion (Plate 2.1). Whoever observes Niśā Maṅgaḷabāra Oṣā has to contribute one decorated *kumbha*, a betel nut and a cloth. The *kumbhas* contain water that has to be replaced every Tuesday. This is done, like all the other preparations, by Māusī. Only she is supposed to approach the goddess and nobody should touch her at this time since this would risk pollution. She also keeps some lithographs of Maṅgaḷā and a bunch of peacock feathers.[15]
>
> While Māusī twists cotton to be put into a small butter-filled lamp, she does not seem to hear my question as to how she had learned to perform the *pūjā*. Her son explains that she had made a wish some 10 years ago and started the worship at that time. 'I knew the *pūjā* from myself, I never asked anybody', she finally answers. 'I had been to Puri in the month of *kārttika*.[16] Everyone talked about the Maṅgaḷā Pūjā there. They told me to

[15] In Orissa, a bunch of peacock feathers is commonly used as a ritual instrument to chase off evil spirits and to give blessings.

[16] Māusī refers to a particular ritual observance that is popular among elderly, post-menopausal women who for this purpose gather in Puri (see Freeman 1980).

**Plate 2.1:** Altar of Mā Maṅgaḷā: the turmeric idol, sacred jars and lamps

go to Kakatpur, to offer and take back a betel nut for worship.' This was about seven years ago. At that time Māusī introduced the worship of the goddess Maṅgaḷā in her locality. Subsequently more and more women joined. From 9.30 A.M. onwards some of them arrive, bow down in front of the goddess and place their offerings on a brass plate in front of the altar. I am told that there should be eight types of fruits, eight stalks of *duba*-grass, puffed rice and flowers, preferably hibiscus (*mandāra*). Most plates contain a coconut, bananas, apples, guavas, etc., but mostly less than eight pieces. The goddess favours 'uncooked' food. Māusī takes some coloured powder and by sifting it through her fingers draws a beautiful diagram in the shape of a flower on the floor. All the lamps are lit; it is 11 o'clock. Māusī rushes to put on a new sari. She comes back with some glowing coir and incense to worship the deity.

The *pūjā* starts in the presence of 10 participants (out of 23) with the shrill and auspicious sound, *huḷahuḷi*. The married women cover their head with their sari. An elderly lady invokes hymns in praise of different goddesses, the others join in: 'Glory to Thee, oh Mā Maṅgaḷā! ... Remembering Her all sorrows will be erased!' After a while somebody starts reciting the story of the beautiful Khulaṇā — a few women listen; yet more participants arrive; there is hardly any space left to sit, the air is hot and filled with smoke. Whenever it is explicitly mentioned in the story, all hoot loudly *huḷahuḷi*.

> After singing and listening for about half an hour, pieces of dried turmeric are collected, seven pieces per person. Subsequently they are put into a huge mortar. While listening to the *Khulaṇā Sundarī*, the women grind it one after another. Some of them sigh, exhausted from moving the heavy pestle. Others take a sieve and separate the powder. Again they will help to pound the dried roots. The grinding of the turmeric takes almost an hour. Even though the recitation of the *Khulaṇā Sundarī* goes on, the attention has turned to the preparation of *paṇā*, a kind of milkshake that serves as an offering to the goddess. Calls such as 'Stir in the puffed rice!' . . . 'Why don't you call for so-and-so?' or 'Where is the other plate?' interrupt the narrative. Some women chat about where to get fancy bangles and the like; laughter; again all join in the singing of hymns.
>
> Māusī crushes some coconuts and sprinkles a little of its water over the image of the goddess. On behalf of the group she offers eight types of fruit (Plate 2.2). She also gives *duba*-grass and some grains of rice with milk. Once again Māusī brings some burning coir and camphor. For this *ārati*-ceremony we have to get up and try to touch Māusī's body. On our behalf she speaks sacred formulas and offers smoke to the deity. A gong is beaten and one lady blows on a conch. We shout a high-pitched *huḷahuḷi*, touch the smoke with our hands and move it towards our foreheads. In a similar fashion flowers are offered. Then Māusī goes onto the veranda and gives water to the sun god. Everyone follows her. Finally all the women return inside. The sacred *bhoga* (the offerings left over by the goddess) and the blessed *paṇā* are distributed. The morning section of the *pūjā* is now over. It is 1.30 P.M., everybody leaves (revised excerpt from my fieldnotes, 5 October 1999).

On the Tuesday afternoons Māusī takes the turmeric powder, mixes it with water and replaces the old image with another one. When the women return in the evening they will see the newly decorated goddess with lots of fresh flowers attached. Then the evening section starts. It is a bit more grand and elaborated concerning the offerings, the number of participants and the time spent reciting the *Khulaṇā Sundarī*. It will not finish before 10 P.M. This sequence is essential to the Niśā Maṅgaḷabāra Oṣā. Since the goddess 'travels in the night' she is particularly accessible to her devotees during the darkness (*niśā*).[17]

---

[17] In Chapter 6 I shall come back to the divine preference for the night and explore how this 'dark' quality is acknowledged and brought about during the Ṭhākurāṇī Yātrā.

**Plate 2.2:** While ringing a bell, Māusī offers fruit to the goddess

I shall not go into a detailed description of this nocturnal *pūjā* since it resembles the morning section to a large extent. The major difference is that instead of crushing turmeric, each woman has to join eight strands of thread by making eight knots, each in one of Maṅgaḷā's names, i.e., the names of the eight Shakta goddesses. With the sacred thread they attach eight pieces of *duba*-grass and eight grains of rice (wrapped into *barakoḷi*-leaves) to a cucumber. After the *pūjā* is over the thread is removed and tied to the upper arm of the respective woman.[18]

While watching the *pūjā* I thought these women to be from the lower sections of society. There were some striking differences to rituals I had seen in middle-class or Brahmin households and in temples. In comparison, Māusī's house was very small; a two-room building with an attached kitchen had to serve as a home for about eight people. There was no space to maintain the strict separation of the sacred domain that is important to pious high-caste people. At night the space facing the altar had to serve as a bedroom, used garments were kept hanging on the wall, small kittens crossed the room while the *pūjā* was in process. All these features are considered polluting and should be avoided where a religious function takes place. To my surprise, Māusī and many of the 23 women who joined the *pūjā* were actually Brahmins (Brāhmaṇa).[19] Moreover, some participants belonged to the Khaṇḍāẏata (previously a warrior caste) and others to the Baṙhei (carpenters). Women of low-ranking communities such as the Bhaṇḍārī (barbers) or Dhobā (washer men, a Scheduled Caste) were not supposed to attend the *pūjā*. But this was not a matter of dispute since many different groups of women in that neighbourhood followed their own Maṅgaḷā Pūjā anyway. Likewise some middle-class Brahmins preferred to perform the ritual among themselves. Māusī's house would certainly

---

[18] The ritual differs slightly on each of the four or five Tuesdays of the month. On the first Tuesday the *kumbhas* are prepared, on the third Tuesday some green grams are put to sprout. The evening section of the last Tuesday is followed by the immersion of the idol, the *kumbhas*, sacred threads and the sprouted green grams.

[19] Māusī belongs to the Haluā-Brahmins who were traditionally farmers (from *hala*, literally: plough). In Orissa there is a large variety of Brahmins and one will find many status differences within this category. On the distribution of castes in southern Orissa, compare the *District Gazetteer* on Ganjam (Behuria 1995: 176–94).

not be considered proper, even though her religiosity was respected. Hence in this case the ritual community resulted from class-based habitus rather than caste affiliation – which is noteworthy since it contrasts with common assumptions on caste ideology. Economically, most of Māusī's attendants were from the lower strata. Their families ran small workshops or other small businesses. Apart from the (at times impure) state of the sacred site, there were other differences between the Maṅgaḷā Pūjā and priest-dominated rituals. The organization of the *pūjā* seemed to be shared among the women: more than five or six felt responsible for the proper procedure, all of them had to prepare the required items and many shouted out from time to time what, in their opinion, had to be done. This feature, however, applies to other votive rites as well.

Generally, the structure of the Maṅgaḷā Pūjā was akin to other rituals that are performed by women on the occasion of a religious fast. This similarity was achieved by the recitation of a legend, the preparation of *kumbhas*, the tying of sacred threads and, above all, the extensive time spent on the worship of the goddess. The offering of food, flowers and light (*ārati*) is common to any Hindu *pūjā*, even if a male priest is involved. Yet in some respects the outline of the Maṅgaḷā Pūjā was very specific – (*a*) It was the *Khulaṇā Sundarī* that had to be recited; (*b*) in accordance with Maṅgaḷā's various names it gave preference to the auspicious number eight; (*c*) women had to tie *duba*-grass, rice and *barakoḷi*-leaves onto a cucumber; and (*d*) they collectively crushed turmeric in order to (re-)create the goddess. The carefully structured procedure of the Maṅgaḷā Pūjā appeared to follow a normative model. Even though I knew that the ritual was introduced only recently, it seemed to repeat or refer to something. I was wondering to what extent written documents prescribed those sequences.

## Story (*kathā*) and Prayers

There are in fact several kinds of texts that *could* be relevant for the performance of the Niśā Maṅgaḷabāra Oṣā: (*a*) the legend of the beautiful Khulaṇā, (*b*) compilations of hymns and prayers, and (*c*) religious digests that also include a sort of *pūjā*-instruction – though the latter were irrelevant to Māusī and her attendants.

The book *Khulaṇā Sundarī* (The Beautiful Khulaṇā) altogether consists of 62 chapters (classified as *chānda*, i.e., stanza) that should be recited in different melody types (*rāga*). According to a popular edition, the book has 156 pages and is therefore difficult to memorize by heart.[20] Although most votaries have a rough idea of the story's plot (it had been made into an Oriya feature film as well), the episodes are recalled only after listening to it once more. The story is divided into five parts (*pāḷi*), to be read out on the four or five Tuesdays of the month.[21] Each part begins with a prayer by the poet (in *chānda* 1, 14, 26, 39, 51). The women read half of it during the morning section and half in the evening. In this way the plot develops over the respective Tuesdays.

(*a*) There was a childless king by the name of Dhaneśvara. None of his riches could cheer him. His queen Naẏanā suggested he gamble with her brother in order to win her sister Khulaṇā as a co-wife. The king won and Khulaṇā joined the palace and became pregnant. In spite of this, Dhaneśvara decided to leave for another country. Only after the news of the birth of a son would he come back. At the time of departure Dhaneśvara prayed to Lord Jagannātha and asked for his blessing. The goddess Maṅgaḷā became angry and decided to teach him a lesson. On his voyage she sent him a vision of a beautiful lady sitting on a lotus flower; a vision he enthusiastically described to Sudarśana, the king of Birupā. Sudarśana was eager to see this image but failed. He accused Dhaneśvara of being a liar and put him in prison. Back home the jealous Naẏanā had started not only to treat Khulaṇā as her servant but to torture her in various ways. Since Khulaṇā worshipped Maṅgaḷā with devotion, the goddess helped her to bear all the burdens and sufferings with ease. Khulaṇā gave birth to a son named Śrīdhara. After Naẏanā tried to poison both of them, they left the palace. Years passed and Śrīdhara grew up.

(*b*) At the age of seven, Śrīdhara decided to search for his father. Before he set out on the voyage, he worshipped the village

---

[20] The full title reads: *The Great and Beautiful Khulaṇā or The Nocturnal Tuesday Fast* (*Bṛhata Khulaṇā sundarī bā niśā maṅgaḷabāra oṣā*, n.d.). Here the book title is abbreviated as *Khulaṇā Sundarī*. According to the catalogue of the British Library, an earlier edition of this book was published in 1978 and its predecessor goes back to 1905.

[21] If the month has only four Tuesdays, the last part is added immediately.

goddess, the god Śiba and Mā Maṅgaḷā. All blessed him and gave him magic weapons: a sword, an arrow and *duba*-grass respectively. Being only a boy, Śrīdhara was accompanied by a guardian called Somanātha. With great difficulties they crossed dangerous oceans and were attacked by hundreds of leeches, the snake demon Kāḷi, giant prawns, and huge crabs. Śrīdhara and Somanātha could only defend themselves thanks to the magic weapons given to them by the gods. Finally they arrived in Birupā. But since Śrīdhara insulted king Sudarśana he was immediately arrested by his soldiers.

(*c*) 27 soldiers were ready to execute Śrīdhara. Once again he prayed to Maṅgaḷā, and at every attempt to behead him the soldiers were killed by their own swords. One by one they died. Only a single soldier was left to inform the king. Now Sudarśana ordered Śrīdhara to be hanged, but by the time he was led to the gallows, his ropes had been untied by the goddess. Then Maṅgaḷā went to the king's palace disguised as an ugly old woman. When she was brutally thrown out, she revealed her true appearance. The king asked for forgiveness and Maṅgaḷā demanded that he should offer his daughter to Śrīdhara in marriage. The king had to agree. At the same time she convinced Śrīdhara to ask for the royal prison as his dowry. The king was surprised by such an unusual request. He learned about Dhaneśvara and set him free. Finally the marriage was celebrated with pomp and splendor.

(*d*) Three months had passed when Śrīdhara dreamt that his mother was very ill. He decided to return to his own country. First Somanātha went as his messenger to give Khulaṇā the happy news. This time the goddess Maṅgaḷā sent eight ghosts to build a new palace. Meanwhile Naẏanā visited Khulaṇā and wondered with whose help she might have obtained this new palace and all those riches. Khulaṇā had to prove her virtue in a series of tests: walking on water, converting iron into rice, staying in a burning house and the like. Finally, with the help of Maṅgaḷā, her fidelity was proven.

(*e*) When Śrīdhara, his wife and his father arrived at the new palace Khulaṇā told him how Naẏanā had tortured her all those years. Dhaneśvara became very angry and wanted to kill Naẏanā. Only Śrīdhara could dissuade him from committing the sin of murder. Finally Naẏanā died a natural death and received

> her punishment in hell. Śrīdhara became the new king and performed all the rites required to thank the god Śiba.[22]

Like other legends, the *Khulaṇā Sundarī* includes several references to a poet (here: Dhībari Bhikārī), yet this does not hint towards authorship in a modern sense.[23] Rather it is a feature of Hindu mythology that most episodes are known in a multitude of versions, and that oral tradition intermingles with written transmission, so that indeed both forms result from a series of authors. In this fashion the legend about the beautiful Khulaṇā has become an integral part of the Caṇḍīmaṅgal, and thus the literary genre *maṅgalkabya* (literally: verses of divine beneficence) written down in Bengali from the fifteenth century onwards.[24] This should not come as a surprise since Bengal and Orissa share many religious and narrative traditions. Moreover, the Maṅgaḷā temple in Kakatpur was under Bengali management until the end of the nineteenth century (Mahapatra 1981/1982: 60). As a genre, the

---

[22] I am indebted to Bandita Panda and Ranjan Das for their repeated help in translating sections of the *Khulaṇā Sundarī* and also while analyzing its potential to shape women's experiences.

[23] At the end of the *Khulaṇā Sundarī* the poet describes himself as a 19-year-old orphan from the fisherman caste (Dhībari), who was asked by his teacher to write down the story of the beautiful Khulaṇā. This biography reflects a narrative pattern where the emphasis of the low-caste status of the devotee (the author) serves to prove the power and grace of a deity, here to enable him to compose *Khulaṇā Sundarī*. Following another rhetoric stereotype, the origin of the book is situated in the reign of the Sūryyabaṃśa dynasty (fifteenth/ sixteenth century). In the history of Orissa this period is known for the renaissance of art, music and literature.

[24] According to the Caṇḍīmaṅgal (for instance by the sixteenth-century Bengali poet Mukundarām Cakrabartī), there once lived a rich merchant named Dhanapati. He was married to both Lahanā and Khullanā, the latter being a devotee of Caṇḍī. When Dhanapati left for a business trip to Simhala, on his voyage he had a vision of a beautiful girl sitting on a lotus flower. Upon his arrival in Lanka he told the king about it. The king was eager to see this vision but was not able to do so. Angered by this fraud he put him into prison. Meanwhile Khullanā gave birth to a son called Śrīmanta. When he had grown up he went in search of his father. The same miracle happened to him. Like his father, he failed to show it to the king of Simhala. This time the king decreed the death penalty. But since Śrīmanta was, like his mother, a true devotee of Caṇḍī, just before his execution the goddess appeared and saved him. His father was freed and they returned home as rich men (see Zbavitel 1976: 165).

*maṅgalkabya* literature emphasizes the rivalry between deities and thus reflects competing religious discourses. Correspondingly, the *Khulaṇā Sundarī* stresses an opposition of the goddess Maṅgaḷā (here associated with Śiba and the village goddess) and the god Jagannātha. While according to the hegemonic Vaishnava belief, Jagannātha is superior to any other deity, but here the supremacy of Maṅgaḷā is demonstrated.[25] However, the women who join the Maṅgaḷā Pūjā do not reflect on this religio-political dimension of the legend.

On the front page of the book women learn why they should pray to the goddess: 'If you sincerely worship Mā Maṅgaḷā, it will be for the well-being of husband and sons. Friends, you won't face any troubles in life, sisters, do this *oṣā-brata*!' In spite of this appeal, the *Khulaṇā Sundarī* is not a manual for the conduct of the *pūjā*. It is a legend and illustrates the power of Mā Maṅgaḷā. Yet, while it describes Khulaṇā and her prayers to the goddess, it also conveys how to worship her (in *chānda* 2, 11, 27, 70, 79): on Tuesdays, on an empty stomach, with some lights, incense, *huḷahuḷi*, offerings, *mandāra*-flowers, and a piece of cloth – features that characterize the worship of several female deities. It refers to *duba*-grass as a magic weapon given by Maṅgaḷā, and the palace built by exactly eight of her supernatural helpers.[26] However, it also shows that Khulaṇā did not worship Maṅgaḷā for the well-being (and safe return) of her husband but rather to be saved from her own suffering! At any rate, the votaries in Māusī's house did not pay much attention to the details of the narrative. Taking a rest from housework, chatting with friends and busy preparing offerings, they could hardly remember in what manner Khulaṇā actually worshipped Maṅgaḷā. When I asked some of the women to explain what happens in the book, they mostly mentioned the conflict between the two sisters, the birth of the son and how Khulaṇā had to suffer. Nobody took the initiative to tell of the events after Śrīdhara left on his voyage, i.e., from the second part onwards. Did they have only the very beginning in mind?

---

25 'From the sky Maṅgaḷā spoke: Oh, Dhaneśvara, did you go mad? Leaving me, you pray to somebody else? To this Jagannātha who is just living in his big temple where he happily eats all the offerings? Has he no feet to walk? Then how will he come to rescue you from trouble.' (*chānda* 6).

26 According to McGee (1987: 229) the incorporation of the performance details of the fast into the story proper is a common format of this literary genre (*vrata kathā*). Alternately, the mode of worship is narrated as a part of the conclusion.

The second type of written sources, recited during the Maṅgaḷā Pūjā, were compilations of different types of hymns (*staba, bandanā, jaṇāṇa, stuti*). The prayers (*stuti*) were not only to adore Maṅgaḷā but also to praise several related deities (Durgā, Mahālakṣmī, Ṭhākurāṇī, Śiba, etc.). A *stuti* commonly describes the appearance of a goddess, enumerates her epithets and hence alludes to her powers, and also includes direct appeals to her grace in the first-person voice. Likewise, the prayer for Maṅgaḷā portrays the goddess as a woman dressed in red with terrifying teeth and tongue, riding on a lion at night.[27] In her eight hands she holds weapons such as a sickle-shaped sword, a curved dagger, a conch, a discus, and a club. This description actually varies from the iconography in her temple in Kakatpur, where the four-armed goddess holds a lotus bud, a rosary and a discus, generally recognized as the full moon.[28] Once I asked Māusī what kind of items Maṅgaḷā usually keeps in her hands. I was astonished to hear her answer: 'She holds the earth, nothing else. She has four arms. She is holding only the earth. She holds neither conch, nor discus, club or lotus.'[29] In other words, none of these descriptions was taken as an imperative when it came to the weekly (re-)construction of the idol. The turmeric representation of Maṅgaḷā had four (empty) arms and a red dress (see again Plate 2.1). It actually corresponds to non-specific images of *ṭhākurāṇī*-goddesses that can be seen at those areas of a temple compound where women carry out their rituals independently, i.e., near a tree or stone next to the main building (where the performance of a *pūjā* usually comes under the authority of a male priest).

Furthermore, the Maṅgaḷā *stuti* describes how the goddess is worshipped in different areas of Orissa as Śāraḷā, Birajā, Carchikā, Bimaḷā, Bhagabatī, Hiṅguḷā, and Samaḷāi. The women in Māusī's group, however, identify the latter with another goddess whose name is

[27] My reference here is the *Sarba Maṅgaḷā stuti* (n.d.), one of the pamphlets used by the votaries described above.

[28] The origin, history and identity of this image are highly contested and reflect the competing religious discourses on Maṅgaḷā. Some scholars believe that the present statue is a substitute and originally represented the Buddhist goddess Tārā (Brighenti 2001: 186).

[29] The weapons associated with Hindu deities commonly hint towards their Vaishnava, Shivaite or Shakta context. Māusī's statement belittles the Vaishnava symbols (conch, discus, lotus). In the same line the prayer stresses Shakta items (sword, dagger, club).

phonetically fairly similar: the goddess Śyāmaḷāẏī (The Dark One, i.e., Kāḷī). In the last 20 years several of the votaries had migrated from Hinjilikatu (near Aska), where there is a large Śyāmaḷāẏī temple. Even though the Maṅgaḷā *stuti* explicitly mentions Samaḷāi residing in Sambalpur, the women are convinced that it refers to Śyāmaḷāẏī at Hinjilikatu (compare Map 2). On each Tuesday of the Maṅgaḷā Pūjā, one prayer is devoted exclusively to this goddess. Thus the worship of Maṅgaḷā serves as a matrix to relocate and recall their former village goddess. In this way it connects the votaries from Hinjilikatu to their birth place.

To sum up, the written sources (*kathā*, *stuti*) were only loosely related to, and vaguely responsible for, the production of the Maṅgaḷā Pūjā. They had suggestive, not authoritative character. To presuppose a text with ritual instructions (*pūjā bidhi*, *oṣā bidhāna*) was not entirely misjudged though. There are several booklets that describe how to worship Maṅgaḷā. Some of these manuals are aimed at scholars and priests well versed in Sanskrit, some in fact address lay devotees.[30] A few also deal with the Niśā Maṅgaḷabāra Oṣā. Yet they do not describe Khulaṇā's fate but narrate completely different stories.[31] The preference

---

[30] For instance, the *Śrī Maṅgaḷā mahāpurāṇa o Śrī Maṅgaḷā mahimā* (n.d.) deals with the temple in Kakatpur, different kinds of worship, the annual Jhāmu Yātrā (walking on glowing charcoal) and several legends and prayers (see also Marglin and Mishra 1991). Being written partly in Oriya and partly in Sanskrit, it is a compendium for the faithful Brahminical scholar and priest. Its style of writing does not appeal to female devotees. Similarly there is the *Śrī Mā Maṅgaḷāṅka pūjā o melā* (n.d.). It includes a whole range of prayers, directions for meditation and also directions on how to worship Maṅgaḷā. This booklet is also mostly written in Sanskrit and for this reason hardly accessible to women. Moreover, it refers to a different ritual to the one performed on the occasion of the Niśā Maṅgaḷabāra Oṣā. None of these booklets mentions the story of the beautiful Khulaṇā.

In comparison the *Mā Maṅgaḷāṅka stuti o melā* (n.d.) is aimed at lay devotees and contains not only prayers and *mantras* but also a summary of various legends concerning the goddess, including some lines about the beautiful Khulaṇā. At the end it describes rules for the collective worship of Maṅgaḷā and mentions general features as well as specific offerings. However, these do not correspond to the Maṅgaḷā Pūjā performed by Māusī.

[31] The story is about a merchant and his son who went to hunt a rhinoceros in order to perform ancestral rites. By accident they kill the favourite cow of the king and are arrested. Thanks to the merchant's wife's worship of Mā Maṅgaḷā,

for one legend or another seemingly varies. In spite of the availability of printed *pūjā* instructions, the performance of the Maṅgaḷā *pūjā* is determined and legitimized in a different manner.

## Women's Voices

After the end of the Niśā Maṅgaḷabāra Oṣā, I visited some of the votaries to find out why and in what way they felt attracted by the ritual in Māusī's house. Their personal commitment to the Maṅgaḷā Pūjā gives some idea how women assess ritual inventions and in what respect they support and take part in this process. One of the first women I spoke to was Rani, a 50-year-old Sarua-Brahmin and mother of six grown-up children. Her husband and her two elder sons run a vegetable shop. Upon my question as to why she had chosen to fast in honour of Mā Maṅgaḷā, Rani told me how for many years she and her husband had tried to buy some land and get their daughters married. When she began to observe the Niśā Maṅgaḷabāra Oṣā about seven years before our conversation, she promised that if her wishes were fulfilled, she would keep on worshipping the goddess on a regular basis. Rani's problems were indeed solved, and when I spoke with her she was quite relaxed about her family's situation, and the Maṅgaḷā Pūjā had become an appreciated social event to her:

> Maṅgaḷā was there for the whole month. We went there, made jokes, we jointly performed the *pūjā*, talked a lot with our friends . . . You have seen how many devotees gathered, how many people were laughing and singing, there was a lot of gaiety. Well, doing the *pūjā* all alone, will it be as pleasant? Whoever . . . performs the *pūjā* on her own, after finishing it she will take the offerings and go to sleep. What else can she do? It is not the same pleasure as if we do it together.

Like several other religious activities, the Maṅgaḷā Pūjā is a welcomed opportunity to interrupt the daily routine. As Leigh Minturn (1993: 178)

---

father and son are repeatedly freed. Finally the king enquires about the reason and instructs his queens to pray to the goddess Maṅgaḷā regularly.

In another legend, Maṅgaḷā disguised herself as an old woman selling berries. She visited a village that was cursed to be barren. There she convinced the king's sweeper woman to buy berries and worship Maṅgaḷā. The sweeper followed her instructions and gave birth year after year. Although the childless king had doubts, he informed his queens to worship Maṅgaḷā. After the birth of sons, the king had to fulfill his promise to Maṅgaḷā and finally received her blessings (a summary of both stories is given by Miśra 1994: 114–17).

has pointed out with reference to Hindu women in Uttar Pradesh, there is no indigenous concept of leisure time, so all forms of recreation are realized in the religious domain.[32] Moreover, the collective performance of rituals serves as an opportunity to leave the premises and to maintain female friendships beyond kinship ties. Regarding the votaries of the Maṅgaḷā Pūjā, I should like to add that these social aspects do not weaken, but rather enhance women's commitment to rituals. However, men had an intuition of this pleasure and, at times, doubted the religious seriousness of their wife or mother. Although explicitly performed for male benefit, men showed reservations against the female practice of fasting. Their objections centred on how harmful it may be for the health. No matter to what extent this argument served as a strategy to keep a woman at home (and at their disposal), the votaries themselves denied this was a difficulty. They did not feel any pain in going without food, but rather gained self-esteem. Rani explained: 'I cannot give this up. Even if I feel sick and I am about to die, I will perform the *pūjā*. Even if [my husband and sons] don't agree I will perform the *pūjā* . . . When I am getting seriously ill and keep on doing the *pūjā*, they get angry. But I don't care.' The conflict about her religious activity became apparent when I asked Rani to recite the hymn in honor of Śyāmaḷāyī. 'Don't ask her to sing, it will never end', her son grumbled in the background; what an offence!

Rani's enthusiasm for the Niśā Maṅgaḷabāra Oṣā was also due to its aesthetic features. She emphasized that it was Māusī herself who had improved the ritual year by year, gradually introducing the binding of knots with a sacred thread, then the device of a cucumber, and, most important, the regular molding of the turmeric idol:

> Nobody does this *pūjā* the way we do. Some perform it by keeping a photo [i.e., a lithograph] of the deity or by making a permanent image out of cement. But only we do it with turmeric . . . [First] we paste the image on the wall. Then we attach its eyes, earrings . . . we use eyes made of silver and possibly a tongue of silver. Then, as if we are folding pleats in our saris, we dress the image.

[32] Strictly speaking, in rural and 'backward' areas of India there is no modern concept of leisure time for men either. However, as Kumar (1995) has argued with respect to men in Benares, the overarching concept of *līḷā* (roughly: play) offers men an ideology of leisure, recreation and being carefree. The discourse on *līḷā* is, according to Kumar (1995: 161), exclusively male or male-centred; playfulness is not the privilege of women. Compare Chapter 7 for the ludic masquerades of men during the celebration of Ṭhākurāṇī Yātrā.

Her statement clearly shows how she appreciates the turmeric image and to what extent the participants at the Maṅgaḷā Pūjā identify with its production – regardless of the fact that the idol is shaped by Māusī's skilled hands alone.

Another day I spoke to Madhu (44-year-old), one of the few non-Brahmin participants in the group. Her family belongs to the carpenter caste (Baṙhei) and still engages in this hereditary business. She had started the Niśā Maṅgaḷabāra Oṣā about five years back because Māusī had requested her to do so ('how can I say no!'). Her husband objected to her fast. Then the family underwent a major financial crisis from which they had not recovered. First they had to take a loan for their daughter's dowry. Then a real estate agent had given them an order for doors and windows for about 90 houses and broke the contract without paying. Finally Madhu's family had to sell their own house and property. 'So I called upon Mā Maṅgaḷā for the repayment of loan and for getting more orders in our business. I am not asking for money to repay everything. Let my children grow up under good conditions so that they will study well, and let us get more work so that we can repay the loan.' In fact several votaries approached Maṅgaḷā to deal with major financial problems that escaped their own capacity for self-help. In this case, the choice of fasting is also influenced by the religious discourse on the faithful Hindu wife (*patibratā*) as a source of prosperity and well-being. Here this ritual competence is an ambivalent gift that may also serve to blame women for social and economic difficulties.

> Even though we had to sell our house I didn't stop worshipping Maṅgaḷā. The Almighty [*bhagabān*] made me like this. By stopping the Maṅgaḷā Pūjā the situation won't get better. If it is not in my luck [*bhāgya*] then I won't get anything. My husband said that there is no improvement in our situation, so why do you continue the Maṅgaḷā Pūjā? But I replied that if it is not in our luck, the Almighty cannot give anything to us. Why should we blame the Almighty? That is why I keep on doing the *pūjā*.

I was impressed by how Madhu accepted her fate, although it made me slightly nervous how she relied on divine help. However, while talking to the votaries I was repeatedly confronted with this kind of conceptualizing of personal crises. As will be shown in the following section, these expressions reflect the rhetoric and subject position transmitted by the *Khulaṇā Sundarī*.

Most of the time it was Suchitra (28-year-old) who recited this legend. She was appreciated for her good voice and pronunciation.

Together with her husband and her two infant sons she lived in a one-room house. They were farmers by caste (Haluā-Brahmins) but her husband had taken up tailoring instead. During my visit to her house it turned out that even she had asked Maṅgaḷā to help her in times of troubles. Her husband's leg had been injured in a car accident and due to an infection it became stiff. For months he was neither able to walk without crutches nor to operate the sewing machine properly. The family had to borrow money for his treatment, among other things, and they were really in dire straits. While Suchitra complained about the situation I asked whether she was disappointed with the goddess Maṅgaḷā. The way she answered already sounded familiar:

> No, whatever is in our destiny [*bhāgya*], it will happen. If we have bad luck why should we curse Mā [Maṅgaḷā]? . . . Whenever we go for a fast we do have something in mind. But in my case everything went wrong. But by condemning the Almighty nothing will happen. It is our bad luck. We have this hardship because it is written in our fate.

In spite of her distress, for Suchitra the Maṅgaḷā Pūjā was also a welcome break from her daily chores. Upon my question as to whether she finds it difficult to perform the fast, she explained 'No, what difficulty should there be? There is nothing [like that]. If you have faith in mind you won't have any problem. I feel "free" [she uses the English term.] . . . That day I won't do any tailoring work.'

She also expressed her preference for Māusī's way of conducting the ritual. Some time back Suchitra had visited the Maṅgaḷā temple in Kakatpur. In a comparison of both forms of worship, she comically illustrated the greedy attitude of the temple priest: 'Give me the fee [*dakṣiṇā*] — ok, the *pūjā* is over!' On our laughter she complained: 'In a hurry they throw incense, lights and all [the other offerings], then they break the coconut [i.e., complete the *pūjā*] and ask for money. Oh it is so different over there!' Obviously Suchitra felt disturbed by the quick ceremony and by the atmosphere. Conversely, she regarded Māusī's inventions and the design of the ritual as an individual contribution to increase the religious value. She praised Māusī's talent at molding the goddess relief: 'she is an expert at it. It looks really good . . . The idol cannot be made by everyone . . . Nobody [in other groups of votaries] knows how to make it . . . To perform the *pūjā* with such a turmeric image is much better [than with a lithograph of the goddess].' From Suchitra's perspective, this form of worship was clearly superior to its temple counterpart and also to other types of Maṅgaḷā Pūjā performed in the neighbourhood.

Finally, Krishnakamini (45-year-old, Khaṇḍāẏata by caste) helped me understand another aspect of Māusī's authority. In a tone which suggested she was sharing a secret, she narrated the mysterious circumstances surrounding Māusī's discovery of a bunch of peacock feathers, then a hymn-book 'lying on the road', the goddess Lakṣmī's paddy plant, and finally the 'toothbrush'[33] of Jagannātha. All these items were considered to be divine gifts and proved Maṅgaḷā's appreciation for Māusī. Krishnakamini also mentioned how Māusī had had a vision of the goddess in her temple in Kakatpur. Maṅgaḷā looked like an old wrinkled woman, dressed in a black sari and bent over a walking stick (a stereotypical description of a goddess in disguise). Krishnakamini continued whispering 'Actually Maṅgaḷā is there in [Māusī's] house', and even more quietly 'She had put the betel nuts [from Kakatpur] under a brass plate in her house. At this place the goddess' idol rose up . . . just by itself. It had a nose, ears, everything. Just like that it grew.' When I later asked the other votaries about these miracles, it turned out that most of the women were familiar with bits and pieces of Māusī's divine encounters. To exchange these rumors seemed to be a common way to acknowledge her competence. Following the logics of the *Khulaṇā Sundarī*, the gift of magic weapons (whether *duba*-grass or in this case a divine toothbrush) is indeed a common means to recognize the support of a deity.

## The Goddess who Guides through Troubles

While talking about the different motives for observing the Niśā Maṅgaḷabāra Oṣā, I noticed how women responded in a somehow standardized manner. There seemed to be a similarity between their ways of expressing personal problems, and how Khulaṇā's suffering was narrated in the book, i.e., the relation between the framing and interpretation of events in the *Khulaṇā Sundarī* and the way women assessed their own experiences. Moreover, whereas I doubted the degree of their attentiveness during the recitation, they were convinced about their knowledge of the legend: 'Anyone who reads the *Khulaṇā Sundarī* will understand it. It contains everything, about the sister's pain and suffering, about her son, their departure.' Were we

[33] Here the English term is used and refers to a thin wooden stick that is used for cleaning teeth.

talking about different stories? I suggest that we were not only reading one and the same written text from two perspectives, we also perceived different cultural scripts. While I was searching for the story-plot, the women at the *pūjā* site objectified the *Khulaṇā Sundarī* as a thematic entity. Their subject matter was how women are capable of bearing their sufferings. Once more I went through the book, this time looking for those passages that might serve women to explain and tolerate the constraints of their lived-in world.

From the beginning of the story, the goddess Maṅgaḷā is praised as the saviour from evil, sorrow, suffering, pain, and danger. 'Khulaṇā . . . tolerated so many troubles. There is no one in this universe who bore so much pain. How you managed to save her, help us like that!' (*chānda* 3) Similar to many young daughters-in-law, Khulaṇā has to face an enormous amount of physical and emotional burden. She is not shown respect for her workload or her mental stress. She becomes a servant to her elder sister and co-wife, who gives her all kinds of inhuman orders. For instance, Naẏanā forces her to carry a water jar of about 150 litres. The book describes many situations of such injustice. '[In despair Khulaṇā] raised her hand and hit her forehead. "Let it burn, my unlucky fate, who I am going to tell about it?" She prays to Mā Maṅgaḷā. Mā Maṅgaḷā will know about her pains.' (*chānda* 8) In asking whom she should talk to, Khulaṇā expresses how useless it would be to complain to someone since nobody would be in a position to change her situation. Maṅgaḷā advises Khulaṇā to keep quiet and to continue to carry the heavy water jar, for it would appear to her 'as light as a small flower'. Magically the goddess reduces Khulaṇā's burdens on many other occasions. As the story develops it becomes clear that Maṅgaḷā does not solve the problems. She neither guards her devotees from difficulties nor does she punish the culprits. She rather guides the votaries through all their troubles. Her blessings work like a painkiller.

Along the same lines, the devotees approach the goddess not to solve their problems but to help them in their distress. One woman told me: 'I have performed this *pūjā* for so many years. None of my wishes has been fulfilled. As you have seen, everything went wrong . . . I keep on doing the Maṅgaḷā Pūjā because I have already performed it for five years. Even now I am doing it happily.' The votaries are quite aware that they cannot expect miracles from Maṅgaḷā. They worship her to feel supported in times of crisis. Since women feel responsible for their family's well-being, they call upon the goddess and seek nothing else but help to bear their fate. The legend implies that suffering has a religious and gendered dimension. On one occasion Khulaṇā responds to Nay̐anā: 'Whatever difficulty and pain you have given me, I tolerate it all because this will count for my *dharma*. Let my body suffer like this, as you are the elder one you will always have this right.' (*chānda* 9) Through the voice of Khulaṇā it is suggested to the votaries that bearing suffering will also 'count for their *dharma*' – the fulfillment of their (female) religiosity and duty. Thus distress is framed as a promise of spiritual reward and an option for women to prove their faith in God. The following quotation even specifies this relationship between gender, suffering and salvation. Khulaṇā considers whether she should escape her ill-treatment:

> 'All my sorrow would immediately stop if I go to my parents' house. But I cannot bear to be considered unfaithful by the whole world, so I won't go. Let her [Nay̐anā] give me as much punishment [as she likes], as it is my fate, my body will bear it. In my parents' house everybody will ask why my husband left. They will blame me for coming back in such a poor state. By hearing this my blood will heat up. [These abuses] will spoil my reputation. I can bear the sufferings but I can't bear these abuses. So I won't go back to my parents' house.' While thinking about all these things she cried and prayed to the goddess. Immediately Maṅgaḷā appeared before her: 'Why are you crying Khulaṇā? It is written in your fate. It is the nature of women to tolerate more pain [than men] and that is why you cancope with it. Since you have had so many pains, oh beautiful one, I will free you from all troubles. Within a few days all your pains will disappear and you will feel happiness in your mind. You will have a son who will free you from all sorrows. Let millions of troubles come upon you, in the end you will come out victorious.' [*chānda* 10]

According to Mā Maṅgaḷā, women can tolerate more pain than men. Yet the *Khulaṇā Sundarī* not only calls on the female devotee to bear her own burdens, but also claims that suffering is a fundamentally female quality – 'women's nature'.[34]

---

[34] Besides, the book suggests that only a son is able to help a woman to escape from her sorrow. However, on the textual level this turns out to be an illusion: Before beginning his voyage, Śrīdhara leaves his mother with the same message: 'We have to bear our sorrow. So mother, please endure all sufferings by chanting [the name of] Maṅgaḷā under her feet. She will protect you

For votaries listening to the legend, the character of Khulaṇā provides a figure to identify with. Her suffering, crying, prayers and calls upon the goddess reflect their own experiences in everyday life. Although the role of Śrīdhara might invite male identification, to the women the main character is Khulaṇā. Even in the further development of the plot (on the following Tuesdays) her sufferings are emphasized. Partly, since Nayanā does not stop threatening Khulaṇā after her departure from the palace, and partly since Khulaṇā's initial torments are narrated on two or three occasions, for instance to Dhaneśvara in the last section of the legend. By either taking the position of the narrator or letting the characters speak for themselves, the book also suggests to its audience how to perceive and classify their own feelings of distress and powerlessness.

While discussing the motives for observing the Niśā Maṅgaḷabāra Oṣā, women often responded in idioms similar to the narrative stance of *Khulaṇā Sundarī*. To them, calls such as 'Oh Mā Maṅgaḷā, save me! I have no friend, brother nor strength. Oh great Mother, save me from this danger!' were not merely narrative phrases. They came to substitute their own voices. I suggest that the formulae in the book serve as a kind of vocabulary, grammar and syntax for women to understand and to conceptualize their own experiences: It prompts the *terms* used to assess individual sensations, mediates how to *relate* these towards one's self and to its origin, as well as how to *assemble* one's experiences in terms of gender and destiny (*bhāgya*).[35] In this way it communicates culturally accepted and appreciated values for dealing with (female) hardship and subordination. By gathering, reading and listening to the *Khulaṇā Sundarī*, women are reminded of their 'female' virtues. They convince each other that there is hope of gaining the goddess Maṅgaḷā as an ally. The ritual also suggests that even in hopeless situations the devotee is capable of taking action. She can get through the troubles by praying to the goddess, and even without taking food she might enjoy it. I should make the point that I do not assume this quality of the

---

from all sorts of dangers. Always keep your mind at the feet of Mā Maṅgaḷā.' [*chānda* 18]

[35] When doing research on votive rites that left devotees with unfulfilled wishes, Pintchman (2006: 230) cites a female interlocutor from Benares who used exactly the same phrases and patterns of relating distress to personal and female destiny.

text to be exclusive to the *Khulaṇā Sundarī*. Still, I believe this text, like many other written and cultural sources, might serve as a framework with which to perceive, assess and reconsider individual emotions and experiences.

## Conclusion: The Personalization of Ritual

The worship of the goddess Maṅgaḷā in the elaborate way described here was only slightly predetermined by written sources. Apart from the overall four-Tuesday structure, neither the *Khulaṇā Sundarī* nor prayers defined the design and sequence of ritual acts. Rather the religious books had inspired several features relevant to the worship of Maṅgaḷā and a *ṭhākurāṇī* in general. The validity of the ritual did not derive from the prescriptive authority of religious texts, although the act of reciting the story (*kathā*) was of great importance and by itself evoked a feeling of sanctity. The impact of the *Khulaṇā Sundarī* on the authentication of the Maṅgaḷā Pūjā escaped notice at first.

The priestly status of the senior lady who directed the *pūjā* was not legitimized by scriptural knowledge either. Her authority arose from her personal commitment towards the Maṅgaḷā Pūjā. The participants appreciated her ritual inventions as a result of her devotion to the goddess. However, these features had to meet the votaries' 'sense of ritual' (Bell, drawing on Bourdieu). Māusī, for her part, denied the responsibility for the development of the *pūjā*. Although in the previous three to five years she initiated most of the present-day ritual sequences (for instance the making of the goddess' image out of turmeric paste and also the tying of a sacred thread to a cucumber), she preferred to regard herself as a divine instrument. Even the participants affirmed to each other that Māusī miraculously found significant items for the *pūjā*, how she had a vision of the goddess, of where Maṅgaḷā 'lived' in her house, etc.

It would be misleading to conceive of Māusī's additions to the ritual structure in terms of artistic creativity or self-expression. Besides the difficulty of pinpointing individual inventions in a society that subscribes to the ideal of non-individuality, her choice of analogies and formal features was neither innovative nor accidental. It reflected familiar ideas, aesthetics and objectifications prevalent in popular religious discourse. With this background, the inspiration to refine the Maṅgaḷā Pūjā was framed in such a way as to prove how the goddess herself had determined the complex procedure of the ritual. Yet to consider Māusī's denial of her initiative as a rhetorical strategy to hide her personal influence in the manipulation of symbols, i.e., to think of it as a kind of pretence, is equally wrong. The Maṅgaḷā Pūjā only became a success because of the convincing performance of the ritual — the sensation of presence that resonated not only to Māusī's self-understanding, but also to the expectations and emotions of the participants. This intuition of the necessity to join, perform and develop a hitherto unknown ritual did not serve particular ideological ends. The votaries did not claim to follow an ancient custom, unlike in the case of those 'invented traditions' (Hobsbawm and Ranger 1983) that construct a link with a fictitious past. Women rather improvised on a culturally established set of ritual figures and parameters. In this respect, the composition of the Maṅgaḷā Pūjā resulted from what I propose to call the 'personalization' of ritual, i.e., the realization of ritual prerequisites in such a way that it evokes and expresses intimate instead of general feelings — a process that contributes to both the validity of ritual *and* religious commitment. I believe this mode of composition neither reflects a substantially new development nor it is limited to women. Rather this way of appropriation is particularly visible against the background of objectified religious knowledge, as in case of the religious digests which enable rituals to travel, and thus to transcend geographical, chronological and possibly social distance.

In the case of the Maṅgaḷā Pūjā, there are basically three ways that deepen the attachment of performers to the ritual and thus shape its personalization: (*a*) the selection of familiar and cherished ritual objects, concepts and sequences (for instance the form and substance of the idol); (*b*) the framing of the *Khulaṇā Sundarī* as a thematic entity dealing with women's burdens and suffering; and (*c*) the conversion of burning issues, emotions and tensions into adequate body practices. This process is based on shared experience rather than on conscious decision-making, as the collective preparation of the goddess image exemplarily shows: Since the crushing of dried turmeric roots matched the women's feeling of tiring and at times endless efforts to perform their daily duties, they might have sensed it appropriate to embody the physical burden of Khulaṇā. During the ritual, an occasion of joy and pleasure, this task was shared among the participants and performed in a very joking and playful manner (see also Hauser 2010b). Hence the big and heavy iron pestle appeared 'as light as a flower', and thus provided the somatic evidence of Maṅgaḷā's presence. As over the years the number of votaries increased, the processing of the turmeric grew into a major act. Since each person has to contribute seven pieces, in the year 1999 the pile of dried roots must have reached, hypothetically, 161 pieces. Even if some participants were prevented from joining the worship, the heap of turmeric was immense. Thus, the time spent on the effort of grinding rose with the size of the goddess' image and again its impression on votaries. The *Khulaṇā Sundarī* for its part provided a matrix of suffering that absorbed not only the day-to-day experiences of participants, it also brought about a sense of coherence that legitimized the collective crushing of turmeric. The personalization of ritual is, hence, substantially different from authorship (that to some extent may antedate production); it authenticates ritual rather than alludes to the concept of individuality.

The performance of the Maṅgaḷā Pūjā also shows how women react to ideal constructions of religion and gender, transmitted by the pious story that accompanies the votive rite. Whereas the women at Māusī's altar do not think about the *Khulaṇā Sundarī* as a text that subverts Vaishnava ideology (the primacy of Lord Jagannātha), they obviously consider the postulated link of femininity, suffering and religious merits. Listening to the text, they learn from Khulaṇā that to tolerate suffering may have soteriological value ('count for *dharma*'). In Hinduism the rationale of austerities and (self-induced) bodily pain as means to acquire spiritual rewards and power is well-known, best exemplified by the idea of asceticism. Similarly, Margaret Egnor (1980: 14) argues that women understand their strength (*śakti*) as a consequence of the suffering that their subordination entailed. The votaries in Māusī's house, however, do not seem to share this interpretation. Even though none of them would openly criticize the religious text, they regard Maṅgaḷā's speech – 'it is the nature of women to tolerate more pain than men' – as a description of unpleasant social reality rather than a precondition to achieve salvation. Unlike the recitation, the intention and enactment of the Maṅgaḷā Pūjā suggests that suffering is not morally superior; the votaries definitely wish to achieve well-being. Like Khulaṇā they worship the goddess to gain divine support in getting through their troubles and difficulties. Rather than self-denial, as fasting could suggest, the psychophysical experience of joining the Niśā Maṅgaḷabāra Oṣā draws the attention of votaries to their own ability to become active and react to even desperate crises in life.

# 3

# Periodically Untouchable: Female Bodies and the Performance of Impurity

So far this book focused on the performance of votive rites (*oṣā-brata*) in their potential to affect and influence the self-understanding of very young women (Chapter 1) and, conversely, of experienced votaries (Chapter 2). Yet the impact of Hindu rituals on female identity in Orissa is not a one-way process. The last chapter emphasized the active part women play in the perpetuation of religious discourse and social negotiation of gender. It revealed how the performance of rituals is clearly characterized by the practitioners' desires, their notions of femininity and their particular location of meanings. This circular character of Hindu rituals as cultural sites, where gender-identity is objectified as well as emergent, could be brought out taking several other examples. However, in this chapter I shall consider the theatrical dimension of day-to-day interactions, and in particular the subtle routine display of menstrual pollution intended to prevent others from touching the menstruant as this would cause the spread of impurity. The concept of purity is crucial for Hindu women and their religious practices since a pure body is the precondition for any form of worship. The following chapter shows how, and in what respect, women identify with the religious and largely Brahminical ideology of purity and pollution that postulates their monthly untouchability, and thus excludes the menstruating women from any religious and several social activities.

With respect to the theoretical approach taken in this book, this chapter has thus the character of an excursus on 'doing gender' in everyday communication. Still, the units of observation and analysis are described as 'scenes' (as if framed), whereas from an emic perspective the behaviour of participants is *not* conceived as performance but rather in terms of social conventions (good manners). In conclusion I shall advance a hypothesis on how these routine enactments vary from self-contained events (cultural performances), in their potential to outline, shape and verify female identity. To anticipate one major effect of this analytic perspective: thinking of menstrual pollution as a performative category allows me to discuss how women perpetuate the discourse on this gendered concept, and also to what extent reflection may provide them with the facility to take action, to structure and frame reality according to their own sense of being. It also shows how by means of regular enactment the sentient body becomes authoritative. Finally I shall consider the processual dimension of this performative practice, and discuss whether alterations of menstrual restrictions allow any conclusions to be reached concerning the concept of pollution and its ability to influence the self-understanding of women in a negative way.

Culture-specific notions of purity and pollution have repeatedly attracted academic imagination. Among these, 'menstrual taboos' constitute a particular apt example to demonstrate women's supposedly irrational belief in, and submission to, tradition. Although anthropological scholarship has critically questioned the assumptions underlying this academic debate (see Buckley and Gottlieb 1988), menstrual restrictions continue to suggest a kind of backwardness, and those practices followed on the Indian subcontinent are no exception to the rule. Gabriella Eichinger Ferro-Luzzi, an anthropologist who in 1971/2 did an intense survey on gender-specific forms of pollution in Tamil Nadu, was puzzled by the 'extraordinary vitality' of these concepts. She identified three reasons for the persistence of menstrual restrictions: first, the 'Indian love for traditions', second, the unobtrusive nature of this type of impurity that does not call for political action against it (as it does in the case of permanent untouchability), and third, an 'appreciable secondary gain' for the menstruating woman (Eichinger Ferro-Luzzi 1974: 154). The author described a great variety of practices and analyzed them in relation to the women's economic situation, their rural/urban background, the size and structure of their family, etc. In spite of missing comparative data, Eichinger Ferro-Luzzi (1974: 156) concludes that menstrual restrictions are changing, and suggests that female forms of pollution may gradually disappear. Her assumption is that educated young women will doubt and finally give up menstrual practices, as if their observance was based on the lack of knowledge and hence the inability to reflect on their meaning.

From the perspective of Indian feminists, the notion of menstrual pollution is just one means among many to control women's behaviours and the spaces they occupy. According to Kalpana Viswanath (1997: 316) it reflects male discourse in that women are merely the sites or the symbols of cultural ideology. Similar to concepts such as honour and shame, the ideal of purity versus impurity produced the idea of the dangerous female body and its potential threat to society. Whereas this cultural discourse legitimized constraints on menstruating women, they themselves felt dirty, embarrassed and scared of pollution (Viswanath 1997: 326). The problem with this feminist position is the presumption that menstrual rules should be given up as if they generally counteracted women's liberation.[1] This stance indirectly subscribes to the norms of contemporary Western society, where monthly bleeding may not interrupt female social behaviour *and working capacity* (see Martin 1987). Moreover, if menstrual practices are considered to be imposed upon women from outside, Indian women are denied the possibility that from their point of view the observance of (some) menstrual practices could also make sense or even result from personal conviction.

The personal experience of menstrual pollution and its relevance for social action are also of concern in cross-cultural psychology, yet again in a negative way. When Richard Shweder (1985) explored how Brahmins in Orissa deal with menstrual impurity, he located their perceptions and pollution concepts in proximity to emotional phenomena like depression. To sense the menstruating body as impure and to observe menstrual restrictions is conceived of as a culture-specific syndrome, and thus pathological.

In this chapter I shall take a different direction and discuss how women in southern Orissa perceive and practically deal with menstrual rules, how they reflect on them and how this influences their sense of self and gender.[2] This is neither to argue for another correlation between the observance of 'menstrual taboos' and the social or psychological status of women, nor do I consider the physical act of

[1] In recent anthropological discourse on menstrual customs the argument of the repressive dimension of menstrual restrictions, in their simpler forms at least, is rejected for being too one-sided (Buckley and Gottlieb 1988: 14).

[2] This chapter is a thoroughly revised and translated version of an article I had previously published in German (Hauser 2006d). A comparative perspective is offered in Hauser (2011a).

menstruation. Rather I shall focus on the cultural notion of menstrual pollution, and how women perpetuate and negotiate this issue in day-to-day communication. I subscribe to the idea that culture-specific tacit knowledge, such as on purity and other sensual categories, is overwhelmingly transmitted not by cognition but rather by means of the lived-in body. The social reality is constructed by the mimetic re-enactment of a pre-structured cultural repertoire, as the following example shows:

> (Scene 1) Just when I am about to hand over the photograph to Gauri, she withdraws her hand. The picture floats down to the ground. I am confused. Then I realize, squat down and display the remaining photographs side by side on the floor so that Gauri can look at them.

In this situation, the notion and reality of ritual pollution is (re-)produced interactively. Gauri allows the photograph to fall on the floor, and therefore, showing not only her interest but also indicating the impure state of her body. By means of non-verbal expression I understood that she did not want to transfer her menstrual impurity onto the photograph presented and hence to me. Her behavior reminded me of the Hindu paradigm of ritual purity, and also evoked a mimetic reaction in that I myself started to avoid bodily contact (in order to show respect for her customs). Placing the photographs on the floor and thus inviting her to merely look at the pictures, I had practically agreed with her pollution! Yet the enactment of cultural values and beliefs does not only reconfirm and establish patterns of behaviour and social routines, it also influences the perception of one's body, time and space, as well as the materiality of artifacts.

As in the episode above, the central theme of this chapter is the subtle ways in which women communicate and objectify impurity, i.e., when and how they recognize and express menstrual pollution through voice, gestures and body language. Considering pollution as a performative category, I shall discuss what kinds of behaviour raise critical reflection, and also how their repetition influences the lived-in body as grounds for experience. It will turn out that rather than a fixed set of menstrual restrictions that limits women during their period, there is a permanent display and deciphering of the female body in its ritual eligibility. This is crucial, because it qualifies non-menstruating Hindu women (rather than men) to bring about auspiciousness. Therefore, the perception of bodily (im-)purity is inherently connected with the self-presentation of women in everyday life, their use of space, their behaviour and also their social interactions. Certainly this presentation of the ritual self is also subject to reflection. Menstrual practices are followed with different intentions and personal attitudes. Although women consider several aspects to answer role expectations related to their period, they hardly question the state of menstrual pollution itself.

One preliminary remark: I did not plan to work on menstrual customs and beliefs. During my stay in Orissa, however, I regularly noticed how social interactions were altered due to menses. The analysis in this chapter is based on these experiences and also on informal talks regarding these incidents. Since I did not carry out (and record) interviews on this subject matter, women's voices are reconstructed and framed in scenes. These episodes were (re-)written on the basis of my field notes. Unlike in other chapters in this book, here the views of urban middle-class women dominate (15 to 40 years old, both single and married, with and without children).

## Purity and Pollution in Hinduism

Menstrual practices in Orissa are related to a culture-specific discourse on purity and pollution (Oriya: *chuā-achuā*, Hindi: *śuddh-aśuddh*) that is commonly associated with Hindu religion. Therefore, it would be misleading to analyze female beliefs and behavioural patterns concerning menstrual impurity separately. Here I should like to point out some of the basic thoughts and implications of the Hindu paradigm of purity. This brief account will only touch on a few arguments from a highly complex academic and also political debate:

One of the central issues in the religious and social life of pious Hindus is to maintain a high degree of purity in one's personal environment. This quality is only partly related to cleanliness and hygiene.[3] Rather it refers to an ideal state that is difficult to achieve and to preserve. Hence the notion of purity guides social behaviour, although it is rarely followed absolutely. The danger of pollution results from bodily emissions, such as sweat, saliva, blood, faeces, hair, finger- and toenails. Moreover, there are polluting events (birth and death), and also polluting substances, for instance alcohol, meat or leather. Thus every Hindu has to cope with pollution in her or his daily routine and life cycle. Some types of pollution are created by the human body itself,

[3] On the notion of purity in relation to other concepts, within the realm of Hinduism, see Michaels (2004a: 184–87) and Malinar (2009).

some are transmitted while drinking water or eating certain foods and also by means of touching, and some result from social relations.

To guard themselves against pollution Hindus may avoid social contact with certain kinds of persons. Nevertheless, in the case of childbirth and death the pollution concerns every family member, no matter whether they were physically present at the crucial time. Some forms of pollution originate from the female life cycle (menarche, menstruation and childbirth). Unavoidable occasions of pollution last for a limited time span only. Their duration may vary according to caste and family tradition. Towards the end of this period, the body is actively purified by bathing or by the ritual use of the so-called 'five products' of the cow: milk, curd, clarified butter, urine, and dung. Yet these ritual practices are not sufficient to compensate for the rather persistent form of pollution, resulting from regular contact with impure substances, and contributing to the assessment of social status. Therefore, members of those communities who by following their hereditary occupation are exposed to pollution, for example sweepers, scavengers, washer men, cobblers, and midwives, are considered highly impure, and thus 'untouchable'. Since pollution may result from contamination by means of social interaction, the estimated level of somebody's (symbolic) purity may serve to explain the avoidance and even discrimination of some individuals or groups.

In the academic discourse on South Asia, the ideal of purity has been identified as one of the guiding principles that structures Hindu religion and society alike, best exemplified by caste hierarchy.[4] The most coherent account of purity and its social relevance can be distilled from a Brahminical perspective, that follows not only ancient theological scriptures but also prevails in many academic accounts, whether in the discipline of Sanskrit studies/Indology, social anthropology or religious studies (Burghart 1990). From this point of view, the degree of ritual purity serves to define the hierarchy of Hindu society, i.e., each caste is ranked according to a system that is presided over by Brahmins – symbolized by the prototypical vegetarian male priest.

---

[4] Most of these studies critically relate to the French sociologist Louis Dumont and his distinguished study *Homo Hierarchicus* (1970). This structural analysis of Indian society is based on the argument that ritual purity/pollution is the fundamental binary opposition organizing caste hierarchy and power. For 'post-Dumontian' approaches towards India, see Searle-Chatterjee and Sharma (1994) and Quigley (1993).

According to the frequency and kind of transactions and services exchanged with others, the status of all the other communities is derived, so that the relative purity of some castes is based on the relative impurity of others. The ideal of purity hence legitimizes the low status of 'untouchables'.

However, this approach is highly problematic and was criticized in many respects as Orientalist fiction (Inden 1990). First of all, this model of Hindu India does not correspond to social reality and its variety of human relationships, social encounters and power plays. The discourse on purity is not superior to or isolated from other strategies to gain status, based on economic, political, demographic or other factors. Moreover, people from different strata do not agree on uniform criteria to measure purity; they might compete over ritual status, or hardly care about this issue at all.

Second, not even the religious domain is configured only by the hierarchical axis of purity and pollution. From a popular or subaltern perspective, the concept of 'auspiciousness' (Oriya: *śubha, maṅgaḷa*, Hindi: *śubh, maṅgal*) seems to be far more influential than the notion of purity, although scholars do not agree whether these two are competing or correlating concepts (Carman and Marglin 1985, Madan 1985, Marglin 1985b, Raheja 1988). On the one hand, purity has an auspicious effect whereas pollution is feared to bring about calamities, such as severe disease, childlessness or a bad harvest. On the other hand, *some* impure events, as childbirth, are also favourable (*maṅgaḷa*) while certain types of worship are inauspicious, for instance death rituals. Whether purity is conceived of as only one or as the central feature of Hinduism is hence highly contested (Searle-Chatterjee and Sharma 1994: 6). Meanwhile, scholars have also reconsidered the supremacy of Brahmins, questioning their power in defining the category and relevance of caste as well as in promoting a particular concept of a Hindu religion (Inden 1990; Quigley 1993; Sontheimer and Kulke 1989; and others).

Apart from the ideological and political impact of the Hindu discourse on purity, there is another dimension of this paradigm that is largely neglected in academic debates: the somatic efficacy of this cultural construct. After all, the perception of pollution (and purity) is only partly defined by a cognitive process. Similar to emotions like disgust or fear, it is grasped intuitively, i.e., located at the sensory level and related to personal experience. Thus the approach taken in this chapter – to show how pollution is mediated, enacted and (re-)produced by means of social interaction, and how reflection may interfere with this everyday performativity – should also inspire the scholarly debate on the role and relevance of purity in South Asia.

Yet, the idea of purity and pollution does not always determine human relationships. Particularly in those spheres of society that are characterized by secularism, mobility and globalization, many ritual procedures to prevent the transmission of pollution are obsolete. In multinational companies nobody cares whether the colleagues who join lunch (commensality) have been in touch with impure substances, people or situations. The relevance of purity is basically limited to the private domain: to the home, family affairs and religious matters. In this context, the display and identification of pure and impure bodies matters. As part of the everyday, it influences the social interactions between women, of women with men, and of women with their children. In the case of a joint family household with several female members, the subtle communication of menstrual pollution will be a regular feature. Anybody may read these signs in order to react accordingly.

The forms of behaviour described in the following sections not only characterize domestic interactions at the time of menstruation, they also occur in other situations where the transfer of pollution is feared, whether due to death or if the persons involved are of extremely different caste status. The photograph mentioned in scene 1, for instance, could have been dropped by a low-caste man as a 'polite' gesture acknowledging the higher status of his counterpart. The *display and deciphering* of pollution is hence a crucial factor when it comes to delineating the social practices of Hindu women *and* men.

## Menstrual Restrictions

Social restrictions for the time of menstruation exist in almost every community all over the Indian subcontinent (Eichinger Ferro-Luzzi 1974: 116).[5] Although several Hindu scriptures include prohibitions

[5] Menstrual practices were recognized and studied in different regions: see Bennett (1983: 215–18), V. Das (1988: 197–98), Fruzetti (1982: 97), Kapadia (1995: 163–78), Puri (1999: 43–73). The accounts of Eichinger Ferro-Luzzi (1974) and Winslow (1980) suggest that menstrual restrictions do not only concern Hindus but also Muslim, Christian, Jain, Buddhist, and tribal women.

relating to menstruation,[6] women learn and transmit them orally and, as is discussed here, by performative means. Varying from caste to caste and from region to region, these practices form several overlapping (and at times inconsistent) sets of rules and prescriptions. The *ideal* version generally refers to: (*a*) the segregation of a menstruating person from others; (*b*) the prohibition of touching substances which may transfer pollution; (*c*) the suspension of any religious activity; (*d*) the omission of body beautification; and (*e*) additional dietary measures. Middle-class women in Berhampur spelt out these rules like this:

(*a*) During the time of her period a woman should withdraw from her family and, if possible, remain in a reserved space or room inside the house. She should avoid any social interaction or at least restrict herself to the most urgent communication. In the Indian joint family system this limitation concerns, first of all, a woman's husband, his brothers and father, and also her own sons and daughters. While growing up, children come to learn that they may not always count on their mother, who once in a month avoids feeding, hugging, dressing and bathing them. For practical reasons, however, a woman will continue to interact with her mother- and sisters-in-law who take care of her children and housework. A menstruating woman is neither allowed to have sexual intercourse nor to sleep in the proximity of her husband. If the couple shares a wooden bedstead (rather than sleeping mats), she has to shift her bedding to the floor. The segregation of a woman during her period should particularly protect those people who are thought to have higher status, like male affines.

(*b*) A menstruant should not touch objects that are considered capable of transferring pollution. In principle this could concern every substance or item, in practice it refers to products appreciated for one reason or another and, above all, to drinking water and food preparations. Hence a woman is not allowed to cook for others, to touch kitchen utensils or to serve food. She takes her meals separately from the family (no commensality)

[6] For the ideal behaviour of a menstruant, according to the eighteenth-century Sanskrit digest *Strīdharmapaddhati*, see Leslie (1989: 283–87). Similar notions can be found in the Mahabharata, the *Laws of Manu* or the *śāstra*-scriptures (Eichinger Ferro-Luzzi 1974: 115).

and uses an old plate reserved for this purpose and cleaned by her only. She is not permitted to fetch water from the well and she should not enter the cooking area. In terms of ritual purity, the kitchen is a highly sensitive site and should be taken special care of. It is considered an almost sacred space often located near a prayer room. Upon the end of menstrual pollution a woman has to purify every object used by her.

(*c*) During menses a woman should interrupt each and every religious activity, i.e., she should skip her daily worship (*pūjā*) at the house altar, stop the observance of a religious fast (*oṣā-brata*) and abstain from the participation in religious ceremonies. One is prohibited to pray, to make offerings and to enter a temple or any other sacred site. A menstruant should also refrain from taking consecrated food (*prasāda, bhoga*) that might be presented to her by others. Some deities are feared for their extreme anger if faced with pollution.

(*d*) A menstruating woman is not allowed to beautify her body. Rather she should avoid attracting attention at all so that, paradoxically, others will notice if necessary. A variety of body markers and practices visualize and thus reveal the duration of menstrual pollution. At the onset of the flow, a woman is to take a 'full bath' including the washing of hair, even if she has already bathed an hour before, it is late at night or there is pressing work to be done. She should change into an old dress not used anymore either for cooking or performing rituals. Moreover, she is to interrupt her usual hygienic routine. This includes her daily bath, brushing her teeth, combing and oiling her hair, applying cosmetics or adorning her body with jewelry. Married women won't apply vermilion in the hair parting and also omit the forehead mark (Oriya: *bindi*, Telugu: *boṭṭu*). None of them will decorate their feet with red dye (*aḷatā*). Telugu women will also abstain from using their favoured turmeric-based facials. The time of menstrual pollution concludes with a second bath. It serves to purify and thus reintegrate a woman into ordinary social life.

(*e*) During the period, some women avoid particular food items, such as onions and garlic. When cooking, they might replace oil with clarified butter (*ghia*) and prefer food that is considered 'cooling' (on the classification of food, see Khare 1976). These

> dietary measures are to counteract the imbalance of humors produced by the 'hot' menstruating body. Occasionally, a menstruant will take her meals before sunset (see Marglin 1995: 112–13; Tokita-Tanabe 1999c: 203).

In short, these rules of behaviour *can* influence women's interactions and their use of space during their menses to a fairly high degree. However, it is highly problematic to make generalizations. I agree with Frédérique Marglin (1995: 126) that even within Orissa there are important differences between attitudes towards menstruation. First, there are several models of menstrual restrictions that vary in detail, duration and commitment according to caste and region. Second, for practical reasons many women are not in the position to abide by the regulations in their entirety. According to Eichinger Ferro-Luzzi's (1974: 129) survey on menstrual pollution among 1200 Tamil women, 19 per cent did not withdraw from social interactions and 21 per cent kept on cooking the meals for their family! Yet in the case of a girl's first menstruation (menarche), the rules have to be followed particularly strictly.

The length of female pollution periods is culturally fixed. Eichinger Ferro-Luzzi (1974: 143–52) has argued that it follows a symbolic number of days. Similarly, menstrual practices in Orissa are only in part related to the physical process of menstrual flow and its hygienic consequences.[7] According to cosmopolitan medical discourse, the menstrual bleeding of human beings lasts between four and six days, though occasionally it finishes in less time or lasts up to nine days.[8] The duration varies individually. The impurity of Hindu women, however, starts with the onset of the menstrual flow and continues for a uniform time span of either three, four or five days, depending on family tradition and caste status. For instance, the menstrual pollution in some Brahmin communities is limited to three days only (Shweder 1985: 204). The comparison of menstrual practices in different parts of South Asia

[7] Women use either rags or sanitary towels to absorb the menstrual blood. In this respect, nobody else is confronted with the blood besides the menstruant.
[8] Even within this medical discourse there are different opinions as to the average duration of menses. Laws (1990: 140) quotes five gynecological studies that claim a norm of four days, five days, two to seven days, one to eight days, and three to nine days. On the normativeness of regular menstrual periods as a product of scientific discourse, see Buckley and Gottlieb (1988: 41–46) and Martin (1987).

suggests that the duration of menstrual impurity increases the low-caste status.[9] After a concluding purification bath, women will again interact, move and behave as usual, no matter whether the bleeding has actually come to an end.[10] This shows how menstrual restrictions refer to a cultural notion of (im-)purity rather than a seemingly pre-modern way of dealing with hygiene (the utilitarian argument).

The Oriya term *raja* signifies not only the menstrual flow but also the vaginal secretion, for instance during sexual intercourse (Marglin 1985b: 58; Tokita-Tanabe 1999c: 200).[11] Although this (menstrual) discharge is considered polluting (*mārā*), it is auspicious (*maṅgaḷa*) in that it provides evidence of the female reproductive cycle and thus alludes to fertility. Thus, the moral quality of *raja* differs from the blood (*rakta*) from a wound. According to Marglin (1995: 121), the latter is not auspicious but considered dirty (*mailā*). However, in daily communication the stigmatizing connotation of *raja* is prevalent. Being 'polluted' (*mārā*) and 'untouchable' (*chuā-achuā*) serve as metaphors for 'menstruation' (*māsika*, literally 'monthly'), and thus contribute on the linguistic level to the identification (and essentialization) of menstruation with pollution (Marglin 1985b: 58).

## The Performativity of Female Bodies

As mentioned previously in the discussion, the concept of purity and pollution influences the social and religious life of Hindus to a large extent. The communication of menses is hence relevant to many kinds of social interaction. Rather than by means of words, the self-presentation of a woman and her body language reveal whether she currently has her period or not. Within the house everybody recognizes the signs of menstrual pollution, whether an unexpected bath or

---

[9] Compare Bennett (1983: 215), V. Das (1988: 197), Eichinger Ferro-Luzzi (1974: 128–29), Fruzetti (1982: 97), Kapadia (1995: 117) and Winslow (1980: 613).

[10] According to Bennett's (1983: 217) study, Chetri-Brahmins in Nepal believe that the fourth day (i.e., *after* the purification bath) is particularly favourable for procreation. In spite of a continuing menstrual flow a man should have sexual intercourse with his wife. A similar notion is mentioned in religious texts (Leslie 1989: 289).

[11] Whereas the Oriya term *raja* names the vaginal secretion independently of its colour, the semantic meaning of the English term 'blood' is based on colour and ignores its bodily origin. In any case, menstrual discharge consists of a *mixture* of mucus, skin particles and blood. On the identity of the female procreated fluid and menstrual blood in old Indian medical works, see R. P. Das (2003).

distancing from the kitchen. If necessary, a woman may also indicate her menses with gestures (such as three raised fingers to signify the third day of bleeding) or describe her state as a 'fever', alluding to the 'hot' menstruating body. According to Veena Das (1988: 198), with the onset of puberty girls start to realize 'that one of the most important ways in which women must learn to communicate is by non-verbal gestures, intonation of speech, and reading meta-messages in ordinary languages [sic].' Thus, most women are aware of their mother's, sisters' or female friends' scheduled time of menstruation. The monthly period is not an anonymous event.

The communication of menstrual pollution is relevant for both genders – the display and recognition concern not only women but, in a complementary fashion, men as well.

> (Scene 2) It is Sunday afternoon; the Mishra family decides to pay their daughter's teacher a surprise visit. The three of them dress up and get on a scooter. Upon their arrival, the teacher's husband (a lawyer by profession) invites them to come in and to take seat. A little later, the teacher appears. She wears a night-dress; her hair looks disheveled. She welcomes the visitors with a few sweet words and disappears in a neighbouring room. Her husband stays back to entertain the guests. He calls his six-year-old son and sends him with a thermos to the tea stall nearby. After a while, the son returns with hot tea. Mrs and Mr Mishra drink tea, eat biscuits and happily chat with the teacher's husband. The children are playing. After more than an hour the guests say goodbye and leave.

That Sunday afternoon nobody mentioned the teacher's menstruation, yet everybody learned about her impurity by non-verbal means and responded accordingly. The teacher herself revealed her bodily condition by her very brief attendance, her uncombed hair and also her night-dress (although this is common casual wear at home). Since she did not return to the guests, the Mishra family could recognize that the teacher did not want to expose them to her pollution. Since there was no other (pure) woman around who could have prepared and served tea, the lawyer asked his son to buy ready-made tea. Since the latter is made by a (male) tea stall owner, it is much more suitable for guests than anything a menstruating woman could have offered. All in all, Mrs and Mr Mishra realized how respectfully they were received in the teacher's house and that she follows a very cultivated lifestyle.

Women mark their bodies in the case of pollution. Most of the time, it is the pure and potentially auspicious female body that is subject to display.[12] It proves not only women's eligibility to perform and participate in rituals, it also alludes to the beneficence of this purity, a gender-specific quality that is even enhanced by marriage. According to Hindu belief, the married woman embodies a virtually holy state, at least as long as her husband is alive. The glance of such a woman (rather than a menstruant or widow) is thought to bring about well-being. She is addressed as Sīmantinī.[13] The paradigmatic proof of her beneficence is the long life of her husband. To indicate this auspicious potential, married women employ vermilion to create a forehead mark and also a red line in the hair parting (see Plate 6.2 or Plate 7.1. in the following chapters). They will wear red bangles or get their feet painted with red *aḷatā*. Some will use turmeric to give the face a yellowish hue or dress in a silk (*pāṭa*) sari. The auspicious state of the Hindu wife is also invoked by a specific way of greeting each other (*oḷaki karibā*). When two married women meet, the younger will touch the feet of the elder, who in response blesses her to be like the divine wife Lakṣmī (*ahya* Lakṣmī *heithā*). If one of them is menstruating, she will either refrain from bowing down at all (in the case of the younger wife) or will withdraw her foot (in the case of the elder). In any case, the greeting as *ahya* (married woman with a living husband) is not only a polite formula. As an illocutionary speech act (Austin) it creates a similarity between a woman and the goddess, and thus has the gender-specific potential of effecting *maṅgaḷa*.

Women not only communicate their monthly pollution, they also commit themselves to displaying the female auspicious state. Many of them feel pretty uncomfortable if their bodily appearance is ambiguous, for instance when the 'bindi sticker' (the self-adhesive dot that often replaces the vermilion mark on the forehead) is lost. Similarly, the red parting of the hair seems to contribute first of all towards women's ritual identity rather than being a symbol used to prolong the life of the husband, as emphasized in hegemonic discourse. This kind of self-presentation in the everyday is of high concern to women. They commonly insist that their daughters, sisters and female friends abide

---

[12] The women I met during fieldwork emphasized an opposition of pollution (*mārā*) and auspiciousness (*maṅgaḷa*) rather than purity, although the latter two notions, i.e., effect and quality, often intermingle (cf. Kapadia 1995: 118–23).

[13] On the concept of the auspicious married woman in eastern and southern India, see Samanta (1992: 61–65), Sudhakar Rao (1996: 73–74) and Reynolds (1980).

by this display of auspiciousness. In any case, the repertoire of signs does not exclusively hint at religion, many features are also employed in the discourse on beauty. During fashion shows (that are condemned by orthodox Hindus) models are often adorned with auspicious symbols.

Considering female self-understanding, it is thus misleading to look solely at the social impact of menstrual restrictions. Rather there seems to be a constant process of marking and deciphering female bodies as either pure/auspicious or as polluted. According to V. Das (1988: 197) Hindu women 'must oscillate' between these two states throughout their lifetime, a process that begins with menarche and lasts until menopause. While her assessment expresses a heavy burden of either hiding the body or emphasizing its sexual productivity, during my fieldwork in Orissa the notion of auspiciousness seemed to be an appreciated source of women's self-esteem. However, the importance given to these contrasting qualities varies according to social context. While in a family photograph, a teenage girl might pose in a pair of blue jeans (a fairly expensive middle-class garment), at a religious ceremony she would certainly wish to emphasize the ritual purity of her body and select her clothing accordingly. Yet, the bodily display of purity and pollution is not limited to ritual contexts. Rather there is a continuum of social situations that vary in their sensitivity to this concept. Therefore, it is difficult to escape the deciphering of female bodies in terms of their ritual eligibility. In comparison with male dress practices, women have far fewer opportunities for a ritually neutral (non-semantic) form of self-presentation, except for, say, professional dress codes that prohibit vermilion and bangles.[14] In line with Judith Butler (1990, 1993) and her studies on gender performativity, I argue that just like the human body, which is permanently marked as either female or male, in southern Orissa female bodies are hardly ever perceived *without* considering their status in terms of (im-)purity.

## Considering Self-Presentation

Women's indication of either the pure/auspicious or the polluted body is based on both tacit knowledge and explicit rules, and thus involves continuous decision-making. Hence, what has been analyzed

---

[14] In order to signify purity, men wear white unstitched cloth (possibly silk). One piece of cloth is folded like a pair of trousers (*dhoti*), another one is wrapped around the shoulders. On the significance of dress for orthodox Hindu women, see Leslie (1992).

so far from a structural viewpoint as culturally and socially appropriate behaviour, is now considered as the result of individual reflection and experience. Many of the women I asked about menstrual practices were actually eager to share their ideas, since they had already defined their own thoughts on this subject. In fact, many regulations are difficult to follow in daily life. Women who breastfeed their baby and female employees have to break these rules regularly. Moreover, if the (joint) family lacks a woman beyond menopause and men leave the premises to work, there might be nobody left who could adequately take care of the preparation of (pure) food. After all, to maintain segregation requires a spacious house and thus sufficient finance. In other words, once in a while every Hindu woman is forced to consider whether and how she can meet menstrual restrictions, and what could happen if she fails to do so (apart from breaking these rules on purpose).[15] There are several circumstances that challenge the normative status of these prohibitions and thus raise attention and self-reflexivity.

Upon the very first menstruation, a girl is puzzled by the prohibitions that limit her freedom of movement that, after all, has already decreased with the first signs of puberty. According to the 15-year-old pupil Uma, for instance, menstrual segregation does not make any sense but rather is a form of punishment ('like in jail'). Reflections on menstrual practices also result from interregional comparison. Women in Ganjam District were certainly aware that some of their menstrual customs contradicted those followed about 150 km to the north, i.e., in Cuttack or in places beyond the Mahanadi river. Menstruants over there were known to sleep in their ordinary bed and to skip the head bath at the *onset* of menstrual flow. Besides, they added cow dung to the purification bath and thus were laughed at in southern Orissa. At any rate, the variation in menstrual restrictions challenges women only in case of migration, i.e., as a consequence of marriage and patrilocal residence. Menstrual practices are also subjected to women's thoughts in the case of competing worldviews. If educated parents introduce their daughter to a biological understanding of the human body and its reproductive cycle, she is likely to question menstrual restrictions, specifically beyond the religious domain. After all, a critical stance towards menstrual practices may also derive from a fairly self-dependent way of life, whether due to gainful occupation or in the case

[15] The violation of these rules is feared to cause sickness and other calamities (*amaṅgaḷa*), see Leslie (1989: 285) and Viswanath (1997: 326–27).

of a nuclear family. If there is only little social control by sisters-in-law or neighbours, women are more likely to take autonomous decisions that ease their daily life. In this case, however, the risk of transferring pollution is also less.

> (Scene 3) I admit to Kabita that in spite of my respect for her religion, many rules she follows during menses seem ridiculous to me. We start talking. The day before, Kabita explains, she had been particularly strict in her observation of the regulations since her husband's relatives had come to visit them. On the one hand, she felt strange that everybody got to know about her bodily condition. On the other hand, she purposely withdrew from any activity in the house to meet each and every expectation concerning her wifely status, and also to avoid quarrels with her sisters-in-law. As a side effect, the two of us could chat freely since she was not obliged to cook and serve guests. Then Kabita reminds me of a situation not long ago, when she was menstruating and everybody had gone out. At that time she didn't hesitate to prepare tea for us.

Unlike Uma, who felt 'like in jail', Kabita takes the opportunity to skip household chores and to enjoy our meeting. In both cases, women follow menstrual restrictions with some reflective distance, keeping in mind the expectations of their family. Whereas the 15-year-old pupil rejects these recommendations in general (if not in an adolescent spirit of rebellion), Kabita not only finds benefit in the interruption of her work routine, she also demonstratively avoids the transfer of pollution and thus proves her status in the family. She did not have an arranged marriage in conformity with caste – a kind of scandal in village terms. Unlike her husband from the Telugu barber caste, she was Oriya Brahmin (hypogamy). In a joint family household of four brothers, their wives and children, Kabita sometimes felt excluded. In this context, the female virtue and pious care for purity shown during the visit of affines emphasized her upper-caste background. Since the relevance and performance of menstrual restrictions reflect the 'habitus' (Bourdieu) of different communities and social strata, the self-conscious display of menstrual pollution can serve as an idiom of social distinction against competing sisters-in-law or a hypercritical neighbourhood.

Although women reflect on their observance of menstrual restrictions, the degree and consequences of this process vary according to context and personality. At times these thoughts may challenge a woman's commitment to menstrual rules, although they don't have to. Rather there is an ongoing decision process as to the display of menstrual pollution and its social consequences. If the performance of regulations indeed creates problems and thus exceeds the capacity of the menstruant, she will switch to the rationality of another moral concept and, for instance, highlight her maternal duty or the social obligation to serve guests.

## Menses and Morality

Whereas practical reasons compel women to consider whether to observe certain menstrual restrictions and skip others, they rarely question the existence of menstrual pollution itself. After all, children grow up with the idea that some persons, items, actions and situations are *mārā* (see Shweder 1985: 206). However, it is by no means obvious in what respect this facticity of menstrual pollution influences women's self-esteem. Basically there seem to be three perspectives from which to assess the social and moral impact of menstrual bleeding: first, to fear the disastrous effects of pollution, second, to appreciate the menstrual flow as an indication of female fertility, and third, to regard menstruation as an unemotional, non-moral medico-biological process.

There is a common saying that is here rendered by a male Brahmin from Orissa:

> If the wife touches her husband on the first day of her period, it is an offence equal to that of killing a guru. If she touches him on the second day, it is an offence equal to killing a Brahman. On the third day to touch him is like cutting off his penis. If she touches him on the fourth day it is like killing a child. So it is a sin.[16]

The comparison of a menstruant's touch with a criminal act seems to be a male trope. The women I had asked about menstrual restrictions never mentioned this statement or any of its variants. However, according to Marglin (1995: 113) and Shweder (1985: 204) *some* Oriya women share the orthodox male view given in this quotation, although

[16] Quoted in Shewder (1985: 203–4), see also Bennett (1983: 216); for textual evidence, see Leslie (1989: 283).

in a moderate way.[17] Thus, it would be sinful (*pāp*) if the menstruating woman were to cook food for others or touch her husband. Lynn Bennett (1983: 216) has pointed out with reference to Nepali Brahmins that unless women disobey menstrual restrictions on purpose, they do not conceive of their actions as the personal sin which the saying accuses them of. Rather the 'danger' and 'sin' of menstrual pollution is regarded as a general formula deriving from religious scriptures, and thus recognized with a reflective distance. In any case, the academic discourse on gender renders several examples of Hindu women who actually believe in these kinds of Brahminical statements. According to V. Das (1988: 200), urban Punjabi women think that their menstrual pollution attracts calamity and they blame themselves if a misfortune befalls the husband. Sanjukta Gupta (1999: 96) claims that women perform religious fasts mainly in order to compensate their female impurity. Karin Kapadia (1995: 163–66) describes a Tamil ritual aimed at Brahmin women after menopause. In order to delete gender-specific pollution forever, it has to be repeated for seven consecutive years. Post-menopausal women, after all, are considered ritually pure and may also qualify as temple attendants (Marglin 1985b: 54).

In Orissa there is also a competing discourse that relates menstruation to both human fertility and the divine feminine force (*śakti*), and thus appreciates the menstrual cycle as a token of women's generative capacity. From this perspective, menstruation is still polluting, but above all it is an auspicious event. According to Marglin (1995: 124), Saṣṭhi, the goddess of children, is also made responsible for regular periods and the healthy growth of a foetus. Menstruation is not only related to fertility, it is also thought to balance the human being with the cosmic rhythm (see Marglin 1985b: 301). Each year women in Puri District celebrate the menstruation of the earth. While men have to leave the village for four days (to avoid pollution), women prepare lavish meals, dress up, sing songs, worship the goddess Haracaṇḍī, and have a wonderful time. In a similar way, Marglin (1995: 121) argues, women's monthly period is a happy occasion. One of her male interviewees claimed that men would try to entertain their menstruating wife and daughters in order to prevent 'inauspiciousness and ill fortune'

[17] There are similar claims with respect to women in other parts of South Asia, see Bennett (1983: 215), V. Das (1988: 199), S. Gupta (1999: 89) and Kapadia (1995: 163).

(ibid.: 99). Even if his statement might refer to the festival of menstruation (Raja Parba) rather than to day-to-day life, it shows that the segregation of menstruating women and their withdrawal from social interaction can be perceived as an interval inherent to the regenerative process.[18] The appreciation for women's menstrual cycle is also emphasized by the celebration of menarche. Unlike in northern India, in many Oriya families the very first menstruation of a girl is concluded with special food, sweets and gifts such as a new dress (Tokita-Tanabe 1999c).[19] In academic discourse the sacredness of menstruation is generally classified as a 'tantric' rather than a Brahminical concept (see Khanna 2000: 116; White 2003: 68–73).

In line with secularized, 'modern' thinking and lifestyles, menstruation is also regarded as a biological process, and thus beyond emotional or moral considerations. Menstrual bleeding is neither associated with evil nor with the feminine divine. Following medical and feminist discourse, menstrual practices are, however, sensed as backward and obsolete. Menstruation is understood as a private domain of experience and concern. Personal hygiene matters rather than ritual impurity (Puri 1999: 60–65). The individual becomes responsible for controlling the bodily process, particularly menstrual odor. Moreover, physical discomfort is framed as a kind of sickness. This perspective implies the objectification of the body as a 'natural' entity that is subjected to the cognizing self. Knowledge about the body is considered as a woman's key to claim control over her personal life and to free her of androcentric norms. Paradoxically this apparently enlightened approach makes the menstrual cycle invisible, emphasizes its concealment and produces shame (see Viswanath 1997: 326–27).

In Orissa any of these three perspectives may influence the perception of the menstruating female body. Yet it would be misleading to conceive of them as clearly separated concepts that could be selected intentionally. Rather these notions shape the feelings and behaviour of Hindu women (and men) without any specific decision process involved. They reflect a variety of congruent and competing beliefs, sayings and arguments that provide both genders with a cultural repertoire for relating to the menstruating body in a way considered

---

[18] On the oral tradition associated with Raja Parba, see Tokita-Tanabe (1999b). There are similar festivals of menstruating temple goddesses in Bengal and Assam (Samanta 1992: 59–61; Tokita-Tanabe 1999c: 216).

[19] On puberty rites in southern India, see Sudhakar Rao (1996: 70–72) and Kapadia (1995: 92–123).

suitable. Relevant here is that women do not legitimate their personal commitment towards menstrual restrictions with reference to one of these approaches. At least, none of my interlocutors gave reason to conclude that she entirely omitted menstrual restrictions *because* she did not believe in pollution. Although several details of these prohibitions raised women's doubts, it was also mentioned that during menses women 'do not feel' like worshipping the gods. In other words: whereas the performance of menstrual restrictions was commonly subject to reflection and required the pragmatic consideration of different moral arguments, the just-mentioned three ways to assess menstrual bleeding only in part influenced and defined women's commitment towards the observance of these rules.

## The Force of Pollution

How a woman feels about menstrual pollution depends basically on her personal bodily experiences. She may go to the office or bathe her infant son and, if undisturbed, she may have no reason to think of segregation. However, the prescribed suspension of the hygienic routine and also the prohibition against the decoration of the body can by itself make women feel bedraggled and practically unclean. Body odor and dirtiness become relevant symptoms in the discourse on purity and pollution, and thus substantiate not only the segregation of a menstruant but also contribute to the embodiment and naturalization of these criteria. Furthermore, women may perceive menstruation as a painful affair and seek medical help. In this case the attention to pain confirms and (re-)enforces that women should withdraw from social activity and observe the expected rules of behaviour. From this perspective, menstrual practices are also regarded as a protective measure.

The cognitive knowledge about menstruation and/or Hindu theological constructs may provide women with reflective distance from the performance of menstrual restrictions, yet it does not annihilate the somatic effects of this discourse.[20] As an embodied practice, the

[20] During fieldwork I could hardly escape this effect. In everyday interaction and also during interviews I became regularly aware of my own ignorance towards Hindu menstrual restrictions. I started to feel uncomfortable whenever I had to attend a ritual during my menses. Although I did not sense any pollution somatically, I felt much better when I could avoid these situations. Whoever does fieldwork on Hindu women's rituals will be faced with the issue of one's own menstruation, see Pintchman (2005: 9–10).

sense for pollution is related to the routine of 'periodically' paying special attention to the body. A student of media and communication, for instance, felt sick for almost two hours after visiting a temple and explained her state as being due to her ongoing menstruation. Although university education and self-reflectivity had empowered her to act individually, she could not ignore her acquired sense of pollution. It is due to the repeated performance of menstrual restrictions, and thus the power of convention, that pollution as a category of practice is realized.

> (Scene 4) The sisters share a room with a big wall cupboard, a rack for clothes and two beds. It is early Tuesday morning. The elder sister Sunita's period had begun and she therefore slept on the floor. She takes her breakfast in the corner of the room, separated from the other family members. Then both of the girls need to study for their exam. The younger sister lifts a textbook and throws it in Sunita's direction. In the same manner she also passes over an exercise book, a rubber and another manual. Sunita catches them adeptly. Instead of concentrating on their studies, the girls get lost in play. Giggling, they jump after the flying items. Finally they calm down. While Sunita takes a serious look at the book, her sister gets ready to leave for college.

The two sisters, 18 and 20 years old, actually follow the behaviour appropriate for menstruating women, yet without giving it a second thought. Their playful way of avoiding the transfer of menstrual pollution via the book turns into a wild, athletic game, and thus becomes meaningful regardless of culture-specific notions of the female body or the idea of subversion. In this way several, if not all, forms of behaviour can be deciphered and contrasted, and thus turned into signs to communicate menstrual pollution. While in Scene 4 the girls invent personal rules for the game, on another occasion the feeling of pollution might compete with or even replace the desire for fun. In any case, the singular act and its interpretation need repetition in order to become, in itself, meaningful.

In one family, for instance, it was assumed that menstrual pollution could be transferred by telephone. Therefore women were not allowed to touch the phone while they were having their periods. Since this practice alluded to other types of precautions taken by menstruating women (such as the prohibition against touching precious items), it made sense to the adolescent daughter. Yet outsiders could not understand or get a feeling for this danger. Although the daughter's schoolmates stopped ringing her up during her menses, they were making fun of these preventive measures. Changing forms to express and to deal with menstrual pollution reveal to what extent the sense of pollution, and thus the credibility of menstrual restrictions, is based on regular repetition and embodiment. To give another example: a few years previously menstruating women had started to replace the red vermilion mark on their forehead with a black one (rather than just abandoning this custom during their period). When dark dots became fashionable and therefore were seen frequently in public, the colour again lost its meaning as a sign of impurity.

One invention, however, has influenced the exposure to menstrual pollution on a large scale. In the 1990s, middle-class women began using hormone tablets in order to control the onset of their menstrual flow. Whenever a woman wants to ensure her auspicious state, for instance in the case of an upcoming marriage party or a religious festival, she might simply postpone her menstruation to a more convenient time. The use of pharmaceuticals was particularly suitable, I believe, since it reconnected the symbolic duration of menstrual pollution to the biological process of bleeding. Though not really healthy, it increased the autonomy of women who could take advantage of a suitable interval for their period. In some strata, however, this option has again created social pressure on those persons who do not intend to manipulate their body in times of ritual duties.[21]

## Conclusion: Acting Natural

In this chapter I discussed several facets that influence the performance of menstrual pollution in everyday life. It was shown how women's observance of menstrual restrictions is linked, for most days of the month, to the self-assured display of female auspiciousness. Due to this gendered ideal, women's self-presentation is almost permanently defined (although to different degrees) in terms of their ritual eligibility. The emphasis women give to the display of their ritualized body is, I assume, not limited to middle-class women in southern Orissa, but rather a general means for orthodox Hindu women to gain self-confidence. To conceive of menstrual practices as a limitation on women's life is, thus, only one side of the coin. Above all,

[21] Even beyond the reach of 'Western' medicine, Hindu women communicate different home remedies in order to manipulate and postpone menstruation (personal communication with Vatsala Iyengar, Bangalore).

the prohibitions at the time of menses also provide benefits (taking a rest from cooking and other work) and invite individuals to take advantage of them. Hence menstrual restrictions do not contribute by themselves to the internalization of gender inferiority.

Since female bodies are more or less permanently enacted and deciphered in terms of (im-)purity, I propose to conceive of this paradigm as a performative category. According to Butler's (1990, 1993) theory on gender performativity, the reality of a performative category is brought forth by the power of discourse. Thus social behaviour is understood as repetition or rather iteration of norms, for instance the enactment of apparently 'feminine' traits – hence a process that by itself creates what it describes, in this case gender. Similarly, I argue that the permanent display and deciphering of bodies and their ritual eligibility *creates* the notion of purity/auspiciousness versus pollution. Furthermore, the repetitive process ends in embodiment, so that the ritual (im-)purity achieves the status of a natural feature and the menstruant's feelings of pain or dirtiness come to serve as evidence. From the perspective of women in southern Orissa, there is no reason to doubt the facticity of pollution. Whereas they certainly reflect on the different ways of coping with menstrual pollution and also question its impact on a variety of social interactions and cultural domains, they cannot escape this discourse. Only a radical change in lifestyle and behaviour might immunize or 'disinform' the body, and thus annihilate both the restraints of being polluted and also the sense of one's gender-specific auspiciousness.

According to Butler, performative categories are brought about by discourse rather than by human subjects who antedate the act. To consider social personae as discursive effects, however, is certainly one of the most controversial points of her theory. Whereas I reject this view with regard to the objectives of this book, and rather explore how women are 'doing gender', in the analysis of menstrual practices the question of human agency hints at another facet. As shown earlier in the discussion, women consider and at times subvert the rationale of menstrual restrictions. Nevertheless, it would be misleading to regard them as autonomous authors of this process. Although they might appear to be inventing new rules, the routine display of pollution contributes by itself to the emergence of new meanings that legitimize this performative practice. Apart from the power of discourse, it is thus the interplay of performance (or theatricality) and its somatic effects that jointly bring about alterations in the way women behave and feel during their menstruation.

Finally, this ethnographic study on menstrual pollution as a performative category also suggests some ideas on the similarities and differences of 'doing gender' in the course of day-to-day interactions. Regarding units of observation and analysis, the distinction between social practices (here: scenes) and cultural performances, which both contribute to the social negotiation of gender, seems artificial. Obviously there is a continuum in the way in that meanings are produced, deciphered, enacted, objectified, and contested. Similarly, religious doctrines are perpetuated within the realm of ritual and beyond. However, this chapter on menstrual pollution clearly showed the extraordinary force of repetition and also the agentive dimension of the human body in creating normative realities, for instance, when following menstrual restrictions half-heartedly and/or on the basis of a natural-scientific approach. In contrast with the extraordinary experiences created by the votive rites described in previous chapters, the facticity of (im-)purity manifests somatically and does not provoke women to reassess their self-understanding as gendered beings. In comparison, the meta-communicative framing of an event (as ritual) seems to offer additional experiential space that playfully seduces participants to relocate the self, i.e., to manipulate emotions, to reframe bodily dispositions and to inspire social relations in hitherto unknown ways. Anthropologists have theorized about these states in terms of subjunctive mood, virtuality and ritual commitment (see Introduction). Women's joy at a *pūjā* site, their liberty to create a mode of worship that resonates with their personal needs, or the metaphorical transformation of their everyday burdens into a competitive game 'as light as a flower' (see Chapters 1 and 2) – and hence the emergence of alternate moods and powers – can be seen as first indicators to support this distinction. However, the next chapters will explore in detail whether rituals can invite women to perceive themselves in substantially different ways than during day-to-day interaction. I shall look at divine possession, i.e., at religious events which not only produce sacred and thus alternative realities, but also personal otherness in its most extreme form.

# 4

# Contested Bodies: Deity Possession as a Religious Idiom

In academic discourse, people who experience spirit possession are commonly regarded as having weak personalities vulnerable to exterior forces. They appear to be under some kind of external control, not only when their body is taken over by a non-human agent, but also in their daily lives, a feature that is often identified as a precondition for their possession. This is particularly so in the case of women, who are considered as the favourite gender of demonic and divine powers. The at times violent and desperate behaviour while possessed is interpreted as a reaction to a woman's lack of recognition in, and exclusion from, many spheres of life.[1] The academic discourse on South Asia is no exception to this: the cultural phenomenon of spirit possession is overwhelmingly seen as involving women who are distressed in some way.[2]

My aim in this (and in the following) chapter is to question the usual assumption that Hindu women are purely the passive victims

[1] For a review of the anthropological discourse on spirit possession, see Boddy (1994), who largely questions the instrumentality of these events and hence its character as an oblique strategy of protest. Behrend and Luig (1999) as well as Mageo and Howard (1996) reflect this debate on the basis of ethnographic examples from Africa and the Pacific respectively. For a feminist critique on the deprivation theory in the academic discourse on possession, see Sered (1994).

[2] Fortunately, some recent research provides more nuanced forms of understanding. For an overview of the present South Asian discourse on possession, see the compilations of essays edited by Assayag and Tarabout (1999) and also by Carrin (1999); cf. Smith (2006: Chapter 2) for a brief survey of ethnographic studies on deity and spirit possession.

of possession, and highlight instead the religious dimension of these events. I argue that women in southern Orissa consider divine possession as essentially religious act that shapes and explains their engagement in rituals, as well as their perspective on Hinduism.[3] This argument is not entirely new. Elisabeth Schömbucher (1993: 261) had already pointed out that in the academic discourse on South Asia there is a tendency to ignore the reality of possession as a religious experience. Recently, Frederick Smith (2006) argued, on the basis of Indian literature from different ages, that ecstatic possession is the most common form of spiritual expression in India. His argument certainly is a challenge to historians of religion, given the fact that several introductions and general books on Hinduism simply skip the subject of possession.[4] However, even Smith's criticism of academic scholars – who obviously have difficulties acknowledging the religious potential of possession[5] – does not explore the issue of gender differences. It is understood that '[p]ossession more often than not involves the feminine – either women are possessed or men are possessed by a form of the goddess'. (Smith 2006: 153) From a gendered perspective on religion and identity, this preponderance of women in (some of the) contemporary traditions of possession in South Asia indeed calls for further investigation.

Focusing on Berhampur and its rural surroundings, I shall evaluate a variety of private and public rituals that *may* include deity possession. It will be shown that from the perspective of women, possession is a rather common religious idiom that is limited neither to a specific ritual event nor to a particular class of persons. Although possession episodes are fairly patterned and also predictable, they create extraordinary experiences for those overwhelmed as well as for onlookers. Moreover, they contribute towards a discourse on the power of deities and the necessity of women's religious commitment and activities to appease them. Against the background of ethnographic vignettes, introduced

[3] An earlier, fairly different version of this chapter has been published in Hauser (2011b).

[4] See, for instance, Michaels (2004a), an otherwise very recommendable introduction to Hinduism.

[5] Although social anthropologists in general classify spirit possession within the religious realm, they are also likely to focus on its social context rather than considering it as embodied knowledge by itself. Hence Lambek (1989) calls for a change in the perspective 'from disease to discourse'.

to illustrate the broad range of possession episodes in southern Orissa, emphasis will be given to the analysis of academic arguments on female possession. This ethnographic survey will be supplemented in Chapter 5. There I explore in detail how individuals actually perceive deity possession, how they sense their bodies being overpowered by an exterior force, and in what ways they personify the divine presence.

The significance of deity possession to women's religious experiences in southern Orissa differs from, and partly contradicts, the notion of female victims in the academic discourse on possession in South Asia. Taking a close look at the ways scholars have represented possessed women and evaluated gender differences concerning the experiential states of those possessed, I shall argue that the contrast emerging in comparison with accounts of possession from other parts of the Indian subcontinent is in some degree due to the dynamics of academic knowledge production itself. Whereas the psycho-medical and also the sociological 'explanations' of possession each have their local counterpart in folk theory, the religious relevance of possession is a matter of social contestation. From a 'high-caste, educated male' perspective (which of course is a label which summarizes a variety of views), possession is denied the status of a religious idiom in its own right. Thus, the apparent importance given to possession in Orissa may reflect women's religious practices even beyond this region, assuming there is a similar emphasis on devotionalism (*bhakti*) and the worship of goddesses (Shaktism).

Before I introduce some exemplary possession episodes, some remarks concerning terminology and classification. As in other languages of the Indian subcontinent, in Oriya there is no exclusive term for spirit or deity possession.[6] Instead people speak of a supernatural being who is likely to 'dance' (*nācibā*) and 'play' (*kheḷibā*), to 'catch' (*dharibā*), 'jump upon' (*ḍeĩki yibā*) or to 'come to the body' (*dehaku āsibā*), regardless of whether or not the human host is prepared for such an encounter, or whether the possessing power is identified as an

[6] The terms for possession in South Asian languages have been rendered by Smith (2006: Chapter 4). He proposes to identify most of these experiential states with the Sanskrit concept *āveśa*, literally 'entrance into', here taken as an umbrella term for 'positive oracular possession'. However, the semantic meaning of this word varies historically and in the Indian languages, as Smith (2006: 14, 119) has pointed out. Similarly, the Oriya term *ābeśa* translates into English as 'attention'. On related terminology in Bengali, see also note 23.

ancestral spirit, ghost, demon or deity.[7] Although people distinguish between forms of possession – beneficial (anticipated by ritual preparations) or unwanted (spontaneous, but also explained with calculable circumstances) – this does not allow any conclusions to be drawn regarding the nature of a particular entity. Rather, the cosmos is characterized as having a continuum of supernatural powers of higher and lower order, some of whom appear to be rather fierce. Non-human beings may also change in status over time. An ancestor who had suffered an inauspicious death might be appeased by rituals and gradually gain a reputation as a powerful guardian, before later being identified with a well-known Hindu deity. Hence disturbing and harmful forms of possession (rather than creatures) are removed or banished.[8] At times, this process may also address a particular type of goddess, known by the generic term *ṭhākurāṇī* (literally: mistress, lady). Even what might be labeled 'exorcism' serves to re-situate a non-human being within his or her own realm, a process performed by those ritual specialists well versed in magical techniques (and addressed as *tāntrika*). Yet any spontaneous and involuntary possession conveys the potential to develop divinatory skills, and most mediums initially underwent a similar ordeal.

In other words, the classification of an event as either 'divine' or 'demonic' possession is partly a matter of context and perspective, as some deities are known for their disturbing powers (on the dark qualities of a *ṭhākurāṇī*, see Chapter 6). Thus, it is difficult to find an appropriate English term that embraces this ambivalence (and goes beyond the Christian connotations of 'devil possession'). Whereas the anthropological term 'spirit possession' generally includes divine beings (see Gold 1988; Mayaram 1999), several scholars working on South Asia employ this term to specify malevolent and unwanted forms (see Claus 1975; Smith 2006). In the latter case, the positive dimension of possession is recognized by a variety of expressions, such as 'spirit

[7] In Oriya, the terms *mahāpuru* (Lord), *mā* (mother), *ṭhākura* or *ṭhākurāṇī* (master/mistress, lord/lady) are used to address a possessing deity; ancestral spirits are referred to as *sajība debatā* (literally: enlivened god) and as *ātmā* (spirit, soul); overwhelmingly fierce entities are classified as *bhūta* (ghost, spirit), as *ḍāhāṇī* (demoness/female ghost) or as *ḍākiṇī* (demoness, witch).

[8] The very notion of 'evil spirits' is, according to Smith (2006: 116), a Western construction imposed on the ethnographic and textual descriptions from South Asia.

mediumship', 'possession mediumship', 'oracular possession' or 'ecstatic possession'. Considering the subject position of possessed persons, scholars speak of 'mediums' or, to acknowledge their competence, of 'shamans'.[9] With respect to Orissa, however, the term 'shamanism' alludes to 'tribal' religions and influences, rather than normative or popular Hindu practices, although these forms certainly may overlap and influence each other.[10] Since the majority of possession episodes, I encountered during fieldwork, were identified with the agency of a goddess, and since the behaviour of female hosts did not suggest any consistent markers to distinguish novices from specialists, I alternately use the terms 'divine possession' and 'deity possession'; the possessed (Hindu) woman is referred to as a 'medium'.

## Occasions and Narratives

At the beginning of my fieldwork, I was not looking specifically for incidents of possession. While watching women's rituals, time after time one of the participants' behaviour changed radically, so that her body was regarded as taken over by a deity. Some of the possessed trembled, jumped wildly or painfully twisted their faces; others had their eyes closed, walked calmly and responded to questions. On the one hand, I had severe doubts about what was happening and therefore shared the uncertainty of several onlookers. On the other hand, I could sense the tension that the incident gave rise to through my own body.

[9] The problem with these terminological distinctions is that they are based on the assumption that possession is an altered state of *consciousness* rather than an embodied practice. As Mary Keller (2002) rightly pointed out, scholars tend to conceive of religion as a mental activity (following Talal Asad, a modern Christian concept) and therefore, while discussing possession, repeatedly get stuck at the question of awareness – in Western discourse the means of human agency.

[10] The distinction between 'shamanism' (referring to spirit journeys while the body remains unconscious) and 'possession mediumship' (the inhabitation of the body by another spirit) goes back to Mircea Eliade. With respect to South Asian ethnography, the usage of these terms – as of 'trance' and 'exorcism' – is rather arbitrary and there is little evidence to support the necessity of these conceptual distinctions (see Tarabout 1999: 10–12). Moreover, to link possession solely to Hinduism is no less problematic since similar forms occur among South Asian Muslims, Sikhs, Buddhists and Christians. Sometimes, the possessing entity and its medium belong to different religions altogether (Mayaram 1999).

I watched the scene full of excitement, at times slightly worried, and more than once I forgot to take any notes. Women encouraged me to tell them what I had experienced and also to test an oracle. Some of them regularly learned that their own and other's behaviour was being driven by a goddess. This divine presence was not at all an unusual topic of conversation. On certain ritual occasions, young girls were encouraged to interpret some of their bodily reactions in terms of non-human agency. The respective female host, her family and others appreciated this kind of divine encounter. Although it constituted an extremely exhausting physical experience, it also contributed towards the self-esteem of the possessed woman. Later, when I began systematically attending rituals to witness manifestations of the divine, one of my research assistants left because she could not bear the, on some occasions, intense drumming and its psychophysical effects – she feared becoming possessed herself. (As a graduate in journalism, she finally joined a private TV channel.)

In the following paragraphs, I give a variety of examples that show when and how women in southern Orissa recognize divine possession, as well as how they conceive of this embodied state and social practice. The descriptions are largely based on women's personal memories, thus, reflecting common ways of talking about possession. My compilation is not exhaustive but rather tries to cover different ritual settings (private, public, spontaneous, institutionalized, individual, and collective).[11] In order to give a short but thorough glimpse, each episode is outlined only briefly.

(a)

> When I devote myself very much to worship [*pūjā*], then the Lord [*mahāpuru*] enters my body. (Basanti, 37 years, tea-stall owner)

It is the duty of a Hindu wife to take care of the family deity. Thus most married women devote some time of the day to pray at the house altar – a place attached to the kitchen or located in a separate

[11] During the course of my fieldwork I was faced with possession in 38 cases (five mediums were men). 33 times the agent was identified as a deity; 24 times as a form of a *ṭhākurāṇī*, twice as Narasiṃha, and four times as ancestral spirit. I also watched several hundred possessed women during the final procession of Ṭhākurāṇī Yātrā. These numbers are not representative of possession in general since I specifically attended *religious* occasions that attracted *women.*

*pūjā* room. During this form of solitary worship, some women face possession. This may happen particularly on those weekdays on which it is especially auspicious to worship a *ṭhākurāṇī* (i.e., on Tuesdays) or the divine man-lion Narasiṃha (on Saturdays). Then possession indicates that a woman favours one of them as her personal goddess or god, a preference that may overlap with the identity of the family deity. Deity possession at the house altar is usually a more or less private religious experience.[12] No special attention is paid to it, although neighbours will gradually get to know about it. For Basanti, who lived with her husband and children in a nuclear family, this encounter with God was a welcomed opportunity to share all kinds of day-to-day problems, whether concerning health or finance. However, she did not remember these incidents by herself. Rather her children told about her frightening appearance while serving Narasiṃha. Basanti was very happy (*khusi*) when she learned about this, yet her husband remained indifferent to it.

In another family, a strange noise was heard from the *pūjā* room, where Sanju was busy with the daily worship of several deities. Since her childhood, she had been vulnerable to possession by Kāḷī and Narasiṃha. Initially her parents tried to save her from such physically exhausting experiences. When they learned from a senior relative that it was not a malevolent spirit (*bhūta*) but rather divine beings manifesting themselves in Sanju's body, she was given care of the house altar. After leaving school she spent several hours a day in prayers and worship on behalf of her extended family. Due to her slightly abnormal physique and poor health, she did not marry but continued to live in her parents' home. Yet her social status was high, since the prosperity of the family business (renting out mechanical equipment) was attributed to the regular divine presence in Sanju's body. Gradually, friends and neighbours came to ask for divine advice and, upon getting it, paid the young woman with food, clothes and other gifts. One might speculate whether Sanju was forced into this role since, due to her physical deficiency, her parents could not find a suitable marriage partner for her. In fact, she planned to leave her family more than

[12] Studies of spirit and deity possession usually stress the performative aspect of this social phenomenon. From this angle, it is quite unusual for the possessed woman to be on her own. Nevertheless, others will notice and share their impressions.

once (for different job offers and also to enter monastic life), but they refused to let her go out of fear that they would 'lose everything'.

(b)

> After one month he appeared in my mother-in-law's dream and asked her: 'Why do you just sit idle? We serve the public!' My mother-in-law could not understand anything. She didn't know how to answer people's questions. He replied: 'You just concentrate on me, call my name and I shall appear through your body'. (Nirmala, 47 years, widow)

Sometimes, the capacity for divine possession is inherited within the family, for instance, if a child has died from smallpox and takes possession of his or her mother and of mothers in later generations. When Nirmala got married, she learned of her mother-in-law's regular possession by the spirit of a deceased son (Nirmala's husband's younger brother). 'I was scared to see this. I knew that the Lord had entered her body but still I was horrified . . . and avoided the *pūjā* room. Then I got used to this. Since I was staying in this house, did I have any alternative?' The ancestral spirit (*sajība debatā*, literally: enlivened god) was identified with Bāidhara, the son of Buṙhī Ṭhākurāṇī, the patron goddess of Berhampur.[13] This goddess is known, among other things, to induce, cure and embody smallpox (*basanta*), and anyone who fails to survive this disease is believed to be her son or daughter. At the age of 30, Nirmala's husband died and a few years later her parents-in-law followed. By that time, Nirmala herself had started to develop divinatory skills. Once a week she answered people's questions and gradually gained a reputation as an oracle. In fact, the divination was the only way she could make a living and raise her four children. Although Nirmala enjoyed the financial benefits of her submission to Bāidhara, she also complained about the physical side effects. The divine encounter produced bodily pain, so Nirmala often avoided possession or limited its duration. At the same time, she felt obliged to

---

[13] Bāidhara is worshipped under a sacred tree within the premises of the Buṙhī Ṭhākurāṇī temple. There devotees had donated a stone idol to him. At first sight he seems to be another form of Bhairaba (Sanskrit: Bhairava) who is also known as a guardian of the goddess (see Chalier-Visuvalingam 1996). The head priest of the Buṙhī Ṭhākurāṇī temple distinguishes both deities though, drawing on the iconography of Bāidhara vis-à-vis Bhairaba in the nearby Śiba temple.

surrender to this god so as to guarantee divine satisfaction and hence blessing. She was looking forward to a daughter-in-law who could release her from this burden, yet she knew that she could not assume her cooperation. 'If she is very stylish, she probably won't like this. If we take measures in order to save my daughter-in-law from being possessed, then he won't come. Otherwise he will not leave her.'

(c)

> Jyotsna (19 years): Mother, Mother, who are you? . . . Mother, who has come? (A woman blows on a conch, while others ululate.)
>
> Nila (17 years, student): Who has come? Hey you, who has come?
>
> Jyotsna: Tell us! If you keep quiet like this, then how will we know?

Possession may occur during semi-public rituals shared by the women of one neighbourhood, for instance on the occasion of the Jahni Oṣā. For one month, unmarried girls meet every evening to worship the goddess Bṛndābatī. At some *pūjā* sites, though not regularly, one of the votaries becomes possessed. Then the girls have to find out who has appeared and why, i.e., what form the goddess has taken and whether her presence is the sign of her grace or anger. One evening, the identity of the deity and the subsequent divination were anything but clear. The votary who had at first impersonated Bṛndābatī as a part of the ritual (Plate 4.1) started to shake her body in a very violent and unpredictable manner. The girls assumed that the goddess had appeared as Bāṭa Maṅgaḷā, a particularly frightening form of the goddess Maṅgaḷā often met at the roadside (*bāṭa*). Here Bāṭa Maṅgaḷā complained about the incorrect *pūjā* she had been offered (Plate 4.2). Then the goddess started to stammer and utter strange noises. She revealed herself as Jāṅī Mā, literally the 'Dumb Mother'. Finally, the possessor was recognized as Bṛndābatī herself, who, through her human host, addressed certain problems in the marriage negotiations of one participant. After half an hour, the exhausted medium lay down and the girls completed the evening's regular program of worship. The discussion as to the meaning of the prophecy continued over the following days. Since the divine utterances had been fragmented and ambiguous, nobody knew for sure whose 'brother had made a mistake', who exactly should be appeased, where and in what way. Nonetheless, in this Jahni Oṣā group and others, the mere possibility of divine possession underlined the significance of the participants' religious practice. Girls felt they had a responsibility to perform votive rites whole-heartedly, since otherwise the goddess would enter their bodies and complain. Hence, their attitude towards possession was one of ambivalence, fear and appreciation at the same time.

**Plates 4.1 and 4.2:** A votary impersonates the goddess Bṛndābatī and becomes possessed by Bāṭa Maṅgaḷā

(d)

> [The goddess] likes dancing, songs and everything. So if we don't dance in front of her, she will not appear at this place. (Babula, 29 years, priest)

On some occasions divine possession is invited by aesthetic means such as rich decoration, figurative masks, elaborate costumes and artistic dancing. Families who, because of a prospective marriage or for any other reason, wish to ensure the divine benevolence may take a procession out to the temple of Buṛhī Ṭhākurāṇī. The priests of this temple, Oriya barbers by caste (Bhaṇḍārī), will organize these processions on suitable days in the month of *caitra* (March/April). They will invoke the divine generative power (*śakti*) in one or more sacred pots that have to be carried by married women on behalf of the family. A few dancers, who remain hidden below huge *ṭhākurāṇī* figures, will commence the pageant. A group of drummers follows. In their midst, a younger male member of the priest's family will dance, dressed up as the goddess Kāḷī. Moving a mask in front of his face, he interacts with the women who carry the sacred pots on their head. Then the remaining family of the sponsor, relatives and friends follow. While proceeding through the lanes of Berhampur, neighbours bow down to the pot bearer(s) and wash her/their feet with sacred water. Regardless of possession, these women are worshipped as an embodiment of the goddess. Moreover, the ritual specialist in the costume of Kāḷī will try to evoke the divine agency in the body of the pot bearer(s), and indeed some of them start to tremble, shriek or communicate in some other way. Neighbours may ask the possessed for their advice and prophecy, while others lay their babies on the road. In response to this act of surrender, the living goddess is to step over them and thus show her grace. If a spectator becomes possessed, the priest will intervene and relocate the divine by 'cooling' the unprepared body with turmeric water. (I shall come back to these pageants in the following chapter.)

(e)

> [I told her:] 'If you are really powerful, then you have to come into my body.'. . . [Finally] the goddess entered my body, so won't I feel happy? (Rajeshvari, 58 years, nurse)

There are several circumstances which influence whether and when a woman should invite or rather avoid goddess possession. During the three weeks of the biennial celebration of Ṭhākurāṇī Yātrā, a festival in honour of the patroness of Berhampur, night after night nine women from the Devāṅgī caste (Telugu silk weavers) carry sacred pots in a procession and are worshipped by the public as human manifestations of Buṙhī Ṭhākurāṇī (see Chapter 6). In this context the goddess is banned from taking possession of the pot bearers. Just before the daily procession, a priest (or rather a *tāntrika*) will seal their bodies. Rather than by pragmatics (daily possession would be physically exhaustive), this rule is governed by the fact that Buṙhī Ṭhākurāṇī has 'adopted' the chief of the Devāṅgī as her father. Since a goddess may possess her children (i.e., devotees) but never her parents – here in a wider sense all Devāṅgī – she is not supposed to overwhelm the pot bearers. During the final night of the festival, however, any women of Berhampur seeking divine favour may go on a fast and join the nocturnal procession. In 2001, several thousands gathered for this event, each carrying a pot invested with the divine generative power (*śakti*). Since these women were not given similar protective measures, in the course of standing and walking in the crowd for hours, about 10 per cent of them became possessed. Whether overpowered by the divine or not, women appreciated this event as a significant religious experience, although due to the crowd the individual transformations were not paid any specific attention. After arriving at the Buṙhī Ṭhākurāṇī temple in the early hours of the morning, not only the sacred pot but also the remaining signs of possession were removed, again by sprinkling turmeric water to 'cool' the body.

In southern Orissa the experience of possession is not restricted to particular castes or social strata. However, the majority of people in Berhampur and the surrounding area belong to the middle-ranking and lower spectrum of the caste society. They are basically artisans, small businessmen, agricultural laborers and farmers, or self-employed in the service industry. In regard to deity possession, caste and class identity does not matter that much.[14] These incidents move Oriya- and Telugu-speaking devotees, women and also men. Yet possession is specifically associated with femininity. The preponderance of possessed women is explained by the goddess's preference for human beings who share her bodily substance, through their sameness of sex and also the consumption of meat. (In southern Orissa only a very few people, some Brahmins and non-Brahmins, are pure vegetarians.) In general, deity possession is considered an *optional* proof of the divine that heightens religious experience and thus is not limited to a specific ritual event. This may vary gradually if prophecy and therefore possession become a regular service on demand (as in Nirmala's case). The local discourse on divine possession involves only certain kinds of deities who are known for their hot temper and demanding character. Thus the man-lion-shaped Narasiṃha, a variety of *ṭhākurāṇīs* and deceased smallpox victims are likely to take possession.[15] Regardless of her or his mood, to experience the divine by means of the lived-in body is conceptualized in terms of pleasure (*khusi*). It is not related to the overpowered individual, her living conditions or social situation. Being selected by a deity is understood to be a result of divine grace, and thus may prove

[14] During fieldwork I spoke to possessed women from the following communities: Karaṇa (accountants), Oṛia (potters, etc.), Bhaṇḍārī (barbers, priests), Devāṅgī (weavers), Liārī (rice processors), Ḍaluā (betel merchants), Hāṙi (sweepers), Telaṅgā (bangle manufacturers, etc.), Gauṙa (milkmen), Haluā Brāhmaṇa (Brahmin farmers) and Kārada (merchants). However, most families had given up their designated caste occupations.

[15] Conversely, the goddess Lakṣmī and male deities such as Nārāẏaṇa, Rāma, Kṛṣṇa or Hanumān will not take a human form.

the piety of a woman. Yet divine possession is an ambivalent gift, since it not only involves the voluntary surrender to an external agency, it also demands unconditional physical self-denial.

On the basis of academic literature, it is difficult to judge whether the ethnographical examples given above are representative of female possession throughout Orissa. Moreover, this Indian state exhibits very considerable cultural diversity, with its dominant Oriya population in the plains, its well-established Telugu diaspora in the south and along the coast, and its various indigenous communities (Adivasi) in the upland interior. The rare and dispersed records on female possession all refer to institutionalized forms. Lynn Foulston (2002: 145–49) mentions the example of a woman who is routinely possessed by the goddess within the premises of a Santoṣī Mā temple. Every Friday, this ritual specialist assumes divine form, proven by eating fire. Being transformed, she is accredited with healing powers and thus draws large crowds of devotees, who seek help with medical problems and also in family affairs.[16] According to James Freeman (1981), who analyzed a fire walking ceremony that failed, deity possession seems to be a low-caste affair. He describes a 70-year-old woman from the untouchable Bauri (Bāurī) caste who acts as a female 'shaman' (*kaḷasī*[17]). As a representation of the goddess Banadurga (Baṇadurgā), it was her task to guide the (male) firewalkers. 'She went into trance, trembling, stretching, and yawning, accompanied by loud drumming, blaring bagpipes and horns, played by Bauri-caste musicians, and a twirling dancing boy, dressed in a women's [sic] garb, performing the *patua* dance'. (J. Freeman 1981: 315). Both instances of deity possession were observed in proximity to Bhubaneswar. In southern Orissa, to the best of my knowledge, this institutionalized form is considered the realm of

[16] Although Foulston (2002: 104) does not provide any details on the background of the medium, she observes that the Scheduled Castes may attend this form of Friday worship but are forbidden to enter the sanctum of the goddess.

[17] The term derives from the word *kaḷasa*, the sacred pot carried by devotees. J. Freeman (1981: 311) translates the role of a *kalasi* (in his spelling) as 'shaman' and as 'shamanistic curer'. As described above, to install the divine power in an earthen pot carried by devote women is common ritual practice in Berhampur. Although I describe these women as pot bearers, they were not considered as *kaḷasī*, a term reserved for professional mediums (or 'shamans', in J. Freeman's parlance).

the men, although in general women are believed to be more eligible for possession than male devotees.[18]

Deity possession among women of a Telugu fishing caste (Vāḍabalija), living along the shores of Orissa, is well documented (Schömbucher 1994a, 1994b, 1996, 1999, 2006). Elisabeth Schömbucher has provided an excellent analysis of the power and poetry of the divine words uttered by these female mediums. The Vāḍabalija consider three classes of non-human beings as liable to possess women: (*a*) regional goddesses (in Oriya classified as *ṭhākurāṇī*) and addressed as 'mother' (Telugu: *ammavāru*); (*b*) Vaishnava male deities such as Narasiṃha; (*c*) immortal beings who have achieved the status of a demigod (Telugu: *vīruḍu*), such as victims of an untimely death (Schömbucher 1996: 243). The Oriya and Telugu women I met during fieldwork basically shared this classification. However, unlike in Berhampur, possession among the fisherwomen seems to be limited to a distinct therapeutic framework, where a male priest (*dāsuḍu*) encourages a female medium (*bhakturālu*) to address the afflictions of various clients. The divine utterances of the possessed person constitute a dialogue that lasts for one or two hours. Its highly stylized and lyrical language inspired Schömbucher to analyze these possession séances as a verbal art, taking into account that the required skills might escape Western notions of aesthetics. In comparison, only *some* possessed women in Berhampur were speaking in tongues and employed familiar religious formulae, yet in a rather brief and much less articulated way.

The mass possession of women in public, as during Ṭhākurāṇī Yātrā, alludes to another type of nocturnal procession in the coastal zone of Andhra Pradesh. According to David Knipe (1989), these pageants are related to death and ancestor worship. They are performed in honour of Vīrabhadra, a divine hero associated with the deification of ancestors who suffered a premature death (similar to Buṛhī Ṭhākurāṇī's smallpox victims). Ahead of those processions one finds musicians and dancers, who wear costumes to impersonate these departed heroes. A crowd of

[18] During the fire-walking festival (Jhāmu Yātrā) in the outskirts of Berhampur, a male priest cross-dresses in order to become an apt vessel for the goddess Ellāmmā, and only he walks on glowing coals. At a similar ceremony downtown, again a male ritual specialist embodies the goddess, yet the act of fire-walking itself has been abandoned (see Hauser 2007). At the yearly Daṇḍa Nāṭa performance, the goddess Kāḷī is known for possessing the male officiant (cf. Schnepel 2008: 70).

devotees follows. In the course of the night, some of these marchers get taken over by the spirits of deceased family members. According to Knipe (1989: 127–28), it is 'most frequently younger mothers in their twenties and thirties, who sway or whirl, slowly at first, then quickly before they abandon the march and fall screaming to the ground'.

Dialogues with immortal beings also characterize the religious practices of Adivasis in Orissa, such as the Sora, who live in the mountains bordering Andhra Pradesh. As Piers Vitebsky (1993) has demonstrated, it is again overwhelmingly possessed women who utter the non-human voice of deceased relatives. In this context the mediums are recognized as shamans (*kuran*) or rather as priestesses in their own right. However, the Sora's spirits (*ılda*) differ from the deified ancestors that are commonly worshipped by their Hindu neighbours.[19]

To make a thorough assessment of divine possession in Orissa, much more comparative research is certainly needed. With respect to the population in and around Berhampur, however, deity possession is not limited to specific religious events, social purposes or strata, but rather serves as a general ritual act that might occur during various forms of worship. It is highly appreciated among women. As a religious idiom of its own, it proves the relevance of their pious dedication and specifically of those religious activities that scarcely find approval in Brahminical male discourse. Whether this commitment to deity possession reflects a regional development, or rather hints at a hitherto silenced and gendered form of Hindu devotion, is discussed in the next sections.

## Female Possession in Academic Discourse

The academic discourse on possession in South Asia is characterized by different theoretical and methodological approaches. Schömbucher (1993: 240) distinguishes four interpretative models: (*a*) the psychological; (*b*) the sociological; (*c*) the cosmological and (*d*) the performative model of possession. These different strands of argumentation reflect not only disciplinary preferences and a chronological development of research paradigms, but also relate to different social contexts and phenomena that are discussed under the heading of possession.[20]

[19] A collection of essays edited by Tina Otten and Uwe Skoda (forthcoming) will give several further examples of possession in tribal communities.

[20] Similarly possession has been evaluated within studies on goddess worship, healing ceremonies and ritual dramas.

Here I shall evaluate central positions taken in this literature regarding possession as a gendered practice.[21]

Some of the pioneering studies on possession in South Asia conceive of these experiential states as a culture-specific form and treatment of psychic disorder. The focus is on *demonic* possession – a form of body experience that is conceptualized in negative terms and demands exorcism. The afflicted person suffers from this state and shows mental and bodily signs of weakness that make normal life impossible and cause alarm in his or her relatives. Throughout the Indian subcontinent a variety of religious institutions specialize in the therapeutic cure of such illnesses, and in this way testify to the prevalence of malevolent possession. Patients are not only taken to Hindu temples – as illustrated by Sudhir Kakar (1982) and, more recently, by Marine Carrin (1999) – but also to Buddhist shrines (Obeyesekere 1977), graves of Muslim saints (Pfleiderer 1988, 1994) and to Christian pilgrimage centres (Stirrat 1992).

Although the patients suffering from demonic affliction are from both genders, academic scholars notice a preponderance of women. With reference to Varanasi, Jonathan Parry (1994: 233) claims that about 70 per cent of victims are female, while over 80 per cent belong to the lower castes. The main argument explaining demonic possession draws on Freudian psychoanalysis. The Indian female self is said to invite this exaggerated behaviour in order to deal with hidden desires, repressed emotions, guilt, fear, and conflict – similar to the gendered phenomenon of hysteria in European medical discourse at the beginning of the twentieth century. To project 'the other' on to the demonic is regarded as a coping mechanism that is successfully dealt with in healing ceremonies, which aim to re-establish the self in relation to family and acquaintances. This approach is identified with psychoanalytically influenced scholars like Sudhir Kakar (1982) and Gananath Obeyesekere (1977, 1981). Although met with criticism, for instance concerning the Western bias, their influential studies keep on inspiring scholars.[22] Following this line, psychiatrist Antti Pakaslathi (1998: 164) has pointed out that affliction by spirits is not limited to

[21] For a review of the 'classical' academic positions followed in the 1950s, 1960s and 1970s, see Schömbucher (1993).

[22] For current psychological views from India compare Pakaslathi (1998) and Chandra Shekar (1989), for recent studies on demonic possession see Dwyer (2003) and Carrin (1999).

the underprivileged. Exorcists of a north Indian temple instead attract clients with an 'average or better than average education', who 'belong to the higher castes' and who are of urban domicile. Regardless of social status, Sarah Caldwell (1999: 228–33) suggests that female possession originates, among other factors, in the traumatic childhood experience of sexual abuse.

Influenced by Ioan Lewis' (1975) deprivation theory, scholars identify demonic possession as a social phenomenon that allows subalterns to raise their voice and pursue their interests against the hierarchy. In his survey on popular Hinduism, Chris Fuller (1992: 233) argues that incidents of possession provide 'culturally tolerated opportunities to complain about female inferiority and subordination within Indian society'. They serve women seeking to escape ill-treatment by their in-laws, to postpone an unwanted marriage or to claim authority in family decisions. Explorations by Claus (1975), Gellner (1994), Obeyesekere (1977) and Pfleiderer (1988, 1994) sustain this argument. More recently, Isabelle Nabokov (1997: 299) has questioned the effectiveness of this kind of 'subversion'. With respect to a case study from Kerala, she claims that demonic possession does not provide women with a means to attain secondary gains, but rather acts to keep them under control.

Looking at shamanic careers, scholars also recorded the transformation of previously suffering victims of demonic possession into ritual specialists, now in control of their ability to host a spirit. This institutionalization of possession may take the form of a regular oracular service at a shrine or of a public display of divine agency during religious festivals. Whereas the potential to gain control over non-human powers seems to be independent of gender and role expectations, female mediumship has raised academic attention fairly often. It will not come as a surprise that scholars concentrated on the socio-political impact of possession. Deprivation and severe troubles in life are often at hand to make sense of a professional approach to possession, since mediums themselves emphasize how the divine call has had a radically positive influence on hopeless economic, medical and social issues – a rhetoric that generally proves the power of a deity. The Rajasthani shaman described by Shail Mayaram (1999), for instance, was troubled by her alcoholic husband who, learning about her vocation, stopped drinking and assisted her in the management of a shrine. Similarly Margaret Egnor (1984) traces the development of a low-caste construction laborer in Madras (Chennai) who, after suffering from poverty and considering suicide, was called by the goddess in a dream. Becoming a divine servant not only gave her mental support, by means of possession she also gradually emerged as a priestess of the goddess Māriamman – a ritual task that appeared to be a viable way of earning a living. Although some professional mediums may gain social reputation and practically intervene in family matters, caste and local politics, their memories and life-stories reflect first of all a religious discourse. Thus, the scholarly comparison of a person's living conditions before and after the growth of mediumship skills risks underplaying the religious experience of a medium in her lived-in world. However, the *form* of possession seems to vary in accordance with social factors. According to David Gellner (1994: 38–39) and Karin Kapadia (1996: 433), the rising status of a medium mostly correlates to the class of divine power that takes possession of her (or him). From that perspective, the identification of a non-human being, for instance a famous pan-Indian goddess, can be understood as a claim to authority.

The institutionalized dialogue with the divine is not limited to ritual specialists of low economic and caste status. Kathleen Erndl's (1993, 1996, 1997) studies on night vigils in honour of the mother goddess reveal that in northwest India, well-to-do and educated Brahmin women may also experience possession and turn into 'living mothers'. In any case, women's experience of possession and their gradual rise to expertise often initiates a complete change of life (whether intended or involuntary), i.e., giving up family ties and adopting an ascetic lifestyle. Still, it is anything but clear whether the scholarly preference for female mediums reflects the local gender distribution among this type of ritual specialists, or whether these women attract attention as exceptions to the rule. However, while studies on malevolent possession emphasize female *victims*, the women described here appear as strategic *agents* who manipulate their environment.

The problem with both the psychological and the sociological perspective on possession is, as Schömbucher (1993: 242) has pointed out, that they regard these experiential states as a 'symbolic expression of other experiences'. In her view, scholars should rather follow a 'performative approach to possession' (1993: 257). They should consider the theatrical aspects of possession, the sequencing of the event, audience reactions and also the divine dialogues as cultural expression in its own right. This perspective was favoured in an exemplarily way by Bruce Kapferer (1983). In his study on exorcism in Sri Lanka, he showed how aesthetics, creativity and humor contribute significantly to the experience and efficacy of the ritual act. Similarly, Richard Freeman (1993: 124) emphasized that possession consists of learned and rehearsed gestures of possession rather than 'trance behaviour' of individuals. On the basis of *teyyam*-performances, a ritual dance that culminates in the speaking in the voice of a god, he observed well-choreographed movements and highly structured recognizable utterances.

Studies focusing on possession as a ritual and aesthetic performance – and thus as meaningful by itself – overwhelmingly identify male mediums to develop artful and ludic ways of expression. Schömbucher's work (1996, 2006) is exceptional since she considers the poetic potential and, in this respect, the authorship of possessed women. Although academic literature gives more hints of a creative role of possessed women (see Osella and Osella 1999: 191–92), scholars seemingly fail to recognize the possession episodes as a cultural site (co-)defined by female performers. Likewise Peter Claus (1975: 56) describes women of a matrilineal community in Karnataka joining the performance of the Siri epic. While mimetically re-enacting the suffering of the heroine, some of them are possessed. Yet according to Claus, these female participants 'are not true specialists because they do not see themselves essentially as priestesses to Siri'. To make it clear, I do not propose translating 'Western' concepts of personhood and art to South Asian contexts. Rather I wish to show how possessed women are represented in academic discourse and in what respect they are conceived of as subjects (compared with male mediums).

Socially widespread and mostly unobtrusive forms of deity possession, like those embedded in women's religious practices in southern Orissa, are rarely reflected by academic discourse. However, Mary Hancock's (1995) study of middle-class women in Madras (Chennai) suggests that such an approach to possession is not limited by region. She discusses how Smārta Brahmin women develop mediumship skills in their devotion (*bhakti*) to a goddess, using these skills for private matters but also offering their help to others. According to Hancock (1995: 63, 70), goddess oracles and their clients are found throughout all castes and social strata. Similar to the examples in Orissa, given in the previous section, this form of religious practice is regarded as compatible with women's roles as mothers and wives.[23]

[23] Recently, Smith (2006) has applied the notion of possession to a continuum of experiential states of the body-mind complex. With reference to *bhakti*

## The Challenge of Ambiguity

In academic discourse, divine possession is mostly recognized in its institutionalized form, i.e., related and limited to *specific* ceremonies ('possession cults'). Only rarely do scholars focus on possession as a type of ritual behaviour as, say, the singing of hymns. This is not only due to research methodology. Although formalized possession routines are to some extent predictable and thus suitable for systematic observation, the scholarly preference also reflects the social contestation of these experiential states within their own context. In this section, I show how local people ('informants') come to support ethnographer's scepticism as to the validity of possession as a *religious* experience, and thus encourage the interpretation of possession as a representation of something else.

Both the psycho-medical and the sociological model of possession have, I argue, a counterpart in local folk theory. Ethnocentric assumptions deriving from (Western) psychoanalysis meet and apparently 'translate' Indian concepts on the female nature and vulnerability. Several scholars have rendered 'cosmological models of possession' (in Schömbucher's classification). They discussed South Asian characterizations of women as highly emotional beings, morally weak, attached to worldly desires, seducible, and therefore likely to face possession (Kapferer 1983: 140; Gellner 1994: 39). These stereotypes are

theology, he includes meditative and devotional practices that serve to evoke an emotional proximity to, if not complete absorption in the divine. His argument is in line with the findings of McDaniel (1989), who in a study on religious ecstasy among Bengali saints has shown how the emotional identification with a god is interlinked with the experience of being overpowered by a deity. 'In devotional ecstasy', McDaniel (1989: 3) explains, 'there is a permeability and openness uniting the person and the divinity, and a sharing of love between them'. Analyzing theological texts, interviews and biographies of two female saints and three contemporary 'holy women' (*sādhikā*), she shows that these renunciants subscribe to a clear hierarchy of these altered states of the body (1989: 229). They privilege emotional experiences classified as *bhāva* (literally: mood, emotion, ecstasy) and downplay a rigid personality change conceived of as *bhor* (literally: engrossed, possession). Although both terms have their Oriya counterpart (*bhāba*, *bhoḷa*), people do not employ them to describe or classify experiential states like possession. By the way, in McDaniel's study women who have experienced the divine in this form are represented as subjects of their own with some freedom and self-determination.

consistent with gendered concepts of the body, such as the menstrual impurity of women, their bodily permeability and specific 'openness' (Osella and Osella 1999: 186–91). In Orissa, the preponderance of female over male possession is legitimized not only with the sameness of sex, but also with shared food habits – the preference for meat, conceived of as humoral disposition representative of women (see Chapter 5).

The sociological approach to possession as a subaltern strategy to acquire secondary gains corresponds in a similar way to 'emic' doubts on the reality of divine overpowering. In fact, local observers do not unanimously agree on the emergence of a divine persona. Deity possession is often subjected to critique and mockery.[24] Even the pious may challenge the authenticity of possession, the standard argument being that it is simply deprived individuals who try to win attention and wealth through this pretence. There is a certain amount of scepticism about the credibility of mediums and religious specialists, a stance taken and related to habitus (Bourdieu) and also to self-presentation.[25]

On the one hand, the perspective on possession is determined by caste and class, and thus reflects processes of status distinction. On the basis of fieldwork in Tamil Nadu, Kapadia (1995: 124, Chapter 6) distinguishes two clearly separated positions. According to 'lower-caste ethos', possession is said to prove a person's piety and true love for God. Thus it constitutes one of the most important forms of *bhakti*. It contrasts with the Brahminical view that denies the religious significance of these bodily experiences and rather emphasizes liturgy authenticated by the Sanskrit scriptures.[26] Similarly Parry (1994: 226–30) shows that from the perspective of Brahmin orthodoxy in Benares, spirit pos-session is considered as 'superstition' and, like impurity, reflects an inferior

[24] See Hancock (1995: 70), Mayaram (1999: 122), Egnor (1984: 28), Kapadia (1996: 435).

[25] Gellner (1994: 39) recognizes another aspect that influences the social contestation of deity possession. According to his study in Nepal, the doubts as to the credibility of possession rise with the status of the possessing entity. The higher a deity, the more skeptical are people of claims to possession. Although this argument sounds convincing, it provokes tricky classificatory problems since the hierarchy of deities is itself a matter of context and perspective (on the 'multiple identities' of Durgā and Kālī, see McDaniel 2004: Chapter 4).

[26] The orthodox standpoint, however, has been challenged by recently. According to Smith (2006), accounts of possession can be found in Vedic, Buddhist, Jain, Tantric and devotional literature, in the epics, in Sanskrit drama, and also in medical texts.

social status. Nonetheless, Brahmin priests may accept ritual specialists exorcizing demons, so long as they do not interfere with their own ritual competence and business, i.e., the negotiation with the divine. It seems that in many parts of the Indian subcontinent, 'high-caste' (or 'middle-class') discourse silences and openly devalues deity possession as an extrovert style of worship associated with the impure, uneducated, lower strata of society (see McDaniel 1989: 240; William Sax quoted by Smith 2006: 170). As a marker of class and caste distinctions, however, the relevance of possession is also subject to social change. Kapadia (1996, 2000: 181–82) shows that divine possession may serve upwardly mobile middle-caste men (non-Brahmin Tamils) to ritually back their new economic status. As a result of this prestige, however, women are banished from these religious events.

On the other hand, the perspective on possession is related to the self-presentation of an interlocutor, whether medium or onlooker. Women who consider themselves to be a deity's vehicle are well aware that their own possession may be ridiculed. In Tamil Nadu, low-caste female possession is mocked at and made fun of (Kapadia 1995: 157, 1996: 435; Egnor 1984: 28). According to Hancock (1995: 70), Smārta Brahmin women under-emphasize their emotionally and aesthetically satisfying experiences during possession in order to avoid doubts being raised as to the genuineness of their transformation. The fear of being stigmatized seems to particularly affect educated and high-caste people, who, refuting deprivation theory, actively participate in rituals that include and require possession in several parts of South Asia.[27] Regarding divine possession by men, William Sax (cf. Smith 2006: 170) points out that although high- and low-caste people are possessed, upper-caste people tend to deny it of themselves and attribute it to the subalterns. However, the assessment of divine presence may also change in the course of time. Pious spectators who are swept away with emotion at the time of the possession episode, Kapadia (1996: 430) notes, might later sneer at the alleged charlatans.

During fieldwork in southern Orissa, I was faced with similar arguments and reactions on the apparent pretence of deity possession and the material gains some individuals received from doing so. A few people clearly appealed to 'our shared scientific knowledge' about these

[27] Scholars have documented Brahminical possession in Himachal Pradesh (Erndl 1993: Chapter 5, 1996, 1997), in Rajasthan (Pakaslathi 1998: 164), in Kerala (R. Freeman (1999: 165–70) and in Tamil Nadu (Kapadia 1995: 150–54).

frauds, anticipating my scepticism. Others collected any news on a priestess in their neighbourhood who gathered crowds of devotees by speaking in tongues. Both priestess and devotees were suspected for being low-caste and uneducated. In general, though these perspectives on possession did not correlate with caste identity, as Kapadia argues with regard to Tamil Nadu, rather most notions on divine possession were in some way ambiguous. Whereas young boys would make fun of a female medium, imitating her behaviour and in particular its transgressive elements, their aunties scolded them. The latter seemed to be glad about having a divine medium around to give advice in several family affairs. They eagerly waited for the moment the goddess would manifest in the respective women. Yet at the same time these aunties requested me to test the medium in order to verify the divine power. If she indeed embodies the goddess, they argued, she would certainly understand German language (my mother-tongue), won't she? My own perspective on their devotion was challenged too.

Ethnographers who study possession are thus confronted with this *locally* contested practice. Their own scepticism as to the reality of this altered state of the body is likely to be manipulated by the respective standpoints of their interlocutors. With reference to anthropological studies on caste, Richard Burghart (1990) has emphasized that scholars tend to imitate the perspective of their mostly high-caste 'informants' (and research assistants, I would add) or, conversely, ignore and exclude their perspective altogether. Although there is nothing like *one* Brahminical or upper-class view, the focus on the dynamics between researchers and their local counterparts in the production of ethnography suggests some self-criticism concerning the acknowledgement of possession as a form of religious experience. Obviously the idea of a uniform 'emic' perspective is an academic construct. In case of contested social and religious practices, however, silencing the diversity of voices is even more problematic. To give examples by two renowned scholars: (*a*) Gellner (1994: 38, 41), in his study on female mediums in Kathmandu valley, reports on 'many Nepalese' claiming that the spread of female mediums was promoted by 'democracy', as if the modern trope of gender equality would explain the increasing number of female ritual specialists. Keeping in mind the relevance of the divine feminine in South Asian religious contexts, one may wonder whose viewpoint has been represented here. Did Gellner speak with the medium and her followers, or did he adopt the perspective of his interlocutors, possibly male and following competing healing traditions? (*b*) Conversely, attending possession séances left an impressive mark on Erndl (1996: 174–75). She decides 'to take seriously the notion of the Goddess as an agent herself rather than simply a symbol or projection . . . as an agent who interacts with both the person possessed and the devotees who worship her.' She obviously identifies with the devotees' perspective and, for her part, neglects any local scepticism about possession.[28] Both authors, in spite of their valuable contributions to the study of possession, seem to give preference to only one line of argument in the local possession discourse. While wondering who actually is performing during possession episodes in Rajasthan, Ann Gold (1988: 59) rightly recognizes '"The spirits themselves" might be a simple, valid response, but even speaking from within the culture, it is not the whole story'.[29] In Chapter 5 I shall come back to this inherently contested nature of deity possession.

## Conclusion: Perpetuating Shaktism

Whereas the overview of scholarly approaches to possession gives some indication of the major social contexts through which possession in South Asia is constituted, the variety of situations that in southern Orissa may evoke divine possession seems to escape any of these patterns and rationales. It would be misleading to reduce this diversity on the basis of social factors. The overpowering by a divine agent can occur on several ritual occasions and serves as an *optional* proof of the divine that heightens the religious experience of mediums and onlookers alike. To communicate with the divine through one's own body is highly respected, particularly among women. It allows encountering the divine in an accessible form that resonates to one's own body and self-understanding. Orthodox high-caste women in principle share this religious discourse, yet only a few of them undergo this personal experience. The realm of devotion is rather defined by demographically dominant social groups. Although deity possession is hardly prevalent among the educated middle-class, it is not merely a sign of low status

[28] Only once Erndl (1996: 183) cursorily mentions that individuals might doubt the validity of deity possession.

[29] This social contestation of possession also alludes to a general anthropological problem: there is nothing like a singular emic voice. Moreover, performers, onlookers and also the ethnographer each produce their own arguments in relation to others.

(unlike in Tamil Nadu, as suggested by Kapadia). At any rate, 'modern' interlocutors will carefully consider their self-presentation when rendering possession episodes. This does not outdate the relevance of deity possession as a religious idiom of its own.

Apart from deities that may 'jump upon' and 'dance' mortal beings, the Hindu cosmology in southern Orissa is populated by several uncanny supernatural entities that cause suffering and disease. On several occasions priests make use of a peacock-feather whisk to wipe out malevolent influences and to protect the human body. This 'brushing and blowing' (*jhaṙā-phunka*) is also performed by (male and female) mediums taken over by a goddess.[30] If possession occurs for the first time, people may call a *tāntrika* to find out whether this condition is caused by a haunting ghost (*bhūta*). Besides, possession is removed in the case of those persons who are not considered eligible to enter this experiential state. Unlike in parts of India with temples widely known for their exorcism rituals, in southern Orissa to drive away spirits, or rather to re-balance the human body is, in general, a two to 10 minute affair that does not raise much attention. As mentioned earlier in this section, there is no clear boundary between desired and harmful forms of possession. In both cases, the behaviour and expressiveness of the body is similar and, like during Ṭhākurāṇī Yātrā, even goddesses can be prohibited from entering pious women. However, certain types of psychophysical affliction are identified within a discourse on black magic (*guṇiā*) and thus regarded as a result of malevolent (super-) human manipulation.

As to the problem of whether this gendered form of divine possession can be considered an Oriyan phenomenon, my analysis has raised several questions and can only suggest some answers that need further clarification. Certainly there are features that may account for the specific regional popularity of divine possession: the importance given to goddess worship (Shaktism) and the popularity of devotionalism (*bhakti*), which emphasizes individual experience of the divine. Yet the *intraregional* variety of possession practices should not be underestimated. At any rate, the previous sections indicated that the contrast between my observations in southern Orissa and the literature on possession also emerges due to the dynamics of anthropological knowledge production itself. Since the religious significance

[30] This ritual act is not limited to Orissa but commonly performed in popular and 'tantric' Hinduism (McDaniel 1989: 13; Gellner 1994: 31; White 2003: 259).

of deity possession is a locally contested issue, it is prone to being overlooked or devaluated by ethnographers. To them the local equivalent of academic psycho-medical and sociological arguments is tempting indeed. Therefore it is likely that women in other parts of Orissa, and even South Asia, may also appreciate the religious experience of divine possession, particularly in its non-institutionalized form. At any rate, the contested character of possession as a religious idiom does not merely result from individual doubts. In the following chapter I shall go even further and argue that divine presence as an objectified state only emerges from social negotiation, and hence by its very nature presupposes some kind of dialogue, publicity and ambiguity.

To women in southern Orissa, incidents of goddess possession transmit fundamental cosmological knowledge about the similarities between and interdependence of women and female deities. Moreover, the occurrence of possession demonstrates the need to engage in the divine dialogue through prayers and elaborate forms of worship, so as to ensure that the goddess is pleased and will take care of her devotees and the territory they live in. Thus, the practice of deity possession does not only express certain ideas about the self, the permeability of human bodies and communication with the divine; it also perpetuates Shaktism in its accessible and embodied form. This religious knowledge includes an inventory of images, observations, emotions, and experiences that outline the character and power of female deities. It is re-enacted, spread and authenticated primarily by possessed women and their (male and female) exegetical supervisors. In the following chapter I shall analyze two case studies that reveal, how women 'learn' to recognize and express divine agency, and how the personal experience of goddess possession affects women's self-understanding and religious self. However, from an ideal 'high-caste male' perspective on Hinduism, this ritual practice can be seen to question hegemonic views on religion and society. Yet it would be highly misleading to regard the challenge of Brahminical (and academic) scholars as a self-conscious religio-political act intended by the respective women. The 'subversive' potential of possession is very limited (compare Chapter 6).

# 5

# (Re-)Calling the Goddess: The Emergence of Divine Presence

In the last decade of the twentieth century, anthropologists came to look at possession phenomena as cultural meta-commentary to consider 'alterity' and 'otherness' (Boddy 1994: 422–26). Similar to European discourses on foreign cultures, the social practice of ('spirit') possession essentially served as a vehicle to reflect upon and verify self-identity and the boundaries between the own and the 'other' (Basu 2002; Behrend and Luig 1999; Boddy 1989; Kramer 1993; Mayaram 1999; Taussig 1993). Studies along these lines emphasize possession in its capacity as a cultural performance, i.e., they focus on bodily practices, mimesis, dramatic techniques and aesthetics that convey extraordinary and apparently alien forms of behaviour as expressions of a constitutive otherness. However, scholars rarely touch the problematic question of in what respect the possessed actively shape these images, or possibly exercise anything similar to authorship. The bodily state of possession is associated with 'passiones' (rather than agency) — the exposure to an unintended mode of action.[1] But who actually (re-)produces the alterity of possession, in what way, and what forms may the 'other' take? Do the possessed merely follow given stimuli or do they have a hand in the emergence of these figures?

To consider the agency of individuals who are regarded as driven by an exterior power may well challenge emic concepts of possession that imply the temporary suspension of the self (and consequently, amnesia). Moreover, it hints at the problematic assumptions of the

[1] The anthropological rediscovery of the concept of passiones goes back to Godfrey Lienhardt, and was put forward to make sense of the images created during possession episodes by Kramer (1993). Schnepel (2006: 125, 2008: 123–27, 2009) has applied the term to the analysis of Dando Nato (Daṇḍa Nāṭa) performances in Orissa.

Cartesian persona concept in Western culture. Here, mind and body are taken to represent intrinsically different faculties of the human being. There is a clear hierarchy of the cognizing mind and the inferior human body devoid of any expressiveness on its own, but rather shaped by cultural and social conditions. Indeed several studies on possession presume a specific (but basically unknown) psychophysical state that is conceived of in cultural terms as deity or spirit possession.[2] From this perspective, to abandon oneself to another force, intention or mood seems to call for an absolute surrender of the body. However, several forms of possession are known to provoke rather patterned forms of behaviour: the host will use highly stylized language, interrupt her or his performance whenever attendants bring offerings, etc. Thus scholars are drawn into obsolete discussions on the levels of 'dissociation', on the difference between possession and shamanism or as to the authenticity of the act. All these arguments collapse due to the naturalist paradigm, i.e., the assumption of a pre-discursive altered state of the body that comes prior to its cultural interpretation. To conceive of an altered state of *consciousness* is also problematic – it connects to religion as a system of belief. Defining religious practice as a result of (privatized) mental activity reflects a post-Enlightenment Christian approach to religiosity (Asad 1993: 45). This historically specific concept may fail to acknowledge the rationale of those forms of worship that are based on (politically informed) routines and embodiment rather than a certain form of awareness.

In anthropology, the approach to the study of possession is gradually changing in that scholars, inspired by phenomenologists like Maurice Merleau-Ponty (1962), fruitfully draw on the analytic concept of embodiment (see Csordas 1990). Michael Lambek (1989: 36), for instance, argues for a thorough 'cultural perspective' on possession that considers the sentient body itself as a mutable product of various historical and structural forces. Following Vincent Crapanzano and Vivian Garrison (1977), Lambek (1989: 45) assumes that possession constitutes a culture-specific system of communication that, by means of performative idioms, can penetrate virtually all areas of life, and thus cannot be reduced to a solely therapeutic, moral, subversive or artistic practice. In addition, he contends that even the seemingly physical dimension of this experiential state is culturally produced. In other

[2] This line of thinking was particularly pronounced by Bourguignon (1976), who distinguished the seemingly physical state of trance from its culture-specific interpretation as possession (for a critique, see Lambek 1989: 37–38).

words, the *perception*[3] of an exterior agent and the sensation of being taken over by that force are themselves brought about and defined by cultural discourse. As an embodied practice, possession is the result of inscribed cultural knowledge. Thus it can be neither reduced to 'natural' bodily symptoms nor to individual intention. In this way, Lambek's claim acknowledges the results of several ethnographic accounts, asking us to regard possession 'beyond instrumentality' (Boddy 1994).

One of the main values of looking at possession as a culturally produced experiential state is that it provides analytic scope for 'a degree of freedom on the part of the human subject' (Lambek 1989: 36). Taking seriously the presence of deities and spirits in the lived-in world, anthropologists may explore how individuals virtually sense, verbalize and experience possession. In other words, how they employ their body to consider respective cultural discourses. The aim of this chapter is to follow this line of thinking and to explore in what way women in Berhampur perceive and bring about the divine other.[4] How do they assess their own somatic reactions, taking into account popular knowledge on Hindu goddesses and on the communication between human and divine beings? I focus on the evaluation of divine presence, i.e., the deciphering of stimuli that is also a way of directing attention and giving way to the agentive dimension of the body. What does the corresponding divine version of human femininity look like? What are the ritual preconditions that encourage women's psychophysical encounters with non-human beings? How do individual experiences resonate with culturally pre-given notions of deity possession? Finally, I wish to reflect on whether and how this bodily experience of radical alterity contributes to verify female identity. It will be shown that rather than being an individual role-play of self and other, this religious practice serves as a paradigmatic way of realizing and sharing the divine generative power (*śakti*) for the benefit of the community.

In the following sections I return to the seasonal processions in honour of Buṙhī Ṭhākurāṇī that were briefly introduced in the last chapter. During these pageants women who carry a sacred pot formally represent the goddess. Some of them may encounter divine possession. I shall focus on two female mediums and their personal experiences while being possessed by a *ṭhākurāṇī*. I assume that the

[3] According to Merleau-Ponty (1962), perception is a *behaviour* produced not by consciousness but by the lived-in body.

[4] An earlier version of this chapter was published in German (Hauser 2004b).

impulses to which they abandon themselves are part of their own lived-in reality.[5] However, it will be shown that the objectification of divine possession is not only a private matter (or a culturally learned 'mental disposition'), but also requires the reconfirmation by religious specialists and devotees alike. In fact, everyone present – whether a family member, a passer-by or a resident – participates in this process, and thus for her or his part contributes to the emergence and authentication of the goddess present. At times, the manifestation of the divine is challenged for religio-political and also very everyday reasons. I argue that deity possession, understood as an embodied practice, is subjected not only to collective exegesis but is intrinsically prone to raise doubts. This *local* verification shows that although divine presence is objectified as a state accessible in social reality, there is no 'emic' rationale to distinguish 'genuine' possession from 'pretense'. Rather, the personification of a *ṭhākurāṇī* is ambivalent: whether an external agent drives the respective woman or she rather actively 'concentrates on the goddess' – and in doing so recalls and re-enacts cultural tropes – escapes the limited capacity of *human* onlookers.

## The Aesthetics of Guise and Disguise

The hot season, and basically the month of *caitra* (March/April), is commonly associated with goddesses classified as *ṭhākurāṇī*. Their hot temper matches a seasonal climate that demands human adjustments – even in the way goddesses are venerated. If not cooled down, they may bring illness, misfortune, disaster, and catastrophe. One way to reassure divine benevolence is to celebrate a procession in honour of these goddesses, and in Berhampur these pageants are dedicated to Buṛhī Ṭhākurāṇī. They are performed on Tuesdays (*maṅgaḷabāra*), the most adequate day to worship such powerful goddesses. Similar to other ritual functions, these processions are known and named by their date, i.e., as *caitra maṅgaḷabāra*. Otherwise, they are termed as a 'pageant' or rather 'journey' (*yātrā*) of Buṛhī Ṭhākurāṇī. Since there is also a biennial festival by the same name (Ṭhākurāṇī Yātrā), here I prefer to speak of 'Tuesday Pageants'. The analysis in this chapter is based on 20 of these pageants that were performed in the years 2000 and 2001. I did not always observe the complete procedure, but while following one procession through the lanes of Berhampur, I could also

[5] However, the subjective reality of deity or spirit possession is as difficult to verify as sensual experiences such as 'true' love and 'real' pain.

watch similar processions on the route. All groups visited a number of goddess temples in order to finally reach the Buṙhī Ṭhākurāṇī temple of Berhampur (see Plate 5.5). At times, Tuesday Pageants had to queue up in front of the temple premises so that the previous group could complete the rituals. Moreover, close to this major temple, the number and density of divine possessions was highest.

To celebrate a Tuesday Pageant is one of the more elaborate and costly forms of Hindu worship, similar to the conducting of a pilgrimage or an animal sacrifice. Generally it is performed by the extended family whenever there is need for divine support, for instance in the case of a prospective wedding or in connection with a religious pledge (*mānasika*). Besides, the Tuesday Pageant may also prevent the disturbance of the family by ancestral spirits who died prematurely due to smallpox (regarded as Buṙhī Ṭhākurāṇī's children). They constitute a class of ambiguous supernatural beings or demigods (*sajība debatā*, literally: enlivened deity) that is both feared and worshipped. Once these uncanny spirits are contented they may prove to be powerful guardians of the family.[6] The head of the family usually takes the initiative to conduct the procession. He or she will consult the priests of the Buṙhī Ṭhākurāṇī temple in the old town, barbers by caste (Bhaṇḍārī). The priest is asked to organize the procession, i.e., to hire dancers and musicians, to perform the required rituals and also to accompany the procession. Depending on financial resources and the size of the family, the Tuesday Pageant will consist of only one or several women carrying sacred pots, and also vary in the number of giant masks and decorative extras. Since each of these pots is delivered to one *ṭhākurāṇī* temple, the number of pots defines the length, route and duration of the procession. Unlike a pilgrimage, an animal sacrifice or other methods of assuring divine benevolence, the procession explicitly aims to catch the attention of onlookers. Its main purpose is to be aesthetically pleasing, not only to devotees but above all to the goddess herself. Similar to the performance of religious plays, the Tuesday Pageant should make her happy. This may happen with a minimum of one sacred pot (bearer). The most elaborate procession I joined, however, consisted of seven pots and continued for about eight hours.

On the agreed Tuesday, the Bhaṇḍārī priest will construct a temporary altar on the premises of his client. In a preliminary ritual he

[6] As in the case of Nirmala's possession by Bāidhara, described in the previous chapter.

will 'install' the divine essence or power (*śakti*) in, to take an average number, two new and richly decorated earthen pots. Each of them has to be taken by a married woman of the family (i.e., a daughter-in-law, mother or aunt). These two women will observe a fast, dress in a (possibly) new sari and, as in other rituals, walk barefoot. On behalf of their entire (joint) family, they will carry the pots on their head and distribute them one by one at the temple of a goddess. Although their role is crucial to the performance of a Tuesday Pageant, the majority of participants are men. At the head of the procession (Plate 5.1) there are one or more dancers with giant *ṭhākurāṇī*-masks, followed by several drummers, who belong to previously untouchable castes (Hāṙi, Bāurī). In their midst there is a ritual specialist dressed up as Kāḷī. He directs the married women who carry the sacred pots. Behind these women, the remaining family members follow, mostly walking in gender-specific groups. Some women may carry additional offerings.

**Plate 5.1:** A Tuesday Pageant with two giant *ṭhākurāṇī*-masks, a ritual specialist in the costume of Kāḷī (here unmasked) and two married women carrying sacred pots

During the procession proper, which will last two to three hours (often exposed to the heat of the midday sun), some of the pot bearers experience a bodily transformation that is understood to mean they have been overpowered by a *ṭhākurāṇī*. The pot bearer is identified with the goddess. In general, this type of possession is welcomed and raises the auspiciousness (*śubha*) of the event. However, the efficacy of the procession is not dependent on deity possession. Even without any change in the bodily state of the pot bearer, she is considered as a personification of the goddess. As argued in the last chapter, divine possession is a religious idiom of its own that may occur during different rituals. It is an optional reaction while being exposed to divine power. Accordingly, it would be misleading to conceive of the Tuesday Pageant as a 'possession cult'. Unlike other ritual settings that invoke deity possession, the Tuesday Pageant stands out since it includes various methods of embodying the divine, varying from play-acting during the masquerade (see *a*, *b*), formal representation of the goddess legitimized by priestly preparations (see *b*, *c*), to the personification of the divine in the body of the pot bearer (see *c*):

(*a*) Those men who lead the procession hidden by huge figures should attract and entertain people. Their giant masks are about 1.3 meters in height and show the goddess' face (and a nimbus behind), torso and four arms holding different kinds of divine weapons. Painted in bright colours, they represent Buṛhī Ṭhākurāṇī (red), Kāḷikā (blue), Śyāmakāḷī (black), Kanaka Durgā (yellow) and other forms of *ṭhākurāṇī*. The deity's skirt covers the person who carries the whole construction on his shoulders. He will orient himself by looking through a small window in the upper part of the goddess' body. To carry and dance with – or rather below – these masks is heavy work and performed by men of lower castes. Their dance adds to the beauty of the procession and should please the goddess, in her ephemeral and manifest version embodied by the pot bearers.[7]

(*b*) The ritual specialist who is costumed as the goddess Kāḷī inhabits an intermediate position. He wears a black skirt, a colourful bib, a necklace of (wooden) skulls and, rising up from

[7] There is no generic term for these dancers and their masks. Both of them can be addressed as *beśa*, literally 'masquerade', 'costume', 'appearance'. This term is used in reference to the ritual specialist dressed up as Kāḷī and for other types of masquerades as well (see Chapter 7).

back, a decorated flat construction that frames his head like a triangle-shaped nimbus (Plate 5.2). He also employs a smaller type of mask as an instrument to hide and reveal his own or

**Plate 5.2:** Kāḷī, impersonated by a dancing ritual specialist

Kāḷī's face. When the Kāḷī impersonator starts to dance, the procession regularly comes to halt. He attracts everybody's attention with a very well-choreographed performance that has lots of acrobatic elements. Encouraged by the intense beating of drums, he jumps here and there, and also twirls around faster and faster. He does the splits, bends forward and uses his mouth to pick up banknotes from the ground. His spectacular dance easily motivates onlookers to place another Rupee note on the road. However, the person who is dressed up as Kāḷī also has a ritual function. He actually belongs to the priests' family. Dancing to please the goddess, he maintains eye contact with the pot bearer. While pulling the mask in front of his face, he communicates with her in a non-verbal way. At times, the dancing Kāḷī succeeds in infecting the pot bearer with the desire to dance as well, and thus induces divine possession. Then he will ask the living goddess about her identity and also transmit her utterances and their meanings to other devotees. He will also safely guide the erratic body through the streets, specifically when there is heavy traffic. As a mediator of divine words, devotees come to wash his feet.

(*c*) The most crucial role with respect to the purpose of the Tuesday Pageant is that of the pot bearer. Each of these women occupies a double role. On behalf of the family she delivers a sacred pot to the temple. Upon her arrival, she will take three circuits around the sanctum of the goddess before she places the pot in front of Bāidhara. Being Buṙhī Ṭhākurāṇī's son he is, like any victim of smallpox, worshipped at a tree or shrine within the premises of the goddess' temple. Finally the woman will enter the main temple building, bow down, and at the feet of the 'Mother' surrender herself and ask for divine blessing. Hence, she maintains and renews the links between a family, including their *sajība debatā* and the tutelary goddess of Berhampur.

Yet the pot bearers are not only mediators essential to the guaranteeing of divine benevolence, they also personify the goddess. From the perspective of devotees, a pot bearer serves as a living sanctified representation of the deity and receives the same attention as an idol in the temple – both embody the divine and are ritually validated by the priest's ceremonial acts. Neighbours and passers-by may come and show their respect to *ṭhākurāṇī*. Devotees wash the feet of the living goddess with

> purified water.[8] They may place the loose end of their sari on the road so that the divine feet can walk on it. Infants are made to lie down and the goddess steps over them without doing them any harm. In this way, devotees show their submission to the divine and the goddess proves her grace. If the pot bearer starts to move in an unusual fashion, she is considered possessed by the goddess. 'The Almighty came', people will comment, 'she will dance' (*mahāpuru āsile . . . nācibe*). Thus the devotees regard the woman who carries the sacred pot not only as a *living form* of the goddess but also identify her behaviour as a result of divine agency. Nobody would think of her actions as play-acting. However, even without this visible bodily transformation, the pot bearer is worshipped as the goddess. The interruption by deity possession may last for a few minutes or continue until the pageant reaches the *ṭhākurāṇī*-temple. In this case, once in front of the altar, i.e., after the woman is released from the obligation to carry the sacred pot, she will gradually regain her consciousness and bodily self-control.

Similar to forms of religious drama, the Tuesday Pageant is characterized by the intermingling of artful play and divine manifestation.[9] As a religious act that should please the goddess, the performance requires decorative and entertaining elements; these features again stimulate the ritual transformation of the pot bearer. It is the concept of dance (*nāca*) that interlinks these modes of divine guise and disguise. Although classified as dance, the goddess' embodiment varies not only in its implications but also in structure and kinetic respects. Whereas both the religious specialist in the Kāḷī costume and the performers below the figurative masks move their bodies (more or less) according to choreographed steps and turns, the 'dance' of the possessed pot bearers is comparatively abrupt, unsystematic and arbitrary (yet also patterned, as I will argue later). Some women proceed straight ahead

---

8 Some women mix water with turmeric that is considered pure and 'cooling', and thus serves as an appropriate substance to appease a goddess.

9 On the emergence of divine presence during Rāmlīḷā performances in Orissa, see Hauser (2006c). Compare Caldwell (1999), Hauser (2008a) and R. Freeman (1993, 1999) for intermingling realities produced by other forms of ritual theatre. On the notion of play (*līḷā*, Hindi: *līlā*) that refers to both stage performance and the essential mode of divine action, see Sax (1995a).

with glassy eyes, some lurch or tremble, some grimace with pain, some keep on nodding their head, some close their eyes, and some shriek or cry. In one procession, the pot bearer started to run, got ahead of the Kāḷī impersonator and the mask dancers, and everybody had to rush after the goddess. At another Tuesday Pageant, the possessed woman jumped wildly up and down, causing her breasts, although more or less hidden by her sari, to swing to and fro in a rather conspicuous manner. Thus the dance of possessed women differs widely, not only from the pre-given steps of the male performers but also from the accepted ideal of female behaviour. The pot bearers seem to lose self-control and behave in a manner they would not contemplate otherwise. Yet, here transgression is regarded as proof of the divine – the goddess herself is dancing.

Summing up, the festive and ritual context of the Tuesday Pageant invites different kinds of identification with the goddess. Although differing in appearance and dynamics, the bodily movements of both the possessed women and also the costumed male performers are classified as a dance. However, the *same* bodily features that in the case of the pot bearers signify divine presence may also hint at malevolent forms of possession. If *spectators* of a Tuesday Pageant start to shake and roll their eyes, the attendant priest will intervene and remove the unwanted supernatural force from the respective woman or man. He will sprinkle some sacred water on their face, speak some ritual formulas (*mantra*) or make them smell red *mandāra* flowers, i.e., he will employ measures to 'cool' the excessively 'hot' body that had attracted the goddess or another other spirit by mistake. As already mentioned, the boundary between ghosts (*bhūta*), spirits of deceased ancestors (*sajība debatā*) and deities (*ṭhākura, ṭhākurāṇī*) is neither impermeable nor permanent. Rather, spontaneous possession of persons who are not ritually prepared is considered inauspicious and malevolent.

## Mimesis and Embodiment

If possession is not only understood as a social phenomenon but also as an embodied practice, the question arises as to whether and in what way a person may feel that she or he is being overpowered. How do women, while carrying the sacred pot on their head, sense and realize the divine presence? The respective criteria are commonly known: the pot bearer should concentrate on the goddess and emotionally surrender to the divine power, and she will then gradually lose consciousness. She won't notice the heavy smoke from glowing resin (*jhūṇā*) near her face, the energetic and penetrating sound of drums or the burning heat of the midday sun. There won't be any thirst or hunger. The 'heaviness' of the sacred pot will cause the body to tremble. Afterwards, the possessed person will not be able to remember anything and will feel very tired. In spite of this general knowledge concerning the divine encounter, bodily behaviour and experiences of possessed women do vary.[10] It is not unusual for them to recall the situation at least in part. Besides, there is a degree of uncertainty as to the somatic reactions upon the invocation of the divine. The following two case studies will show how women do perceive and make sense of their psychophysical state, and thus objectify goddess possession.

### *Basanti*

Basanti and her husband make their living by running a tea-stall.[11] They have four children. Every year, residents in their neighbourhood jointly finance and conduct a Tuesday Pageant. In the year 2000, this procession served to deliver altogether seven sacred pots to different goddess temples in Berhampur. Apart from the obligatory ritual specialist dressed up as Kāḷī, there were three masked dancers representing Buṙhī Ṭhākurāṇī, Śẏāmakāḷī and a ghost (*bhūta*). At this procession, married women from different castes carried the sacred pots on behalf of the entire neighbourhood rather than for their family only. 37-year-old Basanti was one of them. She had already performed this ritual role for 12 years, but this was the first time she had been possessed.[12] When I met her a few days after the pageant and asked about her encounter with the divine, Basanti could remember her bodily reactions fairly well (although initially, she claimed amnesia). While she concentrated on the goddess, and also due to the intense drumming, she got goose bumps. The power of the goddess entered her body 'like a wind' from the sacred pot above her head through the raised arms. She felt very heavy. Basically, Basanti recognized two

[10] The analysis of goddess possession during Tuesday Pageants is based on a series of narrative interviews with five pot bearers. I verified their statements and experiences by consulting two priests, one drummer and two ritual specialists who regularly take the role of Kāḷī.

[11] They were Oṛiā by caste (*jāti*); in earlier times, the family earned their living with pottery.

[12] Yet she was regularly possessed by the Vaishnava deity Narasiṃha (see Chapter 4).

sequences when she felt overpowered by the goddess, lasting a few minutes each. She also noticed which of her neighbours had come to wash her (or the goddess') feet.

After participating in the Tuesday Pageant for so many years, Basanti had challenged the goddess to reveal herself.

> When we reached the beginning of this street, I called upon her. At that time she came. Then near this *pūjā* tent, I again called her to find out whether it was really her who had come. This time she appeared in an angry [*rāgi*] form. Later on, I did not call her anymore because we were about to leave our street. My body was very heavy. Therefore I didn't call her.

In Basanti's view, the goddess showed her mercy (*daẏā*) by coming to her body. As her statement shows, she was not certain as to the facticity of goddess possession and reassured herself by calling upon her a second time. Then her body (i.e., the goddess) was weeping rather than showing signs of anger. However, at the beginning Basanti was not at all sure which supernatural power had taken her body. Since she had called upon Buṙhī Ṭhākurāṇī, she assumed that the goddess would reveal her wild or angry form. When the ritual specialist in the Kāḷī costume started to inquire about the divine intention, there was as yet no complaint from the goddess. Later Basanti learned that the goddess had cried. After consulting her neighbours, she identified the possessor as Kānduri Mā, literally the 'Crying Mother', a form of Buṙhī Ṭhākurāṇī (Plate 5.3).

### Sujata

Sujata, a 33-year-old widow,[13] had initiated and organized a Tuesday Pageant by herself in order to fulfill a religious pledge (*mānasika*) to the goddess Tārā-Tāriṇī, the tutelary deity of her family (*iṣṭadebatā*) and considered another *ṭhākurāṇī*. After the untimely death of her husband, Sujata had pleaded to Tārā-Tāriṇī for help in finding a permanent job to make a living for her two children and herself. The goddess succeeded in providing employment with the municipal cleansing department of Berhampur. Since Sujata's family belongs to the formerly untouchable caste of sweepers (Hāṙi), to collect the rubbish from the

---

[13] According to orthodox Hindus, widows are not eligible to represent the goddess. Several women still do, and not all of them are of low-caste status.

**Plate 5.3:** Possession by Kânduri Mā, the Crying Mother

streets was considered a suitable job. To express her gratitude, Sujata invested five month's salary to conduct a procession that, unlike the common pattern, started from the temple and finished in her home. In the early morning hours, Sujata and her relatives had visited the Tārā-Tāriṇī temple about 35 kilometers away.[14] There, priests had invoked the divine power in two betel nuts, placed in a basket with flowers in order to be taken back home. After arriving in Berhampur, this basket was taken in a procession through the neighborhood and finally served to 'install' the goddess in Sujata's house.

Sujata was not only the sponsor of the Tuesday Pageant, she also carried the sacred basket. Everything was prepared with the greatest care: Sujata was dressed in a red sari and, at the beginning of the procession, had let down her hair so that her appearance already alluded to a *ṭhākurāṇī*. Some male relatives were dressed completely in black. When the goddess, alias Sujata, started walking with the basket on her head, these men raised a sari cloth like a shield above her. Some other saris were put on the floor like a red carpet. Two men with *ṭhākurāṇī*-masks and the Kāḷī impersonator danced in front. Every detail was arranged according to the goddess' liking, for instance using her favourite colours red and black. Most of the time, Sujata walked calmly and with half-closed eyes. She appeared slightly absent. In her hand she held a bunch of peacock feathers. Every once in a while she employed this whisk to bless devotees who had gathered from the neighbourhood. She also began to speak in tongues and thus answered questions raised by women attending the procession. While doing so, the incarnated divinity complained about the inadequate worship that was offered to her — a criticism taken personally by several of the women around. The goddess gnashed her teeth in anger, took the peacock feather whisk and lashed about her. Suddenly, Sujata's mother was possessed as well and both goddesses began 'dancing' with rage (Plate 5.4).

A few days later, Sujata was not able to recall the procedure of the Tuesday Pageant. According to her recollection of events, Tārā-Tāriṇī had overwhelmed her for the whole procession, i.e., for more than one hour. Sujata could not remember anything. Unlike Basanti, Sujata

---

[14] On Tuesdays in the month of *caitra*, the Tārā-Tāriṇī temple celebrates its annual festival and is filled by thousands of pilgrims. Strictly speaking, Tārā-Tāriṇī is a twin goddess characterized by the combined worship of Tara and Tarini (cf. Fischer and Pathy 1996: 35).

**Plate 5.4:** Possession by Tārā-Tāriṇī and, in front, Durgā

did not trace the transformation of her mind and body to a specific somatic feeling; rather it seemed to be a result of lifting the sacred basket on her head. She obviously related her experiential state to the mimesis of divine behaviour, i.e., a form of embodiment that escapes assessment in terms of play-acting since it creates a reality of its own rather than an (aesthetic) illusion. Yet Sujata also emphasized her communication with the goddess. Upon my question about the possibility of the goddess failing to appear, she explains:

> We would think, we have brought you here [addressing the goddess] bearing so much pain and you didn't come to our bodies. By coming to our body, if you could tell us something, then we would be very happy. Why don't you show up? . . . We would doubt whether the goddess had come with us [i.e., from the temple] . . . I would try out all possible means of calling her into my body. I would cry and call her, then she would definitely come.

As mentioned, to cry while embodying the goddess can enable onlookers to recognize the divine presence.[15] Thus crying is both a method to invoke possession and simultaneously proof of being possessed.

Apart from some general knowledge about common signs of deity possession, the religious performance itself provides scope for individual interpretation and also for confusion. The duration of possession can vary and also the character and intensity of its somatic experience, i.e., whether the *śakti* enters the body via hands or head, or to what extent it is related to feeling at all. Moreover, the expressiveness of the medium's body differs in its potential to allude to specific goddesses. Non-semantic bodily behaviour that escapes the assumed divine code of conduct, however, risks remaining unnoticed. Thus possessed women do not merely lose self-control. Rather they act in specific ways that resonate to well-known qualities and images of a goddess. In this respect, the pot bearer needs to meet the expectations of onlookers. After all, they have to be certain about the divine presence as well. With regard to a different tradition of deity possession, Richard Freeman (1993: 134) has put this nicely: 'To be possessed means to perform the possession rituals correctly and manifest possession behaviour'.

The fuzzy memories of being overwhelmed seem to be adjusted in retrospective to cultural norms about divine possession. The relevance and meaning of the pot bearer's bodily reactions emerge largely from conversations with family members, neighbours and ritual specialists. As mentioned earlier, this will contribute to identifying a goddess as Kānduri Mā or also to reconsider personal feelings during the Tuesday Pageant. In one conversation with Sujata about her feelings right after

---

15 Compare Schömbucher (2006: 130–31) for similar descriptions of deity possession by four Telugu-speaking mediums.

the procession, she expressed her ease once she had regained control of her self and body. Immediately her mother interrupted by prompting the immense exhaustion of her daughter – here rhetoric to authenticate the divine presence. Therefore, only those sensations which match the standardized descriptions of possession get emphasized. Finally, these memories will constitute the background of any further bodily encounter of the divine. They might also contribute towards a more refined expressiveness of the body that, after all, brings about those reactions identified with the agency of a goddess. Conversely, singular and individual bodily expressions of the pot bearer could also turn into behaviour associated with a *ṭhākurāṇī*. At times these forms may achieve semiotic character and thus become normative (like weeping).

Women objectify the otherness of their possession behaviour in religious terms. Whether they burst into tears or lash out wildly, it is not recognized with reference to their own self (or as a symptom of suffering or anger), but as proof of a non-human agent taking possession of living carnal vessels. 'It is because of the *bhakti* that she is coming', I was told. Neither Basanti nor Sujata were embarrassed or ashamed when looking at photographs that were taken by me during the possession episode. Although from my perspective their bodies were twisted or disfigured in some of the pictures, both women only recognized features of the goddess. The correspondence of their own facial expression with divine emotions made them happy (*khusi*). However, to identify the transgressive behaviour as an index of divine presence – to see the goddess rather than one's own self – was possible only due to the ritual framework of the Tuesday Pageant, initiated by the invocation of the goddess' power. According to the rationale of possession, the divine will manifest itself neither outside ritual nor in human beings against their will.

Subsequently, women will achieve the ability to sense divine possession. They will acquire basic knowledge about possessive deities, the permeability of the human body, and factors that influence the evaluation and assessment of possession episodes. Whether actively or passively involved, women thus shape a discourse that defines the quality of possession experiences. To make it clear, I do not conceive of these women as self-reflexive creators, although in principle they *could* also act strategically; rather they absorb and put into practice only those notions and aspects of deity possession that seem comprehensible to them on the basis of their own relationship with the lived-in world.

## The Negotiation of Divine Agency

The facticity of divine overpowering does not only derive from embodied notions concerning the permeability of the self and, equally important, the possessive character of female goddesses. It also results from pragmatic and non-religious intentions. Even among devotees, who would consult a medium to get divine advice, there are at times doubts as to the change in persona of the possessed. This ambivalence occurs first at the time of selecting a suitable woman to carry the sacred pot. Young and newly married wives are generally denied this honour. According to the priests of the Buṙhī Ṭhākurāṇī temple, the basic reason is that their possible loss of self-control should not be exposed in public. In this case, the transgression associated with the goddess would leave a stain on a woman's reputation. This risk, however, shows that the distinction of social persona and divine agent is not that clear. The status of a new daughter-in-law is still so fragile that it could be challenged by possession behaviour. In fact, the ritual task of carrying the pot on behalf of the family is mostly given to women who, due to age, sons or any other means, have already gained a respected position.[16] Similarly, the change in persona becomes blurred when the pot bearer belongs to the Scheduled Castes. Extreme differences in social status influence the acknowledgement of divine presence in that some devotees will hesitate or even abstain from washing the feet of the goddess. The only people who performed this ritual service for Sujata, alias Tārā-Tāriṇī, were Sujata's relatives.

Moreover, there are also occasions when the divine presence is challenged in a direct way. Whereas devotees often refrain from expressing their doubts openly – often in fear of divine anger – the priest and also the Kāḷī impersonator may test the medium. They will hide a small item in one hand and ask the pot bearer to identify this object. Unless the woman has the correct intuition and thus proves her divine power, she is asked to stop 'dancing unnecessarily' so that the procession may proceed without delay. At any rate, the emergence of deity possession is not imperative for the ritual success of a Tuesday Pageant.

[16] Contrary to the deprivation theory, which regards possession as a subaltern strategy to challenge hegemonic structures of power (see Chapter 4), the voiceless women of a family may not even get the chance to carry the sacred pot.

The latter is achieved by the beauty and appeal of the procession. In other words, even the faked dance of a pot bearer will contribute to the entertainment of the goddess, just like the choreographed steps of the dancing Kāḷī or the giant *ṭhākurāṇī*-masks. Only human beings who ridicule the power of a deity may fear her divine punishment. From the perspective of devotees who come to bow down before the goddess, the efficacy of worship is dependent neither on the form of embodiment nor on the authenticity of deity possession.

In some cases, however, divine possession is denied for pragmatic reasons. As mentioned earlier in this discussion, priests of the Buṙhī Ṭhākurāṇī temple, barbers (Bhaṇḍārī) by caste, are in charge of organizing Tuesday Pageants (Plate 5.5). They not only offer their priestly services for the proper conduct of the procession, but also send a younger member of their family to dance in the Kāḷī costume. Besides this, they also make, store and rent a variety of *ṭhākurāṇī* masks/figures, for which they hire carriers from the lower castes. In short, directing Tuesday Pageants provides a substantial seasonal income for the priests and their family. Therefore the attending priest also has an economic interest in a spectacular Tuesday Pageant. If the pot bearer gets possessed, he may reassure a skeptical husband or worried relatives so as to encourage their cooperation. He will emphasize the heightened religious experience for onlookers, while considering that the divine presence may also attract new clients. However, there are only a limited number of Tuesdays in the month of *caitra*. Therefore the priests will accept two or even three bookings on the same day. In this case, the Kāḷī impersonator will try to avoid any delay in the procession, even those caused by a (truly) dancing goddess.

No matter whether the goddess manifests herself in a human form or not, the event can be explained in both a positive and a negative way. There is a system of assumptions that guides the evaluation. Thus Buṙhī Ṭhākurāṇī may appear: (*a*) for pleasure and as a sign of her grace; (*b*) upon the call of a sincere devotee; (*c*) due to little or careless worship; and (*d*) due to mistakes in the performance of the ritual. The goddess will select a specific human host: (*i*) if the person is very pious; (*ii*) if she invites divine manipulation; and (*iii*) if she shares her bodily substance. This bodily similarity may originate in the female sex, a 'hot' humoral disposition or the consumption of meat. 'Flesh-eating' (*āmiṣa*) people will attract possession because, according to cosmological constructs, the preference for meat is related to a moral and bodily

**Plate 5.5:** Buṛhī Ṭhākurāṇī in her temple, attended by Bhaṇḍārī priests

disposition,[17] and thus invites non-human beings to take over. These parameters (*a–d*, *i–iii*) outline a discursive field to discuss divine agency and, conversely, reduce the unpredictability of communicating with supernatural entities to only a few factors of influence. The goddess' agency becomes calculable. Moreover, since the goddess can be flattered by 'look-alikes', she is, just like human beings, seducible. The relevance of bodily similarity as the major precondition of divine possession does still create a paradox. The mere sight of a pot bearer and her representative function do not offer any clues as to the agency of either the goddess or the respective woman. Divine manifestation and human creation cannot be differentiated. The opening of the hair bun and also the act of weeping are ambiguous acts in respect to the pot bearer and her condition.

The power to verify the state of possession is not limited to only one person. Even the priest or the dancer dressed up as Kāḷī need the (non-verbal) response of other participants, who may bow down or, conversely, ignore the pot bearer completely. The convincing bodily transformation of the pot bearer, the devotional expressions of passers-by and the enthusiastic dance of the Kāḷī performer mutually and interactively contribute to the realization of divine possession. Virtually everybody can participate in this process, although with varying degrees of authority and bodily impetus. The possession of Sujata's mother, for instance, was not anticipated by the ritual preparations. However, before the priest could intervene, Tārā-Tāriṇī, alias Sujata, had already started to communicate with the other entity and thus proved her divine status. Later the possessing force that 'danced' the mother was identified as Durgā.[18]

[17] This *lāñcuā* (*lāñchuā*, *nāñchuā*) disposition was commonly associated with, but not limited to the female gender. The etymology of the term is obscure. The adjective alludes to demanding and tempting bodies; some people suggested that it means 'bribable'. It was considered an inherited and permanent quality with a slightly negative connotation. A *lāñcuā* body was not related to factors such as caste, class, personality, age or purity. On related cosmological constructs on women's vulnerability to possession by supernatural powers, see Kapferer (1983: 137); Osella and Osella (1999).

[18] This *shared* production of the divine presence differs from those religious performances in which a priest or shaman has to convince the audience about the authenticity of the ceremony by means of his acting. As Schieffelin (1996) rightly argued, these events are risky and may also fail.

## Conclusion: Bodies Beyond the Self

On the previous pages I have demonstrated how deity possession is not only based on a culturally shaped sensorium, creating a lived-in body that is driven by an exterior force; it also emerges from social negotiation. In this respect, the embodiment of possession is only one side of the coin. The subjective experience has to resonate to the interests and expectations of onlookers who confirm the facticity of this condition. In Chapter 4 I had argued that the religious idiom of divine possession is challenged on the basis of a religio-political discourse. However, a close look at the communicative process involved in the emergence of divine presence reveals that deity possession is inherently contested. This experiential state always requires verification by other people and thus is likely to provoke competing views. To put it the other way around: without some doubts among onlookers regarding a particular divine manifestation, the discourse on deity possession may not emerge in its complexities. Unlike criticisms on the religious significance of deity possession by Brahmins or 'modernists', this social process does not cause any disbelief as to the *possibility* of divine manifestation in and through the human body.

Despite the suggestions contained in theories on the nexus of possession and alterity (mentioned at the beginning of this chapter), it would be misleading to conceive of possession episodes in southern Orissa as a social meta-commentary on women's identity, on femininity or on their self-understanding in relation to the lived-in world. The extraordinary behaviour of possessed pot bearers does not emphasize unspeakable aspects of social reality, nor does the expressivity of the body serve as an instrument with which to act out alternative self-images. In southern Orissa, the creation of divine characters is hardly an adequate cultural field to embody forbidding and intriguing otherness.[19] The personification of a deity within a ritual context doesn't really provide the opportunity to consider the *converse* character of the self and the 'other'.[20] Rather, this body practice – and

[19] Thus deity possession in Orissa differs from those theatrical forms that in some African spirit worlds visualize the alterity of colonial regimes or ultimate modernity, classified by Kramer (1993) as 'Fremdbesessenheit', literally: alien spirit possession (cf. Behrend and Luig 1999).

[20] Since during fieldwork I came to know about malevolent forms of possession only occasionally, I do not feel competent to consider in what respect this unwanted form could serve as a cultural vehicle to verify self-identity. At any

its mimetic account of emotions, features and preferences – may be seen as revealing and negotiating the *similarities* that exist between mortal women and goddesses. If relating the possessed body to its non-possessed counterpart at all, the divine feminine visualizes a hypothetical essence of womanhood rather than its constitutive otherness. Goddesses are regarded as categorically, but not intrinsically, different from women. For instance, creativity (at least in a reproductive sense) and anger are thought to be typically female traits (see Nandy 1980: 42). From this angle, deity possession could be seen as a bodily discipline that (re-)enacts and verifies this similarity. Moreover, goddesses are treated like close (rather than alien) social beings who interact with mortal hosts and their families. Women maintain consistent relationships with deities, not only during rituals but also in everyday domestic life. The goddess may become a dear friend. 'She would come (to my body) so that I know that she is there with me', Basanti explains.

Strictly speaking, deity possession is not at all about the self, about self-reflexivity or about individual experience. Being taken over by a non-human agent and thus acting in a more or less unusual way does not provoke any thoughts on the personality and psyche of possessed women – apart from general views on the disposition and seductiveness of the female body. Rather this ritual practice transmits religious knowledge in a theatrical form. The manifestation of divine alterity is understood in its representational character; it is the non-individual semiotic body of the host that is given emphasis. It displays what a goddess may look like (loose hair), her moods (anger, excessive energy) and taste (blood and any red items).[21] The mimetic accuracy in transmitting these features may vary. Whereas Basanti's reactions served as the basis on which to identify divine presence in general, Sujata's possession alluded to familiar iconography. What at first sight appeared to me as a highly predetermined and controlled incident, invited devotees to ask the medium for divine advice. The registration suggested her proficiency in giving way to the goddess. Furthermore, possession episodes transmit formal and aesthetic features that cause this particular bodily condition (like the smoke of resin or a drum rhythm), and also those characteristics that reveal the divine power (anesthesia, amnesia, etc.). In principle, possessed men share this

rate, the bodily expressiveness of divine mediums and other persons suffering from malevolent possession differed only slightly.

21 Male deities and their iconographic marks are visualized in a similar fashion.

bodily inventory, although in different ritual contexts. To sum up, the creation of divine presence by means of the human body is an essentially formalized 'genre', comparable with forms of possession which emphasize the *verbal* communication of religious knowledge (see Schömbucher 2006). Neither divine voice nor divine choreography alludes to the individual who serves as the deity's vessel. Accordingly, mediums remain unaffected by their physical exposure in the course of possession. Whether inflamed with rage or bursting into tears, the subjective experience – the virtuality of ritual, in Kapferer's sense – does *not* spill over into reality.[22] Upon recalling the possession episode in retrospective, the 'autonomous' bodily experience escapes women's self-evaluation.

[22] For a brief discussion of the concept of virtuality and the impact of this perceptual situation on the transformative potential of rituals, see the Introduction to this book.

# 6

# Nocturnal Encounters: Living Mothers and Divine Daughters

Every second year, people in southern Orissa celebrate Ṭhākurāṇī Yātrā, a festival that lasts for about three weeks and attracts more than hundred thousand pilgrims and visitors. It takes place in honour of Buṛhī Ṭhākurāṇī, the tutelary deity of the city of Berhampur and one of the most popular goddesses of the region. According to legend (*kathā*), the festival signifies the goddess's visit to her parental home. Thus, she is transferred from her main temple in the old town to a temporary shrine at her 'father's place', the centre of worship during the festival. There is an elaborate ritual sequence associated with this visit, including regular nocturnal processions with sacred pots that allude to the goddess's circuits and appropriation of territory. This divine movement (*yātrā*) is the central feature of the festival and therefore synonymous with this event and its entertaining aspects.[1] Many streets in the old town are decorated and residents proudly present giant installations of divine characters (*ratha*, literally: chariot) and panoramas of mythological scenes (*kaḷākuñja*). Various types of dance and theatre are performed. There is also a huge fair with rides, food and souvenir stalls, magicians, spectacular exhibitions (among others, of embryos), acrobatic car driving, etc. Towards the end and climax of the festival more and more people visit Berhampur, offer their tribute to the goddess and enjoy themselves. By sunset the streets of the old town are packed. Several men put on a costume (*beśa*) – as a tiger, divine hero or lascivious monk – and mix with the crowd (see Chapter 7).

[1] Thus the term *yātrā* can be translated as 'journey', 'procession', 'festival', and also as 'pilgrimage' or 'theatre'.

The focus in this chapter will be on the regular processions that constitute Ṭhākurāṇī Yātrā.[2] Similar to other important ceremonies forming part of this festival, they take place at night. Moreover, women play a crucial part in the performance of these processions. While most of their roles are confined to a few selected members of the community, each and every female devotee might join the final procession of the festival and proceed through the streets of the town as a personification of the goddess herself. In 2001 about 10,000 women gathered, followed by masses of (predominantly male) spectators. This female primacy during the night contrasts with the general absence of women not only in nocturnal life, but also in the performance of public rituals. Here I shall discuss what qualifies women to engage in these nocturnal activities, and thus what kind of cultural knowledge about gender is produced and enacted in the course the festival. Emphasizing women's experiences during Ṭhākurāṇī Yātrā, I argue that the priority given to (earthly) female ritual roles and also to the (divine) female perspective creates an atmosphere that stimulates and encourages the self-esteem of women who actively participate in the worship of Buṛhī Ṭhākurāṇī, as pot bearers or as residential servants of the goddess.

However, the festival and the priority given to the hours of darkness also reveal some knowledge about the nature of a goddess classified as *ṭhākurāṇī* (literally: mistress, lady). As mentioned before, this type of goddess is feared for her anger, which might cause disease and calamities, and has to be appeased regularly in order to ensure her protective power. Similarly, Buṛhī Ṭhākurāṇī and her manifestations as Kāḷikā, Kanaka Durgā and Śyāma Kāḷī, or related goddesses such as Mā Maṅgaḷā, are ambivalent in character. Although conceived of as divine forces, they also allude to uncanny beings prone to disturbing people. With reference to Ṭhākurāṇī Yātrā it will be shown that the importance of nocturnal worship and also of women as mediators is related to the 'dark' quality of Buṛhī Ṭhākurāṇī, who 'travels through the night' (*niśācara*) and thus is very accessible to her devotees at that time. In this respect, the female participation in the festival is considered a communal service to guarantee the divine benevolence and thus well-being of the town.

## Ṭhākurāṇī Yātrā

At first glance, Ṭhākurāṇī Yātrā represents what Chris Fuller (1992: 131–42) has classified as a 'south Indian temple festival' — a collective

[2] This chapter is a largely extended version of a previous article (Hauser 2005).

celebration of a female village deity – that takes place during the hot season (preferably in the Hindu month of *caitra*), lasts for several days and culminates in an animal sacrifice. Its ritual tasks are shared systematically among different communities, with emphasis given to the dominant caste. Thus it serves as the principal event by which the residents identify themselves with the region that is protected and ruled by the goddess.

Indeed, Ṭhākurāṇī Yātrā is closely interwoven with the history of the locality and also its mixture of Oriya- and Telugu-speaking castes. Considering historical fragments and legendary events, the festival might have originated in the late eighteenth century.[3] In colonial reports, this period of initial British annexation of what came to be known as Ganjam District was characterized by political instability, rebellion and battles between local chiefs (Maltby 1967 [1882]: ix–x). Among others, the ruler (*rājā*) of a 'little kingdom' named Mahurī resisted paying tribute to the colonizers.[4] At this time, according to

[3] To my knowledge, all accounts of Ṭhākurāṇī Yātrā in English language are of recent date, e.g., a report in the *District Gazetteer of Orissa* (Behuria 1995: 243–45. See also Padhi 1979 as translated in Fischer and Pathy 1996: 220–21; and Rath 1987: 109–10). Besides these, several pious chroniclers (for instance Candra 1998, Pātra 1997, Ratha n.d.) describe the procedure of the festival in Oriya. However, rather than references to historical sources or the method of data collection, these booklets include prayers to the goddess and several exaggerations and inconsistencies in the content. Some of these publications are employed in the dispute about the correct performance of the festival (see Chapter 8). Even research scholars at the University of Berhampur in their brief discussions of the festival fail to assess their sources critically (see B. Das 1978: 159–62; Behera 1995: 198–203).

Rājaguru (1992 [1895]: vi–vii), who was based in Parlakimedi, i.e., south of Berhampur, does not explicitly mention Ṭhākurāṇī Yātrā in his early English account on *The Feasts and Fasts of the Uriyas*, though he briefly describes a pot festival: 'Ghata-Parvam . . . [i]s celebrated in honour of the village deity, on the safe return of someone of the family from a long journey or on the recovery from a protected [sic] illness. Coloured earthen pots with handfuls of rice inside and decorated with garlands of flowers are carried by *females* in great procession to the temple of the deity, where fowls and goats are sacrificed, while the pots with their contents are committed to the care of the temple servants.' (my emphasis) If this entry refers to Ṭhākurāṇī Yātrā at all (rather than to the Tuesday Pageant), it is a very general description. Yet following Rājaguru, female pot carriers are not a recent invention.

[4] In relation to other kingdoms in this region, such as Khurda, Jaẏpura (Jeypore) or Vizianagaram, Mahurī was rather small and marginal, but it had access to

one legend, the Mahurī Rājā travelled southwards to the realm of Rajamahendri[5] (Pātra 1997: 8–11).[6] When his royal host made him the gift of a silk cloth, the Mahurī Rājā was amazed by its quality and inquired about its origin. He learned that the fabric was woven by the Devāṅgī (Oriya: Ḍerā) and asked some of these Telugu weavers to migrate to Mahurī. They indeed seemed to have taken him up on his invitation and settled near the Mahurī fort.[7] Moreover, they brought their tradition of pot processions and started to conduct them in honour of the local goddess Buṙhī Ṭhākurāṇī.[8] However, whereas Satīśa Pātra (1997: 14) and others assume 1779 as the initial year of Ṭhākurāṇī

---

the sea and this allowed maritime trade. According to Schnepel (2002: 115), its territory measured 521 square miles (i.e., it corresponded to an area of 37 by 37 km). Although locally the ruler was classified as *rājā* (literally: king), to consider him as a royal power of pan-regional significance is misleading. For 'little kings' and 'jungle kings' in Orissa, see Berkemer (1993, 2004) and Schnepel (2002), for a critical response to this concept of kingship see R. P. Das (1997).

[5] In the present-day anglicized spelling: Rajahmundry (Andhra Pradesh).

[6] Whereas colonial sources identify this ruler as Narayana Deo (Maltby 1967 [1882]: ix), according to oral history he is Harihara Narendra Deba (Pātra 1997: 9).

[7] Considering the war-like situation not only in Mahurī but also in neighbouring kingdoms to the south (Berkemer 2004: 98; cf. Maltby 1967 [1882]), one may speculate about the nature of this visit and the weaver migration. Taking into account that in the eighteenth century the export of cloth was one of the major sources of income for local rulers (by means of taxes, see Berkemer 1993: 228), there may have been an ulterior motive for this 'invitation'. In any case, none of the stories about the origin of Ṭhākurāṇī Yātrā can be related to verifiable historical incidents.

[8] Strictly speaking, it is not that clear whether the Devāṅgī performed the pot processions in honour of their family deity (today identified as Buṙhī Ṭhākurāṇī), and thus transferred the goddess from Andhra to Orissa, or whether she was possibly the patroness of the Mahurī Rājā, i.e., a manifestation of Kaḷuā, who only later achieved the status of an independent deity. Indeed the mythology and iconography of both goddesses is very similar (see Schnepel 2002: 235). In both temples, the priests are recruited from the Oriya barber caste (Bhaṇḍārī). Yet the descendant of the Mahurī Rājā and also the priests in Berhampur's Buṙhī Ṭhākurāṇī temple both conceive of Buṙhī Ṭhākurāṇī as a goddess in her own right and deny any relationship to Mahurī Kaḷuā, who in the ritual calendar is honoured with another *yātrā*.

Whereas some academic scholars such as Rath (1987: 101) conceive of Buṙhī Ṭhākurāṇī as an 'autochthonous' goddess', originally worshipped by 'tribal people of hinterland Ganjam' and only later adopted into the Hindu pantheon, neither the legends about Ṭhākurāṇī Yātrā nor the kind of communities

Yātrā, it must have taken at least another 40 years before the festival could be performed regularly. Only after the disempowerment of local rulers by the British did the political and economic climate permit the establishment of a religious event of a larger size. Over time, the prosperous weaving industry contributed to the rise of Berhampur as a 'silk city', a success attributed to the power of Buṙhī Ṭhākurāṇī. By the beginning of the twentieth century, the fabrication of silk cloth constituted the chief non-agricultural industry in Ganjam District and had attracted several other migrants such as the Kumuṭi, a Telugu business caste (*The Imperial Gazetteer*, Vol. XII 1908: 151–52).

The procedure and organization of today's Ṭhākurāṇī Yātrā reflects this (former) economic and political impact of the Telugu weavers, a community that in 2001 comprised about five thousand people.[9] It is the hereditary headman of this community, the Deśībeherā, who directs the performance of the festival. His wife, the Deśībeherāṇī, plays the most important ritual role. Her task is to offer food to the goddess, and every evening to carry the earthen pot which embodies Buṙhī Ṭhākurāṇī. During Ṭhākurāṇī Yātrā a temporary shrine (*aṣṭhāẏī mandira*) is constructed opposite the family premises, a lane called Deśībeherā Street. Again, the layout of the festival emphasizes the leading position of the Devāṅgī:[10]

(*a*) *The announcement*: After the family priest of the Deśībeherā has fixed the date of the festival, a ritual specialist from the Tuḷābuṇī caste (Oriya cotton manufacturers) will inform the goddess about her journey. After midnight the Tuḷābuṇī will visit the Buṙhī Ṭhākurāṇī temple and talk to her 'in-laws', the

involved in the performance of the festival support this thesis (cf. Brighenti 2001; Eschmann 1978).

[9] Even competing representatives of the Devāṅgī agreed on this estimated number of caste members. With reference to the 'present' occupational pattern of this community, though without any further temporal specification, the *District Gazetteer* mentions that 'about 450 families are depending on this trade in areas under Brahmapur Municipality'. (Behera 1995: 178)

[10] The following summary is based on participant observation during Ṭhākurāṇī Yātrā 2001. Narrative interviews (also in 2003), newspaper articles, photographs, videos, and other documents served to compare the data with previous and subsequent performances. The devotionally inspired festival descriptions by Candra (1998), Pātra (1997) and Rātha (n.d.) were very helpful for the preparation of fieldwork.

priests from the Oriya barber caste (Bhaṇḍārī).[11] Afterwards he will erect an auspicious pole (*śubha khuṇṭi*) in front of the Deśībeherā's house. From this night onwards, the Deśībeherā makes the necessary arrangements for the conduct of the festival (fund raising, construction of a temporary shrine, permissions from municipal authorities, etc.).

(b) *The opening night*: In the afternoon, a class of Telugu priests (Dāmalā, Oriya: Jānī) visit the Deśībeherā's house and guide the preparation of a ritual basket (*cāṅguṙi pūjā*), that later will serve as the vessel of the goddess. The Deśībeherā and his wife take the flame from the goddess's altar (*pīṭham*), light an earthen lamp (*akhaṇda dīpa*, literally: unfading light) and place it inside the basket. In the late evening, a Dāmalā priest clears the area around Deśībeherā Street of evil spirits (*digabandhana*). After midnight the Deśībeherāṇī starts to carry the sacred basket to the Buṙhī Ṭhākurāṇī temple,[12] accompanied by a huge procession of musicians, dancers with giant masks and ceremonial emblems (umbrella, discus, conch),[13] relatives and local honoraries. Upon their arrival in the temple, and with the assistance of Bhaṇḍārī priests, the Deśībeherā's family will offer a cock and a necklace of *iṭāmallī* flowers (among other more common items). Once the first flower drops from the goddess idol back into the basket, it is understood as a sign of divine agreement. In the shape of this 'consent flower' (*ājñā phula*), Buṙhī Ṭhākurāṇī is taken to the temporary shrine in Deśībeherā Street where she is welcomed with an *ārati*-ceremony.[14] From 3 A.M. onwards, the crowd of devotees who watched the procession gets a chance to see (*darśana*) and worship the goddess.

(c) *The installation of sacred pots*: On the evening of the third day, the Dāmalā priests transfer the goddess from the basket into a highly decorated earthen pot (Plate 6.1). Additionally, her 'eight sisters' (*āṭha bhauṇī*)[15] are 'installed' (*sthāpana*) into pots as well.

[11] In local discourse, the identity of Buṙhī Ṭhākurāṇī's husband did not matter.
[12] In 2001 this privilege was shared with the Deśībeherā's maternal aunt.
[13] These masks are also employed during Tuesday Pageants (see Plate 5.1 in Chapter 5).
[14] The performance of *ārati* is a paradigmatic way of worshipping a deity while moving a small light in a clockwise direction in front of the idol.
[15] These sisters are worshipped as a group. Although their number alludes to the eight Shakta goddesses of Orissa (see Chapter 2), there is no consensus as to their identity.

**Plate 6.1:** Buṙhī Ṭhākurāṇī, embodied in a sacred pot, attended by Dāmalā priests

A mask of Bāidhara (Buṙhī Ṭhākurāṇī's son), one of Kāḷimukhī (her daughter-in-law) and the unfading light (*akhaṇḍa dīpā*) complete the altar. From this day onwards, all the deities will receive food offerings from the Deśībeherāṇī (or a female relative) three times a day. The shrine attracts thousands of devotees who, assisted by Dāmalā[16] priests, pay their tribute to the goddesses. The crowd is particularly large during the *ārati*-celebration.

(*d*) *The erection of a flagpole*: On the afternoon of the fifth day, weavers living in Komalabari Street bring a sanctified flagpole (*dharma jhāṇḍa*) that is to enhance religious faith. From this day onwards, and over the following days, well-known decorative and entertaining constructions (*ratha*, *kaḷākuñja*) are put on display.

(*e*) *The pot processions*: From the third night onwards until approximately the twentieth night, depending on the exact duration of the festival, regular pot processions (*ghaṭā parikramā*) will be conducted. Each night Buṙhī Ṭhākurāṇī and her eight sisters are taken through the lanes of old Berhampur. These pots are carried by the Deśībeherāṇī and by women from the chief weaver families. Every night the procession will first pass by the residence of the (former) Mahurī Rājā.

(*f*) *The farewell*: The festival culminates on the final night, when the Telugu weavers and priests conduct the 'return journey' (*bāhuṙā yātrā*) of Buṙhī Ṭhākurāṇī to her Oriya in-laws. This time the pot procession is followed by thousands of women who each carry a sacred pot. On her way, Buṙhī Ṭhākurāṇī briefly visits her 'maternal auntie' (*māusī*) who belongs to the Telugu business caste (Kumuṭi).

Summing up, the festival emphasizes the importance of the Telugu-speaking population and its dominant weaver caste (Devāṅgī), while at the same time it acknowledges the Oriya communities and the higher ritual status of the Bhaṇḍārī priests (barbers), here verbalized in terms of a kinship relation (wife-givers should pay respect to wife-takers). Again the legend of the origin of the festival (discussed in the next section) stresses the superiority of the Devāṅgī.[17]

---

[16] Although there are several communities who by inheritance share the right to conduct the *pūjā* at the temporary shrine, in 2001 it was basically Dāmalā acting as priests (the temple service is divided into shifts that are auctioned among different castes and sub-castes).

[17] However, neither Bhaṇḍārī nor Devāṅgī would take food from each other's house. In this respect, the matter of ritual hierarchy is not so simple. Moreover,

However, the communal services, obligations and rights associated with the proper conduct of Ṭhākurāṇī Yātrā are not only shared between different language and caste groups. There is one more striking division of ritual labor, based on gender. While the headman of the weavers, the Deśībeherā, is responsible for the administrative and financial management of the festival – during Ṭhākurāṇī Yātrā he has to collect subscriptions (*cāndā*) daily – he does not have any religious function. Besides the male priests involved in the conduct of Ṭhākurāṇī Yātrā, the major rituals are performed with the help of Devāṅgī women and, most importantly, the Deśībeherāṇī. The female bias of the festival is not limited to the weaver community but extends to a much broader level of locality. Through worship performed by women, a family maintains ritual relationships with Buṙhī Ṭhākurāṇī as the patroness of the town. The importance given to women characterizes this celebration of a goddess festival but is not limited to Berhampur. Sibendu Manna (1993: 157–60), in his study on Caṇḍī worship in Bengal, mentions a village that celebrates a very similar festival (though on a small scale). Again it is eight women from the silk weaver caste (here: Tantubaya) who carry sacred pots and thus lead the processions. The worship of goddesses classified as *ṭhākurāṇī* is popular among Oriya and Bengali Hindus, and also among several Adivasi communities in this region.[18] Besides, the annual return of a female deity to her parental home is a common motive in several North and East Indian goddess festivals, for instance at Durgā Pūjā, the most important Bengali festival in the ritual year.[19] Thus, Ṭhākurāṇī Yātrā does not follow a *southern* Indian pattern only, though scholars have described fairly similar patterns of goddess festivals in Andhra Pradesh and Tamil Nadu (Handelman 1995; Tapper 1979; for a colonial account compare Elmore 1915: 20–23).

---

although from an ideal-typical Brahminical perspective on caste society, the ritual status of both communities (subsumed as Shudra) would qualify Ṭhākurāṇī Yātrā as a 'subaltern' festival, in comparison to the local distribution of castes and power their rank is fairly average.

[18] See Chaudhuri (1939), J. M. Das (1904), Fischer and Pathy (1996: 32–39), Manna (1993), McDaniel (2004: 34–39), Östör 1980, Schnepel (2002: Chapter 5).

[19] Today the celebration of Durgā Pūjā is not limited to the state of West Bengal; it is also performed in Orissa (see Preston 1980). A similar example from North India is the Nandā Devī pilgrimage that celebrates the divine return of an out-married daughter to her mother's place and back (Sax 1991).

## Divine Daughters Roaming Around

Whereas in the day-time men as well as women from different areas, age groups and social backgrounds come to the festival ground, buy some offerings and worship Buṙhī Ṭhākurāṇī, the goddess herself leaves the temporary shrine every evening in order to visit her devotees. Nine sacred pots, representing Buṙhī Ṭhākurāṇī and her eight sisters, are taken around in a procession through the streets of the old part of Berhampur. To carry one of these pots is a matter of high prestige. The Deśībeherāṇī heads the procession with the main goddess pot (see Plate 6.2); followed by eight selected Devāṅgī women who carry the remaining pots on their heads. Accompanied by huge *ṭhākurāṇī* figures, drummers, priestly attendants and male helpers carrying ceremonial items and the masks of Bāidhara and Kāḷimukhī, they walk barefoot, as on other ritual occasions, on an endless carpet of red and black saris, presented by devotees and spread on the ground by low-caste assistants. First they pass the residence of the Mahurī Rājā, a descendant of the local dynasty, who comes to visit Berhampur for its goddess festival.[20] At his house, a Bhaṇḍārī priest worships Buṙhī Ṭhākurāṇī on behalf of the (former) royal family. Afterwards, the sacred pots proceed for about two or three hours through a few pre-selected streets. The route changes every night, gradually outlining the ritual geography of the divine natal village that is associated with the original settlement. In any case, the procession is not allowed to pass the invisible border between the territories of Buṙhī Ṭhākurāṇī's father and her in-laws, that is, to enter the lanes close to the main goddess temple. After about 20 days, all known quarters (*penṭha*) of the weavers, or in present-day parlance all the '72 streets' should be covered so that each neighbourhood has a chance to receive the divine guest.

When Buṙhī Ṭhākurāṇī visits a street, it is almost exclusively women who worship her on behalf of their families. After eagerly awaiting her visit for the whole day, they come to pray to the goddess in the main

[20] Regardless of the current importance given to the Mahurī Rājā during the celebration of Ṭhākurāṇī Yātrā, the claimed ancestry of the present representative is obscure, and therefore the royal attendance at the festival is not clear. According to Maltby (1967 [1882]: xxxiii), the British bought the kingdom in 1850 after the last ruler of the dynasty died without issue. Therefore the old town and its neighbouring settlements achieved the status of municipality as early as 1867.

**Plate 6.2:** The Deśībeherāṇī carries the main goddess pot

pot and wash the feet of the Deśībeherāṇī with turmeric water. In many streets female devotees need to queue up in order to do this. As an act of pious surrender, they place their infants on the ground to make the goddess step over them (in her embodied manifestation). Whenever she does so, it is considered a sign of her grace and a blessing. The social relationships in the street are enhanced by the collective ritual performance of the women. Moreover, the semi-private zone that commonly limits women's freedom of movement is transformed into a divine space temporarily shared by mortal female beings.

During Ṭhākurāṇī Yātrā the goddess, who in her temple is worshipped by her devotees as a mother, becomes a beloved daughter returning to her place of birth. In excitement people shout: 'Praise to the almighty mistress!' (*mahāpurī sāāntāṇī jaẏ*) While according to public discourse Buṙhī Ṭhākurāṇī visits her pious father, women associate her presence with the freedom of a girl's childhood days. She need not fulfill the expectations of her in-laws by, for instance, staying inside, veiling, showing obedience and working hard, but instead may just 'roam around' the streets. In other words, Buṙhī Ṭhākurāṇī's shift from the Bhaṇḍārī's to the Deśībeherā's care reflects the contrasting code of conduct experienced by Hindu women between their marital and natal homes. This female perspective is also verbalized in devotional poetry, here expressed in the words spoken by Buṙhī Ṭhākurāṇī to her 'father', the Deśībeherā:[21]

> In this world it is not forbidden for a daughter to go to her father's house;
> Every second year I shall come on an auspicious day in *caitra*.
>
> You will invite me and while staying in your home I shall feel happy;
> Look for a good day to take me, oh father, I will stay in your house.
>
> The pain, sorrow and suffering [caused] by a mother-in-law are not there in father's house;
> Going to father's house feels like heaven, my in-law's place is hell.
>
> Make sure you invite me, and for some days I shall enjoy happiness;
> Being my father you would not [visit my temple and] bring me offerings.[22]

The same loving care that a daughter returning home receives from her parents, brothers and other relatives is also shown to Buṙhī Ṭhākurāṇī,

---

[21] These verses are taken from a 24-page booklet on Buṙhī Ṭhākurāṇī that is sold in the market of Berhampur. It includes basic information about Ṭhākurāṇī Yātrā, prayers, hymns and also these verses to illustrate the 'true story' of the goddess (see Ratha n.d.: 17–18).

[22] This last line refers to the legend about the origin of Ṭhākurāṇī Yātrā (see the following lines).

who is welcomed as just another close family member. This reverence shown to a 'daughter goddess' (Schnepel 2002: 237) evokes an emotional commitment fairly different to one related to a demanding divine mother, the other facet of a *ṭhākurāṇī*. As in the goddess's journey, married daughters living outside Berhampur also take the opportunity to visit their family during Ṭhākurāṇī Yātrā. The same notion of divine *and* living daughters visiting their natal home characterizes the Bengali celebration of Durgā Pūjā as well as a few other goddess festivals in northern India (for instance, the Nandā Devī pilgrimage, see Sax 1991).

## Living Mothers Travelling through the Night

On the final night of Ṭhākurāṇī Yātrā, the festival culminates in the 'return journey' (*bāhuṛā yātrā*) of the goddess. The celebrations, continuing throughout the night (and broadcast live by the local TV station), attract thousands of devotees, who in their excitement not only visit the main ritual sites but wander around the illuminated streets. Uncountable groups of people, families and friends, squeeze though the narrow lanes of the old town in order to visit the decorative arrangements made by different neighbourhoods. Food stalls, theatres, colourful masquerades (*beśa*) and comedy contribute further to the festive spirit.

On the ritual level, two events occur at the same time: the public return journey of Buṛhī Ṭhākurāṇī and her eight sisters, and, in almost every household, the private worship of goddess pots, which are finally taken to join the main procession to the Buṛhī Ṭhākurāṇī temple. In the afternoon, priests of the Dāmalā caste initiate both activities with the 'installation' of a thousand-eyed pot (Telugu: *vei kallu ghaṭam*) in the Deśībeherā's house. This perforated (to make the 'eyes') pot made of unbaked clay is said to symbolize the gifts a wife usually brings back home from a visit to her parents (her 'dowry').[23] After midnight, the nine pots at the temporary shrine are worshipped for one final time and then removed. Guided by the thousand-eyed pot, the procession heads for Buṛhī Ṭhākurāṇī's in-laws. This time the procession is particularly beautiful and includes a variety of musicians and decorative elements. It is followed by dignitaries of the old town dressed up as the king (*rājā*),

[23] With reference to the annual festival of Gangamma in Andhra Pradesh, Handelman (1995: 312) notices a similar pot and explains that the eyes signify the sores of small pox. According to Tapper (1979: 19), pustules are metaphorically referred to as 'pots' when associated with this disease.

minister (*mantrī*) and general (*senāpati*), as well as by (male) devotees playfully throwing coloured powders at each other and dancing on the street. On its way, the procession will pass the house of a Kumuṭi family who — as they once saved the divine pot from British soldiers — are considered as Buṙhī Ṭhākurāṇī's maternal relatives. People say that the goddess passes her auntie's (*māusī*) house (rather than her uncle's).[24] Since the old town is packed with people, the procession will take a few more hours to reach the Buṙhī Ṭhākurāṇī temple. There, the Deśībeherā and his family will sacrifice a black male goat as a final offering.

During this last night, the attention of local women is less on the main procession than on the private worship of Buṙhī Ṭhākurāṇī and on escorting her back home. In the previous weeks, several married women will have visited the goddess at her temporary shrine and, near the auspicious pole (*śubha khuṇṭi*) or the flag post (*dharma jhāṇḍa*), promised to carry a sacred pot in order to put the goddess in their debt or to recompense the divine grace. Unlike the vow (*brata*) associated with a set of rituals by the same name (see Chapter 1), these pledges (*mānasika*) are more instrumental in character, in that they link the performance of a devotional act to a specific wish of great importance.

> If somebody does not have a child for five or seven years [she will beg] 'oh Almighty, please give me a son or daughter!' If you act like this [and carry a sacred pot], the goddess will answer your desire; she will definitely give [a baby]. If someone's leg is broken, she will say 'oh Almighty, I offer a [costly] brass pot.' And she will also invest in a silver or golden leg [i.e., a miniature votive offering representing a small leg].

This rather pragmatic approach to worship characterizes the religiosity of several Hindus in this region, yet the method used to express this type of conditional vow varies according to gender. To women of Berhampur, the participation in the return journey of Buṙhī Ṭhākurāṇī is one of the most powerful ways to submit oneself to the goddess and thus to win her support. It is conceived of as a paradigmatic religious exercise.[25] Whereas in case of the Tuesday Pageant the head of a

---

[24] Terms such as '*māusī*'s house' or the divine 'return journey' are reminiscent of the yearly celebration of Ratha Yātrā in Puri, and thus also convey religious prestige.

[25] A typical *male* way to fulfil a *mānasika* is to put on a costume and to engage in role-play during Ṭhākurāṇī Yātrā (see Chapter 7). Several authors have described vows in their importance to female religion and with respect to the

household will select the pot bearer among the married women of a family, to carry a sacred pot during Ṭhākurāṇī Yātrā reflects a woman's personal wish. However, a daughter-in-law is expected to come to share the tradition in a gradual manner.

Women from almost every household will already have instructed a Bhaṇḍārī priest to 'install' their personal sacred pot (*mānasika ghaṭa*) in the morning. As soon as the thousand-eyed pot is prepared at the main festival site, and the news spreads like wildfire, women all over the town start to worship their respective goddess pots at home. Usually this *pūjā* is done in the company of female relatives and friends, so that some families have not two or three but more than 20 sacred pots (Plate 6.3).[26] Whoever has made the vow of carrying a pot will also be fasting. The privately conducted rituals resemble a kind of condensed version of the *yātrā*. The goddess is welcomed, offered food, praised with *ārati* and, finally, given presents to please her in-laws (here a small bow and arrow, i.e., the weapons associated with the goddess). From about 1 A.M. onwards women take their respective *mānasika ghaṭa* and join the public procession, which attracts up to ten thousand pot carriers by sunrise.[27] Even though female police officers and male volunteers guide the masses to form groups and, divided into different sections, to proceed forward little by little, it is almost 5 A.M. when the first pot carriers reach the temple (Plate 6.4). During this procession many of the women not only reach their physical limits, but also are possessed by the goddess.

The carrier of a sacred pot thus turns into the goddess's own vessel. From the individual devotee's perspective, this embodiment of the

---

worship of a goddess (Harman 2006: 28; McDaniel 2004: 34, 53; Pearson 1996: 3; Rodrigues 2005: 78–79); on the role of religious promises in different South Asian religions see Raj and Harman (2006).

[26] If a woman fails to carry the pot herself (due to menstrual impurity or sickness), she can give it to an unmarried young woman or pay a male person to carry it on her behalf. In 2001 about 5 per cent of the pot carriers were men.

[27] My estimation is based on the arrival of these women in the temple. The sound of goddess pots being thrown on the floor (almost every second) for several hours allowed me to calculate the number of participants. I doubt the number of participants reached the alleged 60 thousand pot bearers mentioned by the Oriya newspaper *Sambād* (1 May 2001). With reference to 2003, the Telugu newspaper *Eenadu* (29 April 2003) reported 30 thousand sacred pots. According to the *District Gazetteer of Orissa*, published in 1995, it once had 15 thousand participants on the return journey (Behera 1995: 244). However, there is no information as to the year of observation.

**Plate 6.3:** Private altar with 32 sacred pots in honour of the goddess

**Plate 6.4:** Divided into groups of hundreds, pot bearers approach the temple

female divine power is an extremely impressive experience.[28] At the temple entrance, volunteers wait for the women and assist them in smashing their pots. Many pot bearers need to recover and lie down. The remaining symptoms of possession are removed by sprinkling turmeric water on them in order to 'cool' the goddess.

With regard to the quality and rhythm of time at Ṭhākurāṇī Yātrā, I summarily wish to distinguish three ritual periods: (*a*) during the day, the goddess is worshipped in her temporary shrine, devotees (regardless of gender) bring offerings, and priests conduct the rituals; (*b*) during the first half of the night, Buṙhī Ṭhākurāṇī roams around the streets, and local women honour her like a village daughter; (*c*) after midnight, which is the proper time for the goddess to 'travel' from one place to another, women do not worship Buṙhī Ṭhākurāṇī in a strict sense but rather represent her, and sometimes even physically embody her. It is women's ritual significance that demands and legitimizes their nocturnal presence in public. The successful celebration of the festival – which after all guarantees the prosperity and well-being of the locality by the grace of the goddess – is based on women and their religious roles. They link the patron goddess with her territory as either ritual intermediaries or divine representatives. Moreover, since the washing of feet with turmeric water and the worship of sacred pots belong to the ritual repertoire of women, they feel encouraged in their gender-specific religious practices. However, it is men and male ritual specialists who govern the public discourse of the *yātrā* (see Chapter 8).

## The Darkness of the Goddess

There are certainly many advantages involved in celebrating a festival at night. First of all, most people are free from work, and second, nocturnal darkness provides a pleasant relief from the burning heat of the sun. Moreover, due to the contrast with the daily routine and the effort to overcome sleep, any ordinary action gets transformed into an exceptional event. Indeed, all over India there are certain festivities that take place during the night, such as ritual dramas, folk operas, musical performances or religious ceremonies. With respect

[28] On the occasion of an annual goddess festival, women in Andhra Pradesh are likely to encounter divine possession for the first time (Schömbucher 2006: 124). Similarly, processions in honour of Vīrabhadra attract 'younger mothers in their twenties and thirties' to get overpowered. According to Knipe (1989: 127–28), these (Telugu) women constitute the largest group of possessed devotees.

to Ṭhākurāṇī Yātrā, I argue, the choice of time is neither accidental nor solely practical. The goddess is clearly associated with 'nocturnal qualities' and therefore worshipped preferably late at night.[29]

In Orissa, people know a great number of rather fierce goddesses, who are worshipped for their extraordinary power and at the same time feared for their anger, which might cause disease, epidemics and natural disasters. These goddesses are usually identified by the generic term *ṭhākurāṇī* and can be identified with well-known Hindu goddesses like Bhairabī, Caṇḍī or Kāḷī. In the course of time, some *thakuranis* achieve the status of a village deity and come to be known by a specific name and form of worship, like Buṙhī Ṭhākurāṇī of Berhampur, the 'Old One' (*buṙhī*) and thus most important *ṭhākurāṇī*. Most, if not all, of these goddesses are known for their special relationship with the night. First of all, there are numerous semi-sacred narratives of female divinities who reveal themselves to their devotees through the darkness itself. Similarly the origin of Ṭhākurāṇī Yātrā is explained with reference to a night-time encounter of the Deśībeherā with the goddess in the guise of a helpless girl:

> One dark Tuesday night the Deśībeherā went outside to urinate. In the middle of the road he saw a young girl with long flowing hair. She was weeping bitterly. 'How did you get here?' he asked in surprise. The girl told him that she had lost her way back home and the Deśībeherā felt sorry for her. 'Don't worry', he said, 'come inside and rest. You are like my own daughter; let me take care of you.' He invited the girl to stay overnight and offered to escort her to her parents' house at sunrise. Yet when the Deśībeherā opened the front door to let her in, the girl had vanished. He wondered if he had dreamt the whole incident and went to sleep. The following morning he visited the Buṙhī Ṭhākurāṇī temple as usual. There she was, the same girl. 'Stop coming here', she pleaded, 'how can a father possibly worship his daughter?' The Deśībeherā was

[29] There have been several studies reflecting on time concepts in South Asia. They focus on the idea of cyclical rather than linear time, on the different lunar and solar calendars and their inter-related religious significance, as well as on astrologically defined auspicious moments and periods (see Fuller 1992: 263–66; Marglin 1985b; Östör 1980). They also stress the performance of Hindu festivals as time markers. However, the fact that many of these events take place at night is rarely discussed (for an exception, see Stanley 1977). Therefore, I am indebted to Burkhard Schnepel who inspired me to think about Ṭhākurāṇī Yātrā as an occasion that brings about cultural knowledge about the night and its respective qualities (see Schnepel and Ben-Ari 2005).

> confused. Why should he refrain from his prayers? Then he realized. The girl was Buṙhī Ṭhākurāṇī herself! As he had treated her like his own daughter she revealed to him that she would consider his house as her birth place and, every once in a while, visit him personally. Rather than the Deśībeherā, the first person he met on his way back home should take care of the temple. Again she disappeared. When the head of the weavers left the sacred premises he met a barber and instructed him accordingly. Henceforth, the Oriya barbers serve Buṙhī Ṭhākurāṇī at her temple. Every second year, however, the goddess is invited to the Deśībeherā's house, an event celebrated as Ṭhākurāṇī Yātrā.[30]

Thus the encounter with the divine late at night characterizes Ṭhākurāṇī Yātrā as a re-enactment of this legend, and also legitimizes the complementary ritual roles of the Devāṅgī and the Bhaṇḍārī. However, the relation of a *ṭhākurāṇī* with the night is not only emphasized in narratives. Furthermore, goddesses are known to transmit their messages through dreams and in this way guide their devotees.[31] With reference to Ṭhākurāṇī Yātrā, for instance, many pot carriers will report such a dream when asked about their active participation in the festival. Above all, these goddesses are understood to 'travel through the night', that is, actually to manifest themselves during darkness. It is due to this heightened presence of the goddess that the nocturnal worship is considered to provide the most appropriate access to her divinity. The efficacy of such nocturnal worship (*niśā pūjā*) is highest at midnight. Still, this classification might refer to any corresponding ritual performed after sunset (or exceptionally during the day-time), given that it addresses a *niśā* deity (for instance, Maṅgaḷā, see Chapter 2).

In general, the preference for the nocturnal worship of certain Hindu goddesses becomes most obvious during the 'Nine Nights' (Nabarātri), an important goddess festival celebrated all over northern India, overlapping with regional variants like Durgā Pūjā in Bengal. In several parts of Orissa, this festival is performed on a grand scale lasting from three to 16 nights (see Preston 1980). The peak of this festival comes

[30] This legend, based on oral transmission, is commonly reprinted by local media (for instance, Pātra 1997: 9–13); for variants of this story, see Behuria (1995: 243) or Fischer and Pathy (1996: 220–21). A rather different version is perpetuated among the untouchable Mādigā (see Chapter 9).

[31] It is not only in Hinduism that dreams are considered a source of religious inspiration. For the recent recognition of dreaming as a subject in social anthropology, see Schnepel (2001).

on the 'eighth' (*aṣṭamī*) day of the waxing moon in the lunar month of *āśvina* (September/October), and is marked by a nocturnal animal sacrifice. Yet for south Orissa, Durgā Pūjā is a long way from reaching the importance of the biennial celebration of Ṭhākurāṇī Yātrā. However, even apart from these festivals, there is a ranking of nights depending on their ritual efficacy for the worship of a fierce goddess: devotees in Orissa select Tuesday nights, in the Hindu month of *caitra* (March/April) and those commencing with the entrance of the sun into another zodiac (*saṃkrānti*). These features are also preferred in the case of daytime worship. Furthermore, the hierarchy of nights is governed by the absence of light (a feature whose aesthetic impact diminished with the increased use of electric lights). Whereas the new moon is of heightened importance for the worship of a *ṭhākurāṇī*, full moon is usually avoided. This is particularly noteworthy, since several other Hindu ceremonies specifically take place or begin at this time. However, in the case of *niśā* deities, darkness is required.[32] The beginning and the end of Ṭhākurāṇī Yātrā are both scheduled for the very first dark hours of a Tuesday, possibly in *caitra* and excluding any night with a full moon.[33] On this basis the Deśībeherā's family priest, a Telugu Brahmin (Komma), will fix an auspicious beginning and end of the festival. Apart from these features, and unlike other religious festivals, there is no fixed (Hindu) date for conducting Ṭhākurāṇī Yātrā. Its emphasis on darkness also corresponds to the various epithets of the fierce goddess as she is known in the oral and scriptural tradition: she is Kāḷī (The Black One) or even Śyāma Kāḷī (Dark and Black), Tāmasī (Darkness), or in her most destructive aspect Kāḷarātri (The Black Night).[34]

---

[32] On the association of goddesses with lunar phases, see Kinsley (1998: 45) and Östör (1980: 38, 213).

[33] In 2001 Ṭhākurāṇī Yātrā started immediately after full moon, i.e., on the following Tuesday. According to the Oriya calendar it was performed in the month of *baiśākha* (April/May). Yet the Telugu month starts on new moon rather than on full moon, and thus a fortnight after its north Indian counterpart. Therefore the main portion of the festival took place in the Telugu month of *caitra*. In any case, the focus on the first dark hours of a day contrasts with the general understanding in Orissa and elsewhere in India that the calendrical unit of a day starts at sunrise and that the night belongs to the previous day (on the Hindu calendar, see Fuller 1992: 263–66).

[34] She is also regarded as Yoganidrā/Nidrādebī, the goddess of sleep (see Kinsley 1998: 67–70, 171, 230; Erndl 1993: 23).

The *niśā* way of worship implies certain risks. First, there is the danger of pollution. Once a *ṭhākurāṇī* is worshipped at home, certain precautions have to be taken. If the family deity is of a rather different kind (for instance, Nārāẏaṇa), *pūjā* should be performed at some distance from the house altar. Moreover, while cooked offerings are usually shared among the family members, in the case of a fierce goddess they have to be given away to the washermen (Dhobā) or any other community with a low ritual status.[35] Similarly, during Ṭhākurāṇī Yātrā, low-caste assistants receive the food offerings presented to the goddess and her eight sisters. Furthermore, there are severe consequences for not worshipping a *niśā* deity correctly. For instance, the recitation of *Caṇḍī Paṭha*, one of the most sacred texts in Shaktism, is considered highly dangerous, and the priests warn that its incorrect pronunciation may lead to madness or death. Finally, the danger of a *niśā pūjā* results from its very performance late at night, that is, when creatures like demons, witches and ghosts might disturb the sincere devotees.[36] Thus, the celebration of Ṭhākurāṇī Yātrā requires two kinds of protective ritual. Dāmalā priests, who are known for their magic (*tāntrika*) powers, perform both of them. At the opening of the festival, they will block out any destructive forces by 'binding the directions' (*digabandhana*), a ritual that includes decoy offerings of chicken, alcohol, rice and pulses, that serve to persuade hostile beings to guard the area.[37] Similar to this general protection of ritual space, the Dāmalā also seal the bodily boundaries of the nine pot carriers prior to each nocturnal procession by speaking some formulas (*mantra*) and applying a clod of turmeric paste to each woman's forehead to protect her from possession (see Chapter 8, Plate 8.1).

---

[35] Although the divine appetite for blood sacrifice is recognized, the goddess is generally given vegetarian offerings. So there is no bar on the consumption of her 'leftovers' (*bhoga*, i.e., sacrificial food). Alternately, 'raw' (*kañcā*) food is taken, i.e., fruits and processed sweets. 'Eaten' and thus blessed by the goddess, it does not pollute anybody.

[36] On the accessibility of ambivalently auspicious power that alludes to pollution and divine possession alike, see Stanley (1977: 28–31). Rather than on female deities, his analysis focuses on the worship of Khaṇḍobā in Maharashtra.

[37] For similar precautions taken during the annual festival of a goddess, see Handelman (1995: 291–92), Tanabe (1999: 145) and Tapper (1979: 22). According to White (2003: 259), to fix a sacred space by means of *digabandhana* is a standard preliminary ritual in safeguarding 'tantric' forms of worship.

Yet Buṙhī Ṭhākurāṇī herself is not only regarded as a divine force but is simultaneously identified with demonic and threatening female beings, such as a *yoginī*, *kātyāẏaṇī* or *ḍāhāṇī*, who are all considered as part of the retinue of the deity. When, at the beginning of the twentieth century, J. M. Das (1904: 82) described a *ṭhākurāṇī* as 'a mischievous old witch', this was not (only) derogative but aimed at making clear the sinister aspect associated with this type of goddess. Some of them are thought to originate in the spirit of a deceased ancestress who died prematurely. The actual danger of these goddesses results from their envy. If one goddess is honoured with an annual festival, the greed of neighbouring *ṭhākurāṇīs* has to be satisfied as well. In this respect, whoever is worshipped and feared depends on time and locality. Similarly Buṙhī Ṭhākurāṇī is classified as 'Caṇḍī-Cāmuṇḍā', which might be understood as a dismissive term to signify destructive forces or, conversely, as relating to two specifically powerful goddesses, namely Caṇḍī and Cāmuṇḍā. Their power is highly ambivalent in the sense that some people may approach them not only for spiritual but also for magical purposes (*tantra*). In this case meditation and ascetic practices serve to attain selfish worldly goals like victory over an enemy, or the manipulation and subjugation of others. A similar ambivalence characterizes the group of 'Ten Wisdom Goddesses' (Daśa Mahābidyā) with whom Buṙhī Ṭhākurāṇī is identified in her temple iconography. They represent habits, attributes and other features that are usually considered repulsive or, alternatively, different forms of (secret) knowledge.[38] From the perspective of lay devotees however, the goddess' association with ghostly creatures manifests itself as nocturnal disturbance. In the neighbourhood of the Deśībeherā, for instance, one educated middle-class family did not use the ground floor of their house, since during the night they felt troubled by the rattling of Buṙhī Ṭhākurāṇī's bangles. A magician was called to ban the haunting goddess, but nevertheless the ground floor remained a storeroom only. The ambiguity of this *niśā* quality also reveals itself during the final procession of Ṭhākurāṇī Yātrā. In this case, ordinary women carrying a *mānasika ghaṭa* do not receive the bodily protection measures given to Devāṅgī pot bearers. Hence possession occurs frequently and thus illustrates the exceptional accessibility of power

[38] On the worship of *tāntrika* goddesses, see Kinsley (1998). White (2003) critically discusses 'tantric' forms of worship (and their sexual connotations), not only with respect to popular religious practices but also as a projection of competing religious and academic discourses.

during the night (cf. Stanley 1977). If these women move or shout in wild anger, their behaviour is clearly attributed to the goddess and not regarded as a violation of ideal female modesty.

## Conclusion: Nocturnal Qualities

Ṭhākurāṇī Yātrā is not intended to enlighten or 'domesticate' the night in the sense of avoiding its dark character. Thus it differs from the ritual night vigils (*jāgaraṇa*) known all over India. The emphasis there is on waking, i.e., the denial of sleep, which (in line with abstinence from food) serves as a bodily exercise to adore a deity, for instance on Sibarātri (The Night of Śiba). This can be achieved by singing hymns or by watching spectacular dramatic performances (see Henn 2003). Furthermore, the vigils also serve to keep the gods awake — alert for the proper maintenance and safeguarding of the world. A burning flame may symbolize this, as Kathleen Erndl (1993: 101–3) has shown with regard to vigils for the goddess in northwest India. If the deity manifests herself in the body of a devotee, it is regarded as a sign of this wakefulness. At Ṭhākurāṇī Yātrā, conversely, the nocturnal rituals do not stress the idea of either waking or enlightenment. Instead, it is taken for granted that the goddess travels through the night. There is no need to verify that darkness is the most appropriate time for her worship, since there is no explicit daylight counterpart. The darkness of a goddess is rather seen as one of three complementary essences that constitute the world, each of which is necessary and processual in character. Thus, Shakta theology distinguishes: (*a*) darkness or lethargy (Sanskrit: *tamas*); (*b*) passion or activity (Sanskrit: *rajas*); and (*c*) light or purity (Sanskrit: *sattva*). Each quality corresponds to certain deities, ways of worship and religious goals (see Erndl 1993: 22–30; Kinsley 1998: 42; Östör 1980: 53–56). The *tāmasika* type, for instance, paradigmatically alludes to an animal sacrifice in honour of the goddess Mahākāḷī (a divine embodiment of *tamas*), who specifically helps overcome everyday problems, here an appropriate objective of worship. It is this logic that implicitly makes a nocturnal *pūjā* the most propitious time and context to meet the quality of Buṛhī Ṭhākurāṇī. Like any other period of time (weekdays, months, lunar constellations), night is associated with a particular quality. Thus Ṭhākurāṇī Yātrā is not an attempt to enlighten, pacify or negotiate with darkness, but to emphasize the night for what it is.

In the earlier sections I have shown how the biennial celebration of Ṭhākurāṇī Yātrā is characterized by a division of ritual labor that emphasizes the perspective and role of women. On the one hand, the festive spirit and the emotional commitment to the goddess is associated with the comparatively free code of conduct married women may enjoy while visiting their birthplace, i.e., a mood that also stimulates accompanying children and thus is shared across gender. In this respect Ṭhākurāṇī Yātrā expresses a distinct female viewpoint, although the divine experience does not imply or evoke any social criticism. On the other hand, the procedure of the festival pushes those forms of worship which are associated with, and valued by, women into the spotlight – to carry a sacred pot, to wash divine feet with turmeric water, to embody the substantially female cosmological force (*śakti*). Only with the help of married women the goddess can be appeased and thus guarantee the well-being of the household, the lineage and, in a wider territorial sense, the city. As shown above, women qualify to approach a *niśā* goddess and, as ritual intermediaries, transform her ambivalent and extremely dangerous powers for the good of society. At the same time, pot processions display the male dependency on their wife's and mother's religious engagement. The emphasis on femininity during Ṭhākurāṇī Yātrā creates a *public* mood or rather atmosphere that, unlike non-festive times, encourages women's gendered and religious self. By contrast, for those women who live some distance away from the old town, a visit to the festival site during the night remains a privilege provided by her male family members.

Considering ethnographic studies on other goddess festivals in India, Ṭhākurāṇī Yātrā, with its priority given to female ritual roles, appears to be exceptional. However, this could partly be an effect of a gendered bias shared by male scholars and their interlocutors, as two examples from the neighbouring state of Andhra Pradesh show.[39] When Bruce Tapper (1979: 28) analyzed the pot processions in honour of the goddess Banḍamma, he observed that they regularly stop 'for housewives to worship the pots'. Nevertheless, he concludes that '[d]espite of the symbolism based on female roles the goddess ritual is essentially a male dominated event. It is only men, as representatives of castes and public social categories . . . who conduct the public events in which women remain peripheral.' No doubt the annual processions in honour of Banḍamma are performed by male rather than female pot bearers. Focusing on the communities who *organize* Ṭhākurāṇī

[39] This bias is rarely intentional, since in the presence of men (and anthropologists in general), female 'informants' often downplay their ritual expertise. However, the paradigmatic counterpart in ethnographic research is (still) male.

Yātrā, even the latter is an 'essentially male' festival. Like Tapper, Don Handelman (1995: 321) recognizes a clear majority of female devotees during the yearly celebration of Gangamma. Taking into account the role of costumed men who embody the goddess during processions, he interprets the festival as being 'dominated by men'. In my view both studies *also* suggest reconsidering the perspective of women (whether classified as housewives or devotees), and the impact of their worship on the soteriological success of the goddess festival.[40]

Apart from the essential role married women in southern Orissa play in the worship of a *niśā* goddess, the sheer numerical dominance of female pot bearers during the celebration of Ṭhākurāṇī Yātrā calls for scholarly attention. The ritual primacy given to women in public at night reflects what might be classified as a 'tantric' religious context. I hesitate to use this highly contested label that may describe: (*a*) a variety of popular ritual practices; (*b*) a form of esoteric knowledge and ideology; or (*c*) a specific body of sacred scriptures, i.e., ontologically diverse categories of religion.[41] In Berhampur the term *tāntrika* is also used in reference to black magic or, derogatively, to mean 'mumbo-jumbo'. It carries a stigma.[42] Nevertheless, there is hardly a more adequate term that characterizes Ṭhākurāṇī Yātrā in its capacity to pay obeisance to the divine feminine and its ambivalent powers by means of ritually and emotionally *risky* practices, i.e., acts of worship that (potentially) face pollution and thus reverse the Brahminical emphasis on purity. At the same time, the spirit of the biennial festival is anything but esoteric. In southern Orissa, the performance of Ṭhākurāṇī Yātrā constitutes the most popular religious event. People compare it with the Ratha Yātrā (Car festival) in Puri that draws a pan-Indian audience. Moreover, Ṭhākurāṇī Yātrā of Berhampur has turned into a paradigm by itself. It is the largest among several festivals by this name that are performed at different intervals and places of

---

[40] However, there are goddess festivals whose gender-specific conception has been acknowledged by male ethnographers, for instance the Nandā Devī pilgrimage in the Himalayas, studied by William Sax (1991).

[41] For a discussion of *tāntrika* forms of goddess worship related to 'folk' and *bhakti* strands of Shaktism, see McDaniel (2004); White (2000) gives an overview of recent studies on *Tantra in Practice*.

[42] This stigma is not limited to the regional context but rather related to 'modern' discourse, as McDaniel (2004: 68–69) showed in respect to *tāntrikas* in West Bengal.

southern Orissa (Aska, Icchapuram, etc.).[43] In this respect the feminine perspective emphasized during Ṭhākurāṇī Yātrā reflects mainstream devotional practice rather than exclusive or exceptional cultural knowledge. Even Brahmins will not demonize the worship of Buṙhī Ṭhākurāṇī. The feminine priority is either taken for granted and/or not worth mentioning. Although some men label Ṭhākurāṇī Yātrā as a 'women's festival', this designation does not transmit any message on its religious importance. Both women and men love the festival, yet as the next chapter shows, in part for different reasons.

[43] Possibly it is this whole class of festivals Rājaguru (1992 [1895]: vi–vii) had referred to by the end of the nineteenth century, when he mentioned women who carry sacred pots in great processions (see note 3).

**Plate 1:** Girl adopting the role of goddess Bṛndābatī on the occasion of Jahni Oṣā

**Plate 2:** *Oṣā-brata* rites performed by senior women (here Bālukā Pūjā) serve as paradigm versions for the younger generation

**Plate 3:** Female pot bearer at the Tuesday Pageant

**Plate 4:** During the Tuesday Pageant a devotee places the loose end of her sari on the road to let the living embodiment of *ṭhākurāṇī* walk on it

**Plate 5:** Telugu devotee offering a cock on the occasion of Jhāmu Yātrā

**Plate 6:** Female devotees carrying sacred pots on the outskirts of Berhampur

**Plate 7:** Various types of processions employ a giant mask representing Buṙhī Ṭhākurāṇī

**Plate 8:** Daily pot processions are the main feature of Ṭhākurāṇī Yātrā: the pots embody Buṙhī Ṭhākurāṇī (highly decorated pot at the left) and her eight sisters

# 7

# Divine Play or Subversive Comedy? On Costuming, Gender, and Transgression

This chapter discusses the ludic and entertaining dimension of Ṭhākurāṇī Yātrā, and in particular the masquerades that are considered to be among the main attractions of this festival.[1] A great number of costumed boys and men dressed up as tigers, mythological characters or Hindu deities enliven the public. Others disguise themselves as lascivious monks, as thieves fooling policemen or as members of a mock funeral procession, dancing, joking, and provoking. Women do not participate in these masquerades, although they may enjoy them as onlookers. At first sight, they appear to be doing the 'ritual work', while their sons, husbands and brothers share the 'fun part'. As will be shown further in the discussion, this is not the whole story. Considering the male practice of putting on a disguise actually confirms Ṭhākurāṇī Yātrā as a religious festival that is largely experienced in gender-specific ways.

In anthropological discourse, festivals – as a particular time in human life – are usually seen as calendrical reference points during which a community might enhance and renew social, political and religious values. Furthermore, many scholars stress the potentially conflicting nature of these events (see also Chapter 8). Extravagance, role reversal and transgression are considered as complementary symbolic actions required to challenge, reconfirm and vitalize the prevailing

[1] This chapter is a largely revised version of an article published previously (Hauser 2006b).

moral order.[2] Ludic forms of masking, costuming and disguise have come to serve as paradigmatic examples signifying an interruption of the status quo. Under the influence of Mikhael Bakhtin (1968), the carnivalesque has been conceptualized as a subaltern strategy which allows one to criticize hegemonic discourse, as a vision of egalitarian living (rather than a play of characters), or as the concealment of social personae giving way to uncontrolled bodiliness. Although the question as to whether it should be seen as basically subversive or rather as a conservative social institution has now become obsolete (it might be both), the notion of the carnivalesque certainly carries political connotations (see Gilmore 1998; Kertzer 1988). The transformative capacity, which also has effects for the time after the feast, is attributed to the extreme behaviour of performers and their annoying violation of what is thought to be good manners or style.

The following analysis will show that the political dimension transmitted by the concept of the carnivalesque is fairly misleading when exploring Ṭhākurāṇī Yātrā and the socio-religious impact of these masquerades. Their display, whether offensive or not, serves a religious purpose in the first place. They lead us back to Georges Bataille, who (influenced by the ethnographic studies of Roger Caillois) has offered a very specific notion of transgression. According to Bataille (1997: 248–52), these breaches do not simply ignore rules and regulations, but serve to complete them and are thus paradoxical in their nature. The fear of breaking the moral order is coupled with the hidden desire to do so. Both attitudes together create a feeling of respect. The symbiosis of taboo and temptation manifests itself particularly in the religious sphere. Here transgression constitutes an almost sacred act that is required for the performance of many festivals. If people offended norms either out of ignorance or during non-festive times, it would not be a transgression in Bataille's sense, but a real violation (see Köpping 1998).

The concept of transgression is, like the carnivalesque, a challenge. Following Köpping (2002: 17) one could ask that how expected violations are able to create shocking experiences that 'shatter frames' rather than only reproduce the known? Given the fact that masquerades at Ṭhākurāṇī Yātrā constitute a purely male practice also

[2] See particularly Turner (1969), who regarded transgressions as essential part or phase of the ritual process and thus extended Max Gluckman's argument on 'rituals of rebellion'. For an overview of the anthropology of the festive, see Köpping (2002: 121–38).

raises the question of in what way women relate to transgressions and whether these provoke both genders alike.[3] In the following chapter I shall explore how performers and spectators perceive the playful and at times mischievous aspect of costuming at Ṭhākurāṇī Yātrā. Analyzing the local discourse, I will consider how and by whom transgressions are recognized, given meaning and dealt with. I suggest that masquerades are not only understood in their semiotic sense but also as a body practice in itself. This opens up an ambiguous field of interpretation that allows people to cope with violations displayed and to maintain the ritual scope of the festival.

Furthermore, I shall evaluate these playful breaches as a gender-specific method of authenticating the ritual process. Considering the festival as a site in which to enact and constitute gender differences, I argue that putting on a disguise is regarded as a performative idiom of masculinity. This male body practice has a female counterpart on the final night of Ṭhākurāṇī Yātrā, when thousands of women are possessed and, while being transformed, also violate the behavioural norms associated with femininity. In conclusion I shall reflect on the diversity of female and male transgression, and suggest how these gender-specific body practices contribute in complementary ways to the eternal play evident at Ṭhākurāṇī Yātrā.

## Men and Masquerade

During the festival there are several occasions when people dress up in fancy costumes (*beśa*). Most people do so during the celebration of the first and the final night, on certain auspicious days and towards the end and climax of the three-week-long festival. Yet not everybody goes in for disguise. Unlike carnival traditions with their scheduled parades of costumed people, the time and location of the festival is characterized rather by occasional actors and improvised skits. Among the crowd of ordinary visitors one finds here and there people acting in quite funny ways: the god Rāma passes by on a motorbike; two tigers dance wildly in front of a shopping centre or an election campaigner agitates in favour of drinking, gambling and sexual liberation. In general, people look

[3] Not only in India, masquerades seem to be a preferably male and low status activity. While women are often encouraged to participate, they do so to a much lesser extend than men (see Gilmore 1998: 13–21; Handelman 1990: 145). Theories on transgression and on the rebellious spirit of the carnivalesque thus mostly imply a male bias.

forward to the various disguises that spice up the streets. Newspapers comment on their number and variety. However, while many families and friends go out to discover and enjoy the masquerades, others try to avoid the festival altogether. They are bored or even disturbed by its unpredictable performances. The actors' jokes create a mixture of attraction, excitement and rejection.

The main reason for putting on fancy dress at Ṭhākurāṇī Yātrā is the urgent wish for divine help, i.e., the masquerade should please, amuse and flatter Buṙhī Ṭhākurāṇī and hence gain the favour of the goddess. As mentioned in the previous chapter, to frame a heart's desire as a religious pledge (*mānasika*) is very popular and motivates a variety of devotional practices ranging from fasting to pilgrimage. Usually, a *mānasika* concerns mundane issues such as progeny, recovery from disease, a safe journey or a successful exam, and may derive either from worries about one's own affairs from or those of a loved family member. In this respect, to disguise oneself at Ṭhākurāṇī Yātrā serves as a gender-specific male way of underlining this vow or to pay for the fulfillment of a wish. The religious motive is most explicit in the case of children's costumes. Boys of the age of two to nine commonly dress up as mythological or divine characters: as Kṛṣṇa they will wear blue make-up and play a flute, as Rāma they will carry a bow and arrow, as Duryyodhana they put on a glamorous uniform, while the costume of a holy sage requires an orange robe and a long white beard. Costumes are either improvised or hired at the festival ground. Dressed-up children neither enact the respective mythology nor play with each other. Their disguise is not for fun. The imitation of a divine character serves rather to collect alms from 'seven houses', which are offered to Buṙhī Ṭhākurāṇī at the end of the performance. The act of costuming and begging on behalf of the goddess is expected to protect the child from *basanta*, literally 'spring' and as a derivative 'smallpox', a term used as a synonym for a variety of contagious diseases accompanied by fever and skin rashes.[4] The goddess' heat and anger is understood to cause the pustules. Again, her satisfaction allows recovery from

[4] Smallpox has been eradicated now. It used to be a deadly disease for malnourished children. Moreover, epidemics of smallpox have shaped the history of Ganjam District from at least the nineteenth century onwards. Nevertheless, to worship a 'smallpox goddess' is not only motivated by this specific medical diagnosis (Egnor 1984; for a critique on the problematic label 'smallpox goddess', see Ferrari 2007).

measles, chickenpox or other children's diseases (and, when possible, provides immunity). Thus the disease, at least in its harmless version, is regarded as a desirable form of divine manifestation, similar to deity possession. Like the latter, *basanta* is thought to encourage faith in the goddess. If somebody should die of smallpox, he or she achieves the status of Buṛhī Ṭhākurāṇī's son or daughter. In this respect, the role of this goddess is similar to that of Śītaḷā in other parts of India. The *mānasika* for the good health of a male child is normally made by his mother and the boy is obliged to fulfill the pledge (Plate 7.1). In Berhampur, to have visited the goddess festival in a disguise constitutes a common male childhood experience.[5]

When adult men wish for divine help they might promise to wear a costume at Ṭhākurāṇī Yātrā for an auspicious number of years. In such cases they mostly dress up as a tiger (*bāgha beśa*). This costume has the highest reputation of all masquerades. The tiger represents the favourite animal and carrier of the goddess. Moreover, it is a very elaborate costume, consisting of a time-consuming application of body make-up covering the limbs with tiger-like stripes, highly decorated headgear, a long tail, and a shield of white frangipani flowers covering the upper part of the body (Plate 7.2). During festival time several artists, such as barbers, painters and florists, specialize in transforming men into tigers, a procedure that takes a minimum of half a day. Throughout the following night, the performer should dance continuously and – without taking proper food or rest – stick to his role.[6] In spite of the compelling drums, this needs a lot of strength and discipline. The physical effort is even greater since performers have to cope with itching skin, deriving from sweat or as an allergic reaction to colours suitable for painting walls rather than skin. There are a large number of expenditures involved in this masquerade, for the costume and drummers and to provide a feast for the relatives. Thus, to turn into a tiger is a difficult, painful and expensive affair. Often two or three friends get together to overcome their inhibitions and share the costs.

[5] In principle prepubescent girls can be dressed up as well, but during Ṭhākurāṇī Yātrā 2001 I did not see any of them.

[6] The choreography of this performance is also known as 'tiger dance' (Oriya: *bāgha nāca*, Telugu: *puli veśam*), a particular famous genre in the neighbouring state of Andhra Pradesh (see Rama Raju 1978: 132).

**Plate 7.1:** Painted to resemble a smallpox victim, the boy is taken to the goddess

**Plate 7.2:** Dancing as tiger, the favourite animal of Buṛhī Ṭhākurāṇī

The costume of a child-eating demoness (*pilākhāi ḍāhāṇī beśa*) is comparatively simple and cheap. It needs a black sari, bluish make-up, false long hair, and a huge paper tongue to create an eye-catching masquerade, although a rather gruesome one. The demoness carries a small mirror and a puppet and opts for children as her favourite food. Thus, she might be regarded as the demonic counterpart of Buṙhī Ṭhākurāṇī who, by causing deadly smallpox, seemingly 'eats' children as well. Like the tiger, the demoness attracts audiences by dancing, which requires the company of drummers. However, her performance is less elaborate than the tiger dance and the costume is associated with low social and caste status.

Whether dressed as deity, tiger or demoness, a man should collect alms from 'seven houses' and deliver them to the temporary shrine of Buṙhī Ṭhākurāṇī. Normally the donations are given by acquaintances, who decide on the amount on the basis of their social relationship with the performer, i.e., once a tiger is recognized as a close friend, a distant relative or as the neighbour's servant. Yet many men do not confine their begging to seven places. The loud and potentially threatening dance is used to extract money from onlookers. Therefore many people fear the confrontation with a stubborn tiger or an obtrusive demoness refusing to move on. Some businessmen even close their shops or restaurants. It is difficult to reject the excessive demands of a tiger if customers are attracted by his dance. After all, giving alms is considered a matter of piety — despite the fact that many tigers are suspected of being motivated by the desire for personal profit rather than religious merit.[7]

The costumes mentioned so far are not employed to make fun of the characters displayed. Whether a performer wears female attire, blue make-up, or a lolling paper tongue, it would be highly misleading to perceive the enactment as erotic gender play or grotesque in Bakhtin's sense. Although people agree that masquerades should be entertaining, nobody would want to produce a satire of deities or demons. Conversely, there are several other costumes that are meant to be amusing and foolish in the first place. Many of these represent stereotypes, for instance of hawkers selling fish (curd or perfume), corrupt politicians

---

[7] Once the donation is delivered at the Buṙhī Ṭhākurāṇī shrine, the priests get their share as well. The ritual fee (*dakṣiṇā*) for offering the collected alms differs according to the costume of the donor and thus reflects the religious and monetary efficacy of acting like a tiger or demoness.

or a hypocritical marriage party. The idea of mockery is not consistent. Some individuals change themselves into a perfect image of Mahatma Gandhi or into a modern version of Kṛṣṇa, playing an electric guitar. Another person may wear a number of colourful rags or just pretend to be blind. There are no restrictions on the creation of masquerades.

A few costumes are notorious for their display of devastating insult. They are performed almost exclusively by large groups of young men, who imitate apparently foolish savages, patients enjoying their leprosy, or Muslims mourning a living corpse. These kinds of masquerades consist of 10 to 50 people and are organized from different wards of Berhampur. A few groups have gained a reputation of their own and perform their mockery at every Ṭhākurāṇī Yātrā. The processions of monks (*bauddha sannyāsī beśa*) and of bald-headed priests (*laṇḍā beśa*) have become particularly famous. Both troupes make tremendous fun of religious and clerical symbols. Men wear 'sacred' necklaces made of potatoes, put marks on their forehead to parody those of monastic orders, show off with the latest sunglasses, wrap their robes the wrong way round, hug their (male) girl-friends, and equip themselves with air-filled condoms. In allusion to the sexual drive of clerics, some of these condoms also bulge underneath the robes in fairly obscene ways (Plate 7.3). To join the *laṇḍā beśa* men shave and cut their hair in a variety of shapes such as triangles, squares or stripes, and as such make fun of Vishnuite scholars who keep a small tuft, and the ritual hair sacrifice of Hindus in general. In addition, many participants have provocative and political slogans written on their naked upper body, such as, for instance, 'Bofors' – indicating one of the corruption scandals involving the Indian central government.[8]

## Provoking Discourse

People generally laugh at funny costumes and do not raise objections about the offensive provocations. Local media report on the number and variety of 'wonderful' (*ajab*) costumes, rather than on the content of the performances. Each disguise is implicitly associated with a religious vow. Thus, the hereditary head of the festival, the Deśībeherā, specifically invites people to put on fancy dress, and the local newspapers remind prospective 'monks' of their commitment.

[8] During the administration of Rajiv Gandhi, the name of the Swedish weapon dealer Bofors became a metaphor for political skulduggery and entered the vocabulary of several Indian languages.

**Plate 7.3:** A parody of priests, spiced up with 'sacred' potatoes and inflated condoms

If the range of masquerades is classified at all, people distinguish mythological (*paurāṇika*), social (*sāmājika*) and imaginary (*kāḷpanika*) costumes. Although there are also negative reactions to the provocations, normally people do not blame the performer. His behaviour is legitimized by the character displayed. A child-eating demoness has to be gruesome, tigers usually create trouble and policemen are known to beat people up. However, such reasoning cannot explain the mockery of monks and Muslims, which is justified with reference to 'old tradition'.[9] In any case, the violation of the moral order by costumed people fits well with other forms of transgression, as a peculiar form of social behaviour that is described in social anthropology as allowing anything usually forbidden (at least in public), like the display of obscenity, sexuality, riots, vandalism, or any other kind of symbolic or (even) real disturbance (Köpping 1998: 152). Yet, how do people in Berhampur consider these offensive masquerades and relate them to the ritual framework of the goddess festival?

An advertising leaflet, published on the occasion of Ṭhākurāṇī Yātrā 1999, summarizes the ambivalent audience reaction in a succinct formula: 'Ordinary people turn into artists, intelligent people turn mad!' Whereas 'ordinary people' (*sādhāraśa byakti*) actively participate in the festival, the author expects 'intelligent people' (*mastiṣka byakti*) to reject the practice of costuming. Indeed it seems that, for those who consider themselves the religious elite or of the social middle-class, to refrain from mixing with costumed men is a matter of prestige. However, one should note that the difference between acceptance, involvement and rejection is not just a question of class. Unlike the discrepancy suggested by the author of the leaflet, association and distancing are two different perspectives that might be taken by one and the same person on different occasions.

Usually people stress how difficult it is for a person to change into the role of a tiger, to overcome self-consciousness and dance in public. Therefore, it is more or less accepted that most performers consume a considerable amount of alcohol or cannabis to help stand this masquerade. Disturbances that result from intoxication are regarded as harmless aggressions. One (real) priest was even critical of policemen

[9] As far as I know, there are no records or studies about the origin and history of putting on a masquerade at Ṭhākurāṇī Yātrā. A local chronologist traces the collective costuming as priest and, respectively, as monk back to the years 1936 and 1963 (Candra 1998: 41–42).

beating up presumably drunken tigers roaming around in the middle of the night. In earlier times, he explained, costumed men could have referred to the goddess and remained 'free' (use of the English term in Oriya). Today the police intervene regularly to maintain law and order, and have therefore established an outpost opposite the temporary shrine of Buṙhī Ṭhākurāṇī. In the year 2001, it seemed that their main task was not only to prevent disturbances by intoxicated men but also to mediate in the conflict between competing organizers of the festival (see Chapter 8). In public discourse this quarrel was said to have prevented devotees from disguising themselves (*Sambād*, 21 April 2001). Costuming was recognized as a ritual requirement, i.e., opposed to politics. People explicitly missed the high number of dancing tigers. With respect to the festival as a site for the negotiation of power relations, the politicking of local bigwigs was contested, not the masquerade and the offences that go with it.

'Intelligent people', in turn, seem to have difficulty in dealing with the spontaneous performances of costumed people and their excessive playfulness. In line with this, a fundamentalist Hindu organization tried, though unsuccessfully, to get film music banned from public loudspeakers at Ṭhākurāṇī Yātrā, to avoid 'vulgar scenes' at the festival site (*Sambād*, 18 April 2001). Other attempts to prohibit offence were more effective. Some years ago masquerading as a leper was abandoned in order to show opposition against the discrimination of real victims of leprosy. There are other limitations to mockery. While people easily criticize corrupt politicians at a national level, they might risk severe beating if they made fun of local candidates. Moreover, in order to prevent disguised men from getting away with serious crimes, all 'tigers' now have to register with the police and obtain a permit which has to be shown on demand.

The most common strategy for dealing with offensive masquerades is simply to ignore them. In a brief survey on the festival, a recent *District Gazetteer* lists a variety of costumes, but excluding those which could appear to be distasteful, like the child-eating demoness or the disguise as politician. Costumes are treated only 'as part of the votive offering to the Ṭhākurāṇī' (Behuria 1995: 244). Similarly, an illustrative Oriya booklet on the festival dedicates a whole chapter to masquerades, but focuses only on their religious aspect (Pātra 1997: 29–32). Although the author cannot ignore the popularity of the collective disguise as either monk or priest, he fails to mention *why* people feel so attracted to them. He seems to deliberately misunderstand the provocative spirit of the costumes of the priests, trying hard to explain their unusual haircut as a religious act in honour of the goddess (Pātra 1997: 31). Several people I spoke with during fieldwork felt ashamed about the transgressions invited by the festive context, or at least worried about the conclusions outsiders might draw on learning about them. They did not accept the provocative mockery as part of their own tradition, but rather claimed that it is of 'tribal' origin.[10] Even then, Ṭhākurāṇī Yātrā was regarded as a most important event, which added to the cultural repertoire of southern Orissa, as well as to its tradition of goddess worship.

Women constitute another large group of onlookers, who watch the masquerades from a great distance. They are not allowed to join them, and they do not feel the need to do so.[11] Strictly speaking, women are not even addressed as audience. Although lots of female devotees flock together at the temporary shrine of Buṙhī Ṭhākurāṇī, they do not share the mockery of costumed men. Women are expected to behave decently. When watching funny dresses, they should not burst out laughing. They may enjoy performances, but are usually frightened when directly confronted by obscene jokes or sexual harassment in the predominantly male crowd. Women's role at the festival is confined to the ritual sphere. They gain satisfaction and prestige by serving the goddess and acting as her representative in nocturnal processions.

Thus, it seems that transgressions are a male privilege at the Ṭhākurāṇī festival, and women cannot engage in playful infractions. If they put on a costume and danced on the street it would be a real offence and as such is never approved. Yet, when considering the female way of pursuing a *mānasika* on the occasion of the goddess festival, some of the votaries also cross the line. As elaborated in Chapter 6, about ten thousand women, each carrying a sacred pot, join the final 'return journey' of the goddess. During this procession approximately every tenth devotee gets taken over by the deity. The possessed women

[10] Since several Hindus look down on Adivasis, this attribute seems to reflect a form of 'othering'. According to far-scattered hints in academic literature, masquerades and mockery accompany several Hindu festivities, for instance Daśaharā (Rama Raju 1978: 67), the Bengali Cāraka Gājan festival (McDaniel 1989: 238), Rāmlīlā (Kumar 1988: 190) or the Sāhi Yātrā in Puri (Mukhopadhyay 1978).

[11] One aspect of this rejection could be that the term *beśa*, used in reference to women, alludes to prostitution (Marglin 1985b: 98).

may jump wildly, scream or lash out. These offences against rules of female modesty are anticipated. They are not required, but when they occur they are interpreted as signs of divine presence. As such, female offences do not upset anyone. The occurrence of possession enhances the sacredness of the event. However, unlike male transgressions, female outbreaks are restricted to within the ritual domain and the body repertoire associated with it. They do not trigger controversial debates.

## Role-taking in Hinduism

The masquerades at Ṭhākurāṇī festival need to be understood within a larger context of Hindu devotional practices. Role-taking is considered both a divine play and a ritual technique. Hiding oneself under the garments of another character is a very popular theme in Hindu mythology (Hawley 1995: 123). Many deities are known to disguise themselves in order to fool other gods or to test the faith of their devotees. In the guise of a mendicant, Nārāẏaṇa tests a king's generosity; dressed as a bangle seller, Śiba outsmarts Pārbatī. Kṛṣṇa employs a number of costumes to seduce innocent cowgirls (*gopī*). Such changes of character are ambiguous, they are a play, a sport, they are fun, but they may also have serious consequences. Yet the assumption is that whatever the actions and their result, no (bad) intentions are involved (Sax 1995b: 146). This game, called *līlā* (Skt., Oriya: *līḷā*), can be shared by human beings who through their play become part of the divine world.[12]

Don Handelman's (1995: 293–302) study of the annual festival of the Telugu goddess Gangamma offers a good example of the practice of *līlā*. During the event young boys and men dress up as prince, minister, merchant, ascetic, shepherd, sweeper or snake charmer, and also as ruffians. As in the Ṭhākurāṇī Yātrā, this practice of costuming is connected to a vow. All of these characters are regarded as masquerades of the goddess herself, who is known as 'Mother of Guises' (Veshalamma, in Handelman's spelling).[13] There is no clear distinction between illusion and reality – guise and disguise overlap. In Oriya there is no

[12] On the concept of *līlā* in Hinduism, see Sax (1995a). Although in local discourse the term is associated with specific deities (like Kṛṣṇa or Rāma), its wider sense may include the playfulness of a goddess as well.

[13] For religious masquerades on the occasion of Vīrabhadra worship, compare Knipe (1989).

linguistic distinction either. Both facets of dressing up are called *beśa* (Telugu: *veśam*). Accordingly, Lord Jagannātha, the Oriya deity who attracts pilgrims from all over India, is known for his many costumes, ranging from a golden garment to one suitable for a forest picnic, and from the attire of a tribal warrior to that of the god Gaṇeśa. The accurate arrangement of his dress, cosmetics and decorations follows the instructions in the temple manual and constitutes a significant part of his worship (Schmid 2001: 303–4).

The performance of sacred dramas provides another occasion for humans to slip into divine costume. This happens, for instance, during the yearly performance of the Rāmlīlā, when entire North Indian villages turn into sacred stages for the performance of the life story of the god-king Rāma (see, for instance, Hauser 2006a, 2010a; Hein 1972; Kapur 1990; Lutgendorf 1991). The costumes transform the participants not only into theatre actors, but also enable them to participate in the cosmogonic play. To disguise oneself and join the Rāmlila is considered a pious duty and thus serves as a means for humans to gain religious merits. In Orissa, this is most explicit in the case of devotees who make up the monkey army of the god Rāma. Each year about hundred men take the vow to dress up as monkey. They wear this costume for about 10 days, wander from village to village and collect alms. At night they assemble at the Rāmlila stage to join the ritual drama (Hauser 2008b).[14] A similar form of ritual role-taking is found in Kṛṣṇa devotion. Among some sectarian communities in Bengal and North India, male disciples dress up as the god's female companion in order to participate in the divine liaison. The metaphor of erotic love serves to attain the utmost proximity to the deity and allows participants to become absorbed by this emotional encounter. Here the female dress invites a specific mode of religious realization (Haberman 1988: 137–39). Like changing into the *beśa* of a monkey, it serves to come close to the deity and to benefit from his ultimate presence.[15]

[14] To my knowledge there is no tradition of Ramlila theatre in Ganjam District, yet there are important stages in Asureswar (Cuttack District) and Daspalla (Nayagarh District).

[15] These religious practices are informed and legitimized by sixteenth-century Vaishnava theology that, for its part, had employed ancient Indian dramaturgical theory in order to bestow devotees with a sense of devotional love (see Wulff 1986; Hauser 2006a, 2006c, 2010a).

In general, to get lost in ritual play and to surrender to the divine character also has the potential to evoke possession.[16] During the Oriya performance of Prahlāda Nāṭa – the dramatized encounter of the mythological prince Prahlāda with the demon-king Hiraṇyakaśipu – actors purposely skip the last scene to avoid being taken over by Narasiṃha, the frightful man-lion incarnation of Nārāẏaṇa. However, if deity possession does occur, the audience will appreciate the visitation of the deity as a heightened form of religious experience (see Emigh 1996: 41–60; Hein 1972: 109; Smith 2006: 353). Accordingly, vestimentary practices are employed by male officiants and priests who identify themselves with a goddess, like for instance at the fire-walking festival in Orissa (Hauser 2007), in religious ceremonies among Adivasis in central India (Mallebrein 1999: 141) or among south Indian devotees who turn into 'Goddess-Dancers' (Kapadia 1996). On these religious occasions female attire and hairstyle does not only resemble the gender of the goddess, cross-dressing serves as a technique to encourage possession by her.

Thus there is a recurrent idea of costuming as a ritual body practice. Central to this form of devotional self-identification with the divine is the mimetic process and the human body as an instrument used to gain extraordinary experiences and, by doing so, soteriological merits. The masquerades at Ṭhākurāṇī Yātrā have to be evaluated within this context of role-taking in Hinduism. To grasp their socio-religious impact on non-festive times, I distinguish the semiotic and the processional aspect of costuming.

In its *semiotic* capacity, a disguise is recognized as a manifestation of divine play rather than as a human form of direct or indirect self-presentation. Whether a man dresses as wild tiger or as lascivious monk, in general his masquerade is not assessed in terms of relating his social persona to the character displayed. The costume is neither to hide the known personality of the actor, nor does the type of disguise lead to any conclusion about particular traits in his personality. Onlookers do not consider the dialectics of concealing and revealing the self. In other words, the selection of a particular masquerade and its corresponding behaviour is not normally understood as a result of moral preferences. It either alludes to mythology or displays the painfully

---

[16] On the intertwined modes of embodying and decoding ritual acting, see Hauser (2008a).

comic side of human existence, here ascribed to divine authorship.[17] Therefore, offences against normative values and rules for interaction are not criticized or punished. They reflect the playfulness of the goddess. She is the ultimate actor and the real audience. She has to be amused. Pleased by the festival, Bur̐hī Ṭhākurāṇī will once more take proper care of the town and its inhabitants.

In its *processual* capacity, costuming can be understood as a devotional exercise to express a religious pledge (*mānasika*) or to pay for the fulfillment of a wish. Unlike other ritual forms of role-taking that end in possession, the practice of masquerading at Ṭhākurāṇī Yātrā is not employed to appropriate the nature of another character. To dress like a demoness should not invoke possession by her. Even though people might interpret a mythological disguise as an attempt to share the piety or courage of a particular deity, this is not the general reasoning. The process of role-taking should not emphasize personhood at all.[18] Rather than a journey of self-discovery, role-taking serves as a means to its very annihilation. As a form of temporary denial of the self, costuming can be considered to be a transformative device. In this sense, it is comparable to other male body disciplines like ascetic exercises, wrestling, martial arts or dance.[19] It puts specific attention on the physicality of the body and creates a nearly egalitarian brotherhood where ordinary status differences play only minor roles. Moreover, transformed by a costume, a man turns his back on family life and worldly responsibilities.

As shown previously, the practice of costuming in south Orissa is embedded in a larger religious discourse. It provides justification for offensive masquerades and, as such, perpetuates the paradox of expected violations. I do not claim that reference to this religious context (or any other) creates a uniform reasoning; rather, this is to open a contingent field of interpretation. The emphasis of transcendent playfulness and ritual significance helps people to cope with the

[17] On humour and comedy in Hindu scriptures see Siegel (1987).

[18] This is in fact often overlooked when ritual forms of impersonation are described as play of self and other (see, for instance, Emigh 1996; Sax 1995b, 2002).

[19] On wrestling and ascetic practices see Alter (1992: 214–36); on martial arts and ritual drama compare Zarilli (1990); for Daṇḍa Nāṭa, another Orissan performance genre that combines (male) ascetic exercises with dance and theatre see Schnepel (2008).

irritating performances. Yet, at the same time, the ambiguity of the situation is required to make transgressions what they are: offences that provoke although they are expected. When people debate vulgar gestures, intoxication and exaggerated claims for money, they also consider the possibility that these actions are driven by individual desire. Thereby ambiguity is created, which leaves open the question of who acts — the divine actor or the man behind in the costume?

The differentiation between the semiotic and the processual impact of role-play also helps when comparing the male practice of dressing up with the paradigmatic female way of participating in the festival by means of carrying a goddess pot on the final night. This female 'body technique' (Mauss) to annihilate the self requires a lot of strength. While on a fast, women have to stand and walk for hours. Carrying the sacred pot on their head, they are to concentrate on the goddess manifesting herself inside. Since women are believed to already share the transcendent energy of the goddess, they do not require any specific dress to achieve impersonation. Being female and bestowed with auspicious marks compensates for the lack of any costume when it comes to enticing divine possession. In analogy to some masked men who violate social norms, some pot bearers become possessed. As I have shown in Chapter 5, the behaviour of possessed women is regarded as an allusion to familiar goddess iconography. The extraordinary bodily reactions are regarded as signs of divine identity rather than as a result of human personality. In the case of transgression, however, possession by female participants can create similar uncertainties. In both cases, doubting the true surrender to the deity serves as a means to negotiate the limit of acceptable wildness. No matter whether a woman is overpowered or not, to escort Buṙhī Ṭhākurāṇī on her way home is by itself considered a transformative device. It serves as a religious exercise to either express a vow (*mānasika*) or to give thanks for the goddess' favour — from this angle it again corresponds to the male practice of costuming.

## Conclusion: Gendering *līḷā*

In contrast to carnivalesque traditions, costuming at the goddess festival is not only done for enjoyment but, most importantly, transmits a religious intention. The entertainment is meant to please the goddess, and thus contributes to the soteriological efficacy of the festival. In this respect the semiotic meaning of costumes (and the behaviour of characters displayed) might be neglected in favour of the act of costuming itself, as a form of ritual body practice. Serving as a temporary annihilation of the self, this practice can be compared with other forms of voluntarily chosen religious exercises that transform the person. The temporal denial of human agency reflects the divine taste for ludic role-taking. Comic action and even offensive performances contribute to the eternal play.

With respect to Ṭhākurāṇī Yātrā, the political aspect of the carnivalesque appears to be rather marginal. People do not relate any uprising, debate or movement to the provocative mockery of costumed people. These performances make fun of cultural stereotypes (like the sex-driven monk) but do not question the institution. The festive mood, rather, invites the relaxation of status distinctions. Transgressions by costumed men are expected and conceptualized as a form of humor, possibly contested but without social consequences. In this context the stance of the performer is of little importance. Whether he 'truly impersonates' or 'seriously lives' the confrontation with the moral order is of significance for his personal transformation, but only secondary for the audience and the reorientation of their perception.

As a gender-specific body practice, masquerades do not only express a particular discursive knowledge about male and female codes of behaviour. Rather they verify tacit assumptions and thus modulate the perception of the male body, according to which men can *play* with different appearances and employ them for particular (ritual) purposes. Even the everyday guise of a man does not lead to a conclusion about his nature (though it may indicate status). This is fundamentally different with women. Female corporeality is thought to transmit a moral message about the person, at best about her auspiciousness (see Chapter 3). Dress, body decoration and behaviour are seen as an index of a woman's character. Seemingly, the female body visualizes the essential qualities of the person. This gender concept is supplemented by the notion of possession. Women's bodies are thought to be more permeable than male ones. They do not need costuming to attract and integrate divine power, quite unlike male ritual specialists who personify the goddess. However, not every woman in the final procession is overpowered, and possession does not only happen to women. Yet possession and costuming both contribute to the idea of male bodies as bounded entities. Although male selves get absorbed in performance every now and then, they are not forced to do so; their bodies are comparatively more independent. This makes men eligible for costuming. Thus, the performance of a disguise at the festival perpetuates (hyper-) manliness, although the actor might wear the attire of a *female* demon.

Transgression, for its part, is not simply an indication of masculinity. Rather the modalities of going beyond the limits vary according to gender. As shown previously in the discussion, wearing masquerade dress and carrying a sacred pot are structurally similar in that both serve as a religious exercise to fulfill a religious pledge. Both can invite 'wild' behaviour. However, female and male forms of transgression differ in their social impact. Male violations are conceptualized in terms of humor and, nevertheless, create a public debate about the limits of this role-play. In contrast, transgressions by possessed pot carriers do not provoke any discourse. Women who violate the ideal of female modesty cause neither laughter nor public outrage. Their at times grotesque bodiliness is ascribed to the goddess's ambivalent nature that also legitimizes women's participation in the nocturnal public in general (a transgression by itself). Moreover, carrying a sacred pot constitutes a ritual exercise that, in principle, can be shared by men. In several parts of South India, men in fact dominate processions in honour of a goddess (see Kapadia 1996). Within the context of Ṭhākurāṇī Yātrā, both male and female ways of exceeding the limits contribute towards the sacredness of the event in complementary ways. Both kinds of transgressions are re-enacted and refreshed in the course of the festival. Unlike some forms of global art, the provocations do not gradually expand or dissolve moral limits. Their transformative potential reveals itself first of all to the performer and her or his religious self.

In respect to ritual drama in Benares, Nita Kumar (1995: 158) has argued that the concept of *līlā* perpetuates a highly gendered discourse. Women are excluded from most events classified as *līlā*; nor do they actively participate in the production and reproduction of the discourse on *līlā*: 'Playfulness is not the prerogative of women, as is not lack of worry [sic], carefreeness, abandon . . . women are not part of this vision of the good life [i.e., līlā] as subject participants'. (Kumar 1995: 163) On the one hand, this is also true for Ṭhākurāṇī Yātrā, where only men dress up, while female transgressions are contained within the ritual domain. On the other hand, this is only one side of the coin. Women can certainly experience the performance of Hindu rituals in very pleasurable, playful and sensuous ways. This is most explicit in Kṛṣṇa devotion (see Tokita-Tanabe 1999b: Chapter 1). However, they prefer to do so among themselves, rather than in the company of men. In this sense, female laughter is hardly public. From another perspective, Ṭhākurāṇī Yātrā serves as a cultural site where the divine play itself is constructed in gender-specific ways: in the course of male masquerades and, most prominently, by means of possessed pot bearers. In this case, possession as a religious form and female practice is not a given.[20] If a woman has vowed to carry a sacred pot, she will do so. In this posture she is regarded as the *representation* of the goddess. However, considering the nocturnal processions by the nine Devāṅgī women, deity possession is anything but predestined. The divine power should manifest itself in the pot but not in the women. None of the Devāṅgī women *personify* Buṛhī Ṭhākurāṇī and her eight sisters. Similarly, the Deśībeherāṇī is treated as the (adopted) mother of the goddess but not as her embodiment (see Chapter 8). Thus Buṛhī Ṭhākurāṇī's 'return journey' differs from Tuesday Pageants. Looking at this final night, female devotees instead take the procession as a religious site to define their encounter with the divine feminine in this specific bodily and thus personal form. In this respect, not only male but also female corporeality creates how the divine play manifests itself.

[20] Kapadia (1996, 2000: 181–82) observed that Tamil women are gradually banned from the participation in pot processions once the event is given prestige.

# 8

# The Limitations of Ritual: Female Politics and the Public

Several religious festivals in South Asia (and elsewhere) have their own history of conflicts and Ṭhākurāṇī Yātrā is no exception. A public performance of this size commonly involves immense monetary transactions, encourages competition and rivalry, and raises questions of hierarchy, status and privileges (see also Fuller 1992: 136). Thus it alludes not only to devotion and transcendence but also to basic human longings and shortcomings. With the spiritual purpose in mind, participants often silence, downplay and condemn these conflicts; the sacred character of the event should remain free of mundane distractions. Still, it is expected that some people may look for personal advantage. In present-day local discourse, this is often verbalized as the intermingling of two cultural domains, of 'religion' and 'politics', or rather of two historical periods and their moral quality – 'tradition' (*paramparā*) and 'modernity'.[1] The conflicts thus generate a debate as to the rightful performance of Ṭhākurāṇī Yātrā.

Whereas the pot processions and also the masquerades constitute gender-specific sites for experiencing Ṭhākurāṇī Yātrā, the dispute about the correct procedure of the festival involves both men and women, particularly those individuals who share the responsibility of its direction. In this chapter I shall concentrate on the role of the

[1] With respect to pre-modern and present-day India, academic scholars have argued that it is misleading to conceive of religion and politics as two separate cultural domains since one entails the other (see Sax 2000: 39). As will become clear further in the discussion, I generally subscribe to this view. Nevertheless, priests and their clients employ this distinction to assess ritual practices, no matter whether their definition as opposites derives from a Western post-Enlightenment discourse.

Deśībeherāṇī and her female relatives (affines), and consider in what ways they relate to the unpopular conflicts. The interdependency of both genders for the successful celebration of Ṭhākurāṇī Yātrā, and hence the religious benefit for the community at large, becomes particularly clear when considering her personal situation. I shall demonstrate that to refuse cooperation in religious functions or to deny somebody her or his honorary rights is a way of exercising immense power. Moreover, as shown in previous chapters, women often gain authority due to reference to the divine, i.e., by alluding to the goddess herself as the driving force of their actions. This capacity to act in cooperation with divine consent I have termed ritual agency. Focusing on the performance of Ṭhākurāṇī Yātrā, the limits of ritual agency and also of women's empowerment by means of their religious engagement become obvious. What happens to the Deśībeherāṇī in the public space of Ṭhākurāṇī Yātrā, I contend, resembles the experience of several women who, if in a desperate and marginalized position, devote themselves to religious matters. Their ritual activities are likely to be denigrated as a strategy to achieve personal profit. In spite of what simplistic and polemic statements of this kind suggest, the performance of rituals does not generally improve a woman's status, with regard either to family politics or to finance. Although heightened ritual competence at times initiates a new form of livelihood, this is exceptional. In this respect the performance of rituals is not a very effective tool for the enforcement of social claims. Nevertheless, it may serve as a source of improved reputation and self-confidence.

To write about conflicts and to expose living individuals to academic discourse also raises ethical questions. In the case of Ṭhākurāṇī Yātrā it is difficult to render personal features anonymous since the respective women are well-known. However, by the year 2001 the disputes about the festival, and particularly concerning the marriage crisis of the leading couple, had already created a public debate, and both the Deśībeherā and the Deśībeherāṇī informed the media about the lack of cooperation of their spouse. The following chapter is written on the basis of these intimate and yet public arguments, transmitted in newspaper articles[2] and also orally to everyone who spent any time

[2] In this chapter I evaluate articles from the Oriya newspapers *Anupama Bhārata* (19 April 2001), *Dainika Āśā* (12 March 2001, 12 April 2001, 17 April 2001, 24 April 2001, 25 April 2001), *Dharitrī* (15 April 2001), and *Sambād* (24 March 2001, 1 April 2001, 10 April 2001, 12 April 2001, 14 April 2001, 16 April 2001, 21 April 2001,

in Deśībeherā Street. Certainly, the general dispute about Ṭhākurāṇī Yātrā also influenced the fieldwork situation. Whereas it was possible to communicate with *either* the Deśībeherā *or* the Deśībeherāṇī – and also with those at the margins of the conflict – interviews with other female pot bearers did not materialize. Moreover, several details of the festival were emphasized or silenced after considering their impact on (my presumable position in) the ongoing conflict. In any case, the aim of this chapter is to search neither for the 'true' culprits nor for the one and only 'correct' procedure of Ṭhākurāṇī Yātrā. Rather I shall explore how the role and behaviour of prominent female ritual specialists is framed and evaluated in local discourse, on the basis of culturally pre-structured arguments, rhetoric formulas and acts of legitimization. It will be seen whether and on what basis the Deśībeherāṇī and her female affines are regarded as powerful, and what kind of effects their religious engagement can produce in everyday life. I argue that ritual honours bestow the performer with 'social immunity' – particularly relevant if the non-ritual sphere is characterized by conflicting interests and severe disputes. Considering the inherently political nature of ceremonial processions in India, women's interest in ritual honours also constitutes a genuine way to manifest and claim 'real' power and authority.

## The Family Drama

In 2001 the realization of Ṭhākurāṇī Yātrā was challenged by a severe marriage crisis of the leading couple, i.e., the Deśībeherā and the Deśībeherāṇī. Their personal situation raised practical problems regarding the celebration of the festival. It also confronted people with the risk of breaking with tradition (*paramparā*), and thus infringing heavenly 'rules and regulations' (*bidhi-bidhāna*) for the worship of Buṛhī Ṭhākurāṇī. The family dispute turned into a public affair and, to make matters worse, was then stirred up by the media. In this context, the position of the Deśībeherāṇī was extremely fragile. Although she represented the most important female ritual specialist, she also faced the stigma of being an abandoned wife and single-parent mother.

24 April 2001, 25 April 2001, 30 April 2001, 5 May 2001). As far as I know from Telugu journalists, the Telugu papers reported on Ṭhākurāṇī Yātrā in a very similar fashion. In the pan-regional English press, however, the marriage crisis of Deśībeherā and Deśībeherāṇī was mentioned only briefly, without personal names and details (*New Indian Express* 11 April 2001, 24 April 2001).

In 1995, at the age of 18, she had married the present Deśībeherā. It seemed to be a promising match since the marriage qualified her groom to perform his inherited assignment as the leader of the Devāṅgī (Telugu weavers). He was thus authorized to conduct Ṭhākurāṇī Yātrā in collaboration with his wife, and a few weeks after the wedding, the festival did indeed take place. In the following year the Deśībeherāṇī gave birth to a son. In 1999 Ṭhākurāṇī Yātrā was already overshadowed by the couple's marriage crisis, and hence the temporary absence of the Deśībeherā. His daily tasks were performed by members of the organizing committee, and to fulfill the 'rules and regulations', the infant boy had to replace his father. In the beginning of 2001 the Deśībeherāṇī and her son stayed at her parents' house; the couple appeared to be ready for a divorce.

During the preliminaries of Ṭhākurāṇī Yātrā, the Deśībeherā took formal steps to advance this separation. Turning to the district administration he obtained an eviction order against his wife. With the help of police, he opened the room where she had locked her belongings. This act was legitimized by the coming festival. Since her room was attached to the goddess shrine (*pīṭham*), the locked doors hindered the rituals scheduled for the initial night of Ṭhākurāṇī Yātrā, i.e., the installation of the sacred basket (see Chapter 6). According to the press, the Deśībeherā was planning to conduct the festival at any rate, considering the transfer of his wife's ritual tasks to somebody else, if necessary (*Dainika Āśā*, 12 March 2001). Subsequently, the Deśībeherāṇī appealed to the district magistrate. She strongly opposed the illegal eviction, also using arguments concerning Ṭhākurāṇī Yātrā (rather than family law). She claimed that her husband had denied her the privileges of a Deśībeherāṇī, i.e., to be treated like the mother of Buṛhī Ṭhākurāṇī, to carry the main goddess pot during the nocturnal processions and to stay at the *pīṭham* house – the family premises that in the course of the festival turned into public space. These rights were promised to her in the course of the marriage proposal. Once the petition reached the High Court of Orissa, the nature of the case was thus characterized as the 'right to worship the Goddess'.[3]

Finally, the Collector (the district chairman and magistrate) gave the order for Ṭhākurāṇī Yātrā to be conducted jointly. Whereas the Deśībeherā was asked to account for the funding, the Deśībeherāṇī was entitled to perform the 'rituals as per practice'. In the presence of

[3] Source: O.J.C. No. 3856 of 2001, High Court of Orissa, Cuttack, 29 March 2001.

10 respected residents of the old town, the couple signed a *Memorandum of Understanding for Restoration of Marital Life* so as to guarantee the smooth performance of the festival. He agreed 'to solve all the problems created by his mother and sisters', she promised 'not to go to her parents' house very often'.[4] This fragile reconciliation was strengthened by the foundation of an organizing committee with a great number of advisers, chairmen and secretaries from municipal boards, political parties and business and caste organizations. However, the troubles continued even after the onset of Ṭhākurāṇī Yātrā. Again both husband and wife were considering their complaints in religious terms: She would cause delays during the pot procession, change the course of the nightly processions arbitrarily and therefore skip a number of roads where devotees were waiting. She had chosen unknown rather than legitimate women to carry the remaining goddess pots, and failed to offer the sacrificial food. He was blamed for accusing the eight pot bearers in filthy language and for wrongfully giving ritual honours to his sister (who did not formally belong to the Deśībeherā's dynasty). Moreover, he would refuse to hand out the jewelry that was considered part of the Deśībeherāṇī's attire and thus essential for the pot procession. Only after police intervention did the Deśībeherāṇī get to wear the golden ornaments and the nocturnal rituals could then proceed.[5]

These conflicts arising on the occasion of Ṭhākurāṇī Yātrā were well-known throughout the old town. Women in the neighbourhood of the Buṙhī Ṭhākurāṇī temple commented:

> Yes we know about the quarrel. The problem is that [out of jealousy] the mother-in-law is not able to stand the daughter-in-law, so that the [husband] wonders whether to leave his mother or his wife. Well, he left his wife. Mother and son, they drove away the daughter-in-law. But when the festival time came, the Collector said that *only after fetching your wife* will I give the permission to carry out the pot processions. *Then the Deśībeherā bowed down to the feet of his wife and called her back.* (my emphasis)

Besides the initial formulaic statement that alludes to a potential conflict in many joint family households, the assessment of the Collector's

[4] *Memorandum of Understanding for Restoration of Marital Life* (handwritten), 9 April 2001.

[5] These accusations were also published by the Oriya newspapers *Sambād* (12 April 2001) and *Dainika Āśā* (24 April 2001).

role and also the Deśībeherā's alleged reaction show how these women certainly recognize the power offered by the ritual status of the Deśībeherāṇī.

Indeed, the family conflict was not limited to the troubles between the Deśībeherāṇī and her husband but also concerned her tense relations with his mother and his maternal aunt. Both women are the natural daughters of a previous Deśībeherā who had died in 1983. Since he did not have a male heir, he had adopted his grandson (younger daughter's son, i.e., the present Deśībeherā) and thus left close family members with competing claims to inherited rights, a point I shall come back to later. In this context, the mother of the present Deśībeherā had taken hold of the daily food offerings to Buṙhī Ṭhākurāṇī (and the eight sisters), an act that subverted the ritual priority of the Deśībeherāṇī. Similarly, the maternal aunt had succeeded in carrying the sacred basket (and pot, respectively) on the initial and final night of Ṭhākurāṇī Yātrā, i.e., during the most significant processions of the festival. Previously she had lost a lawsuit against her younger sister about the legitimate succession of the latter's son rather than the son of the first-born, i.e., her own boy (*Anupama Bhārata*, 19 April 2001). It was decided to compensate her with the lifetime honour of carrying the basket/main pot on the first and the last night of the festival. By 2001, both sisters were in their fifties and defended their ritual privileges, not only against the Deśībeherāṇī but also with respect to their formal eligibility. On the one hand, neither of them belonged to the (late) Deśībeherā's lineage (*gotra*), a status they had lost after their marriage.[6] On the other hand, they had by now become widows. From a conservative standpoint they therefore lacked the auspiciousness to carry, for instance, a goddess pot.[7] However, for both sisters it was a matter of devotion *and status* to join the festival and remain close to Buṙhī Ṭhākurāṇī. While in 2001 their participation did not raise any *public* criticism, it revealed the hierarchy of the women in the extended family of the Deśībeherā and in this respect was noticed in the neighbourhood.

[6] At marriage every bride shifts from her natal to her marital lineage (*gotra*). In this respect, daughters are considered part of their future husband's family.

[7] Whereas from a high-caste perspective widows should not represent the goddess, in practice they do so on several occasions (compare Sujata's case in Chapter 5). On the auspiciousness of married women whose husbands are alive, see Chapter 3.

The tense situation apparently culminated in what came to be known as a faked goddess possession. At the beginning of one nocturnal procession, opposite the Mahurī Rājā's residence, the Deśībeherāṇī 'couldn't proceed further as she fell unconscious', the local newspaper reported (*Sambād*, 14 April 2001). According to eyewitnesses the Deśībeherāṇī started to stumble and two men, who were standing close to her, got hold of the goddess pot. The pot bearer, however, fell down on the ground. When she was asked what had happened, the Deśībeherāṇī complained in a way that alluded to Buṛhī Ṭhākurāṇī. 'In my house [i.e., the *pīṭham* house] nobody is worshipping me properly! . . . The divine light (*akhaṇḍa dīpa*) was left to be extinguished! . . . Why are you offering me sacrificial food (*bhoga*) twice? . . . Why are you people avoiding me?' She was gnashing her teeth and pushing people. By means of this (seemingly) divine uttering, the Deśībeherā and his relatives were reprimanded for their insufficient religious commitment. Above all, the speech was conceived of as a direct criticism of the Deśībeherā's mother, who had not transferred the honourable duty of serving the goddess' daily food on to her daughter-in-law. When, a few days earlier, the Deśībeherāṇī had given the *bhoga* herself, her mother-in-law did not concede this privilege, and the divine meal was offered twice.

After some time the Deśībeherāṇī regained consciousness and, in tears, proposed to return to the temporary shrine (*aṣṭhāẏī mandira*). That evening the goddess pots did not visit any of the scheduled streets. Women were kept waiting in vain and were unable to show their reverence to the goddess. Despite this embarrassing situation, the divine intervention itself appeared fairly natural. A neighbour commented: 'If she is not well or if her mind is disturbed, she will not proceed any further but return from the [Mahurī] Rājā's premises to the temporary shrine'. Significantly, the personal pronoun in this statement is ambivalent. It could refer to both, the goddess and the Deśībeherāṇī.

According to male ritual specialists, the Deśībeherāṇī had actually only pretended to be possessed:

> We presume that [she] acted like this in order to insult her husband . . . Knowledgeable people, meaning my father, my uncles and educated people did not believe it. Since she carried the pot on her head, the goddess will be inside the pot [rather than inside her body].

Being possessed, however, the Deśībeherāṇī had not only questioned how she was treated in her husband's house but also the competence of the Dāmalā priests. These men are in charge of sealing the body of the Deśībeherāṇī and of the other eight pot bearers against possession by supernatural powers. In accordance with the legendary origin of Ṭhākurāṇī Yātrā, the goddess is not allowed to possess her 'parents', i.e., the Deśībeherā and his wife, or the remaining pot bearers either.[8] Therefore a Dāmalā priest performs a protective ritual ahead of each pot procession, in which he speaks some sacred formulas (*mantra*) and attaches a lump of turmeric paste to the person's forehead (Plate 8.1). If the divine should still overpower the pot bearer this would certainly disgrace the priest. Whereas in other processions (like the Tuesday Pageant) the altered state of the body usually authorizes the pot bearer and her utterings to reveal divine truth, in this case the response was different. The Deśībeherāṇī was blamed for play-acting. Onlookers were not prepared to listen to divine words.

The possession incident thus called on two competing principles: (*a*) it alluded to ritual agency, associated with the female pot bearer; and (*b*) it challenged *ritual expertise*, personified by the Dāmalā priest. Whereas several women in the old town who had witnessed or heard about the incident considered the manifestation of the divine, the public privileged the male priestly competence and thus disqualified the respective (and in this context female) body practice and method of authentication. The Deśībeherāṇī was criticized for not considering her self-presentation and instead acknowledging her submission to the divine! However, the debate as to the credibility of the possession also shows that the potential of the Deśībeherāṇī had posed a real threat.[9]

Despite her still young age, the Deśībeherāṇī seemed to follow the 'rules and regulations' of the festival as sincerely as she could. Yet according to local spokesmen she did not earn any credits by doing so. Why? Apparently there were several reasons. First, social conflicts are often said to originate from quarrels between women. In this respect the Deśībeherāṇī rather than the Deśībeherā is always more likely to become the scapegoat. People were also of the opinion that 'in . . . their

[8] As shown in Chapter 6, this rule does not apply to women in general. During Buṛhī Ṭhākurāṇī's return journey on the final night of the festival, several pot bearers were possessed. In any case, they do not take any protective measures to prevent goddess possession.

[9] Here the competing viewpoints on the reality of deity possession are also shaped by gender. Questioning the authenticity of an oracle is yet a common objection whenever divine mediumship is employed in the public arena as an instrument of policy-making (see, for instance, Sax 1991: 100, 185).

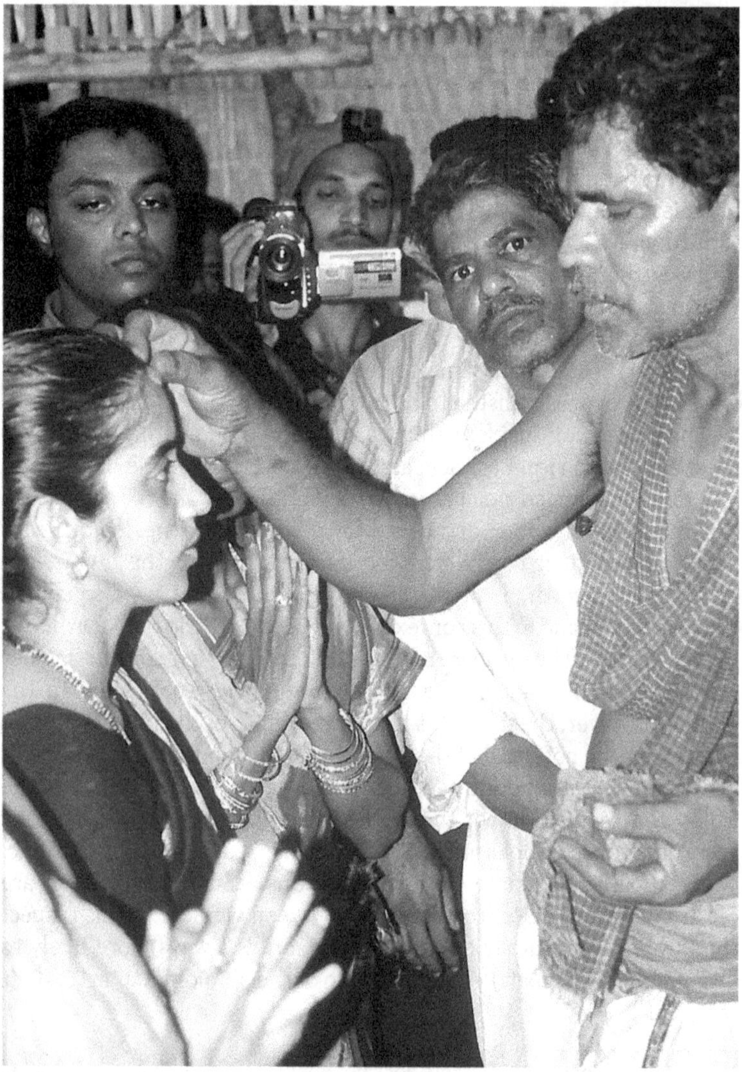

**Plate 8.1:** Dāmalā priest seals the body of the Deśībeherāṇī, documented by a local television reporter

family the ladies always dominate'. Second, the Deśībeherā and the Deśībeherāṇī had each assembled leading figures to join the organizing committee, yet these members were associated with different political factions. Whether they publicly defended or blamed the Deśībeherāṇī reflected their own allegiance to the ruling party or, conversely, the opposition.[10] This intermingling of 'feminist' arguments and party politics certainly caused scepticism. Yet there is also a third dimension to the criticism the Deśībeherāṇī had to face. Being the Deśībeherā's wife and 'adopted mother' of the goddess makes her first of all a representative, who in the 'public arena' (Freitag) serves the deity on behalf of the community.[11] In this context, her private suffering and struggle do not matter, and if anything leaks to the public this will cause disagreement. Moreover, while acting in her capacity as Deśībeherāṇī any statement is likely to be deciphered in political terms, and in this case as a metaphor for quarrels and factions *within* the community. This will by itself stir emotions and anger. Subsequently by uttering complaints, though regarding the proper worship of the goddess, the Deśībeherāṇī had entered a *political* minefield. Her rhetoric alluded to a series of previous conflicts within the community when Ṭhākurāṇī Yātrā served as a site to negotiate monetary and political interests.

## Fencing Traditions

The analysis of the twentieth-century history of Ṭhākurāṇī Yātrā shows that disputes about the correct performance of the festival are neither new nor originate in the 'poor' behaviour of specific women. Rather they are connected to political and financial conflicts within the Devāṅgī and other communal bodies participating in the performance of Ṭhākurāṇī Yātrā.

The *present* series of conflicts goes back to the death of the former Deśībeherā in 1983. Since he did not have any male offspring who could become the next leader of the Devāṅgī, the old man had adopted his grandson (the present Deśībeherā). Yet since this boy was still a minor and unmarried, he could not take his office. In 1985 the late Deśībeherā's nephew (younger brother's son) became the (interim) Deśībeherā.

10 Tokita-Tanabe's (1996: 98) study on village politics had shown that disparate factions tend to associate with political parties although they do not necessarily identify with their policies. In this respect, party affiliation only objectifies a sense of belonging based on caste, economic interests and local socio-political claims.

11 There is an extensive debate on the variable and changing perception of public space in South Asia. For the impact of collective action, religious ceremonies and public performances as a form of political engagement and identity formation see, for instance, Freitag (1989, 1991).

The late leader's widow and his daughters went to court. They lost the litigation about the succession, but in 1993 they resumed the case and eventually won. By that time the grandson had grown up and was waiting to get married. However, the conflict about the succession had divided the community. Several representatives of the Devāṅgī, men assigned as 'Senāpati' (literally: General), were in favour of the interim Deśībeherā. They cut off their social relations with their late leader's descendants. People hesitated to give their daughter in marriage to the young outcast. However, this possible stigma was compensated by the status of a Deśībeherāṇī which a wife would receive, so finally a suitable bride was found. In 1995 the newly married candidate succeeded in becoming the Deśībeherā and from then on, in cooperation with this wife, conducted Ṭhākurāṇī Yātrā. Nevertheless, his position was still disputed by some.

In 2001 the reunification of the Deśībeherā and his wife 'for the sake of the festival' motivated parts of the Devāṅgī community to revive a pending case concerning their righteous leader. The interim Deśībeherā and his people were eagerly waiting to provide evidence of mistakes in the performance of Ṭhākurāṇī Yātrā, in order to disqualify the 'false' Deśībeherā. Their criticisms referred to the following points:

(*a*) The *route* of the pot procession:
How many and which streets are visited?
Who is authorized to select the route every evening?

(*b*) The *qualification* and selection of pot bearers:
Besides the Deśībeherāṇī, who may carry the main goddess pot?[12]
Who is eligible to take the other eight pots, any Devāṅgī women or Senāpati wives only?
Who is entitled to select these women?

(*c*) The *nomination* of the Deśībeherā:
Can leadership ever devolve to an adopted son?
Has the adoption case been legally confirmed?
Does the leadership require the approval of other authorities, such as the Senāpatis or the Mahurī Rājā?

---

[12] Menstrual pollution or sickness may prevent the Deśībeherāṇī from carrying the main goddess pot herself.

In this respect, several issues raised during the private conflict between the Deśībeherā and his wife had indeed resembled and related to established idioms of power relationship verification during the goddess festival.

The disputes about Ṭhākurāṇī Yātrā and its correct performance in fact go back to the beginning of the twentieth century (at least), and concern not only the Devāṅgī but also other castes and interest groups living in the old town. According to journalistic investigations there were altogether 20 litigations related to Buṛhī Ṭhākurāṇī and her biennial festival, starting from 1900 onwards.[13] This certainly hints at the attractive financial benefits and also at the political significance associated with Ṭhākurāṇī Yātrā and the position of the Deśībeherā. In the history of India, Hindu temples, their administrative networks and also religious festivals served as pivotal redistributive institutions

---

[13] The Oriya newspaper *Anupama Bhārata* (19 April 2001) gives a list of the respective case numbers, years and courts (here given in Anglicized spelling):

1. O.S. 40 of 1900, Berhampur Subdivision Magistrate;
2. O.S. 613 of 1912, Berhampur Subdivision Magistrate;
3. O.S. 283 of 1913, Berhampur Subdivision Magistrate;
4. O.S. 554 of 1923, Berhampur Subdivision Magistrate;
5. O.S. 342 of 1924, District Munsif;
6. O.S. 192 of 1928, Subdivisional Magistrate;
7. O.S. 499 of 1931, Subdivisional Magistrate;
8. O.S. 266 of 1942, Subdivisional Magistrate;
9. O.S. 88 of 1951, District Munsif;
10. T.S. 2 of 1970, District Munsif (Berhampur);
11. T.S. 3 of 1970, District Munsif (Berhampur);
12. T.S. 35 of 1985, Subordinate Judge (Berhampur);
13. T.S. 88 of 1998, Subordinate Judge;
14. Civil Revision 89 of 2000, District Court;
15. Second Appeal 64 of 1995, High Court of Orissa (Cuttack);
16. M.C. 140 of 1995, High Court of Orissa (Cuttack);
17. M.C. 142 of 1997, High Court of Orissa (Cuttack);
18. M.C. 97 of 1999, High Court of Orissa (Cuttack);
19. O.J.C. 3856 of 2001 High Court of Orissa (Cuttack);
20. A-A8 of 1998, Endowment Court (Berhampur).

I could verify the nature of only some of these cases. They concerned land rights associated with the office of the Deśībeherā, the management of the Buṛhī Ṭhākurāṇī temple, the financial administration of Ṭhākurāṇī Yātrā, and the succession of the Deśībeherā.

(Appadurai and Appadurai Breckenridge 1976: 203; Freitag 1991: 74; Talbot 2001: Chapter 3). From this angle the long-standing conflicts over Ṭhākurāṇī Yātrā characterize neither the Devāṅgī nor the inhabitants of Berhampur in particular. To substantiate this assertion and shed some light on the historical setting that is likely to have inspired the development of Ṭhākurāṇī Yātrā, I shall advance two arguments[14] – the first concerning the contested nature of the festival, and second referring to the inherently political nature of processions.

At first sight, the conflicts over Ṭhākurāṇī Yātrā reflect a gradual change in the way people memorize their past. Whereas cultural knowledge has been transmitted for several ages by means of performances such as rituals, celebrations and festivals, and thus by *incorporated* practices (see J. Assmann 1992; Connerton 1989), the advance of the Oriya printing press during the late nineteenth century and the rise in the number of people with the ability to read and write initiated a new way to memorize, store and transmit significant incidents, structures and procedures. Considering the slowly growing literacy rate, this transformation of the memory culture in fact continued even after Indian independence (1947).[15] The development from hitherto embodied to inscribed knowledge also implied a shift in perspective. Unlike recent publications on Ṭhākurāṇī Yātrā that describe a variety of features as if they represented general understanding (see, for instance, Pātra 1997), the oral and bodily knowledge about the performance of the festival was partial rather than objective or homogenous.[16] Each participating group experienced the festival from its respective and disparate perspective. In this regard the *shared* knowhow concerning the performance of Ṭhākurāṇī Yātrā, or the basis of consensus, was rather limited. Except for the very general procedure,

---

[14] As shown in Chapter 6, there is only little reliable information to trace and contextualize the origin of Ṭhākurāṇī Yātrā. Relating orally transmitted legendary events to the political circumstances of colonial annexation the festival seems to have taken form in the course of the nineteenth century, though it is ascribed to the year 1779 (Pātra 1997: 14).

[15] In 1951 the overall literacy rate in Orissa was only 15.80 per cent (females: 4.52 per cent). In the following decades it gradually rose to 21.66 per cent (1961), 26.18 per cent (1971), 33.62 per cent (1981), 49.09 per cent (1991), and to 63.61 per cent in 2001 (Government of Orissa 2004: 137). The percentage of literates varied according to gender, district and rural/urban area.

[16] However, even embodied knowledge is objectified vis-à-vis mnemonic devices such as images, objects and locations.

I believe, the details of the festival were hardly of *common* interest. There was no privileged viewpoint from which to grasp the festival in its complexity. In this respect, the conflicts about Ṭhākurāṇī Yātrā reflect a shift from situated 'functional memory' to objectified 'stored memory', to use Aleida Assmann's (1999) categories.

Even in 2001, the different classes of priests considered the festival basically from their subjective position. Whereas the Dāmalā knew the significance of the thousand-eyed pot on the final day (see Chapter 6), Oriya ritual specialists were not even aware of its proper name. Similarly, the untouchable Mādigā (Telugu cobblers) narrated their own story to explain and highlight their participation in the festival. According to their view, Bur̥hī Ṭhākurāṇī took shelter in the house of a Mādigā who, due to his poverty, went to the Deśībeherā and asked him to take care of the goddess (for a comparison with the more frequent legend see again Chapter 6). When Mādigā drummers accompany the nocturnal pot processions, they thus re-enact their own bond with the goddess and their initial visit to the Devāṅgī leader.[17] In other words, each communal unit which participated in the festival had only a vague sense of what the others were actually doing and how they rationalized this contribution.

The change in the perception of the past was antedated and stimulated by colonial categories introduced through the Anglo-Indian judicial system (see Appadurai and Appadurai Breckenridge 1976: 200; Presler 1987: 59–61; Price 1991: 112, Rogers 1992: 193–96). With reference to temple administration in nineteenth-century south India, Arjun Appadurai (1981: 17) argues that this 'fresh set of concepts' allowed emerging communal factions to reframe their participation in the temple redistributive system in terms of legal claims. As a result, the colonial court was forced to act in accordance with 'the structural and cultural needs' of these new civic agents, largely merchants, urban guilds and ambitious artisan groups. Thus, major conflicts between trustees, temple servants, donors and worshippers were wide-spread (Appadurai and Appadurai Breckenridge 1976: 204–5).

[17] This subaltern view did not create any social dispute. All of the recent Deśībeherās relied on Mādigā drummers and also on a Mādigā ritual specialist who during the divine 'return journey' carries a bush that is decorated with decoy offerings in order to prevent unwanted creatures from disturbing the procession.

Similarly, in case of Ṭhākurāṇī Yātrā the Indian court was given the authority to decide about the correct performance of the festival. Although largely in a post-colonial setting the juridical system still had to review the inherited honours and shares, and thus delineated the vision of an eternal original. During the litigation in 1985, for instance, some features of the festival apparently achieved canonical status, such as the Senāpati status of the eight pot bearers, or the authority of the Mahurī Rājā. Henceforth the importance and emphasis given to these features was taken for granted, regardless of their relevance in the past and approval by the court (which did after all have to clarify questions of leadership).[18] In some respects, the judicial discourse itself produced 'true' and 'false' evidence, like a route chart for the pot processions, a family tree of the Deśībeherā, letters of authorization and photographs. The testimony of plaintiffs and defendants on the sensed past of the festival gradually achieved the status of objective facts. In recent years the ability to follow the previous Ṭhākurāṇī Yātrā came to legitimize the respective organizers. Meanwhile, the festival is documented not only by the local press but also by private television channels (BTV, ETV, see Plate 8.1).[19]

Considering the chain of conflicts associated with Ṭhākurāṇī Yātrā, the changing memory culture and also the colonial introduction of new categories still reveal only one side of the coin. Scholarship on state formation in pre-modern India has shown that ritual performances and ceremonial processions can be considered as paradigmatic institutions, not only to authorize royal authority but also to define, shape and structure political or 'civic' society (Dirks 1987; Freitag 1991; Price 1991: 111; Price 1996: Chapter 5; Sax 2000; Schnepel 1996; Sutherland 2003). Ritual functions and theatrical forms of enactment thus *constituted* polity and sovereignty rather than reflected or symbolized antecedent social structures. In pre-colonial India, Nicholas Dirks (1987: 289)

[18] Source: T. S. 35 of 1985, Subordinate Judge, Berhampur.

[19] To the best of my knowledge, there is no (visual) documentation of performance details before 1983, i.e., the lifetime of the last commonly accepted Deśībeherā. Otherwise, I assume, these pictures or texts would have been used in the litigations already. However, for the same reason people might hold back their documents. In respect to the annual festival of the goddess Rāmacaṇḍī in Khurda District, Tanabe (1999: 62) described that the details of rights and responsibilities were recorded in notebooks from 1974 onwards. Meanwhile, these notes achieved authoritative character and superseded memories of previous performances.

asserts, *pūjā* (worship) was the root metaphor for political relations. Hence processions were not only promoting 'communitas' (Turner); their character was competitive in the first place. As a cultural site, they served various interest groups to express collective values and to verify self-defined identities in relation to each other. To negotiate the right to offer service to a deity and to sponsor particular ritual acts hence *produced* the political landscape of the community, mobilized alliances, fostered oppositions and challenged power. This political instrument proved to be particularly important for new social bodies that emerged while established rulers lost their power in the colonial encounter. In the course of the nineteenth century, claims to representative functions in the public also came to downplay political deprivation caused by British rule (see Freitag 1991; Price 1991).

Taking present-day processions as an entrée through which to explore civic society and its political constitution in the history of India, Peter Sutherland (2003: 32) argues that 'processional practices integrated Hindu rural politics in a world-ordering scale of peasant, monarchical, imperial and cosmic formations' from at least the nineteenth century until independence. He specifically focuses on the processional movements of deities in order to outline 'geometries of power' (see also Sax 2000). Taking his perspective, the itinerary of Ṭhākurāṇī Yātrā would suggest two overlapping patterns of past political and economic authority: (*a*) a hierarchical and reciprocal relation between the Oriya barbers (Bhaṇḍārī) and the Telugu weavers (Devāṅgī),[20] manifest in the dyadic travel from the 'in-laws' to the 'parents' and back; (*b*) the interdependence of various communities, possibly through the cloth industry, visualized in the nocturnal circumambulatory movement of the goddess pots. Since, due to colonial trade a local chief could benefit from his new role in revenue collection and trade expansion (Berkemer 1993: 228), the visit to the Mahurī Rājā's residence at the beginning of each nocturnal journey might have been an articulation of this (limited) power. Apart from theorizing about the assumed historical setting of Ṭhākurāṇī Yātrā, the disputes about its proper performance in the last decades show that the spatial movement of the goddess (pots) is also a *contemporary* instrument to maintain and raise status.

[20] Considering the relevance of these two castes in particular, one could debate whether they represent Oriya- versus Telugu-speaking residents, ritual specialists versus artisans, original inhabitants versus immigrants, or possibly two communities that gained status in nineteenth-century civic society.

The attention on the variety and the selection of visited streets indeed relates to the different Devāṅgī habitats (*penṭha*), i.e., units that vary historically in size and number. These *penthas* are almost synonymous with those neighbourhoods who contribute to the splendor of Ṭhākurāṇī Yātrā by constructing colourful statues of deities (*ratha*) and dioramas that display mythical events (*kaḷākuñja*). The devotional and financial investment of these communal bodies is reconfirmed by the direct visit of Buṙhī Ṭhākurāṇī in the shape of the main sacred pot, so that the married women in the respective streets will get a chance to win the favour of the goddess on behalf of their family.

If ceremonial processions are conceived not only as occasions that reflect authority in a symbolic way but as culture-specific sites with which to bring about power by performative means, the long-standing conflicts about the correct performance of Ṭhākurāṇī Yātrā fail to identify either 'corrupt' communities or 'selfish' individuals. The analysis of processions in the past rather invites us to rethink the present-day discourse on the role and behaviour of the Deśībeherāṇī during Ṭhākurāṇī Yātrā, especially with respect to her husband.

## Conclusion: Ritual Agency Exposed

The previous section has shown that the subject matter of the correct performance of Ṭhākurāṇī Yātrā is neither trivial nor can it be regarded as a mere symbolic field for acting out other kinds of conflict. The route of the nocturnal procession, the identity of the eight pot bearers, and also the choices exercised by the Deśībeherāṇī (or the Deśībeherā), all refer to political realities. It is not only that this goddess festival, like any other ritual performance, is embedded and situated in non-ritual structures of power and authority. Hence I do not wish to emphasize the 'political impact' or 'instrumental use' of Ṭhākurāṇī Yātrā as a separate feature. Rather I hope to have shown that in this context processions are an essentially political genre, no matter whether they are enacted to please the goddess. It is at the very heart of this cultural institution to reveal and to give reality to power structures. There is no alternative 'pure' way to perform the goddess festival. Nevertheless, in public discourse it was suspected that the Deśībeherāṇī followed 'selfish interests' rather than devoting herself to communal needs.

Similar to rituals within the private or semi-private space of a household, the public celebration of Ṭhākurāṇī Yātrā serves as a field where selected women enact, consolidate and verify their social position. The Deśībeherāṇī could make herself heard; she could pursue personal matters concerning her family by considering unpleasant realities (here: the eviction, the missing jewelry) in terms of denied religious honours. By doing so she followed a pre-existing discourse on religious traditions that cause both obligations and legitimate privileges in the lived-in world; for instance, to be treated as the mother of Buṙhī Ṭhākurāṇī. The Deśībeherāṇī could raise her voice only because of her exposure to the public of Ṭhākurāṇī Yātrā, i.e., because of her essential role in the conduct of this goddess festival. Like worldly diplomats, the ritual tasks provided the Deśībeherāṇī with what I call social immunity. Her person was required to maintain good relations with the deity, hence the Deśībeherāṇī was not judged in terms of her vulnerable position within the family. This kind of diplomat status is not limited to the Deśībeherāṇī or the performance of Ṭhākurāṇī Yātrā. In southern Orissa, married women in general are regarded as intermediaries of the divine feminine. On behalf of the family, their worship guarantees the goddess' benevolence. Therefore, I suggest, religious commitment may endow any woman with social immunity, no matter whether the performance of rituals itself empowers them in non-ritual spheres too. Similarly these female ritual specialists will risk public criticism once their behaviour as their family's representative will indicate some kind of personal side effect.

In any case, the Deśībeherāṇī was not the only woman who exercised ritual honours. In fact she openly competed with her mother-in-law over offering the sacrificial food. The elder woman recognized this claim to power and, for her part, responded in the same ritual mode, successfully. Similarly, the Deśībeherā's maternal aunt could assert her authority by means of carrying the sacred pot during the return journey of the goddess and thus at the climax of the festival. The Deśībeherāṇī had to accommodate her, due in part to the lack of support by her husband. In another instance her ritual agency was devalued completely. Although elsewhere oracles are employed in public rituals so that the divine voice may join and direct local politics (see, for instance, Berti 1999), the audience in Berhampur was not prepared to listen to the goddess. The altered state of the Deśībeherāṇī during one of the nocturnal processions did not meet established patterns. Moreover, the possession incident challenged the ritual expertise of the Dāmalā. Confronted with male priestly proficiency, the reality of deity possession was exposed as a mean trick. Nevertheless, many women *and* men related this pot bearer's collapse to the religious idiom of possession rather than framing it in terms of physical weakness or mental stress.

Apart from this power play in the course of Ṭhākurāṇī Yātrā, did the ritual role of the Deśībeherāṇī provide her with some means to achieve a permanent solution in her marriage crisis? As a matter of fact, she was able to revoke the eviction order and take further steps to restore her family life. Rather than Indian family law, the right of worship 'as per tradition' – and thus her appeal to communal interest – offered her a real opportunity to react. All in all though, I still had severe doubts about the future of the couple. Considering the local discourse, the Deśībeherāṇī stabilized her position within the extended family. The following Ṭhākurāṇī Yātrā in 2003 remained largely undisturbed by marital conflicts. The Deśībeherāṇī carried the main goddess pot, the daily route of the procession was announced on a blackboard, and the Deśībeherā selected the eight pot bearers. The couple had obviously accommodated themselves to the public interest.[21] The Deśībeherāṇī succeeded in carrying the sacred basket (and the main pot) even during the most important nights, and thus asserted herself against her husband's maternal aunt.[22] Conversely, she had left the selection of pot bearers to the Deśībeherā. No matter whether the spouses could or could not compromise at a personal level as well, to leave the office of the Deśībeherāṇī did not seem to be an alternative.

Like the Deśībeherā, the formal leader of the festival, his wife was also prone to being manipulated by different factions. Thus her privileged position served others to get involved in politics within the old town. Yet the case study shows that women are not only subjected to politics but also may actively relate to communal affairs, for instance by recruiting pot bearers or by skipping roads. Yumiko Tokita-Tanabe (1996) has argued that women join village politics in their own gender-specific ways. Rather than offering their opinion in public and overwhelmingly male debates, they prefer to pull strings backstage. In this informal and private realm the performance of rituals serves as

[21] However, since I did not attend Ṭhākurāṇī Yātrā in 2003 personally but returned to fieldwork four month later, the local assessment of the Devāṅgī leaders could also have been influenced by the temporality of remembrance. Unpleasant features tend to fade away.

[22] According to the press in 2005 and 2007, the festival was performed as per tradition and the Deśībeherāṇī (again) carried the sacred basket during the opening night (*The Statesman*, 20 April 2005; *The Hindu*, 9 April 2007). By 2009 several amateur videos on Ṭhākurāṇī Yātrā were uploaded on the Internet (*YouTube*). These local documentaries also showed that the respective couple was in charge in 2009 and 2011 as well.

a cultural site to negotiate power relationships in a very subtle form. The collective observance of a votive rite in the neighbourhood, for instance, will raise questions concerning from which families women are able to join the ritual, who is to provide what kind of materials, whose house may function as an appropriate place of worship, etc. Thus any semi-private form of worship also reflects and manipulates social alliances and controversies (Tokita-Tanabe 1996: 112, 116–17). According to Tokita-Tanabe, female activities at the backstage and the male public method of negotiating politics are complementary. The study of Ṭhākurāṇī Yātrā clearly shows that the negotiation of power and hierarchy through ritual is not limited by gender. Nor is women's ritual relevance restricted to the private realm or home. Any exposure to the public, whether among neighbours or at the communal level, may provide women with social immunity. At the same time, being in public is also risky, in that women's ritual agency is contested once it is assessed in terms of a power play. Then any religious commitment is likely to be denigrated as selfish interest.

# Afterword

In the course of this book I have explored a variety of religious and semi-religious events that involve women as ritual specialists, as embodiments of the divine and as more or less active participants, at times conjointly with men. Each chapter located bodily, affective and cognitive moments that influence the perception of performance reality and its effects on women's understanding of gender and Hinduism. The underlying question was how the performance of rituals offers women in southern Orissa the opportunity of verifying their sense of self vis-à-vis the world, and how they react to apparently restrictive and omnipotent role expectations conveyed by Hindu religious discourse.

Rather than summarizing what has been said before, this conclusion will reconnect some of the findings from the previous chapters to the question of ritual and its impact on female identity as it was outlined in the Introduction. I shall resume the concept of 'doing gender' and, taking the example from southern Orissa, relate it to the perceptual situation created by framed events such as rituals. Before doing this, I wish to consider the limitations and the situated character of my research results since cultural practices are neither static nor timeless.

## Locating Validity in Post-Colonial Society

This study does not make any claims about the 'nature' of women in southern Orissa.[1] It is not about Hindu women as a specific bounded group that differs substantially from women in northern Orissa or from women who identify with an alternate religious tradition. Nevertheless, the study gives insight into a female world largely determined by Hindu rituals and thus may raise the question of whether and in what respects to generalize its contents. It will not come as a surprise that I hesitate to give a straightforward answer.

[1] Though the anthropological study of bounded groups and static 'identities' has been questioned as a dubious endeavour (see Brubaker and Cooper 2000), even self-reflexive language use is ambivalent, since it is fairly difficult to avoid generalizing phrases like 'Hindu women' or 'women in southern Orissa'.

First, the modern Indian state of Orissa exhibits a large diversity of cultural forms that are commonly distinguished in terms of region (coastal belt, hill tracts, north and south), religious affiliation (Vaishnava, Shivaite, Shakta, other religions), ethnic and social boundaries ('tribal', 'Hinduized' or Brahminical practice), not to speak of even more contested categories such as 'Aryan' versus 'Dravidian' origin. The scattered literature on women in this region substantiates this diversity of living forms and religiosity.[2] Assuming the perspective of the educated middle-class in Bhubaneswar, the capital of Orissa, several issues described in the previous chapters appear strange, traditional, unorthodox or even backward. The activities of pious women are preferably addressed as 'culture' (the English term has entered several Indian languages) rather than as part of Hindu religion. Still I am uneasy about classifying the religious practices of women in Berhampur and its rural surroundings as subaltern, a label that suggests a clear hierarchy of religious practices defined by the elite, constituted by the Brahmin caste, upper class and men.

On the one hand, I described viewpoints and routines from a variety of castes, some clearly privileged, some stigmatized, but mostly belonging to the demographically dominant spectrum of caste society, consisting of artisans, small businessmen, peasants, and service castes. Women of these communities in fact share many religious forms, yet with different emphasis. Whereas certain Brahminical ideals influence women regardless of their caste, for instance in the case of menstrual restrictions, Brahmin women are not immune to the discourse on deity possession. Even their religiosity and ritual commitment is pervaded by the possibility of divine manifestation though, as I have shown, divine possession certainly is a contested practice. However, the majority of women mentioned in this book are neither Brahmin nor 'untouchable' (Scheduled Caste), neither very rich nor the poorest of the poor.[3] Due to lack of money and time, women at the very bottom

[2] Compare Marglin (1985b) on the vanished tradition of temple dancers in the Jagannātha temple of Puri; Schömbucher (2006) on female mediums among a Telugu-speaking fishing-caste in Puri; Seymour (1999) on Brahmin urban women in the capital of Orissa, Tokita-Tanabe (1999a) on rural women, their rituals and agency in Khurda District; and Otten (2006) on women's healing practices among the Ronā, an indigenous community living in the hinterland of Orissa.

[3] Though, from a European or Anglo-American perspective, the majority of people in southern Orissa are fairly poor, regardless of their local status.

of the society engage themselves in labor rather than rituals. Although caste identity authorizes some women in taking specific ritual roles, such as the Devāṅgī pot bearers at Ṭhākurāṇī Yātrā, in general social status rather than caste determines participation in collective rituals. Women who most actively participate in religious functions and also define the discourse on female religiosity are, to the best of my knowledge, from this dominant spectrum of caste society. Thus the situation in southern Orissa differs from Tamil Nadu, on which basis Karin Kapadia (1995: 5) argues that a sharp dichotomy exists between Brahminical and lower-caste values. This polarization does not characterize and divide forms of female religiosity in Berhampur and the surrounding area, though there certainly are class distinctions and contested viewpoints. Religious practices are not stratified along linguistic affiliation either. Several rituals are observed jointly by Oriya- and Telugu-speaking women, some rituals are performed on different dates, and some by only one language group. In any case, there are several kinds of women who prefer the performance of rituals in their own 'tradition' (*paramparā*). Similarly women from the educated *economic* elite[4] generally abstain from those ritual sites clearly identified with the lower strata. Regarding the position of a woman within the hierarchy of a joint family, lack of status (for instance, due to widowhood or as a new daughter-in-law) is neither a bar to joining rituals nor a specific trait of female participants.

On the other hand, I have reservations about classifying the *female* perspective on religion by itself as subaltern, since this presupposes that in social practice (rather than academic theorizing) there is a superior male view on what Hinduism should be to women. Though there certainly are prominent Hindu scriptures on women's moral and religious duties (for an eighteenth-century Sanskrit treatise on how women ought to behave, see Leslie 1989), one feature of female religiosity in southern Orissa is women's degree of autonomy in defining the scope and meanings of Hinduism. This is not 'subversive' in the first place, since ritual performers are eager to follow the 'rules and regulations', admittedly an often imagined authority. Moreover, on the basis of regular ritual performances women conceive of

[4] This elite is often identified as 'middle-class', yet in local perspective these people constitute the upper segment of society rather than the intermediate strata.

themselves as the more religious gender.[5] In other words, they do not regard themselves as inferior 'others' to (orthodox) male believers. At the same time, men do not feel any need to convince their mother, wife, daughters or daughters-in-law in religious matters. Rather they acknowledge, and gain prestige from, the religious reputation of a female family member. Although some men are prone to denigrate women and their activities in general, this attitude does not stem from a different viewpoint on religiosity.[6] In fact, men at times share the female perspective, for instance, regarding Ṭhākurāṇī Yātrā as a religious event that requires the participation of women to be soteriologically successful. However, it would also be misleading to classify the ritual activities of female Hindus as what Susan Sered (1994) has called a 'religion dominated by women'. Rather, several (gendered) views on Hinduism coexist, and their assessment varies according to perspective, time and circumstances.[7] Thus the contrast drawn through this book of women's position(s) vis-à-vis those of male Hindus should be seen as a heuristic tool rather than as a dichotomy that hints toward a normative model of Hindu orthodoxy.

Characterizing female religious practices in southern Orissa as 'popular' religion is, though more appropriate, also tricky. If this term is understood in opposition to 'elite', it conveys the same problematic connotations as the label 'subaltern'. Yet, if 'popular' Hinduism is understood vis-à-vis a religion defined by theological scriptures, some of the urban elite in Bhubaneswar can be said to follow popular forms of worship as well. All the same, several apparently 'folk' practices have their counterpart in written tradition, for instance votive rites (see McGee 1987) or deity possession (see Smith 2006). In short, I repudiate a sharp and simplifying dichotomy of either elite/scriptural or subaltern/popular religion. Rather several, partly overlapping and competing strands of Hinduism, liturgy and oral tradition influence

[5] This viewpoint is not limited to Orissa, as Pintchman (2005: 187, 190) has shown with reference to Hindu women in Benares.

[6] However, the performance of ritual certainly is a site to negotiate social and power relations (see Chapter 8). Similarly, some men try to prevent their wife or mother from observing so *many* fasts since this would cause health problems. Women generally reject this criticism, well aware that this male advice finally limits their personal self-determined sphere of life.

[7] The phenomenon that Hinduism can integrate a variety of religious traditions is well-known and, in academic parlance, termed as 'inclusivism' (Hacker), cf. Michaels (2004a: 5–12, 336).

religious practice. In general, this does not matter to believers as long as relevant practices can be subsumed within one's own tradition. Thus the goddess Maṅgaḷā can be conceived of as a Vaishnava and, conversely, a Shakta deity. Similarly, Ṭhākurāṇī Yātrā can be situated within the theological strand of goddess worship (Shaktism), within a specific 'tantric' path to salvation, or more generally as a celebration of unrestrained devotion (*bhakti*). However, if the adjectives 'subaltern' and 'popular' are understood as references to mainstream religious practices, the ritual performances described in this book can be certainly subsumed. Nevertheless, from the perspective of a male Brahmin priest, some of the ways in which women in southern Orissa interpret Hinduism will appear unorthodox – and possibly, upon taking a closer look, his own wife's mode of worship too.

Let me try to situate the features of this ethnography in a temporal perspective. Although the religious activity of Hindu women in the first place alludes to a paradigmatic vision of tradition, the form of this commitment is related to and defined by its respective social, historical and political context. As Partha Chatterjee (1989) has pointed out, the nationalist movement in nineteenth-century India strongly advanced the identification of the 'new Indian woman' with religious values. While men aligned themselves with secularized modern society, women were made responsible for the maintenance of 'tradition'. Yumiko Tokita-Tanabe (1999a: 3), who largely follows Chatterjee in her study on Oriya women in Khurda District, regards the present-day space for women to exercise agency – by and large the religious realm – as being a result of colonial experience as well as a process used to overcome this experience. Indeed the distinction of the socio-religious and the politico-economic sphere and its association with tradition and, respectively, modernity was shaped, if not invented by colonial administration. In nationalist discourse, however, the two spheres were identified with a division of space, and thus fully merged in the contrast of the spiritual 'home' (*ghara*) versus the material 'world' (*bāhāra*, literally: outside). The home was transformed into a gendered site in which the female care for religion served to resist the foreign influence in the politico-economic sphere (cf. Chatterjee 1989: 624).

On this background, the religious commitment of women in southern Orissa and their confidence as ritual performers is also specific to the post-colonial situation. The current freedom of women to perpetuate their form of Hinduism has been probably benefited from the (post-) colonial division of cultural space and men's sole orientation towards the outside world. One could even argue that with the growing secularization of modern Indian society, women's influence in religious matters is increasing. In southern Orissa, neither new job opportunities nor any other inventions are replacing the religious sphere as one of the major fields of female self-realization (in addition to the care for the family).[8] Whereas a woman's activity in the religious realm is highly appreciated, her commitment in other spheres of life risks being criticized as 'selfish'. At present, the sons of the former priest elite embrace more lucrative careers brought about by the recent form of globalization. They try to enter, for instance, the software industry. On certain religious occasions, this results in a shortage of priests. Again women are ready to replace their functions whenever required, and in metropolitan Indian cities such as Pune, they already receive formal training to do so (*BBC News*, 26 April 2001).

The division of space, as emphasized in the nationalist discourse, only partly describes women's present-day religious practices in southern Orissa. Although most of their rituals are performed in private, some public activity outside the home is also required. On the final day of several votive rites, women immerse sacred pots or temporary altars in a nearby pond, and thus naturally pass public places. Certainly, the gradually increasing density of Berhampur's city architecture might have contributed to the diffusion of space. Yet the successful performance of a Tuesday Pageant or of Ṭhākurāṇī Yātrā is inherently based on women's participation in *communal* rituals. Vice versa, women may also employ their religious commitment in order to leave the house, to meet neighbours or to cultivate female friendships beyond kinship ties. In this respect the inner/outer distinction reflects imagined and flexible rather than concrete boundaries.

At present, images of femininity in India are changing rapidly, especially since the 1990s, when liberalized economics and private television channels started to conquer the subcontinent (see Poggendorf-Kakar 2002, Puri 1999; Sunder Rajan 1993). Women in Berhampur and its rural surrounding are confronted with these media versions of the new urban middle-class (pan-)Indian woman.[9] In the years 1999 to 2003 (when I

[8] Nevertheless, it would be misleading to conceive of Hindu women's ritual performances as a form of individual self-realization that characterizes large strands of present-day 'Western' society. Female religious activities are mostly embedded in and conceived of as communal service.

[9] On the problem of the label 'middle-class', see note 4.

did fieldwork), these new images of femininity did not really challenge women's commitment to religion, at least among those strata that most actively engage in rituals. Elite girls for their part would observe the Jahni Oṣā and, on another occasion, visit one of the first commercial Internet access points in Berhampur. Even young and, according to local classification, 'modern' women did not (publicly) belittle the performance of votive rites or the carrying of a sacred pot during a religious procession. However, the 'Westernized' newly rich have an impact on the assessment of hitherto mainstream religious practices. For instance, some families have started to avoid Ṭhākurāṇī Yātrā, an attitude legitimized by the disturbing crowds on the streets, a situation that puts them in unwilling contact with lower-caste people and obscenities by masked men. Conversely, by the time this manuscript was revised for print (2011) there were already two Internet pages dedicated to Buṙhī Ṭhākurāṇī and her biennial festival (www.thakuraniyatra.in, www.thakurani.com).

In the end, my hesitation in generalizing the ethnographic features described in previous chapters is related to the objective of this study. The aim of my endeavor was to shift scholarly attention from making general claims about the effects of Hindu rituals on the position of women to the respective actions involved in women's understanding of themselves, with respect to gender stereotypes advanced by Hindu orthodoxy. Drawing general conclusions from this study thus concerns the *process* of doing gender rather than the character of women's self. As I shall elaborate in the following section, Hindu rituals do not simply form women's identity, rather female devotees fashion rituals that mold their world (cf. Bell 1997: 73). Women in southern Orissa, and I guess even beyond, are not forced to follow pre-given gender roles blindly but relate to Hinduism in such a way that resonates to their own understanding of themselves as gendered beings. These ways of doing gender are not limited to women of a particular caste who happen to live in southern Orissa at the turn of the twenty-first century. In the following paragraphs I shall substantiate this conclusion with respect to the ethnographic site and also from a theoretical perspective.

## Ritual and Identity

At the beginning of this book, I introduced the concept of doing gender in order to investigate how women during the course of a ritual perpetuate and negotiate images of femininity prevalent in Hindu religious discourse. The assumption was that gender is a routine achievement that results from seen, but mostly unnoticed, everyday activities that mark a person as female or male (e.g., the mode of walking in public). 'Doing gender' thus refers to the re-enactment of socially appropriate gender-specific behaviour that, by means of mimesis, becomes inscribed on the body. As embodied practice it generally escapes awareness, yet due to its mostly contingent, and at times ambivalent, character it may also become subject of human reflection and be converted into strategically articulated performance. The second strand of my argumentation concerned ritual as a particular type of cultural performance that is prone to transform the perception of its participants and, consequently, influences their view on the self, vis-à-vis the lived-in reality. I emphasized those approaches to ritual that consider its psychophysical effects, such as the 'virtuality' of the event, the 'subjunctive mood' and the authority given to non-expected experiences that befall the participant ('passiones'). So let us see how the concept of doing gender can illuminate some of the processes and mechanisms in which the performance of Hindu rituals in southern Orissa affects its participants and their sense of self and gender.

As was shown in the case of the Jahni Oṣā, women certainly reflect on gender stereotypes that arise on the occasion of specific ritual practices. While according to male-dominated public discourse this votive rite helps unmarried girls to obtain a good husband, the performers themselves reject this rationale. They might even make fun of those participants who seem to follow this goal excessively. Moreover, the ritual procedure itself pronounces fasting as a self-dependent form of female religiosity rather than as a pious strategy to enable (a good) marriage. The votaries were convinced that 'boys are not able to fast', due to their lack of self-discipline. Only girls had the strength (*śakti*) to do so. Similarly, women define their own thoughts on the allegedly 'evil' potential of menstrual pollution, a common trope in Brahminical ideology. Whereas menstruating women try to refrain from worshipping, cooking and social interaction, this does not have any negative effect on their self-esteem. Menstrual impurity is no reason to consider either one's own person or the female gender as 'sinful' or disadvantaged. Rather women identify, in between their periods, with the auspiciousness associated with the fertile female body – a gender-specific moral gift that lacks a male counterpart. Hence women emphasize and display the purity and beneficence of their body whenever possible. They also seek to share the divine female energy (*śakti*). This is explicit at many ritual occasions, for instance, when women are to carry a sacred pot. Unlike the day-to-day counterpart, this act of holding an earthen pot on top of the head draws the attention of the pot bearer and onlookers alike to the sacredness of the generative power. This 'subjunctive' state encourages reflective distance, on the power of the feminine divine, on sharing this potential but also on one's own gender role.

The self-conscious identification with particular religious paradigms is delineated and constrained by Hindu doctrine that emphasizes the institution of marriage and motherhood as normative to fulfill the cosmological disposition as a woman.[10] In general, women do not wish to follow male forms of commitment to the divine, such as wearing a costume at Ṭhākurāṇī Yātrā. Although some of them are critical about the paradigmatic concept of wifely devotion to a husband (*patibrata*), the gender-specific performance of votive rites serves indeed as a means of self-realization. In the course of the ritual year with its variety of fasts and festivals, women select those that resonate to their personal situation and self-understanding. In this respect 'doing gender' and the experience of the gendered self during ritual is determined by the individual degree of self-awareness. As has been shown, the women among whom I worked conceive of several religious ideas, procedures and role expectations in their own ways. This is most explicit in the case of the (re-)interpretation of the moral and religious duties of a wife (*strīdharma*). Female ritual performers understand these obligations as a source of self-esteem. The well-being of others, and hence society in general, is regarded as the result of women's sincere observance of fasts. In reference to the common wordplay about god *Śiva*, who without his consort is merely a corpse (*śava*), a young woman explained: 'A man is nothing, the woman is the force (*śakti*). If he is good it is so because of his wife. Whatever prosperity he gains in his life, it is because of her.' This gendered (and tantric) bias in the interpretation of female *śakti* is not made explicit and it would be misleading to conceive of it as strategic or even subversive acts. Rather women understand and define religious norms in such a way that these correspond to their own sense of piety and feeling of self-worth.

[10] However, the ideology of marriage and motherhood provides Hindu women with a means to gain enormous respect, social recognition and also power that is absent in those post-modern realms and in a society where divorce is frequent and children are few.

Throughout the study I have attempted to emphasize that, in regard to the social negotiation of gender, ritual performances cannot be seen merely as a site of self-presentation or as a result of discourse. Instead I would suggest looking at ritual as a framed event, constituting a particular perceptual situation that privileges somatic attention given to performative effects: the *force* evoked by joining a pot procession of thousands, the *tension* produced by deciphering the divine utterings of a medium, the *sense of carefreeness* while decorating the altar. Any of these emotional and somatic states is brought about and authorized by the sacredness of the event, i.e., the conception of worship as a form to communicate with god. This view on the somatic results does not outdate the impact of self-reflexivity or religious doctrine. Rather, in order to grasp the variety of social effects caused by a specific ritual, I have found it helpful to consider the following analytic distinctions within performance: representational practice, discursive practice, and aesthetic practice. As shown in the previous chapters, several apparently 'conservative' rituals have had the potential to evoke highly satisfactory experiences. They could be the provocation of laughter, the promise of relief from everyday burdens or confront participants with thrilling proximity to the divine. However, in respect to the 'side-effects' of ritual on the self-understanding of performers in the lived-in world, the most crucial consequence of this perceptual situation was apparently a change in the sense of agency, for instance, after being selected as pot bearer in a Tuesday procession, thus serving as representative of a family on whose behalf the ceremony is performed.

As has been argued prominently by Caroline Humphrey and James Laidlaw (1994), ritual action is characterized by the release from individual utilitarian acting associated with the social persona in favour of a stipulated program of acts. Considering the experiences of practicing Hindu women in southern Orissa, to perform a ritual and put aside one's personal interests – and possibly one's subordinate social status – has, I would conclude, a paradoxical effect. The ritual both *enhances* and, on another level, *suspends* the awareness of being an agent of one's own, and by this means it influences the self-understanding of ritual performers in such a way that stands out against non-ritual times.[11]

[11] As it should be clear by now I conceive of agency as an imagined property that can be associated with different persons and collectives, but also with non-human entities (see Gell 1998).

Let me illustrate this finding:

On the one hand, women who join rituals largely negotiate gender roles by being physically involved in practices that *differ* from their everyday experiences. They get exposed to decision-making, become aware of their responsibility as ritual actors, and experience themselves to be in sole control of a certain meaningful and authoritative space (like during the worship of sacred pots ahead of Buṛhī Ṭhakurāṇī's return journey). Some women start to compose devotional songs or self-consciously improve the aesthetics of a *pūjā* site (for instance, during the Jahni Oṣā). Others take leadership roles and achieve priestly status (such as Māusī), thus indirectly questioning the religious monopoly of male religious specialists and temple servants. Similarly, being transformed into a representative or even embodiment of the divine allows access to the urban public, not only in the case of the Deśibeherāṇī. Thus, female ritual performers do not only achieve agency by means of their submission to the divine (i.e., ritual agency), they also gain self-confidence from their primarily 'non-intentional' (Humphrey and Laidlaw) bodily encounter within the ritual realm. They submit their ordinary self to the ritual reality and assume a 'subjunctive mood', yet the psychophysical experiences that befall the performer are characterized by being capable of influencing the lived-in world (and possibly the gods too).[12] This confidence of the sentient body, I believe, continues to have an effect even in non-ritual times. It does not only alter the perception of the self and social reality, it also affects social behaviour and relationships. Women who regularly engage in worship earn respect within the realm of their family and neighbourhood, regardless whether some male relatives might depreciate it as 'waste of time'.

On the other hand, the performance of *familiar* bodily routines within the ritual frame may also contribute to the negotiation of religious ideas on gender. When participants of the Maṅgaḷā Pūjā employ a heavy pestle to jointly crush enormous piles of dried turmeric – required to renew the image of the goddess – they allude to women's tiring work in daily life. Yet since votaries do so as part of the ritual, this burden appears 'as light as a flower'. Women's joy and commitment to this

---

[12] This performative effect should not be confused with the soteriological merit that some rituals and religions promise in exchange of voluntary self-abandonment; however this effect may prove the divine presence to devotees.

ritual act clearly indicate that they do not consider suffering as a way to salvation, as the religious discourse on austerities suggests. Though personal distress motivates women to join the Maṅgaḷā Pūjā, the very experience at the ritual site is characterized by joyful activity and a refreshing interruption of routine work.

What happens in both of these cases can be described with Kapferer's (2005, 2006) notion of virtuality as an experiential sphere that suspends external reality and brings about its own modalities of human experience, 'a dynamic that allows for all kind of potentialities of human experience to take shape. It is, in effect, a self-contained imaginal space – at once a construction, but a construction that enables participants to break free from the constraints or determinations of everyday life . . .' (Kapferer 2006: 673). No matter whether the ritual addresses virgins in search of a husband or women suffering from a crisis, the celebration (still) provides performers with satisfying psychophysical experiences. Given the authorization of the human body, as suggested by the ritual frame, these unexpected experiences are prone to have a significant impact on the self. They encourage somatic learning. This ritual experience differs from 'doing gender' in ordinary social interaction in which exceptional bodily reactions and gestures that befall the gendered self evoke embarrassment or, at best, remain interruptions to the norm. As it was shown with regard to (im-)purity as performative category, the lost *bindi* sticker (the self-adhesive dot that replaces the vermilion mark on the forehead) is regarded as a slip-up and causes unpleasant ambiguity. The context of this episode does not provide additional experiential space motivating the re-orientation of the self. At any rate, during day-to-day social interaction the bodily sensations are likely to be downplayed and silenced rather than heightened as some kind of guidance. In other words, the specific potential of rituals to shape notions of self and gender derives from the attention given to somatic experience.

However, the ritual frame may also require the absolute suspension of the human self, most pronounced in the case of deity possession. As shown in this study, even possessed bodies transmit and negotiate gender norms, for instance with regard to the iconography of a goddess and the female ability to share her divine power. Whether the goddess weeps or bursts out in rage, after the end of the ritual these emotions do *not* continue to have an effect on the mood and self-understanding of the human host. Instead mediums experience, to some extent, fatigue and amnesia. Here the virtuality of ritual does *not* spill over into reality, probably for the good of these women and their sense of self-understanding. Serving as a temporary vehicle of the divine is rather regarded as a source of prestige.

Summing up, the potential of doing gender within the ritual context does not only consist of self-conscious identification with or, possibly, critical reflections on gender models transmitted by Hindu ideology, but primarily in the enactment of exceptional forms of and attitudes to body practices and behaviour. The link between the individual and her (or his) actions is (gradually) resolved, and this allows experiencing a sense of agency that is *not related to everyday personhood*. The ritual release from the ordinary subject position either activates or ignores the body as an experiencing agent. Most of these non-expected somatic experiences – such as the affective, energetic and motorial sensations – are capable of influencing the aftermath of a ritual. They encourage the readjustment of the gendered self with respect to others.

Whether the confidence and strength women in southern Orissa may gain by means of their regular performance of Hindu rituals is conceived as a form of empowerment is primarily a matter of interpretation. Nevertheless, a woman's engagement with Hindu rituals also improves her ability to act on her lived-in world. In this book I identified three basic ways to do so. First, the 'personalization' of ritual, i.e., the validation of ritual acts on the basis of personal circumstances – for instance in case of Māusī (Chapter 2). This process fosters a devotee's dedication to ritual and thus its capacity to bring about extraordinary experiences. Furthermore, proficiency in worshipping the gods provides a woman with 'ritual agency', i.e., the freedom to make decisions and to take actions in ordinary life that are legitimized by her submission to the divine – a mode of action that cannot be denied by social superiors. Sanju (Chapter 4), who refrained from marriage and cared for the joint family's house altar; Uma (Chapter 1), who visited her friends each night to join the Jahni Oṣā; or the Deśībeherāṇī, who finally got to wear the family jewellery have illustrated in what respect ritual expertise may empower women (Chapter 8). After all, the ritual engagement will invest the performer with 'social immunity', a sort of protection that is particularly relevant in times of severe social conflicts. However, as was shown in the last chapter, the capacity of rituals to bestow women with a substantial tool to improve their social situation or to carry out their own will against others who might oppose it is fairly limited. Nevertheless, I suggest that women in southern

Orissa who abstain from the religious domain, no matter for what reason, lose a source of self-esteem and confidence that allows for reframing and also practically influencing the lived-in world. Unless they gain another source of power women are much more tied by gender restrictions that, after all, shape secularized spheres and sections of society as well.

At any rate, it is important to keep in mind that Hindu women themselves do not regard rituals as a way of negotiating self and gender. Rather the religious realm is appreciated for providing experiences beyond the limited scope of individuals. What has been described here as effects of framing and performativity proves, ritually speaking, nothing more than the power of the divine.

# Bibliography


Alter, Joseph S. 1992. *The Wrestler's Body: Identity and Ideology in North India.* Berkeley: University of California Press.

Appadurai, Arjun. 1981. *Worship and Conflict Under Colonial Rule: A South Indian Case.* Cambridge: Cambridge University Press.

Appadurai, Arjun and Carol Appadurai Breckenridge. 1976. 'The South Indian Temple: Authority, Honour and Redistribution', in *Contributions to Indian Sociology* (N. S.), 10 (2): 187–211.

Appadurai, Arjun, Frank Korom and Margret Mills (eds). 1991. *Gender, Genre and Power in South Asian Expressive Traditions.* Philadelphia: University of Pennsylvania.

Asad, Talal. 1993. *Genealogies of Religion: Discipline and Reasons of Power in Christianity and Islam.* Baltimore: John Hopkins University Press.

Assayag, Jackie and Gilles Tarabout (eds). 1999. *La Possession en Asie du Sud: Parole, Corps, Territoire.* Collection Purusartha 21. Paris: École des Hautes Études en Sciences Sociales.

Assmann, Aleida. 1999. *Erinnerungsräume: Formen und Wandlungen des kulturellen Gedächtnisses.* München: Beck.

Assmann, Jan. 1992. *Das kulturelle Gedächtnis: Schrift, Erinnerung und politische Identität in frühen Hochkulturen.* München: C. H. Beck.

Babb, Lawrence A. 1975. *The Divine Hierarchy: Popular Hinduism in Central India.* New York: Columbia University Press.

Babb, Lawrence A. and Susan S. Wadley (eds). 1995. *Media and the Transformation of Religion in South Asia.* Delhi: Motilal Banarsidass Publishers.

Bailey, F. G. 1996. 'Cultural Performance, Authenticity, and Second Nature', in David Parkin, Lionel Caplan and Humphrey Fisher (eds), *The Politics of Cultural Performance.* Providence: Berghahn, 1–18.

Bakhtin, Mikhail M. 1968. *Rabelais and His World.* Cambridge, Mass.: M.I.T. Press.

Bal, Mieke. 2002. *Kulturanalyse.* Frankfurt/Main: Suhrkamp.

Banerjee, Sumanta. 1989. *The Parlour and the Streets: Elite and Popular Culture in Nineteenth Century Calcutta.* Calcutta: Seagull.

Basu, Helene. 2002. 'Afro-indische Besessenheitskulte im interkulturellen Vergleich (Sidi-goma in Indien; zar in Ostafrika; candomblé in Brasilien)', in *Zeitschrift für Ethnologie* 127, 41–55.

Bataille, Georges. 1997. *The Bataille Reader.* Ed. by Fred Botting and Scott Wilson. Oxford: Blackwell.

Becker, Judith. 2004. *Deep Listeners: Music, Emotion, and Trancing.* Bloomington: Indiana University Press.

Behera, Purnima. 1995. *A Socio-Cultural Study of Ganjam*. Berhampur: Berhampur University. Unpublished PhD thesis.

Behrend, Heike and Ute Luig (eds). 1999. *Spirit Possession in Africa*. Madison: University of Wisconsin Press.

Behuria, Nrusinha Charan (ed.) 1995. *Orissa District Gazetteers: Ganjam*. Cuttack: Gazetteers Unit. Department of Revenue, Government of India.

Bell, Catherine. 1992. *Ritual Theory, Ritual Practice*. New York: Oxford University Press.

——. 1997. *Ritual: Perspectives and Dimensions*. New York: Oxford University Press.

Bennett, Lynn. 1983. *Dangerous Wives and Sacred Sisters: Social and Symbolic Roles of High Caste Women in Nepal*. New York: Columbia University Press.

Berkemer, Georg. 1993. *Little Kingdoms in Kalinga: Ideologie, Legitimation und Politik regionaler Eliten*. Stuttgart: Franz Steiner Verlag.

——. 2004. 'Jaypur Parlakimedi Vizianagaram: The Southern Gajapatis', in Angelika Malinar, Johannes Beltz and Heiko Frese (eds), *Text and Context in the History, Literature and Religion of Orissa*. Delhi: Manohar, 93–117.

Berti, Daniela. 1999. 'Un résolution d'un conflict villageois dans la vallée de Kullu (Himachal Pradesh)', in Jackie Assayag and Gilles Tarbout (eds), *La Possession en Asie du Sud: Parole, Corps, Territoire*. Purusartha 21. Paris: École des Haute Études en Science Sociales, 61–100.

Bharati, Agehananda. 1985. 'The Self in Hindu Thought and Action', in Anthony J. Marsella, George DeVos and Francis L.K. Hsu (eds), *Culture and Self: Asian and Western Perspectives*. New York: Tavistock, 185–230.

Boddy, Janice. 1994. 'Spirit Possession Revisited: Beyond Instrumentality', in *Annual Review of Anthropology* 23, 407–34.

——. 1989. *Wombs and Alien Spirits: Women, Men and the Zār Cult in Northern Sudan*. Madison: University of Wisconsin Press.

Bose, Mandakranta (ed.) 2000. *Faces of the Feminine in Ancient, Medieval, and Modern India*. New Delhi: Oxford University Press.

Bose, Shib Chunder. 1883. *Hindoos as They Are*. Calcutta: Thacker, Spink and Co.

Bourdieu, Pierre. 1977. *Outline of a Theory of Practice*. Cambridge: Cambridge University Press.

Bourguignon, Erika. 1976. *Possession*. San Francisco: Chandler & Sharp.

Brighenti, Francesco. 2001. *Śakti Cult in Orissa*. New Delhi: D. K. Printworld.

Brubaker, Rogers and Frederick Cooper. 2000. 'Beyond "Identity"', in *Theory and Society* 29, 1–47.

*Bṛhata Khulaṇā sundarī bā niśā maṅgaḷābāra oṣā kathā*. Kaṭaka: Bīṇāpāṇi pustaka bhaṇdara napani (n.d.).

Buckley, Thomas and Alma Gottlieb. 1988. 'A Critical Appraisal of Theories on Menstrual Symbolism', in Thomas Buckley and Alma Gottlieb (eds), *Blood Magic: The Anthropology of Menstruation*. Berkeley: University of California Press, 3–50.

Burghart, Richard. 1990. 'Ethnographers and Their Local Counterparts in India', in Richard Fardon (ed.), *Localizing Strategies: Regional Traditions of Ethnographic Writing*. Washington, D. C.: Smithsonian Institution Press, 260–79.

Butler, Judith. 1990. *Gender Trouble: Feminism and the Subversion of Identity*. New York: Routledge.

——. 1993. *Bodies That Matter: On the Discursive Limits of 'Sex'*. New York: Routledge.

Butzenberger, Klaus. 2002. 'Identitätskonzeptionen in Indien', in Klaus-Peter Köpping, Michael Welker and Reiner Wiehl (eds), *Die autonome Person - eine europäische Erfindung?* München: Fink, 29–43.

Caldwell, Sarah. 1999. *Oh Terrifying Mother: Sexuality, Violence and Worship of the Goddess Kali*. New York: Oxford University Press.

Calhoun, Craig (ed.) 1994. *Social Theory and the Politics of Identity*. Oxford: Blackwell.

Candra, Śarata. 1998. *Oṙiśāra śaktipīṭha*. Brahmapura: Śāraśvatī Pablikesan.

Carlson, Marvin. 1996. *Performance: A Critical Introduction*. London: Routledge.

Carman, John B. and Frédérique A. Marglin (eds). 1985. *Auspiciousness and Purity in India*. Leiden: Brill.

Carrin, Marine (ed.) 1999. *Managing Distress: Possession and Therapeutic Cults in South Asia*. Delhi: Manohar.

Chalier-Visuvalingam, Elizabeth. 1996. 'Bhairava and the Goddess: Tradition, Gender and Transgression', in Axel Michaels, Cornelia Vogelsanger and Annette Wilke (eds), *Wild Goddesses in India and Nepal: Proceedings of an International Symposium Berne and Zurich, November 1994*. Bern: Lang, 253–301.

Chandra Shekar, C. R. 1989. 'Possession Syndrome in India', in Colleen A. Ward (ed.), *Altered States of Consciousness and Mental Health: A Cross-Cultural Perspective*. Newbury Park: Sage, 79–95.

Chatterjee, Partha. 1989. 'Colonialism, Nationalism, and Colonialized Women: The Contest in India', in *American Ethnologist* 16, 622–33.

Chaudhuri, Nanimadhab. 1939. 'Cult of the Old Lady', in *Journal of the Royal Asiatic Society of Bengal, Letters* 5 (3): 417–25.

Chitgopekar, Nilima. 2002a. 'Indian Goddesses: Persevering and Antinomian Presences', in Nilima Chitogepekar (ed.), *Invoking Goddesses: Gender Politics in Indian Religion*. Delhi: Shakti Books, 11–42.

—— (ed.) 2002b. *Invoking Goddesses: Gender Politics in Indian Religion*. Delhi: Shakti Books.

Claus, Peter J. 1975. 'The Siri Myth and Ritual: A Mass Possession Cult in South India', in *Ethnology* 14, 47–58.

Coburn, Thomas B. 1991. *Encountering the Goddess: A Translation of the Devī-Māhātmya and a Study of its Interpretation*. Albany: State University of New York.

Cohen, Anthony P. 1994. *Self Consciousness: An Alternative Anthropology of Identity*. London: Routledge.

Connerton, Paul. 1989. *How Societies Remember*. Cambridge: Cambridge University Press.

Crapanzano, Vincent and Vivian Garrison (eds). 1977. *Case Studies in Spirit Possession*. New York: Wiley.

Csordas, Thomas J. 1990. 'Embodiment as a Paradigm for Anthropology', in *Ethos* 18, 5–47.

——. 1993. 'Somatic Modes of Attention', in *Cultural Anthropology* 8 (2): 135–56.

—— (ed.) 1994. *Embodiment and Experience: The Existential Ground of Culture and Self*. Cambridge: Cambridge University Press.

Das, Bitchitrananda. 1978. *History of Mohuri, 1767-1850*. Berhampur: Berhampur University. Unpublished PhD thesis.

Das, Jamini Mohan. 1904. 'Note on the Grām Devatī or Tutelary Village Deity in Orissa', in *Journal of the Asiatic Society of Bengal* 72 (3): 81–85.

Das, Rahul Peter. 1997. 'Little Kingdoms and Big Theories of History', in *Journal of the American Oriental Society* 117, 127–34.

——. 2003. *The Origin of the Life of a Human Being: Conception and the Female According to Ancient Indian Medical and Sexological Literature*. Delhi: Motilal Banarsidass.

Das, Veena. 1976. 'Masks and Faces: An Essay on Punjabi Kinship', in *Contributions to Indian Sociology* (N. S.) 10 (1): 1–30.

——. 1988. 'Femininity and the Orientation of the Body', in Karuna Chanana (ed.), *Socialisation, Education and Women: Explorations in Gender Identity*. Delhi: Orient Longman, 193–207.

Dash, Kunja Behari. 1991. *Folklore of Orissa*. Bhubaneswar: Orissa Sahitya Akademi.

Dash, L. N. 1993. *Women, Family Life and Rural Welfare*. Delhi: Manak Publications.

Denton, Lynn T. 2004. *Female Ascetics in Hinduism*. Albany: State University of New York Press.

Desjarlais, Robert, R. 1992. *Body and Emotion: The Aesthetics of Illness and Healing in the Nepal Himalayas*. Philadelphia: University of Pennsylvania Press.

Dirks, Nicholas B. 1987. *The Hollow Crown: Ethnohistory of an Indian Kingdom*. Cambridge: Cambridge University Press.

Dobia, Brenda. 2000. 'Seeking Ma, Seeking Me', in Alf Hiltebeitel and Kathleen M. Erndl (eds), *Is the Goddess a Feminist? The Politics of South Asian Goddesses*. New Delhi: Oxford University Press, 203–38.

Doniger, Wendy and Brian K. Smith. 1991. 'Introduction', in *The Laws of Manu*. London: Penguin, xv–lxxii.

Dumont, Louis. 1970. *Homo Hierarchicus: The Caste System and its Implications*. Chicago: University of Chicago Press.

Duvvury, Vasumathi K. 1991. *Play, Symbolism, and Ritual: A Study of Tamil Brahmin Women's Rites of Passage*. New York: Peter Lang.

Dwyer, Graham. 2003. *The Divine and the Demonic: Supernatural Affliction and its Treatment in North India*. London: Routledge Curzon.

Egnor, Margret T. 1980. 'On the Meaning of Śakti to Women in Tamil Nadu', in Susan S. Wadley (ed.), *The Powers of Tamil Women*. Syracuse, N. Y.: Syracuse University, 1–34.

——. 1984. 'The Changed Mother, or What the Smallpox Goddess Did When There Was No More Smallpox', in E. Valentine Daniel and Judy F. Pugh (eds), *South Asian Systems of Healing*. Contribution to Asian Studies 18. Leiden: E. J. Brill, 24–45.

Eichinger Ferro-Luzzi, Gabriela. 1974. 'Women's Pollution Periods in Tamilnad', in *Anthropos* 69, 113–61.

Elmore, Wilber Theodore. 1915. *Dravidian Gods in Modern Hinduism: A Study of the Local and Village Deities of Southern India*. Lincoln, Nebraska: University of Nebraska.

Emigh, John. 1996. *Masked Performance: The Play of Self and Other in Ritual and Theatre*. Philadelphia: University of Pennsylvania Press.

Erndl, Kathleen M. 1993. *Victory to the Mother: The Hindu Goddess of Northwest India in Myth, Ritual, and Symbol*. New York: Oxford University Press.

——. 1996. 'Śerāṅvālī: The Mother Who Possesses', in John S. Hawley and Donna M. Wulff (eds), *Devī: Goddesses of India*. Berkeley: University of California Press, 173–94.

——. 1997. 'The Goddess and Women's Power: A Hindu Case Study', in Karen King (ed.), *Women and Goddess Traditions in Antiquity and Today*. Minneapolis: Fortress Press, 17–38.

Eschmann, Anncharlott. 1978. 'Hinduization of Tribal Deities in Orissa: The Śākta and Śaiva Typology', in Anncharlott Eschmann, Hermann Kulke and Gaya Charan Tripathi (eds), *The Cult of Jagannath and the Regional Tradition of Orissa*. Delhi: Manohar, 79–97.

Eschmann, Anncharlott, Hermann Kulke and Gaya Charan Tripathi (eds). 1978. *The Cult of Jagannath and the Regional Tradition of Orissa*. Delhi: Manohar.

Falk, Nancy A. and Rita M. Gross (eds). 1980. *Unspoken Worlds: Women's Religions Lives in Non-Western Cultures*. San Francisco: Harper & Row.

Ferrari, Fabrizio M. 2007. '"Love Me Two Times." From Smallpox to AIDS: Contagion and Possession in the Cult of Śītalā', in *Religions of South Asia* 1 (1): 81–106.

Fischer, Eberhard and Dinanath Pathy. 1996. *Murals for Goddesses and Gods: The Tradition of Osakothi Ritual Painting in Orissa, India*. New Delhi: Indira Gandhi National Centre for the Arts.

Fischer-Lichte, Erika. 2002. 'Grenzgänge und Tauschhandel: Auf dem Wege zu einer performativen Kultur', in Uwe Wirth (ed.), *Performanz: Zwischen Sprachphilosophie und Kulturwissenschaften*. Frankfurt/Main: Suhrkamp, 277–300.

——. 2004. *Ästhetik des Performativen*. Frankfurt/Main: Suhrkamp.

Flood, Gavin D. 2003. 'Introduction: Establishing the Boundaries', in Gavin D. Flood (ed.), *The Blackwell Companion to Hinduism*. London: Blackwell, 1–19.

Flueckiger, Joyce B. 1991. 'Literacy and the Changing Concept of Text: Women's Ramayana Maṇḍalī in Central India', in Joyce B. Flueckiger and Laurie J. Searle (eds), *Boundaries of the Text: Epics Performances in South and Southeast Asia*. Ann Arbor: University of Michigan Press, 43–60.

——. 1996. *Gender and Genre in the Folklore of Middle India*. Ithaca: Cornell University Press.

Foulston, Lynn. 2002. *At the Feet of the Goddess: The Divine Feminine in Local Hindu Religion*. Brighton: Sussex Academic Press.

Freeman, James M. 1980. 'The Ladies of Lord Krishna: Rituals of Middle-Aged Women in Eastern India', in Nancy Auer Falk and Rita M. Gross (eds), *Unspoken Worlds: Women's Religious Lives in Non-Western Cultures*. San Francisco: Harper & Row, 110–26.

——. 1981. 'A Firewalking Ceremony That Failed', in Giri Raj Gupta (ed.), *The Social and Cultural Context of Medicine in India*. New Delhi: Vikas Publication House, 308–36.

Freeman, Richard. 1993. 'Performing Possession: Ritual and Consciousness in the Teyyam Complex of Northern Kerala', in Heidrun Brückner, Lothar Lutze and Aditya Malik (eds), *Flags of Fame: Studies in South Asian Folk Culture*. South Asia Studies, 27. Delhi: Manohar, 109–38.

——. 1999. 'Dynamics of the Person in the Worship and Sorcery of Malabar', Jackie Assayag and Gilles Tarbout (eds), *La Possession en Asie du Sud: Parole, Corps, Territoire*. Collection Purusartha 21. Paris: École des Haute Études en Science Sociales, 149–81.

Freitag, Sandria B. 1989. *Collective Action and Community: Public Arenas and the Emergence of Communalism in North India*. Berkeley: University of California Press.

——. 1991. 'Enactments of Ram's Story and the Changing Nature of "the Public" in British India', in *South Asia* 14 (1): 65–90.

Friedson, Steven M. 1996. *Dancing Prophets: Musical Experience in Tumbuka Healing*. Chicago: University of Chicago Press.

Fruzetti, Lina M. 1982. *The Gift of a Virgin: Women, Marriage, and Ritual in a Bengali Society*. New Brunswick, N. Y.: Rutgers.

Fuller, Chris J. 1992. *The Camphor Flame: Popular Hinduism and Society in India*. Princeton: Princeton University Press.

Geertz, Clifford. 1966. 'Religion as a Cultural System', in Michael Banton (ed.), *Anthropological Approaches to the Study of Religion*. London: Tavistock Publications, 1–46.

Gell, Alfred. 1998. *Art and Agency: An Anthropological Theory*. Oxford: Clarendon Press.

Gellner, David. 1994. 'Priests, Healers, Mediums and Witches: The Context of Possession in the Kathmandu Valley, Nepal', in *Man*, N. S. 29 (1): 27–48.

Giddens, Anthony. 1991. *Modernity and Self-Identity: Self and Society in the Late Modern Age*. Cambridge: Polity.

Gilmore, David D. 1998. *Carnival and Culture: Sex, Symbol, and Status in Spain*. New Haven: Yale University Press.

Goffman, Erving. 1959. *The Presentation of Self in Everyday Life*. New York: Doubleday & Company.

——. 1979. *Gender Advertisements*. London: Macmillan.

Gold, Ann G. 1988. 'Spirit Possession Perceived and Performed in Rural Rajasthan', in *Contributions to Indian Sociology* (N. S.) 22 (1): 35–63.

——. 1994. 'Gender, Violence and Power: Rajasthani Stories of Shakti', in Nita Kumar (ed.), *Women as Subjects: South Asian Histories*. London: University Press of Virginia, 26–48.

Goody, Jack. 1977. 'Against "Ritual": Loosely Structured Thoughts on a Loosely Defined Topic', in Sally F. Moore and Barbara G. Myerhoff (eds), *Secular Rituals*. Assen: Van Gorcum, 25–35.

Government of Orissa. 2004. *Orissa Human Development Report*. Bhubaneswar: Government of Orissa.

Gross, Rita M. 2000. 'Is the Goddess a Feminist?', in Alf Hiltebeitel and Kathleen M. Erndl (eds), *Is the Goddess a Feminist? The Politics of South Asian Goddesses*. Sheffield: Sheffield University Press, 104–12.

Guha, Ranajit (ed.) 1998. *A Subaltern Studies Reader, 1986–1995*. Delhi: Oxford University Press.

Gupta, Lina. 1991. 'Kali, the Savior', in Paula M. Cooey, William R. Eakin and Jay B. McDaniel (eds), *After Patriarchy: Feminist Transformations of the World Religions*. Maryknoll: Orbis, 15–35.

——. 1997. 'Hindu Women and Ritual Empowerment', in Karen King (ed.), *Women and Goddess Traditions in Antiquity and Today*. Minneapolis: Fortress Press, 85–110.

Gupta, Sanjukta. 1999. 'Hindu Woman, the Ritualist', in Harald Tambs-Lyche (ed.), *The Feminine Sacred in South Asia/Le sacré au féminin en Asie du Sud*. Delhi: Manohar, 88–99.

Haberman, David L. 1988. *Acting as Way of Salvation: A Study of Rāgānugā Bhakti Sādhana*. New York: Oxford University Press.

Hall, Stuart and Paul du Gay (eds). 1996. *Questions of Cultural Identity*. London: Sage.

Hancock, Mary E. 1995. 'The Dilemmas of Domesticity: Possession and Devotional Experience Among Urban Smārta Women', in Lindsey Harlan and Paul P. Courtright (eds), *From the Margins of Hindu Marriage: Essays on Gender, Religion and Culture*. New York: Oxford University Press, 60–91.

Handelman, Don. 1990. *Models and Mirrors: Towards an Anthropology of Public Events*. Cambridge: Cambridge University Press.

Handelman, Don. 1995. 'The Guises of the Goddess and the Transformation of the Male: Gangamma's Visit to Tirupati, and the Continuum of Gender', in David Shulman (ed.), *Syllables of Sky: Studies in South Indian Civilization*. Delhi: Oxford University Press, 283–337.

Hardenberg, Roland. 1998. *Die Wiedergeburt der Götter: Ritual und Gesellschaft in Orissa*. Hamburg: Kovač.

Harman, William P. 2006. 'Negotiating Relationships with the Goddess', in Selvy J. Raj and William P. Harman (eds), *Dealing with Deities: The Ritual Vow in South Asia*. Albany: State University of New York, 25–41.

Hart, Lynda and Peggy Phelan (eds). 1993. *Acting Out: Feminist Performances*. Ann Arbor: University of Michigan Press.

Hauser, Beatrix. 2004a. 'Creating Performative Texts: The Introduction of Maṅgaḷā pūjā in Southern Orissa', in Angelika Malinar, Johannes Beltz and Heiko Frese (eds), *Text and Context in the History, Literature and Religion of Orissa*. Delhi: Manohar, 203–38.

——. 2004b. 'Göttliches Gestalten: Zur Besessenheitserfahrung von Frauen in Orissa, Indien', in Michael Schetsche (ed.), *Der maximal Fremde: Begegnungen mit dem Nicht-Menschlichen und die Grenzen des Verstehens*. Grenzüberschreitungen 3. Würzburg: Ergon, 139–60.

——. 2005. 'Travelling Through the Night: Living Mothers and Divine Daughters at an Orissan Goddess Festival', in *Paideuma: Mitteilungen zur Kulturkunde*, 51: 221–33.

——. 2006a. 'Ästhetik im Transit: Indische Konzeptionen der Ramlila-Aufführungspraxis', in *Paragrana: Internationale Zeitschrift für Historische Anthropologie*, 15 (2): 133–48.

——. 2006b. 'Divine Play or Subversive Comedy? Reflections on Costuming and Gender at a Hindu Festival', in Ursula Rao and John Hutnyk (eds), *Celebrating Transgression: Method and Politics in Anthropological Studies of Culture*. New York: Berghahn, 129–44.

——. 2006c. 'Durch den Körper sehen: Zur Präsenz der Götter bei der indischen Ramlila', in Erika Fischer-Lichte, Robert Sollich, Sandra Umathum and Matthias Warstat (eds), *Auf der Schwelle - Kunst, Risiken, Nebenwirkungen*. München: Fink, 143–59.

——. 2006d. 'Periodisch unberührbar — zur körperlichen Performanz menstrueller Unreinheit in Südorissa (Indien)', in Ursula Rao (ed.), *Kulturelle VerWandlungen: Die Gestaltung sozialer Welten in der Performanz*. Berlin: Lang, 67–99.

——. 2007. 'Tribal or Tantric? Reflections on the Classification of Goddesses in Southern Orissa', in Georg Pfeffer (ed.), *Periphery and Centre: Studies in Orissan History, Religion and Anthropology*. Delhi: Manohar, 131–52.

——. 2008a. 'Acting like God? Ways of Embodying the Divine in Religious Play and Deity Possession' in *Diskus* 9. http://www.basr.ac.uk/diskus/diskus9/hauser.htm (last accessed on 9 January 2012)

——. 2008b. 'Dem Spiel ergeben: Zum theatralen Entwurf devotionaler Liebe bei der indischen Ramlila', in Anke Henning, Brigitte Obermayr, Antje Wessels and Marie-Christin Wilm (eds), *Bewegte Erfahrungen: Zwischen Emotionalität und Ästhetik*. Zürich: Diaphanes, 201–14.

Hauser, Beatrix. 2008c. 'How to Fast for a Good Husband? On Ritual Imitation and Embodiment in Orissa', in Alexander Henn and Klaus-Peter Koepping (eds). *Rituals in an Unstable World: Contingency-Hybridity-Embodiment*. Frankfurt/Main: Peter Lang, 227–45.

——. 2010a. 'Dramatic Changes? The Experience of a Religious Play in the Mega-City of Delhi', in Angelos Chaniotis et al. (eds), *Body, Performance, Agency and Experience*. Ritual Dynamics and the Science of Ritual, Vol. II. Wiesbaden: Harrassowitz, 459–79.

——. 2010b. 'Performative Constructions of Female Identity at a Hindu Ritual: Some Thoughts on the Agentive Dimension', in Anette Hoffmann and Esther Peeren (eds), *Representation Matters: (Re)articulating Collective Identities in a Postclonial World*, Thamyris Intersecting no. 20. Amsterdam: Rodopi, 207–21.

——. 2011a. 'Das Vermitteln der Regel(n): Menstruelle Unreinheit in der performativen Praxis indischer Frauen', in Peter Burschel and Christoph Marx (eds), *Reinheit*. Wien: Böhlau, 197–217.

——. 2011b. 'Divine Possession as a Religious Idiom: Considering Female Ritual Practice in Orissa', in Hermann Kulke and Georg Berkemer (eds), *Centres Out There? Facets of Subregional Identities*. Delhi: Manohar.

Hawley, John Ss. 1995. 'Every Play a Play Within a Play', in William S. Sax (ed.), *The Gods at Play: Līlā in South Asia*. Oxford: Oxford University Press, 115–30.

Hein, Norvin. 1972. *The Miracle Plays of Mathurā*. New Haven: Yale University Press.

Henn, Alexander. 2003. *Die Wachheit der Wesen: Politik, Ritual und Kunst der Akkulturation in Goa*. Münster: Lit.

Hiltebeitel, Alf and Kathleen M. Erndl. 2000a. 'Introduction: Writing Goddesses, Goddesses Writing, and Other Scholarly Concerns', in Alf Hiltebeitel and Kathleen M. Erndl (eds), *Is the Goddess a Feminist? The Politics of South Asian Goddesses*. New Delhi: Oxford University Press, 11–23.

—— (eds). 2000b. *Is the Goddess a Feminist? The Politics of South Asian Goddesses*. Sheffield: Sheffield University Press.

Hobart, Angela and Bruce Kapferer (eds). 2005. *Aesthetics in Performance: Formations of Symbolic Construction and Experience*. New York: Berghahn.

Hobsbawm, Eric and Terence Ranger (eds). 1983. *The Invention of Tradition*. Cambridge: Cambridge University Press.

Howes, David. 1990. 'Controlling Textuality: A Call for a Return to the Senses', in *Anthropologica*, 32 (1): 55–73.

—— (ed.) 1991. *The Varieties of Sensory Experience: A Sourcebook in the Anthropology of Senses*. Anthropological Horizons, 1. Toronto: University of Toronto.

Humes, Cynthia Ann. 1997. 'Glorifying the Great Goddess or Great Woman? Hindu Women's Experience in Ritual Recitation of Devi-Mahatmya', in Karen King (ed.), *Women and Goddess Traditions in Antiquity and Today*. Minneapolis: Fortress Press, 39–63.

Humphrey, Caroline and James Laidlaw. 1994. *The Archetypical Actions of Ritual: A Theory of Ritual Illustrated by the Jain Rite of Worship*. Oxford: Clarendon Press.

Huyler, Stephen P. 1994. 'Tulasī: A Survey and Case Study of Ritual Terracotta Planters for Tulasī, the Goddess Incarnate as a Basil Bush', in Bridget Allchin (ed.), *Living Traditions: Studies in the Ethnoarchaeology of South Asia*. New Delhi: OUP & IBH Publications, 323–49.

Hymes, Dell. 1975. 'Breakthrough into Performance', in Dan Ben-Amos and Kenneth S. Goldstein (eds), *Folklore, Performance and Communication*. The Hague: Mouton, 12–74.

Inden, Ronald B. 1990. *Imagining India*. Oxford: Basil Blackwell.

*Jahni oṣā bā tuḷāsī pūjā kathā*. n. d. Brahmapura: Ragunātha pustākalaẏa.

Jameson, Frederick. 1991. *Postmodernism, or the Cultural Logic of Late Capitalism*. Durham: Duke University Press.

Jayakar, Pupul. 1989. *The Earth Mother*. Delhi: Penguin.

Jenkins, Richard. 1996. *Social Identity*. London: Routledge.

Kakar, Sudhir. 1982. *Shamans, Mystics, and Doctors: A Psychological Enquiry into India and its Healing Traditions*. Bombay: Oxford University Press.

Kapadia, Karin. 1995. *Siva and her Sisters: Gender, Caste and Class in Rural South India*. Boulder (Colorado): Westview Press.

——. 1996. 'Dancing the Goddess: Possession and Class in Tamil South India', in *Modern Asian Studies*, 30 (2): 423–45.

——. 2000. 'Pierced by Love: Tamil Possession, Gender and Caste', in Julia Leslie and Mary McGee (eds), *Invented Identities: The Interplay of Gender, Religion and Politics in India*. Delhi: Oxford University Press, 181–202.

Kapferer, Bruce. 1983. *A Celebration of Demons: Exorcism and the Aesthetics of Healing in Sri Lanka*. Bloomington: Indiana University Press.

——. 2005. 'Ritual Dynamics and Virtual Practice: Beyond Representation and Meaning', in Don Handelman and Galina Lindquist (eds), *Ritual in Its Own Right: Exploring the Dynamics of Transformation*. New York: Berghahn, 35–54.

——. 2006. 'Virtuality', in Jens Kreinath, Jan Snoek and Michael Stausberg (eds), *Theorizing Rituals, Vol. 1: Issues, Topics, Approaches, Concepts*. Numen Book Series: Studies in the History of Religions 114–1. Leiden: Brill, 671–84.

Kapur, Anuradha. 1990. *Actors, Pilgrims, Kings and God: The Ramlila at Ramnagar*. Calcutta: Seagull.

Kaufmann, Jean-Claude. 2005. *Die Erfindung des Ich. Eine Theorie der Identität*. Konstanz: UVK.

Keller, Mary. 2002. *The Hammer and the Flute: Women, Power & Spirit Possession*. Baltimore: The John Hopkins University Press.

Kertzer, David I. 1988. *Rituals, Politics, and Power*. New Haven: Yale University.

Khanna, Madhu. 2000. 'The Goddess-Woman Equation in Śākta Tantras', in Mandakranta Bose (ed.), *Faces of the Feminine in Ancient, Medieval, and Modern India*. New Delhi: Oxford University Press, 109–23.

Khare, R. S. 1976. *Culture and Reality: Essays on the Hindu System of Managing Food*. Simla: Indian Institute of Advanced Study.

King, Karen (ed.) 1997. *Women and Goddess Traditions in Antiquity and Today*. Minneapolis: Fortress Press.

Kinsley, David. 1998. *Tantric Visions of the Divine Feminine: The Ten Mahāvidyās*. Delhi: Motilal Banarsidass Publishers.

Knipe, David M. 1989. 'Night of the Growing Death: A Cult of Vīrabhadra in Coastal Andhra', in Alf Hiltebeitel (ed.), *Criminal Gods and Demon Devotees: Essays on the Guardians of Popular Hinduism*. Albany: State University of New York, 123–56.

Köpping, Klaus-Peter. 1998. '"Jenseits": Bataille und die Transgression des Sprechens über das Erotisch-Heilige', in *Paragrana*, 7 (2): 152–76.

——. 2002. *Shattering Frames: Transgressions and Transformations in Anthropological Discourse and Practice*. Berlin: Reimer.

——. (ed.) 1997. *The Games of Gods and Man: Essays in Play and Performance*. Hamburg: Lit.

Köpping, Klaus-Peter, Bernhard Leistle and Michael Rudolph. 2006a. 'Introduction', in Klaus-Peter Köpping, Bernhard Leistle and Michael Rudolph (eds), *Ritual and Identity: Performative Practices as Effective Transformations of Social Reality*. Berlin: Lit, 9–30.

——. (eds). 2006b. *Ritual and Identity: Performative Practices as Effective Transformations of Social Reality*. Berlin: Lit.

Köpping, Klaus-Peter and Ursula Rao (eds). 2000. *Im Rausch des Rituals: Gestaltung und Transformation der Wirklichkeit in körperlicher Performanz*. Münster: Lit.

Kotthoff, Helga. 2002. 'Was heißt eigentlich "doing gender"? Zu Interaktion und Geschlecht', in Jiřina van Leuuwen-Turnovcová et al. (eds), *Gender-Forschung in der Slawistik: Beiträge der Konferenz Gender-Sprache-Kultur*. Wiener Slawistischer Almanach, Sonderband 55, 1–27.

Kramer, Fritz W. 1993. *The Red Fez: Art and Spirit Possession in Africa*. London: Verso. (German Original 1987).

Kripal, Jeffrey J. 2000. 'A Garland of Talking Heads for the Goddess: Some Autobiographical and Psychoanalytic Reflections on the Western Kali', in Alf Hiltebeitel and Kathleen M. Erndl (eds), *Is the Goddess a Feminist? The Politics of South Asian Goddesses*. New Delhi: Oxford University Press, 239–68.

Kulke, Hermann and Burkhard Schnepel (eds). 2001. *Jagannath Revisited: Studying Society, Religion and the State in Orissa*. New Delhi: Manohar.

Kumar, Nita. 1988. *The Artisans of Banaras: Popular Culture and Identity, 1880–1986*. New Jersey: Princeton University Press.

——. 1994a. 'Introduction', in Nita Kumar (ed.), *Women as Subjects: South Asian Histories*. London: University Press of Virginia, 1–26.

——. 1995. 'Class and Gender Politics in the Rāmlīlā', in William S. Sax (ed.), *The Gods at Play: Līlā in South Asia*. Oxford: Oxford University Press, 156–76.

Kumar, Nita. (ed.) 1994b. *Women as Subjects: South Asian Histories*. London: University Press of Virginia.

Kurtz, Stanley N. 2000. 'In Our Image: The Feminist Vision of the Hindu Goddess', in Alf Hiltebeitel and Kathleen M. Erndl (eds), *Is the Goddess a Feminist? The Politics of South Asian Goddesses*. New Delhi: Oxford University Press, 181–86.

Laderman, Carol and Marina Roseman (eds). 1996. *The Performance of Healing*. New York: Routledge.

Lambek, Michael. 1989. 'From Disease to Discourse: Remarks on the Conceptualization of Trance and Spirit Possession', in Colleen A. Ward (ed.), *Altered States of Consciousness and Mental Health: A Cross-Cultural Perspective*. Newbury Park: Sage, 36–61.

Laws, Sophie. 1990. *Issues of Blood: The Politics of Menstruation*. Basingstoke: Macmillan.

Leslie, Julia. 1989. *The Perfect Wife: the Orthodox Hindu Woman According to the Strīdharmapaddhati of Tryambakayajvan*. Delhi: Oxford University Press.

——. 1992. 'The Significance of Dress for the Orthodox Hindu Woman', in Ruth Barnes and Joanne B. Eicher (eds), *Dress and Gender: Making and Meaning*. Oxford: Berg, 198–213.

—— (ed.) 1991. *Roles and Rituals for Hindu Women*. London: Pinter Publishers.

Leslie, Julia and Mary McGee (eds). 2000. *Invented Identities: The Interplay of Gender, Religion and Politics in India*. New Delhi: Oxford University Press.

Lewis, Ioan M. 1975. *Ecstatic Religion: An Anthropological Study of Spirit Possession and Shamanism*. Harmondsworth: Penguin.

Lutgendorf, Philip. 1991. *The Life of a Text: Performing Rāmcaritmānas of Tulsidas*. Berkeley: University of California Press.

MacAloon, John J. 1984. 'Introduction: Cultural Performance, Cultural Theory', in John J. MacAloon (ed.), *Rite, Drama, Festival, Spectacle: Rehearsals Toward a Theory of Cultural Performance*. Philadelphia: Institute for the Studies of Human Issues, 1–15.

MacCormack, Carol P. and Marilyn Strathern (eds). 1980. *Nature, Culture and Gender*. Cambridge: Cambridge University Press.

Madan, Trilokhi Nath. 1985. 'Concerning the Categories *śubha* and *śuddha* in Hindu Culture: An Exploratory Essay', in John B. Carman and Frédérique A. Marglin (eds), *Auspiciousness and Purity in India*. Leiden: Brill, 11–29.

Mageo, Jeannette Marie and Alan Howard (eds). 1996. *Spirits in Culture, History, and Mind*. London: Routledge.

Mahapatra, L. K. (ed.) 1981/1982. *Man in Society: Bulletin of the Department of Anthropology, Utkal University* 2. Bhubaneswar: Department of Anthropology, Utkal University.

Malinar, Angelika. 2009. 'Reinigung und Transformation von "Unreinem" im Hinduismus', in Angelika Malinar and Martin Vöhler (eds), *Un/Reinheit: Konzepte und Praktiken im Kulturvergleich*. München: Fink.

Mallebrein, Cornelia. 1999. 'Tribal and Local Deities — Assimilations and Transformations', in Vidya Dehejia (ed.), *Devi: The Great Goddess. Female Divinity in South Asian Art*. München: Prestel, 137–56.

Maltby, T. J. (1882) 1967. 'Extracts from The Ganjam District Manual', in M. Ahmed (ed.), *Census of India, 1961, Orissa: District Census Handbook Ganjam, Vol. II*. Cuttack: Orissa Government Press, V-XXXIV.

Manna, Sibendu. 1993. *Mother Goddess Caṇḍī: Its Socio Ritual Impact on the Folk Life*. Calcutta: Punthi Pustak.

Marglin, Frédérique A. 1985a. 'Types of Oppositions in Hindu Culture', in John B. Carman and Frédérique A. Marglin (eds), *Auspiciousness and Purity in India*. Leiden: E. J. Brill, 65–83.

——. 1985b. *Wives of the God-King: The Rituals of the Devadasis of Puri*. Delhi: Oxford University Press.

——. 1995. 'Gender and the Unitary Self: Looking for the Subaltern in Coastal Orissa', in *South Asia Research*, 15 (1): 78–130.

Marglin, Frédérique A. and Purna Chandra Mishra. 1991. 'Death and Regeneration: Brahmin and Non-Brahmin Narratives', in Diana L. Eck and Françoise Mallison (eds), *Devotion Divine: Bhakti Traditions from Regions of India. Studies in Honour of Charlotte Vaudeville*. Groningen: Egbert Forsten, 209–30.

Marriott, McKim. 1976. 'Hindu Transactions: Diversity Without Dualism', in Bruce Kapferer (ed.), *Transaction and Meaning*. Philadelphia: Institute for the Study of Human Issues Press, 109–42.

Martin, Emily. 1987. *The Woman in the Body: A Cultural Analysis of Reproduction*. Boston: Beacon Press.

Mayaram, Shail. 1999. 'Spirit Possession: Reframing Discourses on the Self and Other', in Jackie Assayag and Gilles Tarabout (eds), *La Possession en Asie du Sud: Parole, Corps, Territoire*. Collection Purusartha 21. Paris: École des Hautes Études en Sciences Sociales, 101–32.

McDaniel, June. 1989. *The Madness of the Saints: Ecstatic Religion in Bengal*. Chicago: University of Chicago Press.

——. 2003. *Making Virtuous Daughters and Wives: An Introduction to Women's Brata Rituals in Bengali Folk Religion*. Albany: State University of New York Press.

——. 2004. *Offering Flowers, Feeding Skulls: Popular Goddess Worship in West Bengal*. New York: Oxford University Press.

McDermott, Rachel F. 1996a. 'Popular Attitudes Towards Kālī and Her Poetry Tradition. Interviewing Śāktas in Bengal', in Axel Michaels, Cornelia Vogelsanger and Annette Wilke (eds), *Wild Goddesses in India and Nepal: Proceedings of an International Symposium Berne and Zürich*, November 1994. Bern: Lang, 383–415.

——. 1996b. 'The Western Kālī', in John S. Hawley and Donna M. Wulff (eds), *Devī: Goddesses of India*. Berkeley: University of California, 281–313.

McGee, Mary. 1987. *Feasting and Fasting: The Vrata Tradition and Its Significance for Hindu Women*. Ann Arbor, Michigan: University Microfilms.

McGee, Mary. 1991. 'Desired Fruits: Motive and Intention in the Votive Rites of Hindu Women', in Julia Leslie (ed.), *Roles and Rituals for Hindu Women*. London: Pinter Publishers, 71–88.

——. 2000. 'Introduction: Invented Identities: The Interplay of Gender, Religion, and Politics in India', in Julia Leslie and Mary McGee (eds), *Invented Identities: The Interplay of Gender, Religion and Politics in India*. New Delhi: Oxford University Press, 1–56.

McKenzie, Jon. 2001. *Perform of Else: From Discipline to Performance*. London: Routledge.

Mead, George Herbert. 1934. *Mind, Self and Society*. Ed by Charles W. Morris. Chicago: University of Chicago Press.

Menon, Usha and Richard A. Shweder. 2000. 'Power in its Place: Is the Great Goddess of Hinduism a Feminist?', in Alf Hiltebeitel and Kathleen M. Erndl (eds), *Is the Goddess a Feminist? The Politics of South Asian Goddesses*. Sheffield: Sheffield University Press, 151–63.

Merleau-Ponty, Maurice. 1962. *Phenomenology of Perception*. London: Routledge. (French Edition 1945).

Michaels, Axel. 2004a. *Hinduism: Past and Present*. Princeton: Princeton University Press.

——. 2004b. 'Indology and the Cultural Turn', in Angelika Malinar, Johannes Beltz and Heiko Frese (eds), *Text and Context in the History, Literature and Religion of Orissa*. Delhi: Manohar, 457–81.

Michaels, Axel, Cornelia Vogelsanger and Annette Wilke (eds). 1996. *Wild Goddesses in India and Nepal*. Bern: Lang.

Mines, Mattison. 1994. *Public Faces, Private Voices: Community and Individuality in South India*. Berkeley: University of Berkeley.

Minturn, Leigh. 1993. *Sita's Daughters: Coming Out of Purdah. The Rajput Women of Khalapur Revisited*. New York: Oxford University Press.

Miśra, Nirmaḷa. 1994. *Oṣā brata gapa*. Brahmapura: Tārātāriṇī pustakālaẏa.

Morris, Rosalind. 1995. 'All Made Up: Performance Theory and the New Anthropology of Sex and Gender', in *Annual Review of Anthropology* 24, 567–92.

Mukhopadhyay, Durgadas. 1978. 'Sahi Yatra', in Durgadas Mukhopadhyay (ed.), *Lesser Known Forms of Performing Arts in India*. New Delhi: Minimax, 119–23.

Nabokov, Isabelle. 1997. 'Expel the Lover, Recover the Wife: Symbolic Analysis of a South Indian Exorcism', in *Journal of the Royal Anthropological Institute* (N. S.) 3, 297–316.

Nandy, Ashis. 1980. *At the Edge of Psychology: Essays in Politics and Culture*. Delhi: Oxford University Press.

Obeyesekere, Gananath. 1977. 'Psychocultural Exegesis of a Case of Spirit Possession in Sri Lanka', in Vincent Crapanzano and Vivian Garrison (eds), *Case Studies in Spirit Possession*. New York: Wiley, 235–94.

——. 1981. *Medusa's Hair: An Essay on Personal Symbols and Religious Experience*. Chicago: University of Chicago Press.

Ojha, Catherine. 1981. 'Feminine Asceticism in Hinduism: Its Tradition and Present Condition', in *Man in India*, 61 (3); 254–85.

Orsini, Francesca (ed.) 2006. *Love in South Asia: A Cultural History*. Cambridge: Cambridge University Press.

Ortner, Sherry B. 1996. *Making Gender: The Politics and Erotics of Culture*. Boston: Beacon Press.

Ortner, Sherry B. and Harriet Whitehead (eds). 1981. *Sexual Meanings: The Cultural Construction of Gender and Sexuality*. Cambridge: Cambridge University Press.

Osella, Caroline and Filippo Osella. 1999. 'Seepage of Divinised Power Through Social, Spiritual and Bodily Boundaries: Some Aspects of Possession in Kerala', in Jackie Assayag and Gilles Tarabout (eds), *La Possession en Asie du Sud: Parole, Corps, Territoire*. Collection Purusartha 21. Paris: École des Hautes Études en Sciences Sociales, 183–201.

Östör, Ákos. 1980. *The Play of the Gods: Locality, Ideology, Structure and Time in the Festivals of a Bengali Town*. Chicago: University of Chicago Press.

Otten, Tina. 2006. *Heilung durch Rituale: Vom Umgang mit Krankheit bei den Rona im Hochland von Orissa*. Berlin: Lit.

Otten, Tina and Uwe Skoda (eds). Forthcoming. *Dialogues With Gods: Trance and Possession in Orissa*. Berlin: Weissensee.

Pakaslathi, Antti. 1998. 'Family-Centred Treatment of Mental Health Problems in the Balaji Temple in Rajasthan', in Asko Parpola and Sirpa Tenhunen (eds), *Changing Patterns of Family and Kinship in South Asia*. Studia Orientalia, 84, 129–66.

Parker, Andrew and Eve K. Sedgwick (eds). 1995. *Performativity and Performance*. New York: Routledge.

Parry, Jonathan. 1994. *Death in Banaras*. Cambridge: Cambridge University Press.

Pati, Biswamay. 2001. *Situating Social History — Orissa (1800–1997)*. New Delhi: Orient Longman.

Pātra, Satīśa. 1997. *Pāramparika ṭhākurāṇī yātrā o mā'ṅka mahimā*. Brahmapura: Siddhabīra pablikeśans.

Pearson, Anne M. 1996. *Because It Gives Me Peace of Mind: Ritual Fasts in the Religious Lives of Hindu Women*. Albany: State University of New York.

Pfleiderer, Beatrix. 1988. 'The Semiotics of Healing in a North Indian Muslim Shrine', in *Social Science and Medicine* 5, 417–24.

——. 1994. *Die besessenen Frauen von Mira Datar Dargah: Heilen und Trance in Indien*. Frankfurt/Main: Campus.

Pintchman, Tracy. 1994. *The Rise of the Goddess in Hindu Tradition*. Albany: State University of New York Press.

——. 2000. 'Is the Hindu Goddess Tradition a Good Resource for Western Feminism?', in Alf Hiltebeitel and Kathleen M. Erndl (eds), *Is the Goddess a Feminist? On the Politics of South Asian Goddesses*. New Delhi: Oxford University Press, 187–202.

Pintchman, Tracy. 2005. *Guests at God's Wedding: Celebrating Kartik Among the Women of Benares.* Albany: State University of New York Press.

——. 2006. 'When Vows Fail to Deliver What They Promise: The Case of Shyamavati', in Selva J. Raj and William P. Harman (eds), *Dealing with Deities: The Ritual Vow in South Asia.* New York: State of New York Press, 219–34.

Poggendorf-Kakar, Katharina. 2002. *Hindu-Frauen zwischen Tradition und Moderne: Religiöse Veränderungen der indischen Mittelschicht im städtischen Umfeld.* Stuttgart: Metzler.

Presler, Franklin A. 1987. *Religion Under Bureaucracy: Policy and Administration for Hindu Temples in South India.* Cambridge: Cambridge University Press.

Preston, James J. 1980. *Cult of the Goddess: Social and Religious Change in a Hindu Temple.* New Delhi: Vikas.

——. 1983. 'Goddess Temples in Orissa: An Anthropological Survey', in Giri Raj Gupta (ed.), *Religion in Modern India.* Main Currents in Indian Sociology 5. New Delhi: Vikas, 229–47.

Price, Pamela G. 1991. 'Acting in Public versus Forming a Public: Conflict Processing and Political Mobilization in Nineteenth Century South India', in *South Asia,* 14 (1): 91–121.

——. 1996. *Kingship and Political Practice in Colonial India.* Cambridge: Cambridge University Press.

Puri, Jyoti. 1999. *Woman, Body, Desire in Post-Colonial India.* London: Routledge.

Quigley, Declan. 1993. *The Interpretation of Caste.* Oxford: Clarendon Press.

Raheja, Gloria G. 1988. *The Poison in the Gift: Ritual, Prestation, and the Dominant Caste in a North Indian Village.* Chicago: University of Chicago Press.

Raheja, Gloria G. and Ann G. Gold. 1994. *Listen to the Heron's Words: Reimagining Gender and Kinship in North India.* Berkeley: University of California Press.

Raj, Selva J. and William P. Harman (eds). 2006. *Dealing with Deities: The Ritual Vow in South Asia.* Albany: State University of New York.

Raja Rao, E. 1999. 'The Telugu Diaspora in Orissa', in Dinanath Pathy and Ramesh P. Panigrahi (eds), *The Continuity in the Flux: Orissa.* New Delhi: Harman Publishing House, 209–14.

Rājaguru, Śyāmasundara. (1895) 1992. 'The Feasts and Fasts of the Uriyas', in *Abhinaba Bhañjabhāratī* 4–9, i–xx.

Rama Raju, B. 1978. *Folklore of Andhra Pradesh.* Delhi: National Book Trust. Revised Edition.

Ramaswamy, Vijaya. 1997. *Walking Naked: Women, Society, Spirituality in South India.* Shimla: Indian Institute of Advanced Study.

Rao, Sudhakar N. 1996. 'Transformative Rituals among Hindu Women in the Telugu Region', in *Contributions to Indian Sociology* (N. S.), 30 (1): 69–88.

Rao, Ursula. 2006. 'Einleitung: Zwischen Struktur und Kontingenz', in Ursula Rao (ed.), *Kulturelle VerWandlungen: Die Gestaltung sozialer Welten in der Performanz.* Berlin: Lang.

Rapport, Nigel. 1997. *Transcendent Individual: Towards a Literary and Liberal Anthropology.* London: Routledge.

Rath, Asoka Kumar. 1987. *Studies on Some Aspects of the History and Culture of Orissa*. Calcutta: Punthi Pustak.

Ratha, Rabindra Nātha. n. d. *Brahmapura Buṙhī Ṭhākurāṇīnka yātrāra itihāsa*. Brahmapura: Sannyāsī Press.

Raut, Laksmi Narayan. 1988. *Socio-Economic Life in Medieval Orissa (1568–1751)*. Calcutta: Punthi Pustak.

Reynolds, Holly B. 1980. 'The Auspicious Married Women', in Susan S. Wadley (ed.), *The Powers of Tamil Women*. Syracuse, N. Y.: Syracuse University, 35–60.

Rodrigues, Hillary. 2005. 'Women in the Worship of the Great Goddess', in Arvind Sharma (ed.), *Goddesses and Women in the Indic Religious Tradition*. Leiden: Brill, 72–104.

Rogers, John D. 1992. 'Gambling in Colonial Sri Lanka', in Douglas Haynes and Gyan Prakash (eds), *Contesting Power: Resistance and Everyday Social Relations in South Asia*. Berkeley: University of California Press, 175–212.

Roy, Manisha. 1975. *Bengali Women*. Chicago: Chicago University Press.

Samanta, Suchitra. 1992. '*Maṅgalmayīmā, sumaṅgalī, maṅgal*: Bengali Perceptions of the Divine Feminine, Motherhood and "Auspiciousness"', in *Contributions to Indian Sociology* (N. S.), 26 (1): 51–75.

Sangari, Kumkum and Sudesh Vaid (eds). 1989. *Recasting Women: Essays in Colonial History*. New Delhi: Kali for Women.

*Sarba Maṅgaḷā stuti*. n. d. Kaṭaka: Pustaka bhaṇḍāra.

Sax, William S. 1991. *Mountain Goddess: Gender and Politics in a Himalayan Pilgrimage*. New York: Oxford University Press.

——. 1995b. 'Who's Who in the Pāṇḍav Līlā?', in William S. Sax (ed.), *The Gods at Play: Līlā in South Asia*. Oxford: Oxford University Press, 131–55.

——. 2000. 'Conquering the Quarters: Religion and Politics in Hinduism', in *International Journal of Hindu Studies*, 4 (1): 39–60.

——. 2002. *Dancing the Self: Personhood and Performance in the Pāṇḍav Līlā of Garhwal*. Oxford: Oxford University Press.

——. (ed.) 1995a. *The Gods at Play: Līlā in South Asia*. Oxford: Oxford University Press.

Schechner, Richard. 1985. *Between Theater and Anthropology*. Philadelphia: University of Pennsylvania.

Schieffelin, Edward L. 1985. 'Performance and the Cultural Construction of Reality', in *American Ethnologist*, 12 (4): 707–24.

——. 1996. 'On Failure and Performance: Throwing the Medium Out of the Seance', in Carol Laderman and Marina Roseman (eds), *The Performance of Healing*. New York: Routledge, 59–90.

——. 1997. 'Problematizing Performance', in Felicia Hughes-Freeland (ed.), *Ritual, Performance, Media*. London: Routledge, 194–207.

Schmid, Anna. 2001. 'Lord Jagannātha in Pictorial Representations: A Collection of Cloth Paintings (*pata citras*) from Orissa', in Hermann Kulke and Burkhard Schnepel (eds), *Jagannath Revisited: Studying Society, Religion and the State in Orissa*. New Delhi: Manohar, 297–316.

Schnepel, Burkhard. 2009. 'Zur Dialektik von *agency* und *patiency*', in Klaus-Peter Köpping, Burkhard Schnepel and Christoph Wulf (eds), *Handlung und Leidenschaft. Jenseits von actio und passio*. Paragrana 18 (2). Berlin: Akademie-Verlag, 15–22.

Schnepel, Burkhard (ed.) 2001. *Hundert Jahre 'Die Traumdeutung': Kulturwissenschaftliche Perspektiven in der Traumforschung*. Köln: Köppe.

—— Schnepel, Burkhard. 2002. *The Jungle Kings: Ethnohistorical Aspects of Politics and Ritual in Orissa*. Delhi: Manohar (German Original 1987).

——. 2006. 'The "Dance of Punishment": Transgression and Punishment in an East Indian Ritual', in Ursula Rao and John Hutnyk (eds), *Celebrating Transgression: Method and Politics in Anthropological Studies of Culture*. New York: Berghahn, 115–27.

——. 2008. *'Tanzen für Kali': Ethnographie eines ostindischen Ritualtheaters*. Berlin: Reimer.

Schnepel, Burkhard and Eyal Ben-Ari. 2005. 'Introduction: "When darkness comes...": Steps Toward an Anthropology of the Night', in *Paideuma: Mitteilungen zur Kulturkunde* 51, 153–64.

Schömbucher, Elisabeth. 1993. 'Gods, Ghosts and Demons: Possession in South Asia', in Heidrun Brückner, Lothar Lutze and Aditya Malik (eds), *Flags of Fame: Studies in South Asian Folk Culture*. South Asia Studies, 27. Delhi: Manohar, 239–67.

——. 1994a. 'The Consequences of not Keeping a Promise: Possession Mediumship among a South Indian Fishing Caste', in *Cahiers de Littérature Orale* 35, 41–63.

——. 1994b. 'When the Deity Speaks: Performative Aspects of Possession Mediumship in South India', in Josef Kuckertz (ed.), *Jahrbuch für musikalische Volks- und Völkerkunde* 15. Eisenach: Karl Dietrich Wagner, 124–34.

——. 1996. 'Die Göttin und ihr Medium: Über Autorenschaft bei medialer Besessenheit', in Renaud van Quekelberghe and Dagmar Eigner (eds), *Jahrbuch für Transkulturelle Medizin und Psychotherapie: Trance, Besessenheit, Heilrituale und Psychotherapie*. Berlin: Verlag für Wissenschaft und Bildung, 241–55.

——. 1999. '"A Daughter for Seven Minutes": The Therapeutic and Divine Discourses of Possession Mediumship in South India', in Jackie Assayag and Gilles Tarbout (eds), *La Possession en Asie du Sud: Parole, Corps, Territoire*. Collection Purusartha 21. Paris: École des Haute Études en Science Sociales, 33–60.

——. 2006. *Wo Götter durch Menschen sprechen: Besessenheit in Indien*. Berlin: Reimer.

Searle-Chatterjee, Mary and Ursula Sarma (eds). 1994. *Contextualising Caste: Post-Dumontian Approaches*. Oxford: Blackwell.

Sered, Susan S. 1994. *Priestess, Mother, Sacred Sister: Religions Dominated by Women*. Oxford: Oxford University Press.

Seymour, Susan C. 1999. *Women, Family, and Child Care in India: A World in Transition*. Cambridge: Cambridge University Press.

Sharma, Arvind (ed.) 2005. *Goddesses and Women in the Indic Religious Traditions*. Leiden: Brill.

Sherma, Rita DasGupta. 2000: '"Sa Ham — I Am She": Woman as Goddess', in Alf Hiltebeitel and Kathleen M. Erndl (eds), *Is the Goddess a Feminist? The Politics of South Asian Goddesses*. New Delhi: Oxford University Press, 24–51.

Shweder, Richard A. 1985. 'Menstrual Pollution, Soul Loss, and the Comparative Study of Emotions', in Arthur Kleinman and Byron Good (eds), *Culture and Depression: Studies in the Anthropology and Cross-Cultural Psychiatry of Affect and Disorder*. Berkeley: University of California Press, 182–215.

Siegel, Lee. 1987. *Laughing Matters: Comic Tradition in India*. Delhi: Motilal Banarsidass.

Singer, Milton. 1959. 'Preface', in Milton Singer (ed.), *Traditional India: Structure and Change*. Philadelphia: American Folklore Society, ix–xxii.

——. 1972. *When a Great Tradition Modernizes*. New York: Praeger.

——. 1992. 'Cultural Performance as a Blurred Genre: Remarks to Inaugurate a Conference', in Joan L. Erdman (ed.), *Arts Patronage in India: Methods, Motives and Markets*. Delhi: Manohar, 19–27.

Smith, Frederick M. 2006. *The Self Possessed: Deity and Spirit Possession in South Asian Literature and Civilization*. New York: Columbia University Press.

Sökefeld, Martin. 1999. 'Debating Self, Identity, and Culture in Anthropology', in *Current Anthropology*, 40 (4): 417–47.

Sontheimer, Günther D. and Hermann Kulke (eds). 1989. *Hinduism Reconsidered*. Delhi: Manohar.

Srinivasan, Nirmala. 1990. 'The Cross-Cultural Relevance of Goffman's Concept of Individual Agency', in Harold Riggins (ed.), *Beyond Goffman: Studies on Communication, Institution, and Social Interaction*. New York: Gruyter, 141–61.

Srubar, Ilja, Joachim Renn and Ulrich Wenzel (eds). 2005. *Kulturen vergleichen*. Wiesbaden: Verlag für Sozialwissenschaften.

Stanley, John M. 1977. 'Special Time, Special Power: The Fluidity of Power in a Popular Hindu Festival', in *Journal of Asian Studies*, XXXVII (1): 27–43.

Stirrat, R. L. 1992. *Power and Religiosity in a Post-Colonial Setting: Sinhala Catholics in Contemporary Sri Lanka*. Cambridge: Cambridge University Press.

Sunder Rajan, Rajeswari. 1993. *Real and Imagined Women: Gender, Culture and Postcolonialism*. London: Routledge.

——. 2000. 'Real and Imagined Goddesses: A Debate', in Alf Hiltebeitel and Kathleen M. Erndl (eds), *Is the Goddess a Feminist? The Politics of South Asian Goddesses*. Sheffield: Sheffield University Press, 269–84.

Sutherland, Peter. 2003. 'Very Little Kingdoms: The Calendrical Order of West Himalayan Hindu Polity', in Georg Berkemer and Margret Frenz (eds), *Sharing Sovereignty: The Little Kingdom in South Asia*. Berlin: Schwarz, 31–61.

Syed, Renate. 2001. *'Ein Unglück ist die Tochter': Zur Diskriminierung des Mädchens im alten und heutigen Indien*. Wiesbaden: Harrassowitz.
Talbot, Cynthia. 2001. *Precolonial India in Practice: Society, Region, and Identity in Medieval Andhra.* New Delhi: Oxford University Press.
Tambiah, Stanley J. 1979. 'A Performative Approach to Ritual', *in Proceedings of the British Academy* 65, 116–42.
Tanabe, Akio. 1999. 'The Transformation of Śakti: Gender and Sexuality in the Festival of Goddess Ramachandi', in *Senri Ethnological Studies* 50, 137–58.
Tapper, Bruce E. 1979. 'Widows and Goddesses: Female Roles in Deity Symbolism in a South Indian Village', in *Contributions to Indian Sociology* (N. S.), 13 (1): 1–31.
Tarabout, Gilles. 1999. 'Prologue: Approches anthropologiques de la possession en Asie du Sud', in Jackie Assayag and Gilles Tarbout (eds), *La Possession en Asie du Sud: Parole, Corps, Territoire*. Collection Purusartha 21. Paris: École des Haute Études en Science Sociales, 9–30.
Taussig, Michael. 1993. *Mimesis and Alterity: A Particular History of the Senses.* New York: Routledge.
Tewari, Laxmi G. 1991. *A Splendor of Worship: Women's Fasts, Rituals, Stories and Art*. Delhi: Manohar.
*The Imperial Gazetteer of India. Vol. VIII: Berhampore to Bombay*. New Edition. Published under the Authority of his Majesty's Secretary of State for India in Council. Oxford: Clarendon Press 1908.
Tharu, Susie J. and K. Lalita (eds). 1993. *Women Writing in India. Vol 2.* London: Pandora Press.
Tokita-Tanabe, Yumiko. 1996. 'Village Politics and Women: Towards a Gendered Analysis of "Faction" in Rural Orissa', in *Journal of the Japanese Association for South Asian Studies* 8, 90–122.
——. 1999a. *Body, Self and Agency of Women in Contemporary Orissa, India*. Tokyo: University of Tokyo. (Unpublished Ph.D. thesis).
——. 1999b. 'Play and Eros: Girls' Swing Play and Swing Songs in Orissa, India', in *Journal of the Japanese Association for South Asian Studies* 11, 25–50.
——. 1999c. 'Women and Tradition in India: Construction of Subjectivity and Control of Female Sexuality in the Ritual of First Menstruation', in Masakazu Tanaka and Musashi Tachikawa (eds), *Living with Śakti: Gender, Sexuality and Religion in South Asia*. Senri Ethnological Studies, 50. Osaka: National Museum of Ethnology, 193–220.
Turner, Victor. 1969. *The Ritual Process: Structure and Anti-Structure*. New York: Aldine.
——. 1982. *From Ritual to Theatre: The Human Seriousness of Play*. New York: PAJ Publications.
——. 1984. 'Liminality and the Performative Genres', in John J. MacAloon (ed.), *Rite, Drama, Festival, Spectacle: Rehearsals Toward a Theory of Cultural Performance*. Philadelphia: Institute for the Studies of Human Issues, 19–41.

Turner, Victor. 1991. 'Are There Universals of Performance in Myth, Ritual, and Drama', in Richard Schechner and Willa Appel (eds), *By Means of Performance: Intercultural Studies of Theatre and Ritual.* Cambridge: Cambridge University Press, 8–18.

Viswanath, Kalpana. 1997. 'Shame and Control: Sexuality and Power in Feminist Discourse in India', in Meenakshi Thapan (ed.), *Embodiment: Essays on Gender and Identity*. New Delhi: Oxford University Press, 313–33.

Vitebsky, Piers. 1993. *Dialogues with the Dead: The Discussion of Mortality Among the Sora of Eastern India*. Cambridge: Cambridge University Press.

Wadley, Susan S. 1980a. 'Hindu Women's Family and Household Rites in a North Indian Village', in Nancy A. Falk and Rita M. Gross (eds), *Unspoken Worlds: Women's Religions Lives in Non-Western Cultures*. San Francisco: Harper & Row, 94–109.

——. 1983. 'Popular Hinduism and Mass Literature in North India: A Preliminary Analysis', in Giri Raj Gupta (ed.), *Religion in Modern India*. Main Currents in Indian Sociology, 5. New Delhi: Vikas, 81–103.

—— (ed.) 1980b. *The Powers of Tamil Women*. Syracuse, NY: Syracuse University.

West, Candace and Don H. Zimmerman. (1987) 2002. 'Doing Gender', in Sarah Fenstermaker and Candace West (eds), *Doing Gender, Doing Difference: Inequality, Power and Institutional Change.* New York: Routledge, 3–25.

White, David Gordon. 2003. *Kiss of the Yoginī: 'Tantric Sex' in its South Asian Contexts*. Chicago: University of Chicago Press.

—— (ed.) 2000. *Tantra in Practice*. Delhi: Motilal Banarsidass.

Willems, Herbert and Martin Jurga (eds). 1998. *Inszenierungsgesellschaft: Ein einführendes Handbuch*. Opladen: Westdeutscher Verlag.

Williams, Ron G. and James W. Boyd. 1993. *Ritual Art and Knowledge: Aesthetic Theory and Zoroastrian Ritual*. Columbia: University of South Carolina Press.

Winslow, Deborah. 1980. 'Rituals of First Menstruation in Sri Lanka', in *Man* (N. S.) 15, 603–25.

Wulff, Donna Marie. 1986. 'Religion in a New Mode: The Convergence of the Aesthetic and the Religions in Medieval India', in *Journal of the American Academy of Religion*, 54 (4): 673–88.

Young, Katherine K. 2002. 'Women and Hinduism', in Arvind Sharma (ed.), *Women in Indian Religions*. Delhi: Oxford University Press, 3–37.

Zarilli, Phillip B. 1990. 'What Does it Mean to "Become the Character": Power, Presence, and Transcendence in Asian In-Body Disciplines of Practice', in Richard Schechner and Willa Appel (eds), *By Means of Performance: Intercultural Studies of Theatre and Ritual.* Cambridge: Cambridge University Press, 131–48.

Zbavitel, Dušan. 1976. *Bengali Literature*, History of Indian Literature, Vol. 9. Wiesbaden: Harrassowitz.

# About the Author

**Beatrix Hauser** is Adjunct Associate Professor (*Privatdozentin*), Institute of Social and Cultural Anthropology, Martin-Luther-University, Halle-Wittenberg, Germany. She holds a PhD and a *Habilitation* in social anthropology. Her research interests lie in anthropology of the body, of religion, of theatre and performance, visual anthropology, transculturality and gender. She has published numerous articles in various international journals and edited volumes, and is the author of *Mit irdischem Schaudern und göttlicher Fügung: Bengalische Erzähler und ihre Bildvorführungen* [With Earthly Dread and Divine Decree: Bengali Storytellers and their Scroll Performances] in German (1998); and *Yoga Traveling: Bodily Practice in Transcultural Perspective* (edited volume, forthcoming).

# Index

aesthetics: of guise and disguise 147–54; importance of 26–27, 131, 144; of *pūjā* site 246
ancestral spirit 39, 121, 125, 148
Appadurai, Arjun 7n9, 228, 229
auspiciousness, concept of 5, 32, 54–55, 96, 99, 107, 115–16, 150, 213, 221, 243
authentication, of ritual 35, 223

Bakhtin, Mikhael 196, 202
Bataille, Georges 34, 196
Beautiful Khulaṇā (*Khulaṇā Sundarī*), legend of 62–63
Bell, Catherine 29n37, 35, 54, 90, 242
Bennett, Lynn 100n5, 104, 110n16, 111
*bhakti* 51, 64, 120, 136, 138, 142, 161, 240
Bourdieu, Pierre 3,12, 17, 22, 35, 54, 61, 90, 109, 138
Brahminical doctrine 2, 5
Brahminical ideology, of purity and pollution 93
Brahmins, supremacy of 99
*brata* 39, 182 *see also vrata*
Bṛndābatī, goddess 36, 41–43, 45, 49, 60; joint prayer to 52
Burghart, Richard 98, 140
Buṙhī Ṭhākurāṇī (deity of Berhampur) 13, 33–34, 125, 127–31, 146–48, 150, 152, 155–56, 170, 172–82, 185–87, 194, 202, 206–7, 211–12, 215, 218–23, 227, 229, 232–33, 242; possession of 128, 146; assumptions 163; powers of 190–91; during Ṭhākurāṇī Yātrā 178–81
Buṙhī Ṭhākurāṇī temple 125n13, 127–29, 162 *see also* Ṭhākurāṇī Yātrā festival; performance of Tuesday Pageants 147–54, 182–83
Butler, Judith 12, 18, 22, 107, 116

*caitra maṅgaḷabara* 147
Caldwell, Sarah 7n9, 134, 153n9
Caṇḍīmaṅgal 78
*Caṇḍī Paṭha* 189
Carrin, Marine 118n2, 133
Cartesian notion of the autonomous person 18
Cartesian persona concept 145
Chatterjee, Partha 3, 8n11, 48n21, 240
churning of curd (*dādhimanthana*) ritual 43–44
class-based habitus 75
Claus, Peter 121, 134, 136
collective agency, notion of 19
cooling food 58
costuming, as a ritual body practice 210 *see also* masquerades
Crapanzano, Vincent 145
Csordas, Thomas 17, 29, 145

Daśaharā festival 45
Dāmalā priests 174, 176, 189, 222–23, 229, 233
Daṇda Nāṭa (ritual dance in Orissa) 29, 144n1
Dash, Kunja Behari 40n11, 56–57
Das, Veena 19, 110n5, 104n9, 105, 107, 111
death rituals 99
deity possession 119; among women of Telugu fishing caste 131; Bāidhara deity 125; Basanti,

case of 124; Bāṭa Maṅgaḷā deity 126; Buṙhī Ṭhākurāṇī deity 128, 146; at the house altar 124; Kali deity 124, 127–28, 131n18, 149, 152–58, 162–63, 165, 186, 188; Narasiṃha deity 124, 129, 131; Sanju, case of 124; Tārā-Tāriṇī 156; Vīrabhadra deity 131
demonic possession 32, 121, 133–34
devotionalism *see* devotional love (*bhakti*)
devotional love (*bhakti*) 44n16, 51, 120, 142, 208n15
*dharmaśāstra* 4n2
doing gender: concept of 12, 17, 23; within the ritual context 243–49
dreams, as a source of religious inspiration 187
*duba*-grass 71–72, 74–75, 77, 79, 86
Durgā Pūjā 45, 177, 181, 187–88

ecstatic possession 119, 122
Eichinger Ferro-Luzzi, Gabriela 94, 100, 101n6, 103, 104n9
embodied practice, possession as 154–61, 183–85; Basanti, case study 155–56; challenges of facticity of divine overpowering 162–65; Sujata, case study 156–61
exorcism 27n35, 121, 122n10, 133, 135, 142

female art forms 8
female bodies, performativity of 104–7
female identity *see* gender-identity
female mortality rate 3
female religious practices 5, 55, 239
female spirit possession, academic discourse on 132–36; in Kathmandu valley 140; relevance in South Asian religious contexts 140–41
female virtues 89
fire-walking festival (Jhāmu Yātrā) 131n18
Fischer-Lichte, Erika 23, 27
five products of cow, ritual use of 98
Flueckiger, Joyce 7n10, 9, 15n22, 67n9
folk theory 120, 137
Foulston, Lynn 130
Freeman, James 43n15, 56, 70n16, 130
Freeman, Richard 136, 139n27, 153n9, 160
Fuller, Chris 134, 170, 186n29, 188n32, 216

Garrison, Vivian 145
gender-based social inequality 3
gender fluidity, theory of 20
gender-identity 2–3, 9–11, 18
gender performativity, concept of 18
goddess devotion, social implications of 7
Goffman, Erving 11, 19, 21
Gold, Ann 7n9, 8, 121, 141
Gupta, Sanjukta 41, 55, 111

Hancock, Mary 136, 138n24, 139
Handelman, Don 25n33, 177, 181n23, 189n37, 193, 197n3, 208
hegemonic gender ideology 59
Hindu doctrines, influence on present-day conceptions of gender 1, 3, 5
Hindu goddesses, theology and symbolism of 6
Hinduism 2, 119, 236, 238–40, 242; austerities and (self-induced) bodily pain 92; concept of *līlā* in 208n12; female deities in 6; purity and pollution in 97–100; role-taking in 208–12; sacred scriptures and texts 64–67; votive rites in 55–59; women and 3–9
Hindu mythology 41, 43, 78, 208

Hindu rituals 119; commitment 28; concept of 29; impact on female identity 93; Jahni Oṣā (religious fast) *see* Jahni Oṣā (religious fast); joy of 59–61; Karvā Cauth 55; *nabakaḷebara* 69; non-discursive aspects of 25; performance of 32; secular 29; Somnātha Brata 55; use of five products of cow 98
*huḷahuḷi* 42, 45, 53–54, 71–72, 79
Humes, Cynthia Ann 6n8, 7, 65, 66n6
Humphrey, Caroline 28–29, 37, 245, 246

Inden, Ronald 19, 99

Jagannātha, Lord 68, 76, 79, 86, 92, 209
Jagannātha temple 14, 69, 237n2
Jahni Oṣā (religious fast) 30–31, 36–38; bodily experiences 50–55; celebration of 41; and girl's identification as a ritual performer 54–55; performance of 39–46, 59–61; reason for observing 47; rituals, rationalizing of 46–50
Jhāmu Yātrā 81n30, 131n18
joint family system 48, 56, 101, 109

Kakar, Sudhir 133
Kālī, worship of 6–7
Karvā Cauth 55
Keller, Mary 122n9
Khanna, Madhu 3, 5, 6n8, 112
*Khulaṇā Sundarī* (book) 75–76
*Khulaṇā Sundarī*, legend of 62–64, 72, 75–79, 84, 86–89; impact on authentication of Maṅgaḷā Pūjā 90
Knipe, David 131–32, 185n28, 208n13
Kṛṣṇa, Lord 41, 43, 49, 51, 198, 203, 208–9, 214
Kumāra Pūrṇṇimā 45, 49

Laidlaw, James 28–29, 37, 245–46
Lambek, Michael 119n5, 145–46
*Laws of Manu* (200 BCE–200 CE) 4
Lewis, Ioan 134
*līlā*, practice of 208–9
liminality, concept of 26–27
low-caste female possession 139

McGee, Mary 4–5, 9, 20, 39n6, 56, 59n35, 66–67, 79n26, 239
Mahurī Rājā 172, 178, 222
*mānasika* 39, 43n14, 46, 148, 156, 182–83, 190, 198–99, 207, 211–12
*maṅgaḷabāra* 68, 147
Maṅgaḷā, goddess 31, 42, 46, 49, 62–63; altar of 71; who guides through troubles 86–90; worship of *see* Maṅgaḷā Pūjā
*maṅgaḷkabya* 78–79
Maṅgaḷā Pūjā 63, 67–75, 81; expectations and emotions of the participants in 91; impact of *Khulaṇā Sundarī* on authentication of 90
Maṅgaḷā temple, in Kakatpur 69
*manusmṛti* 4n2
*mārā* 104, 106n12, 110
masquerades 196; as an act of role-taking 208–12; audience reaction to 205; boys 198; of child-eating demoness 202; classification 205; as divine character 198, 210; donations received 202; female devotees and 207; as females 202; and idea of mockery 203; men and 97–203; offensive provocations and 203–8; *processual* capacity of 211–12; from protection aspect 198–99; religious motive 198; *semiotic* capacity of 210, 212; at Ṭhākurāṇī Yātrā 198–99; as tiger 199
menstrual impurity 10n12, 95–97, 104, 138, 243

menstrual pollution: communication of 105; comparison of menstruant's touch with a criminal act 110; cultural notion of 93, 95–96; duration of 102, 104; force of 113–15; menses and morality 110–13; and performativity of female bodies 105; self-presentation during 107–10; social and moral impact of 110
menstrual restrictions 100–104; biological understanding of human body and its reproductive cycle 108; relevance and performance of 109; self-presentation during 107–10; social impact of 107; women's observance of 115; *see* menstrual taboos
menstrual taboos 32, 94–95; *see* menstrual restrictions
Merleau-Ponty, Maurice 145, 146n3
Minturn, Leigh 58, 82

*nabakaḷebara*, ritual of 69
Nabokov, Isabelle 134
Nandy, Ashis 20, 167
Niśā Maṇgaḷabāra Oṣā 31, 62, 70, 72, 89; personalization of ritual 90–92; story (*kathā*) and prayers relevant for 75–82; women's voices 82–86
*nisa* way, of worship 188–89
Nocturnal Tuesday Fast *see* Niśā Maṇgaḷabāra Oṣā
nocturnal worship, of Hindu goddesses 170, 187

Obeyesekere, Gananath 133–34
*oṣā-brata* 39, 57, 60, 62, 79; different types of 40; *see also* Niśā Maṇgaḷabāra Oṣā
oracular possession 120n6, 122

Pakaslathi, Antti 133, 139n27
Parry, Jonathan 133, 138
passiones, concept of 29
Pati, Biswamoy 66
*pativrata*, ideal of 4–5, 55
Pearson, Anne 39n6, 40n9, 55n29, 56–58, 67, 183n25
personal hygiene 112
possessing power 120–21
possession mediumship 122
Prahlāda Nāṭa, performance of 210
public debate, of Ṭhākurāṇī Yātrā festival 218–25
purity and pollution, concept of 32, 93–94; in Hinduism 97–100; ritual use of five products of cow 98

*raja*, moral quality of 104
Rāmlila, performance of 209
religious diet 54, 58
religious doctrines, effect on women's self-understanding 22
religious knowledge, democratization of 65
religious practices of women 236–37; Brahminical ideals, influence of 237–38; and images of femininity 242–49; in modern Indian society 240–42; self-conscious identification in 244–46; in southern Orissa 239–41; subaltern aspect of 134, 138–39, 196, 237–40; subjunctive mood of 243–44; viewpoints and routines of different castes 237–38
religious texts: consumption of 64–67; positive effects of women's access to 67
rites of passage, three-stage model of 26
ritual: agency; 31, 35, 55, 60, 61, 217, 223, 232–35, 246, 248; authentication of 35, 223; competence

53–54, 59–60, 63, 84, 139, 217; pollution, notion and reality of 96; transformation 23–30; *see also* Hindu rituals
role-taking, in Hinduism 208–12

sacred scriptures and texts: consumption of 64–67; positive effects of women's access to 67
*Śakti*, concept of 5, 7
Santoṣī Mā 130
*sattva* nutrition 58
Sax, William 21n28, 26n34, 139, 153n9, 177n19, 181, 193n40, 208, 211n17, 216n1, 223n9, 230, 231
Schechner, Richard 26
Schömbucher, Elisabeth 15n22, 119, 131–32, 133n21, 135–37, 160n15, 168, 185, 237
secular rituals 21, 29
self, performance of 17–23
self-conscious display, of menstrual pollution 107–10
self-understanding of performers 245–46
Sered, Susan S. 9, 118n1, 239
Shakta centres, in Orissa 69
Shaktism 68, 120, 141–43, 189, 240
shamanic careers 134–35
shamanism 122, 122n10, 145
Shweder, Richard 7n9, 95, 103, 110
Smārta Brahmin women 139
Smith, Frederick 118n2, 119, 120n6, 121, 136n23, 138n26, 139, 210, 239
social contestation, of deity possession 137–38, 138n25
social hierarchy, of women 4
social immunity 35, 218, 233, 235, 248
social practice, patterns and strategies of 29
somatic mode of attention 29
Somnātha Brata 55
South Asian characterizations, of women 137
spirit mediumship 121–22
spirit possession, cultural phenomenon of 118–22; academic discourse on 132–36; ancestral spirit 125; attitude towards 127; in Benares 138–39; caste and class, significance of 138–39; contribution 119; cosmological aspect of 163–65; devotional expressions of passers-by, significance of 165; episodes in southern Orissa 120; gendered perspective 119; lower-caste ethos 138; mass possession of women in public 131; Nirmala, case of 125–26; performative approach to 135–36; psychological model of 133–34; as ritual and aesthetic performance 127–28, 136; during semi-public rituals 126; sociological explanations 120, 134–35, 137–38; Sora, case of 132; as superstition 138–39; women's personal memories 123–29
*strīdharma* 4, 56, 60, 63, 244
*stuti* 80–81
supernatural being 2, 34, 120, 148
Sutherland, Peter 230, 231
Syed, Renate 3
Śyāmaḷāẏī, goddess 81

Tewari, Laxmi 39n6, 56
*ṭhākurāṇī* 68, 121, 124, 127, 146–50, 152
Ṭhākurāṇī Yātrā festival 33–34, 128, 131; announcement 173–74; change in perception of 229–32; competing principles of possession incident 223; conflicts over 227–29; debate

about correct procedure 216; economic and political impacts of 173; erection of a flagpole 176; farewell event 176; features of 169; female bias of 177–83; festivities at night 185–86; gender-based division of ritual labour 177; history 171–72; installation of sacred pots 174–76; litigations related to 227, 229–30; marriage crisis of Deśībeherā and the Deśībeherāṇī 218–25; nocturnal qualities of 185–91; opening night 174; political and financial conflicts within community 225–32; position of the Devangi in 173–76, 178; pot processions 172, 172n8, 176; private worship of goddess pots 181; public criticisms about 217–18, 226; return journey (*bāhuṙā yātrā*) of the goddess 181–85; ritual periods 185
theology of subordination 5
time concepts, of Hindu festivals 186n29, 188
transformation, ritual 23–30
transgression, concept of 26, 34, 154, 162, 195–97, 205, 207–8, 212–14
Tuḷasī (Indian basil plant): religious significance of 42; worship of 41, 44, 45, 60

Vāḍabalija 131
Vaishnava goddess 68
Viswanath, Kalpana 95, 108n5, 112
votive rites, in Hinduism 55–59; classification and socio-religious significance of 56
*vrata* 39, 55–56, 66

Wadley, Susan 5, 39n6, 40n9, 56, 57, 65n4, 66–67
women: access to religious literature, positive effects of 67; discrimination against 3; and Hinduism 3–9; oral tradition, regional diversity of 67
worship, general techniques of 53

For Product Safety Concerns and Information please contact our EU representative GPSR@taylorandfrancis.com
Taylor & Francis Verlag GmbH, Kaufingerstraße 24, 80331 München, Germany

www.ingramcontent.com/pod-product-compliance
Lightning Source LLC
Chambersburg PA
CBHW050702280326
41926CB00088B/2422
* 9 7 8 1 1 3 8 6 6 5 0 3 3 *